Archaeology and
Biblical Interpretation

ARCHAEOLOGY AND BIBLICAL INTERPRETATION

Essays in Memory of D. Glenn Rose

Leo G. Perdue
Lawrence E. Toombs
Gary L. Johnson
editors

Unless otherwise indicated Scripture quotations are from the Revised Standard Version of the Holy Bible, copyright, 1946, 1952 and © 1971, 1973 by the Division of Christian Education, National Council of the Churches of Christ in the U.S.A. and used by permission.

Acknowledgment is made to the following for permission to reprint:

To the American Schools of Oriental Research for Fig. 10: Schematic section of the excavations by Petrie and Bliss (*AASOR* 43, 1978, p. 114); Fig. 12: Schematic plan of lower wall system, Field III (*AASOR* 43, 1978, p. 113); Fig. 18: Simplified section through Field III (*AASOR* 43, 1978, p. 133); Fig. 24: Plan of the environs of Araq el-Emir (*AASOR* 47, p. 2); Fig. 45: Spread of Iron II (*BASOR*, 204, Dec. 1971, p. 3).

To the Joint Expedition to Shechem for Fig. 44: Site plan of the Shechem mound (copyright © 1987 Joint Expedition to Shechem) and Fig. 45: Spread of Iron II (copyright © 1971 Joint Expedition to Shechem).

To Massada Press and Jewish History Publications (Israel—1961) Ltd. for permission to include in expanded and revised form "The Last Years of the Kingdom of Judah," originally published in *The Age of the Monarchies: Political History,* volume 4–I of *The World History of the Jewish People,* edited by Abraham Malamat (Jerusalem: Massada, 1979).

Library of Congress Cataloging-in-Publication Data

Archaeology and Biblical interpretation.

    Bibliography: p.
    Includes index.
    1. Bible—Antiquities.   2. Rose, D. Glenn, d. 1982.
I. Rose, D. Glenn, d. 1982.   II. Perdue, Leo G.
III. Toombs, Lawrence E., 1919–   IV. Johnson,
Gary L. (Gary Lance), 1941–
BS621.A69   1987   220.9'3   87–16817
ISBN 0–8042–0003–3

CONTENTS

III. Selected Topics in Archaeology and Biblical Interpretation

LIST OF FIGURES

LIST OF TABLES

Archaeology and
Biblical Interpretation

D. Glenn Rose

D. GLENN ROSE

IN MEMORIAM

The professional life of D. Glenn Rose was distinguished by high standards of personal excellence, responsible and meticulous scholarship, enthusiasm for interdisciplinary study, and commitment to theological education. Reared in Louisiana, Missouri, Dr. Rose received his A.B. degree in 1953 from Bethany College, Bethany, West Virginia, an institution of higher learning affiliated with his denomination, the Christian Church, Disciples of Christ. He later attended Yale Divinity School on a Danforth Scholarship, earning a B.D. with honors in 1955. Then followed two graduate degrees from Yale: an M.A. in 1956 and a Ph.D. in 1959. His dissertation, "The Use of Exodus Imagery in Isaiah 50—55," typified his early training and interest in biblical exegesis and theology. Indeed biblical studies continued to provide the intellectual crucible in which his expanding interests were forged.

Accepting a post in religion at Transylvania University in Lexington, Kentucky, another institution of the Christian Church, Dr. Rose soon became the chair of the Division of Humanities. In this context two distinctive features of his career took shape. The first was his effort as an ordained minister of the Christian Church to make the best of biblical scholarship available to students and laity by means of publications, lectures, and sermons. The second was his excitement in studying the Bible within the broad context of the humanities, particularly western literature. The fresh insights from disciplines outside traditional biblical studies provided for Dr. Rose a constant source of stimulation which extended, invigorated, and redefined his exegetical and theological understandings and abilities.

In 1963 Dr. Rose joined the faculty of Phillips University Graduate Seminary in Enid, Oklahoma, one of four seminaries of the Christian Church (Disciples of Christ), and was promoted to full professor in Old Testament in

1965. In 1980 his faculty honored him by naming him Distinguished Professor of Old Testament and Archaeology and bestowing upon him the seminary's only endowed chair, the Darbeth Chair. The seminary, set within a university context, provided the distinctive environment in which Dr. Rose's interests, training, and skills matured and came to fruition. As a teacher he instilled in a generation of seminary students a respect for careful scholarship and a sense of excitement resulting from the critical engagement of theological issues. A concern for the welfare of students was matched by a stern expectation which drew forth their best efforts. He was an active supporter of the advancement of women in his calm, practical mentoring and in straightforward advocacy.

It was his unabated enthusiasm for learning, including areas outside his graduate training, that sparked his scholarly development and achievements during these years as a seminary professor. Dr. Rose's first research leave (1967–68) combined a summer program in Near Eastern civilization at the Hebrew Union Biblical and Archaeological School in Jerusalem with a year's research in Old Testament theology and rabbinic Judaism at Mansfield College, Oxford University. His summer in Israel kindled an interest in archaeology which led in the summer of 1969 to his participation as a volunteer in the Gezer excavations. After this experience, field work became his passion. Dr. Rose then participated in the Joint Expedition to Tell el-Hesi as an area supervisor during the 1970 and 1971 seasons and as a field supervisor in 1973. In the summer of 1974 he began work as a field supervisor at Idalion on Cyprus. When the excavation was interrupted by the outbreak of war, Dr. Rose returned to the States and participated as a volunteer at the Koster excavations in Illinois where he gained firsthand experience in "new archaeology." Ever seeking to integrate and combine areas and approaches, Dr. Rose spent his second research leave (1974–75) again at Mansfield College where he began to construct a synthesis between Old Testament theology and prehistoric archaeology. With fresh insight he returned to Hesi in 1975 with a keen interest to combine the theories, methods, and techniques of American prehistoric archaeology with those operative in Palestinian archaeology. In 1975 Dr. Rose was chosen project director for the Joint Archaeological Expedition to Tell el-Hesi. In this capacity he combined extraordinary administrative gifts with a rigorous demand for meticulous detail in field operations and recording. Throughout these years as his responsibilities in the Hesi excavations grew, he produced a variety of reports and articles detailing the field work at Hesi and reflecting on the relationship of archaeological methodology and evidence to related disciplines. Under his direction the excavations at Hesi evidenced a high degree of interdisciplinary research. Ever the teacher concerned with the training of a new generation of scholars, Dr. Rose's leadership was largely responsible for the distinctive reputation Hesi developed for educating volunteers. Biblical studies and archaeology, modern literature and biblical themes, theology and prehistory, scholarly methodology and theological education were bipolarities which provided the creative tension for Dr. Rose's thought.

In the summer of 1981 Dr. Rose began his third research leave by directing the seventh season of excavations at Hesi. This was to be followed by a semester in residence at the W. F. Albright Institute of Archaeological Research as the Annual Professor, during which he was to complete work on the hellenistic volume for the Hesi publications. He planned to return to Mansfield College during the spring of 1982 in order to continue work on a manuscript on creation theology in Genesis 1—11, drawing on the insights of structural anthropology. However, these projects were not completed. A few days after concluding the seventh season of excavation, Dr. Rose was working on a rough draft of the project director's report in the apartment of the Annual Professor in the Albright Institute when he died of a heart attack. He was fifty-three.

The three sections of this volume represent appropriately the three areas of archaeology and biblical studies which characterized Professor Rose's activities: methodology, field work, and interpretation. The five essays in Section I discuss the distinctive features of the so-called "schools" which continue to evolve in Palestinian archaeology. Dr. Rose's article provides a fitting summary to the other scholars' discussions of the Albright school, G. Ernest Wright, Israeli archaeology, and the "new archaeology." The seven articles in Section II deal with specific excavations and their results for understanding the biblical world. Representative of this section is the essay by Professor Joseph Callaway who places the evidence of the Ai excavation within the book of Judges rather than in Joshua 7—8. Professor Rose's own field work is represented by the two articles by former Hesi colleagues Ralph Doermann and Valerie Fargo, which concentrate on Hesi's status as an Iron Age fortress. Section III includes integrative articles on archaeology and biblical interpretation which vary from Walter Rast's discussion of the relation between the Sodom saga and the excavations at Bab edh-Dhra to Yigal Shiloh's documentation of underground water systems in Iron Age Israel.

This collection of essays, written by distinguished scholars who respected and valued Professor Rose's work in Bible and archaeology, demonstrates the high esteem in which he was held by his professional peers, but it also evidences the breadth and variety which characterized his own intellectual appetite. It is to the memory of the strong intellectual traditional and compassionate humanity which he embodied that this collection is dedicated.

I. ARCHAEOLOGICAL SCHOOLS AND BIBLICAL INTERPRETATION

Chapter 1

BIBLICAL INTERPRETATION AND THE ALBRIGHT SCHOOL

George E. Mendenhall
University of Michigan

This essay in honor of D. Glenn Rose, who was taken untimely from his loved field of scholarly work, is a highly subjective contemplation upon the topic assigned. It is necessarily so, for any attempt to summarize the vast output of the second and third generations of those whose skills and methods derived from W. F. Albright must inevitably be in large part an exercise in autobiography. The main theme of this essay could well be summed up by the couplet that the late Malcolm Kerr quoted in his inaugural address as the president of the American University of Beirut:

> We deprecate with vague inanities
> Man's inhumanity to the humanities.

That the humanities are in trouble, if not a disaster area, in the academic scene is a proposition that can hardly be proven—but then it is worth considering at least that the concept of "proof" is hardly relevant to any significant area of the humanities that deals with values which are themselves powerful determinants of overt behavior. The trouble in academia is reflected in the outside world as well.

"The past is not dead," said William Faulkner, "it is not even past." This quip from one of his plays seems very relevant to the current state of the so-called "Albright school" of archaeological and biblical studies. Many of the scholarly products of the second generation and even the third generation of the Baltimore school constitute elaborations upon themes that Albright himself originated during his lifetime of extraordinarily original and creative work in at least three fields: archaeology, history, and philology. What seems to be most characteristic today of the "Albright school" is the fragmentation of these three interrelated scholarly fields, which were and ought to be mutually supportive, into independent academic disciplinary specializations. Thus the past is not dead: it has merely disintegrated like much of academia, especially the humanities.

The area of field archaeology is of crucial importance because it is the indispensable means for the retrieval of data that must be dealt with by the other two fields. Though Albright himself in one of his early articles maintained that field archaeology should be kept quite distinct from philology, very soon his mind changed and the rest of his scholarly life was spent in the correlation of archaeological with literary evidence. It is a sad commentary on this aspect of the humanities that perhaps the mainstream of archaeological scholarship seems determined to turn the clock back to the precritical situation of the nineteenth century by making archaeology completely independent of literary studies. This recidivistic tendency can be explained in part by the enormous influence of the "hard" sciences, the incredible successes of which have induced scholars who deal with the world of human beings to imitate their presuppositions, their procedures, and, too often, their values which have resulted in the human ability to return life on this planet to the level of microbes.

Since anthropological archaeology has dealt very largely with preliterate or nonliterate societies and their artifacts, it is not surprising that they have been able to develop means by which to extract the maximum of information from minimal evidence. The fact that most of the results are the sort that cannot be said to transcend common sense is obscured by the enormous elaboration of "scientific" technology employed to retrieve the evidence. Because this branch of the "social sciences" has always dealt with preliterate, primitive societies, it has never been able to cope with history or even to come up with a "scientific" accounting for the process of cultural change, which would seem to constitute one primary subject matter of history itself. Much less has it been able even to imagine what is necessary in order to arrive at some understanding of the human historical process, which is one of the main themes of the Bible. In this respect it is disconcertingly similar to most modern theology which also cannot cope with and often enough displays an Olympian contempt for "mere history."

It is a tempting conclusion that in many archaeological fields the point of diminishing returns was reached decades ago, especially in Palestinian archaeology. This contrasts most sharply to the situation elsewhere in the Near East where startling if not revolutionary discoveries have been made in the past fifteen years, and there still remain many entire regions that have barely been explored if at all. Though it may well be said that in Albright's day it was hardly possible to avoid being a pioneer in the discovery of new horizons of ancient cultural history or even in the development of new archaeological methods and means for the interpretation of archaeological evidence, the question may now be legitimately raised whether the enormous elaborations of methodology and of excavation technique have really been accompanied by a similar increase in the understanding of ancient cultures and the historical process, with which Albright was so enormously fascinated. It is a constant in all fields of academic enterprise—and probably always has been since the "wisdom literature" of the ancient Near Eastern cultures—that a specialized field of competence constitutes the claim to fame of its practitioner, and therefore all fields that do not fall within that field are automatically dismissed as trivial, irrelevant, or even amusingly old-fashioned.

It is worth considering that the greatest gap between the work of Albright and his students and what seems to be the mainstream of most contemporary archaeology lies in the nature of the goals and purposes. The enormous obsession with academic prestige—and consequently funding—that made out of archaeology "not a science but a vendetta," as Sir Mortimer Wheeler well put it, has meant that many of its practitioners could not afford to pay much attention to matters that didn't happen to be currently fashionable in peer circles or, above all, in those bureaucratic hierarchies that dole out grants for excavations and research. The enormous elaboration of technique and technical instrumentation that has characterized the "new archaeology" has been accompanied, necessarily it seems, by some naiveté in matters pertaining to the humanities. At the same time few, if any, are asking why such large sums of money should be spent on digging up the "dead and primitive past" at all, and this is particularly true of Palestine which always was, as Dever accurately observed, "culturally and economically a provincial back-water."

It is not difficult to understand why this development has taken place in academia. To be sure, the constant battle for funds and prestige has much to do with it, but this is a constant and has had similar effects in other fields dealing with the humanities. The very existence of high technology, of the elaboration of scientific methods that have had impact not only on society as a whole but also specifically on Palestinian archaeologists and their conception of their task, has preempted the attention and interest of scholars. What is sad about it is not the neglect of much literature and art, for archaeologists are all too aware (or should be) that fashions in these areas are not very long lasting. It is probably a very important aspect of the current difficulties facing the humanities that they have become almost exclusively identified with the manipulation of verbal and visual symbols. It should be quite clear from any examination in depth (which has repeatedly been done) that what is admired about a great quantity of modern visual and literary overproductivity is not its intrinsic value to persons but its social instrumental value measured by the currencies of publicity, prestige, and the consequent money.

What is sad about the current plight of the humanities is the inability to exercise some value judgments about the ultimate worth of what they do or to show some understanding of what an inhuman world needs in order to make and keep this planet livable. One major reason for that inability is precisely the fragmentation of learning that has already taken place. It is simultaneously a social phenomenon and an ideological phenomenon that is operative not only in academia but also in the world at large. For, if it is the enormously enhanced capacity to predict that characterizes science, it is only to be expected that "science" is regarded as the basis of predictability in the *human* sphere of experience. As a consequence, every attempt is made in nearly every sphere of academic activity to become "scientific." It is a sad response to an inner emptiness, to an inner insecurity which derives from the idea that there is no transcendent value that can be regarded as a safe and reliable base for decision making either in private life or in the public life of academia, much less in that of political power structures. Consequently, the vagaries of fads and fashions take over, and no one is able to understand why some academic fad becomes obligatory: it simply becomes the thing to which one must adapt and show one's expertise by the highest competence in manipulating the new. The result is quite predictable. As Dean Inge has well put it, "He who espouses the 'spirit of the age' soon finds himself a widower."

It is this academic compulsion for prestige that makes prisoners of its practitioners, that makes extremely difficult the consideration of really new alternatives, and, at the same time, that contributes greatly to the increased public reluctance to pay for this kind of effort. The great contrast between the enormous effort put into the recovery of the ancient world and the increasing realization that that world was little different from our own, so far as human beings are concerned, raises a very good question: why bother, when you can make a lot more money manufacturing computer chips or software programs that enable you to sort the "facts" much more efficiently?

At this point we return to the second great concern of Albright which is so unfashionable among those circles that deal with the Bible at all; namely, history. The correlation of empirical reality with the biblical text and the consequent process of historical synthesis or reconstruction were and presumably still are the hallmark of the so-called "Albright school." The long-lived contribution of John Bright's *A History of Israel* in successive editions is a lasting monument to this concern for the inseparable tie between biblical studies and history but even more to the fact that the history must change as new *evidence* comes to light—over against the usual process of changing history when modern political ideologies change. In view of the fact that the only empirical reality that is accessible for the biblical period is that made available through archaeological investigation, it must be emphasized as strongly as possible that the empirical reality now known is as far removed from that available in the 1930s when the "Albright school" had its beginnings as our present-day knowledge of outer space is from that now remote era.

It is not at all surprising—indeed it is only to be expected as it is in almost every other field of academic research—that the conclusions reached a half century ago on the basis of barely emergent archaeological discoveries did not remain viable for more than a few decades at most and were vigorously combated the whole time. After all, it is generally admitted in many non-humanistic academic disciplines that the life expectancy of a technical training is about five to ten years. In very rapidly developing fields such as computer science and engineering there are only two categories: either experimental or obsolete.

It is probably through the writings and excavations carried out by G. Ernest Wright that the "Albright school" received its clearest definition, at least so far as the outside scholarly world was concerned. Elaborating upon Albright's thesis concerning the identification of the LB–Early Iron destruction levels with the "Israelite Conquest of Palestine," Wright's work was accepted as fact by a couple of generations of seminarians, at least in America. Even earlier, Albright's thesis was powerfully reinforced by Nelson Glueck's interpretation of his archaeological explorations in Transjordan. The discovery of an increase in population there in the Early Iron Age was naturally identified with the arrival of the seminomadic Israelites, Moabites, and Edomites. The excitement and exhilaration of those early days of archaeological exploration and excavation combined with the interpretation and reinterpretation of the biblical text have now largely, it seems, disappeared with the refutation of one identification after another. Now there is almost a backlash against identifying anything in excavations with the biblical text except, of course, in Israel and among the fundamentalists.

Again, this is probably not something consciously engaged in out of principle but rather a process of conforming to the mainstream of recent cultural developments in the modern Western world, two of which are of particular importance here. First is the alleged "secularization" of the Western world which is usually equated with the drop in church attendance. This parochial view of secularization is entirely out of touch with historical reality, both biblical and modern. What has in fact happened is a rapid and radical change in the conventional public opinion concerning *what* is "sacred." The only distinction between the secular and the sacred that can be seen to be operative across chronological and geographical boundary lines is the difference between that which is *conventionally* regarded to be of crucial importance to individuals and the social organization with which they identify themselves and that which is merely trivial or disposable. The one thing sacred in the modern Western world is the existing political state (none of which existed in its present form three centuries ago), and this is the one ecumenical theology that cuts across *all* religious and "ethnic" boundaries. Unfortunately, this ecumenical theology is absolutely incapable of cutting across *any* political boundary, and it can operate only for the purpose of supporting politically organized violence in the form of law as well as war. No one needs a political theology of this sort in order to conform to the economic demands of that sacred entity—no one other than usurpers in both ancient and modern times.

The second cultural development that has made it difficult for anyone with academic pretensions to engage in "biblical archaeology" is the increasing inability or unwillingness in contemporary society to face facts and to value the experience of the past. This chronological provincialism so characteristic of high school children seems epidemic in modern society, and history, if it is to be tolerated at all, must be confined within the safe limits of the political ideology or used merely to illustrate the correctness of some form of determinism that happens to be currently fashionable in academia. Thus the human and ethical dimensions with which the Bible is so enormously concerned are of no interest to the archaeologist who has to jump on the ecology bandwagon to prove he or she is "up to date."

Certainly there is nothing wrong about a concern for ecology, but it is no substitution for recognition of the fact that ecological calamities are in the Bible already regarded as predictable consequences of irresponsible behavior —the curses for violation of covenant—and this process is identified as acts of God. Curiously enough, this is the exact opposite of the modern concept that regards acts of God as unpredictable, arbitrary events (in French: *force majeure*) that relieve persons of legal responsibility. In this respect the modern person is ideologically a throwback to ancient Bronze Age mythical thought where also the gods were mere functions of the political boundary line and useful explanations for the occasional disaster.

It is worth considering at least that it is this withdrawal from reality, this inability to face facts when they have to do with a "Sacred Book," that brings about an unbridgeable gulf between the material reality of excavations and the "spiritual" reality of the Bible. It is only the fundamentalist (whether religious or political) who unashamedly makes such identifications and proclaims them absolutely true, with the backing of all the financial and social pressure resources of the social group with which the fundamentalist identifies.

So far as the "Albright school" is concerned, its overshadowing, if not demise, at the present time is largely to be attributed to this change in the *Zeit-geist*, the enormous increase in knowledge that has taken place since the 1940s and the enormous increase in the number of scholars working in the academic field, the vast majority of whom derive from academic traditions that do not regard the ancient realities of the extra-biblical world as at all necessary to the understanding of the Bible.

In addition, the integrative and synthesizing purpose of Albright's own work are a methodical procedure which makes such enormous demands on its practitioners that there are very few scholars broadly enough trained and experienced to be able even to value such an enterprise, much less engage in it. Also, this approach itself flew directly in the face of long-range trends toward a higher and higher degree of specialization typical of many if not all academic fields. Last but not least is a factor that seems by far to be the most important: such a method is foreign to many religious traditions, for both history and a modern type of biblical criticism have rarely been integrated into the thought systems of modern theologians—to say nothing of the laity—and as a matter of fact these methods are anathema to many religious sects whose attitudes and policies cause still further antipathy to the Bible.

The result is what can be seen in almost any issue of any biblical journal— a modern day docetism that treats biblical texts as though they were somehow completely unrelated to the everyday processes of ancient life and experience and as though their only purpose was to give aid and comfort to twentieth-century human psyches and their accidental social organization with which they happened to be affiliated often enough merely by the accident of birth. The similarity to medieval methods of biblical study is apparent enough: the Bible cannot say anything that is not in conformity with contemporary ecclesiastical or political authority. The dehumanization of the Bible is illustrated at the opposite poles of the modern religious spectrum: on the one hand, a prestigious theologian can complain that "modern biblical studies have reduced Sacred Scripture to the relativities of ancient history," while, on the other hand, the same rejection of "mere history" and the humanities is characteristic of the present-day fundamentalist militancy.

The same is true of any academic approaches to the Bible. The liberationists start with a modern political concern usually intimately connected with a power struggle and use the Bible as an authority for their claims to enhanced political or purchasing power. Whether Marxist or not, their "theology" is derived from the modern ideology, and it is perennially possible to find in the thousand-year range of biblical experience something to exploit for a modern purpose that may well be totally irrelevant or even diametrically opposite to that which concerned ancient people.

The rudimentary nature of the social sciences in general at Johns Hopkins during the eminent achievements of W. F. Albright is perhaps responsible for one of the two or three most significant lacunae in his work, and for that he has received considerable criticism. Utilization of the work of Levy-Bruhl is not the kind of procedure that could have been very impressive to those sophisticated in social sciences in the fifties and sixties. It must be noted, however, that at least a beginning in the utilization of some social science questions and methodology can be seen in the work of W. F. Albright. As is the case with regard to the archaeological recovery of ancient cultures and their histories, Albright came at a time when the social sciences were themselves quite elementary. It is partly for that reason that, though stimulated by them, he was very far from a slavish imitation or subjugation by those passing fads or fancies. Perhaps more important is the fact that the social sciences could not and cannot cope with the problems of value with which the Bible is inseparably associated and with which the civilized world in the late 1930s was inevitably involved.

It is, thus, a gross misconception of the nature and substance of Albright's own contribution to biblical and ancient studies to identify it merely with a working hypothesis that identified the LB–Early Iron destruction levels with the ancient Israelite "conquest" of Palestine. Though there are no doubt many persons engaged in academic endeavors who still accept this thesis as "scientifically" demonstrated, it seems to me and to very many scholars that it is both far too simplistic a concept to account for historical and social phenomena of that extremely traumatic period and completely irrelevant to the sudden emergence of a new religious ideology that furnished the bonding power necessary to the existence and continuity of a new kind of community and society that called itself "Israel."

To put the problem another way, the very progress of archaeological investigation of the ancient world, especially that of Palestine proper, has forced a shift of attention away from the mere correlation of words in the Bible with archaeological artifacts to a far more difficult and demanding attention to extremely complex processes of history and to the interconnections between ideology as a determinant of behavior (not merely as "symbols") and the social bonding that happened at that specific time and place. It seems that this kind of historical research into the inner workings and structure of the early biblical community is either too difficult or of no interest to the mainstream of contemporary biblical and ancient scholars who evidently find it much more rewarding to come up with a new technology for analyzing ancient broken dishes or to discover new "patterns" in the ancient manipulation of words.

This breakdown into antiquarian technology on the one hand and literary criticism on the other hand demonstrates at least two things to me. It shows the feedback mechanisms at work in the present scene, whereby those who engage in a particular type of scholarly activity are rewarded by other scholars who also engage in the same field of research. It also shows the breakdown of scholarship into the mutually exclusive parochialisms that the academic world calls "schools." For this reason it is questionable whether there ever was any justification for the idea that there was an "Albright school."

A school is characterized by a substantive dogmatic content that must be defended at all costs, and this, in my experience, is the exact opposite to everything that Albright and his scholarship stood for. Perhaps some aspects of the scholarship of some of his students might have at one time been properly described as a school, but there is little of that left now that is very significant in the scholarly world. It is precisely the openness to new evidence, to new working hypotheses, to new or, even more properly, old understandings of the ancient world that are new only to us that characterized Albright and his work and that therefore prevented that tradition from degenerating into a mere school, the primary functions of which have to do not with the discovery of truth but with tribal bonding for purposes of winning in academic power struggles.

The disadvantages of that kind of academic stance are apparent: it is very weak in the contemporarily powerful demands for social bonding, for a psychological security in the knowledge that one belongs to a powerful academic subculture that is able to guarantee the rewards of jobs, prestige, and power. It is a part of the comedy of this academism that throughout his scholarly life Albright had to suffer constant attacks on his work on the grounds that "he changed his mind." This kind of humility before the facts runs diametrically in opposition to the usual academic obsession with being the authority on something or other—and, usually, the more authoritative, the more trivial.

The present state of the "Albright school" is perhaps not too different from what it used to be: non-existent, except in the sense that it eschewed and vigorously rejected any idea that any modern ideology, especially political, had a monopoly on the truth or its approaches. The enormous potential and realization of new understandings that resulted have been ingrained into biblical studies to an extent probably not realized by those of the younger generation who cannot remember what biblical scholarship was like before Albright. What is sad is the fact that there are too many schools who are busily engaged in trying to force the Bible and its traditions into some such parochial pettiness or to utilize some ridiculous nineteenth-century ideology to "explain" what will probably continue to be one of the greatest mysteries of human history; namely, how a community came into existence that itself transcended the power politics of its day to create a religious tradition that for three thousand years and more has continued in spite of the constant attempts on the part of ambitious Caesars to subjugate it to some passing political and parochial interest.

At a time when the entire ancient world was just opening up its secrets to scholarship through excavations, decipherments, and philology, *pure* research was both necessary and justifiable on the grounds of a considerable interest, curiosity, and stimulus especially where the Bible was concerned. The discovery that the biblical texts did indeed have some connection with the real experience of real people, albeit long ago, had a considerable impact on those who went through the process of finding out that the "sacred words of the Sacred Book" did at least at one time have a direct and immediate tie to experience and did not emerge merely, as the old theology would have it, from the "Sacred Scribes' direct pipeline to Heaven." As mentioned above, most conservative religious organizations, though gratified at the fact that archaeology seemed to "prove the Bible," stayed very far away from the central issue, which was that the biblical tradition was intimately connected in origin with immediate experience and represented a reaction to as well as an interpretation of that continuum of experience. In fact, there is evidence for a whole series of reinterpretations that took place through the millennium of Old Testament history. In effect, the meaning of sacred Scripture had to be correlated with the experience that it interpreted and gave expression to, but it is likely that there is little in the modern academic or religious scene to which this correlation appeals. The idea that the relationship between text and ancient context must be considered in the interpretation of biblical passages is considered too limiting on the creative endeavors of the modern exegete.

The present state of the "Albright school" is not, therefore, a result of any inadequacies in its goals, methods, and results. It is the result of a cultural disintegration that increasingly is both unwilling and unable to cope with historical reality, either modern or ancient. It is the extreme of irony that the biblical tradition itself almost certainly originated out of the experience of ancient peoples who had gone through this process to its logical culmination.

The disintegration of society into smaller and smaller power units is probably what brought about the destruction levels of the Late Bronze Age. It is worth considering that when this process is taking place there is a strong tendency for the "preservation" of the pathetic symbols that had functioned in the arena of social bonding in the past, but the purpose of the social bonding is a question that cannot be asked except in the obvious case of the socially organized violence that is always engaged in for the sake of "self-preservation." What societies cannot recognize, and some academicians and theologians as well, is the fact that all human social entities are ideologically bonded, even, and perhaps above all, kinship relationships. If the ideology is abandoned then so are the kin, as well as all other social and human relationships and obligations. It follows that the most important and culminating goal of biblical studies is biblical theology. Though Albright never made any claims in the field of theology, his interests in the history of religion that never reached fruition attest to his recognition of its overarching importance.

The formative period of the "Albright school" did not, as usually is the case, last very long, but the scholarly world is not the same even though many antihistorical thinkers, both religious and antireligious, proceed as though it were by going back to the nineteenth century for their ideological inspiration, resurrecting Herder, Wellhausen, Nietzsche, Darwin, Kierkegaard, Marx, Weber, or whoever. The older process of direct identification of something in an excavation with passages in the Bible has made its contribution, in spite of the fact that many specific conclusions reached have not proven to be tenable any longer. It is usually the case also in other fields of scholarly inquiry that the more that is learned about a particular area of experience, the larger the arena of the unknown is opened up. Things are never quite the same, but nevertheless the possibilities of future understanding are greatly enhanced, not diminished, by the enlarged sphere of understanding. As the known context enlarges, so also do the demands upon both method and substantive mastery of a multitude of "facts." Getting to know and, in some measure, to understand the concrete realities of that ancient world and the historical process that resulted from ancient peoples' systems of values is a difficult and often enough tedious and frustrating task. It is both much easier and more comforting to cut the Gordian knot by concentrating upon some particular aspect of antiquity as a specialization, and this procedure is of course both necessary and inevitable. The problems arise when scholars act and proceed as though their own field of expertise constitutes the entire universe of that which is important.

One main area of future development would seem to lie in the historical investigation of the relationship between social organization and the ideology that undergirded if not produced it, and this is the problem of biblical theology as well as its future program. For it is obvious that not only were the social organizations of Old Testament times quite ephemeral from the perspective of the ages, but also the same process is operative to the present day. The contemporary fundamentalist obsession with identifying something in the Bible with modern experience is merely a present-day regurgitation of the ancient myth-making mentality that identified ultimate value with the parochial interests operating within the social boundary line and could not cope with the relationship between cause and effect on the historical level. This inability to face facts in a too complex and frightening world results in the imposition of an a priori dogmatic system upon the ancient *and* modern reality and in the Orwellian rewriting of history to make it fit orthodox political party lines. It is evidence of the ideological, intellectual, and, often enough, moral bankruptcy that usually accompanies such a myth-making mentality. It is not surprising that apocalyptic is so fashionable at present.

Chapter 2

THE INFLUENCE OF G. ERNEST WRIGHT ON THE ARCHAEOLOGY OF PALESTINE

Philip J. King
Boston College

G. Ernest Wright was a versatile scholar, distinguished as both a field archaeologist and a biblical theologian; he was also a charismatic teacher. On the occasion of Wright's death in 1974 Frank M. Cross, his colleague and friend, stated in a tribute at the Memorial Church, Harvard University, "Ernest Wright is best known as an archaeological scholar, and his contributions to Near Eastern archaeology remain as his most imposing and enduring scholarly monument."

Born in 1909, Wright received sound biblical training in the Presbyterian tradition at McCormick Theological Seminary in Chicago. The Seminary curriculum also included courses in biblical archaeology taught by Ovid R. Sellers, the excavator of Beth-zur (Khirbet et-Tubeiqeh) in the Hebron region. Wright's interest in archaeology continued to develop at Johns Hopkins University where he pursued the doctorate in Near Eastern studies under William F. Albright. Wright became closely identified with his mentor, perhaps more so than Albright's other students, because of archaeology. Albright had already established his reputation as the leading American archaeologist in Palestine. Concentrating on prehistory Wright focused on early ceramic typology; his dissertation, *The Pottery of Palestine from the Earliest Times to the End of the Early Bronze Age* (1937), served as a framework for all subsequent studies on the subject.

Another formative influence on Wright the archaeologist was his participation in the seminars on the prehistoric archaeology of the Near East and the Aegean which were conducted by Henri Frankfort at the Oriental Institute of the University of Chicago. Among the contributing members of the seminar was anthropologist Robert J. Braidwood. After World War II Braidwood undertook, in Wright's words, "full regional and ecological surveys and excavations." Braidwood's name is associated in a special way with Jarmo, a prehistoric site east of Kirkuk in Iraq. Dating as early as 7000 B.C.E. Jarmo contained evidence of one of the first village-farming communities. Wright was impressed with the interdisciplinary character of Braidwood's field staff, consisting of both natural and social scientists. In Wright's estimation Braidwood's expeditions were the model for all field projects in archaeology.

Wright had his first experience in field archaeology during the 1934 campaign at Bethel, a well-known religious center in biblical times. Identified with the modern village of Beitin, ten miles north of Jerusalem, Bethel was being excavated by Albright. In addition to Wright, John Bright and James B. Pritchard were among the members of the Bethel staff; all were learning the techniques of field archaeology.

Between 1928 and 1933 Elihu Grant of Haverford College directed five campaigns at Beth-shemesh, identified with Tell er-Rumeileh and situated about twelve miles west of Jerusalem in the northeastern Shephelah. Wright did not participate in the field work, but he assisted with the preparation of the reports on the basis of materials and records from the dig. By reworking the pottery and the stratigraphy Wright brought order out of chaos and thus salvaged important data for the archaeology of Palestine.

As early as 1938 Wright made an enduring contribution to Near Eastern archaeology by launching on behalf of the American Schools of Oriental Research (ASOR) a popular journal entitled the *Biblical Archaeologist*. The *Bulletin of the American Schools of Oriental Research (BASOR)*, which began to appear in 1919, had been serving scholars well; over time, however, it became too technical for the popular reader interested in following developments in biblical archaeology. There was a real need for a more general publication suited to the layperson. Ernest Wright was the ideal person to edit such a journal; a scholar who never lost the common touch, he was always able to translate the results of technical research into the language of the nonspecialist.

The first issue of the *Biblical Archaeologist* (1938) consisted of a mere four pages—a striking contrast with the current issues. Wright's article, "Herod's Nabatean Neighbor," appearing in the initial issue, was the first of thirty-six which Wright contributed to the journal in as many years. Wright continued as a member of the editorial board until 1962, when he resigned after twenty-five years of selfless service.

The bibliography of Ernest Wright appearing in his memorial volume, *Magnalia Dei. The Mighty Acts of God* (1976), consists of more than 300 titles; it is an impressive testimony to his contribution to books and journals relating to biblical and Near Eastern studies. His best-known and most enduring contribution to archaeology is his volume entitled *Biblical Archaeology*; first published in 1957, it was later reprinted, revised, and expanded. This book was a standard textbook in archaeology classes for two decades. Wright's other book-length archaeological publications are the *Westminster Historical Atlas to the Bible* (edited with Floyd V. Filson) and *Shechem: The Biography of a Biblical City*.

After having taught at McCormick Theological Seminary for two decades Wright went to Harvard University in 1958 where he became the mentor to an entire generation of archaeologists. He directed a number of dissertations on archaeological topics, including ceramic typology. William G. Dever acquired his special interest in MB I pottery as a result of his thesis topic on the subject which Wright had suggested; so, too, John S. Holladay who wrote on the pottery of northern Palestine in the ninth-eighth centuries B.C.E. Joe D. Seger and others also chose dissertation topics on ceramic typology.

Wright was a truly charismatic teacher who inspired his students with enthusiasm for the Bible and archaeology. At Harvard it was not unusual for him to leave the lecture hall to the applause of the students. Not only did he take a great deal of personal interest in them, but also he was the rare teacher who encouraged his students to surpass him.

In the memorial service for Ernest Wright at St. Andrew's Church in Jerusalem on September 8, 1974, William Dever, director of the Albright Institute of Archaeological Research, paid tribute to Wright as a teacher, observing that "of all his achievements, that as a teacher will live longest." He went on to give personal witness:

> I have no hesitation in saying that had it not been for Ernest Wright and his encouragement, I would not be in the field of archaeology today, or even necessarily in academic life. I owe him literally everything, and this tribute today is a pathetically small measure of my gratitude. Dozens of his students could give the same testimony.

Wright's influence as a teacher of archaeology was not confined to the classrooms at Harvard but also carried over into the field, especially at Tell Balatah (biblical Shechem) in central Palestine, where between 1956 and 1968 he established his own "school" of Syro-Palestinian archaeology. Wright conceived of Shechem as the training ground for Americans in the post-World War II period. He wanted aspiring archaeologists to learn how to dig according to the best methods available. As Frank Cross observed, "Shechem gave Ernest Wright the opportunity to develop and test new methods of digging."

Shechem, strategically located at the pass between Mt. Gerizim and Mt. Ebal, was an important political and religious center which began its history as a city around 2000 B.C.E. In view of Shechem's role in biblical history it seemed appropriate that Wright direct the long-term dig there. Like Wright, Ernst Sellin, who excavated the site earlier in the century, was also a biblical scholar. After a twenty-year absence from the field Wright arrived at Shechem in the summer of 1956 at the urging of his colleague, Frank Cross. Wright began by conducting a three-week exploratory dig with the assistance of Bernhard W. Anderson and Robert J. Bull of the Drew University faculty.

Reexcavating Tell Balatah was a challenging task; the German archaeologists who had worked there earlier misdated several of the architectural features of the ancient city and left inadequate records. Unfortunately, Sellin's files as well as several small objects from the site had been destroyed by fire when the Americans bombed Berlin in 1943. The only continuity with the German campaigns was in the person of Hans H. Steckeweh; architect-director at Shechem during the 1934 season, he joined Wright's staff for the 1957 campaign. Steckeweh had also worked with Albright at Bethel in order to learn Palestinian pottery.

At Shechem Wright combined the best techniques of digging and recording known in Palestine. Basically he followed the Reisner-Fisher method with the refinements introduced by Kathleen Kenyon. Albright's emphasis on ceramic typology also played a large role, while the project's organizational structure was modeled on Yigael Yadin's at Hazor.

In Wright's estimation George A. Reisner was "one of the greatest geniuses" produced by field archaeology in modern times. Reisner began his archaeological career in 1897 at the pyramids of Giza in Egypt; he excavated in Egypt almost continuously until the outbreak of World War II. He also found time to teach Egyptology at Harvard during an occasional semester and to be curator of the Egyptian collection at the Museum of Fine Arts in Boston. More important, he played a major role in setting standards for Egyptian excavations. A pioneer in archaeological method, Reisner's lasting contribution to the discipline was the debris-layer technique of digging; it consists of separating the occupational layers of a tell's superimposed strata, much the same way one distinguishes the layers of a cake. In the process of separating the layers of debris the excavator must note carefully the location of all artifacts. Reisner combined this method with a detailed recording system which included photographs, a daily written report, maps, architectural plans, and find-spots; a registry of objects containing descriptions of all the artifacts was also kept. Reisner trained a good staff, consisting of native Egyptians who were able to assume responsibility in the field and to serve as foremen or technical men (as they are called on digs in Arab lands).

In 1909–10 Reisner interrupted his Egyptian projects to excavate at Samaria (modern Sebastiyeh) in Palestine. Clarence S. Fisher, an architect from the University of Pennsylvania, ably assisted Reisner on this dig. When Reisner introduced his techniques of digging and recording at the Samaria project, a new day had dawned for Palestinian archaeology, marking the beginning of the systematic excavation of Palestinian tells.

At the end of the Samaria project Reisner returned to Egypt, but his influence on Palestinian archaeology continued to be felt through his architect, Fisher, who spent most of his life in Palestine. Fisher's success in applying Reisner's methods was responsible for the coinage of the term "Reisner-Fisher" method. By participating in almost every dig conducted under American auspices in Palestine between World War I and II, Fisher played a prominent role in the development of Palestinian archaeology. As professor of archaeology at the American School in Jerusalem Fisher acted as adviser to all digs affiliated with ASOR; he also devised a master plan for the systematic coordination of archaeological research in Palestine.

Albright, who called Fisher "one of the most thorough scientific archaeologists of America," learned much from him about excavation technique, pottery chronology, and other aspects of field work. Profiting from the experience of senior colleagues such as Fisher, Albright built on their work and then made his own contribution to Palestinian archaeology. At Tell Beit Mirsim, twelve miles southwest of Hebron on the edge of the Shephelah, Albright developed and refined the ceramic index for Palestine, a process which Flinders Petrie began at Tell el-Hesi in 1890. By classifying the stylistic changes in potsherds, Albright constructed his ceramic typology which he then correlated with the stratigraphy of Tell Beit Mirsim. Through a combination of stratigraphy, typology, and other means, he was able to assign relative dates to the occupational levels of Tell Beit Mirsim.

The Wheeler-Kenyon method is comparable to that of Reisner-Fisher; in fact Wright saw practically no difference between them. In principle they are the same, emphasizing the separation of layers of debris. Samaria served as the laboratory for both methods, with Reisner digging there in the first decade of the century and Kenyon in the 1930s. However, the Wheeler-Kenyon method came into greatest prominence at Tell es-Sultan (Old Testament Jericho) where Kenyon directed the excavations between 1952 and 1958 on behalf of the British School of Archaeology in Jerusalem. Kenyon learned her stratigraphic technique from Mortimer Wheeler, a distinguished but controversial British archaeologist; they had dug together at the Romano-British town of Verulamium in England in the 1930s. The first complete statement of Kenyon's method appeared in her *Beginning in Archaeology* published in 1952, the year she began her Jericho dig.

At Jericho Kenyon ran a deep trench across the mound, but not in the crude way of excavators before World War I. Her procedure was a model of stratigraphic control and careful recording as she went about digging the site in stratified layers within five-meter squares. When this grid method is utilized, sections are automatically formed on the four sides of the five-meter square. These exposed vertical surfaces, called balks, serve as indicators of the successive strata that have been dug.

Wright had many differences with Kenyon during their archaeological careers, but he readily acknowledged her achievements at Samaria and Jericho when he said:

> I have no hesitation in affirming that the Kenyon work at Samaria is one of the most remarkable achievements in the history of Palestinian excavation. The publication of *Samaria III*, when considered together with the extraordinary work done at Jericho between 1952 and 1958, makes her one of the leading field archaeologists of our generation (1959: 17).

At Shechem Wright gave special attention to pottery, the hallmark of the Albright tradition. The potsherds were analyzed daily and their description recorded in detail. Edward F. Campbell, associate director of the Shechem project, has described the pottery reading process at Shechem as "a conversation between the dirt and the artifacts"; a careful correlation of the sherds and the strata can help correct errors in digging. At Jericho Kenyon did not neglect pottery analysis, but it was not accorded the same prominence as it was at Shechem.

Before launching his Shechem expedition in 1956 Ernest Wright paid a visit to the great Israeli dig at Hazor, north of the Sea of Galilee. Yigael Yadin, one of Israel's distinguished archaeologists, directed the Hazor excavations. Wright was impressed with Hazor's organizational structure—a reflection, no doubt, of Yadin's own military background. Teamwork was also much in evidence at Hazor; in fact the original members of the Hazor team are today's leading archaeologists in Israel. At Shechem Wright implemented the team approach. As director he had no interest in being the dig's factotum; he wanted every staff member to share responsibility for digging the site and publishing the results. Today teamwork is the rule on almost all excavations in the Near East; the complexity of the field operations would not allow otherwise.

By 1964 when the dig was well underway the Shechem team saw the need for a topographic survey of the Shechem region as a supplement to excavating: instead of studying Tell Balatah in isolation one could then view it in a regional context. Edward Campbell was entrusted with this survey which resulted in the mapping of about fifty neighboring sites. Today the regional survey is an integral part of almost every excavation project in the Near East because, unlike the individual site, it can answer a broad range of questions about a region's political and cultural history.

Reflecting Braidwood's influence, Wright was aware of the need for specialization on archaeological field projects and was eager to introduce interdisciplinary archaeology at Shechem. However, he was unable to persuade specialists in the physical and social sciences to take part in a dig pertaining to the historical periods in Syria-Palestine; they were more at home at prehistorical sites. When Wright was digging at Shechem in the late 1950s the "new archaeology," as the interdisciplinary approach is called, was not ready to take root in Palestine. Interdisciplinary archaeology became an integral part of an American excavation for the first time at Gezer in the late 1960s; since then almost all Syro-Palestinian digs have been interdisciplinary.

In an attempt to assemble an interdisciplinary team for Shechem Wright searched in 1960 for a geologist who would undertake a survey of the entire Shechem region; at the same time he was eager to engage a paleobotanist and a zoologist. Eventually Wright secured geologist Reuben G. Bullard, who had already been working at Gezer. Bullard raised a whole new set of questions for the consideration of the archaeological staff at Shechem; at the same time he provided valuable information about the source of the building stones used in the Shechem fortifications and identified the ingredients of clay found in the Shechem pottery. The presence of the geologist on the dig brought a new dimension to the archaeological process.

Besides the light it cast on ancient Near Eastern history from the third millennium onward, the Shechem project under Wright was responsible directly or indirectly for establishing a number of other excavations such as Gezer, Taanach, Ai, Tell el-Hesi, Heshbon, Shema, and Caesarea. The directors and several staff members of these digs were trained at Shechem, and in all cases Wright continued to confer with the core staff of these satellite projects.

In the academic year 1964–65 Ernest Wright was visiting director of the Hebrew Union College Biblical and Archaeological School which Nelson Glueck had established in Jerusalem. During that year Wright had the opportunity to study firsthand the topography of the land of Israel. In addition to considering the topography and territorial history of, the Philistine plain, he concentrated on the region around Lachish in the Shephelah. He was especially interested in determining the relationship of Tell el-Hesi to Lachish. From his topographical study he concluded that Hesi was one of several tells in the area which had served as outposts of Lachish in the Iron Age.

In April 1965 Wright undertook a campaign at Tel Gezer, eighteen miles northwest of Jerusalem, with the collaboration of Nelson Glueck, president of the Hebrew Union Colleges and the famed explorer of Transjordan and the Negev. The Irish archaeologist R. A. S. Macalister had excavated Gezer between 1902 and 1909. His was a large-scale project but suffered from the fact that he worked alone. The study of Gezer had been suggested to Wright during his student days as a possible dissertation topic, but he did not pursue it at the time.

Two of Wright's Harvard graduate students, William G. Dever and H. Darrell Lance, who accompanied him to Jerusalem for a year of study in 1964–65, were searching for an archaeological field project. Wright suggested Gezer as a site needing reexcavation. During the first season in 1965 Wright was field director; afterward he relinquished the post to Dever who became director, with Lance as associate director. Under their joint leadership the first phase of the new excavations at Gezer continued through 1971. Having learned the techniques of stratigraphic digging, recording, and pottery analysis at She-chem, the new generation of archaeologists at Gezer applied the method practiced at Shechem and also improved upon them. Wright and Glueck, the founders of the Gezer project, continued to act as official advisers, visiting Gezer each season to plan strategy with the staff and to address the volunteers as part of the lecture series in the field-school program.

Among American field projects in the Near East, Gezer pioneered in the interdisciplinary approach to archaeology. When geologist Reuben Bullard joined the Gezer project he was the first of a variety of specialists, including physical and cultural anthropologists, paleoethnobotanists, and zoologists, who eventually became an integral part of almost all excavations in the Near East.

The excavations at Tell el-Hesi were a direct outgrowth of the Gezer project; Ernest Wright spurred the long-term Hesi project. Located midway between Ashdod and Beer-sheba, Hesi is the 37 a. mound where Flinders Petrie, distinguished Egyptologist, pioneered Palestinian archaeology. He and his successor, Frederick J. Bliss, laid the foundation for the stratigraphy and typology of Palestinian archaeology at Tell el-Hesi beginning in 1890; despite their good work they left many questions unanswered. Compared with other sites excavated before World War I, Hesi was dug well; the early projects suffered from lack of method and inadequately trained excavators. In order to clarify or correct the interpretations of the early archaeologists, Wright en-couraged the reexcavation of sites such as Shechem, Taanach, Ai, Gezer, and Hesi.

The Hesi project, inaugurated in 1970, became a model of interdisci-plinary archaeology. With natural and social scientists and archaeologists working side-by-side at the site, Wright's dream of ecological archaeology in the historical period was fulfilled; the "new archaeology" had finally taken root in Palestine.

Heshbon, located about fifteen miles southwest of Amman in Jordan, was the site of a large-scale dig after the Six Day War of 1967. Siegfried H. Horn, the project director, chose Heshbon in order to illuminate the early history of Transjordan, especially the Israelite conquest and settlement, events that con-tinue to perplex biblical scholars. Several of the Heshbon core staff had trained at Shechem under Ernest Wright.

The archaeology of Jordan owes much to the Heshbon expedition, espe-cially for its pioneering efforts in interdisciplinary research. This was the first truly interdisciplinary project in Jordan on a large scale. Heshbon's environ-mental studies included work on the climate, geology, and soil; hydrology, phytogeography, and zoogeography were also pursued. The Heshbon expedi-tion pioneered methods and procedures for processing large quantities of animal remains; it was also the first to introduce ethnoarchaeology, the ethnographic study of material and social life in the present for the purpose of aiding integration of evidence from the past.

In 1966 Ernest Wright was elected to the presidency of the American Schools of Oriental Research in recognition of his contribution to the archaeology of the Near East. A vigorous president, he was intent upon improving the standards for field archaeology; he also had an overall plan for excavations in Israel and the Arab world. Concerning standards, Avraham Biran, director of the Department of Antiquities in Israel, recalled that Wright had insisted on several occasions, "I will not have incompetent work in the name of ASOR," and "I will not support an excavation which is not directed in accordance with the highest degree of scholarship."

Shortly after his election to the ASOR presidency Wright had to deal with the aftermath of the Six Day War; it radically changed the geographical boundaries within which ASOR had been operating since the sovereignty of Israel in 1948. Transcending political considerations, Wright devised a plan that made it possible for ASOR-affiliated archaeologists to work on both sides of the Near Eastern dividing "wall." Such accommodation is no small achievement in that part of the world. Wright's principal concern was that archaeological field work continue; ASOR archaeologists have been excavating uninterruptedly in Israel and the Arab lands since the Six Day War.

Frank Cross once stated, "One of the greatest needs of biblical archaeology is to learn more about the Phoenicians." Sharing Cross's conviction, Wright was eager to work in Lebanon, the homeland of the ancient Phoenicians. Excavating in Lebanon is full of promise because of its rich mixture of Phoenician, Hittite, Egyptian, Greek, Roman, Byzantine, and Arab cultures. The undug tells of Lebanon conceal material capable of shedding enormous light on the history of the Phoenicians, who had been both sea traders and colonizers.

Unfortunately the vicissitudes of the Near East prevented Wright from sponsoring a project in Lebanon in his quest of the Phoenicians. However, he was not impeded from pursuing them in the colonies they established on Cyprus and in Carthage. Wright also envisioned that, after having studied the Phoenician occupation at Carthage in Tunisia, he would move to Sicily and finally to Spain in pursuit of the Phoenicians, but time ran out before he could realize this ambition.

When Paul Lapp, a most promising Palestinian archaeologist, drowned off the northern coast of Cyprus in 1970, he was just about to begin a long-term dig at Idalion, an ancient city about twelve miles south of modern Nicosia in Cyprus. The occupation of the site extended from the thirteenth century B.C.E. to the Early Roman period. An independent kingdom from 700 B.C.E., Idalion was eclipsed about 450–25 B.C.E. by the Phoenician kingdom of Kition on the southeast coast near modern Larnaca. As part of his long-term plan to investigate Phoenician history in the Mediterranean region, Ernest Wright assumed responsibility for the Idalion dig in place of Lapp.

The systematic excavation of Cyprus has a short history. The Swedish Cyprus Expedition, working in Cyprus from 1927 to 1930, set the archaeology of the island on a scientific foundation, but some of their conclusions needed, to use Wright's word, "overhauling." Earlier the archaeology of Cyprus was at the mercy of amateurs who occupied themselves with treasure-hunting and grave-robbing. More recently several native Cypriots, especially the present director of the Department of Antiquities, Vassos Karageorghis, and his predecessor, Porphyrios Dikaios, have done impressive archaeological work on the island.

The Idalion project gave Wright the occasion to restudy and reclassify the pottery of Cyprus on the basis of controlled stratigraphic excavation. In Wright's characteristically blunt estimate Cypriot pottery chronology was in a chaotic state. The Idalion project was Wright's opportunity to assemble the interdisciplinary staff he wanted for Shechem fifteen years earlier. In addition to the excavators, the Idalion staff included the following specialists: geologist, agronomist, metallurgist, physical anthropologist, paleozoologist, artist, and conservator. The geologist was able to identify the source of clay used in making the pottery of the Late Bronze Age; the agronomist carried out paleo-botanical investigations and pollen analysis; the metallurgist did preliminary research on the ancient Cypriot copper industry. Archaeologists and specialists alike contributed to the interpretation of the excavation's results. After Wright's unexpected death the Idalion project lost its momentum and never achieved his expectations which may have been somewhat unrealistic from the beginning. A few weeks before he died Wright stated:

> Idalion, Cyprus is my most ambitious undertaking in archaeology. It is com-
> pletely interdisciplinary. I like variety of background and training within the
> staff so that no one becomes a "yes-man;" and, through the interchange of
> people from a variety of backgrounds, no one will become fixed on too narrow a
> base (1975: 115).

Today Carthage, on the northern coast of Africa, is a residential suburb of the city of Tunis. Most historians believe that the Phoenicians of Tyre founded Carthage in 825 or 814 B.C.E. By 1972 its rich history had hardly been tapped, and the ancient sites were on the verge of complete displacement by ubiquitous modern developers. In desperation UNESCO launched an international cam-paign to save Carthage from depredation; nine countries, including the United States, responded to the appeal. Wright died before the UNESCO project was finalized, but his successor in the ASOR presidency, Frank Cross, assured ASOR's participation. Between 1975 and 1979 two archaeological teams exca-vated at Carthage under the auspices of ASOR. Lawrence E. Stager focused on the commercial harbor and the precinct of Tanit, also called the Tophet. The

Tophet designated the infamous site where children had been sacrificed to the Carthaginian fertility goddess, Tanit. John Humphrey excavated a nearby site of the Late Roman, Vandal, and Byzantine periods.

While excavators may sometimes prefer to dig sites of certain archaeological periods instead of others, all periods are important and must not be neglected. As president of ASOR, Ernest Wright recognized that some periods were, in his words, "archaeological dark ages"; among these were early Judaism, primitive Christianity, and classical Graeco-Roman antiquity. Wright encouraged younger archaeologists to undertake projects that would illumine these obscure periods; at the same time he urged classicists, early Christian historians, and specialists in early Judaism and the New Testament to join efforts in these undertakings.

Tell er-Ras, the northernmost peak of Mt. Gerizim, was excavated by Robert J. Bull as part of the overall Shechem project. This site yielded hellenistic and Roman remains, including the foundations of a Greek-style temple. On the basis of numismatic and literary evidence, Bull conjectured that the temple, dedicated to Zeus Hypsistos, had been erected by Emperor Hadrian in the second century C.E. According to the excavator, the Roman Zeus temple had been constructed over the Samaritan sanctuary, an earlier edifice dating from 335–30 B.C.E., which the Hasmonean ruler John Hyrcanus destroyed in 128 B.C.E.

Pella took its name from Pella of Macedonia, the birthplace of Alexander the Great. A city of the Decapolis, Pella served as a refuge for Christians fleeing Jerusalem at the beginning of the Jewish revolt against Rome in 66 C.E. Occupation at Pella extended almost continuously from the third millennium B.C.E. to the late medieval period, although Pella was never rebuilt after the earthquake of 747 C.E. Its long history notwithstanding, Pella was best known as a Graeco-Roman city.

Robert H. Smith of the College of Wooster began a full-scale excavation of Pella just before the Six Day War of 1967. The project soon came to an abrupt halt and could not be resumed until 1979. This time the dig took the form of a joint project sponsored by the College of Wooster and the University of Sydney, with J. Basil Hennessy directing the work of the Australians.

As president of ASOR Ernest Wright encouraged the investigation of ancient churches in Transjordan. In the early Byzantine period (324–491 C.E.) Christianity won its struggle against paganism; as a result many churches were built, especially during the late Byzantine period (491–640 C.E.). Remains of these churches have been unearthed at such well-known sites as Madeba, Heshbon, Jerash, Umm el-Jimal, Umm Qais, Pella, Dibon, and Siyaghah. Bastiaan van Elderen has been actively engaged in the excavation of several churches adorned with beautiful mosaics. At Swafiyeh on the outskirts of

Amman he uncovered an elaborate mosaic belonging to a Byzantine church. He also excavated a church at Tell Masuh about three miles east of Heshbon; the church may date to the early fourth century. Because Christianity made great inroads into Transjordan, several more churches remain to be excavated there.

Caesarea Maritima, the magnificent ancient city on the Mediterranean coast, was built by Herod the Great between 22 and 10 B.C.E. in honor of his patron, Caesar Augustus. This 8,000 a. site, one of the largest commercial centers of the ancient Near East, served as the capital of Syria-Palestine for over six hundred years. An important center of early Christianity, Caesarea was the city where Paul was imprisoned for two years before successfully invoking his right as a Roman citizen to appeal to the emperor. There was a substantial Jewish community at Caesarea, living in tension with the Gentiles who were in the majority.

At the request of the Israel Department of Antiquities and with strong support from Ernest Wright, Robert Bull undertook a salvage operation at Caesarea beginning in 1971. The project was necessitated by the encroachments of the local kibbutz, which was cultivating a banana plantation and a citrus grove on the ancient site. The construction of a resort hotel also threatened the archaeological remains. Among Bull's discoveries was the first Mithraeum unearthed in Roman Palestine. Its remains were found in one of the barrel-vault warehouses in the immediate vicinity of the Caesarea harbor. Roman soldiers had used this sanctuary, dating from the late third and early fourth centuries C.E., for the worship of Mithra, an ancient Persian warrior deity of light and truth. The cult of Mithraism was prominent in the Roman Empire and for a time it rivaled Christianity.

Two German archaeologists, Heinrich Kohl and Karl Watzinger, pioneered the exploration of synagogues in Palestine during the early part of the present century. Jewish scholars living in Palestine before the establishment of the state of Israel also took an interest in the ancient synagogues. A leader in this field, Eliezer L. Sukenik, assisted by Nahman Avigad, was engaged in the excavation of several synagogues. Ernest Wright was responsible for a resurgence of interest in synagogue remains beginning in 1970. At Wright's initiative one of his students, Eric M. Meyers, began a long-term project of excavating synagogues in upper Galilee. The first synagogue he investigated was at Khirbet Shema; as the name suggests this site is associated with the burial of Shammai, a member of the Pharisees and a leading Jewish sage who lived in the first century of the era.

The excavators cleared an important public building at Shema; it turned out to be the first broadhouse synagogue uncovered in Galilee. A broadhouse synagogue has its focal point situated on the longer rather than on the shorter wall; traditionally the short wall was the sacred wall. According to Meyers, the remains of the first synagogue at Shema date to the late third century C.E.; a second synagogue built on the ruins of the first was completed by the mid-fourth century and was then destroyed by earthquake in 419. The scientific significance of the Khirbet Shema project resides in the fact that the synagogue at this site was the first ever to be dated through excavation; i.e., on the basis of sealed pottery and coins found beneath the synagogue floor.

The second synagogue site to be excavated was at Meiron, a northern Palestinian Jewish center, across the valley from Khirbet Shema. Two-thirds of the facade of this majestic synagogue still stands to the height of the lintels; hardly anything else survived with the exception of some column bases. In contrast to the synagogue at Khirbet Shema, the Meiron synagogue was a standard basilica type, rectangular in shape with two rows of columns running the length of the room and dividing the structure into a nave and two side aisles. Using sealed remains the archaeologists dated this synagogue to the late third century C.E.

Meyers also dug at Gush Halav (Giscala), five miles northwest of the famous Jewish center of Safed. Two synagogues were discovered, one buried beneath the village church, the other standing on the slopes above the Gush Halav brook. Concentrating on the latter, the excavators are inclined to date this basilical synagogue about 250 C.E.

In 1980 Meyers and his team moved to Khirbet en-Nabratein (Nevor-raya), a short distance southeast of Gush Halav. The synagogue and associated village date to the late Roman–early Byzantine period. The current work of excavation and reconstruction at Nabratein reached its climax when the archaeologists discovered a portion of the aedicula or Torah shrine (known also as the Holy Ark), which dates to the third century C.E. and is in the form of a pediment featuring rampant lions.

Besides investigating individual synagogues in upper Galilee, the excavators conducted a surface survey of the ancient sites in upper and lower Galilee and in the Golan Heights as a way of recovering the material culture of Syria-Palestine in the Roman and Byzantine periods. This combination of regional survey and site excavation has shed new light on several aspects of Jewish life in Galilee before the Arab conquest in 634 C.E. When the Romans destroyed the Second Temple in 70 C.E. Galilee became the center of Jewish life and scholarship in Palestine. That situation prevailed until the accession in 527 C.E. of the Byzantine emperor Justinian the Great who repressed and persecuted the Jews. With the Arab conquest Galilee became a deprived region and the Jewish presence came to an end.

Throughout his life Ernest Wright never lost his enthusiasm for biblical archaeology; he also remained open to new ideas. As time passed he recognized the limitations of archaeology, as he acknowledged in a well-known article entitled "What Archaeology Can and Cannot Do":

With regard to Biblical events, however, it cannot be overstressed that archaeological data are mute. . . . Yet the mute nature of the remains does not mean that archaeology is useless. . . . What archaeology can do for Biblical study is to provide a physical context in time and place which was the environment of the people who produced the Bible or are mentioned in it (1971: 73).

Wright's statement resembles one made by Roland de Vaux, the distinguished French biblical historian and archaeologist: "Archaeology does not confirm the text, which is what it is, it can only confirm the interpretation which we give it" (1970: 78). The similarities between Wright and de Vaux are striking: both were trained biblical scholars deeply involved in the archaeology of Palestine; both appeared to have been more confident of the probative value of archaeology as a discipline in their early years than they were later in life; both wrote about the limitations of archaeological evidence in their mature years.

On the occasion of the memorial service for Ernest Wright at St. Andrew's Church in Jerusalem, William G. Dever said, "He [G. Ernest Wright] was, indeed, mentor of an entire generation of American archaeologists, and for that, perhaps even more than for his other achievements, future generations of scholars will remember him, as we do today, with affection and gratitude." Ernest Wright had trained so many students capable of continuing his work that his death, though tragic, was not so devastating as expected; his students filled the vacuum he left. Therein lies his greatest contribution to the archaeology of Palestine.

BIBLIOGRAPHY

Cross, F. M., Lemke, W. E., and Miller, P. D. (eds.)
  1976   *Magnalia Dei. The Mighty Acts of God: Essays on the Bible and Archaeology in Memory of G. Ernest Wright*. Garden City, NY: Doubleday.

Kenyon, K.
  1952   *Beginning in Archaeology*. London: Phoenix.

Vaux, R. de
  1970   On Right and Wrong Uses of Archaeology. Pp. 64–80 in *Near Eastern Archaeology in the Twentieth Century: Essays in Honor of Nelson Glueck*, ed. J. A. Sanders. Garden City, NY: Doubleday.

Wright, G. E.
  1937   *The Pottery of Palestine from the Earliest Times to the End of the Early Bronze Age*. American Schools of Oriental Research, Publication of the Jerusalem School. Archaeology 1. New Haven, CT: American Schools of Oriental Research.
  1938   Herod's Nabatean Neighbor. *Biblical Archaeologist* 1: 3–4.
  1957   *Biblical Archaeology*. Philadelphia: Westminster.

1959   Israelite Samaria and Iron Age Chronology. *Bulletin of the American
            Schools of Oriental Research* 155: 13–29.
1964   *Shechem: The Biography of a Biblical City*. London: Duckworth.
1971   What Archaeology Can and Cannot Do. *Biblical Archaeologist* 34: 70–76.
1975   The "New" Archaeology. *Biblical Archaeologist* 38: 104–15.

Wright, G. and Filson, F. V. (eds.)
1945   *The Westminster Historical Atlas to the Bible*. Philadelphia: West-
            minster.

Chapter 3

THE BIBLE AND ISRAELI ARCHAEOLOGY

Ephraim Stern
Institute of Archaeology
Hebrew University

For many years the American archaeological study of Palestine revolved around discussions of the relationship between archaeology and biblical studies. The main proponents of this approach were the founding fathers of American biblical archaeology, W. F. Albright and G. E. Wright (e.g., Albright 1966a; 1966b; 1969; Wright 1969; 1970; 1971; Cross 1973). With the death of these scholars we are again witnessing a renewed flood of articles and discussions on related subjects. Not long ago, a complete issue of *BA* was devoted to a reassessment of the subject defined as "Biblical/Palestinian Archaeology: Retrospects and Prospects." It comprised a series of articles dealing with the different aspects of Palestinian archaeology and particularly with the connection between the "new" field archaeology and traditional biblical archaeology. Even this *Festschrift*, dedicated to the memory of the outstanding archaeologist, Glenn Rose, has set aside an entire section in which this matter is debated.

All of the above articles stress the existing need to reassess the purposes of biblical archaeology and especially to reevaluate the connection between field archaeology and traditional biblical archaeology. The essence of this problem has been, in my opinion, exceptionally well defined by H. Darrell Lance in his incisive paper in *BA* (1982). Lance describes our present state as a "particular moment," a period of "hesitation and uncertainty" which requires a rethinking of aims. Among the factors which, in his opinion, are the causes for the present state of American biblical archaeology he cites the change of generations; i.e., the passing of the founding generation of this discipline, whose enthusiasm attracted numerous disciples and whose opinions were always persuasive. Its passing also witnesses the "end of the era of biblical theology which confidently spoke of the acts of God in history" and which emphasized the towering importance of historical and archaeological research for biblical studies. Lance also dwelt on the problem of the information explosion as one of the main causes for the present state of confusion and loss of direction by biblical scholars of the present generation in the light of the flood of new archaeological material. He also rejects the new approach advocated by D. L. Holland (1974), William G. Dever (1974; 1982), and Larry E. Toombs (1982), which calls for the need for an autonomous discipline of Syro-Palestinian archaeology and the abandonment of the term biblical archaeology which in this age of specialization has supposedly become obsolete. Lance considers this approach a confusion of terms.

Though I agree with most of Lance's arguments concerning the relationship between biblical and Palestinian archaeology, it is not my intention to enter into this argument which seems to me to be a purely American controversy. I shall accordingly confine myself to a discussion of Israeli research and its connection with archaeological-biblical study which in my judgment occupies a unique position.

The exclusively American nature of this controversy is also evident from the dearth of reaction in Israeli journals. All my efforts to uncover some discussion of this problem in Israeli publications of recent years yielded only two or three articles on possibly related subjects. One, by the late Yohanan Aharoni (1973), concentrates on the distinctive features of Israeli excavation techniques. An article by Anson Rainey (1975), which describes current American archaeological projects, naturally touches more on the subject, and a recent joint article by Ofer Bar-Yosef and Amihai Mazar (1982), which is completely nonpolemical, presents an overall summary of the development and achievements of Israeli archaeology and thus frees this writer from reiterating a full review of it here.

The sole article by an Israeli archaeologist containing an attempt to express an opinion on the current controversy among American scholars is that of David Ussishkin in the same issue of BA in which Lance's article appeared (1982). This contribution was not conceived on the initiative of the writer but, like the present article, was solicited for the purpose of presenting an additional aspect of the subject.

Indeed, it is not by chance that this debate has elicited no echo whatsoever among Israeli scholars for, in my opinion, there is no feeling of crisis in Israel concerning traditional biblical archaeology (and consequently the expression, this "particular moment," has no significance); rather the opposite is true. Israeli archaeology today enjoys a large measure of continuity both in field techniques and, primarily, in its aims. It is in fact experiencing an unusual period of vitality and growth.

I will attempt to describe the situation in Israel against the background of Lance's presentation of the problems which have led, in his opinion, to the current confusion in American archaeology, noting in turn its continuity along-side its constant growth, its capacity to assimilate new schools of technique without abandoning its dependence on traditional biblical archaeology, its unique body of amateur enthusiasts, and its manner of coping with both the information explosion and the problem of specialization, while at the same time noting its weaknesses.

Israeli archaeology is fortunate in having successfully passed through the change of generations with practically no crisis. In Israel now, too, the generation working in the field and directing the major excavations is for the most part not the same one that was active a few years ago (cf. Ussishkin 1982: 93). Here, too, there are significant differences of personality, enthusiasm, methods of work, etc., between the two generations, but much more remarkable is its element of continuity. One of the main reasons is that the former generation of teachers is fortunately still active in the field, especially in guiding the younger scholar. Their personal influence remains great, and the young archaeologist does not hesitate to seek their help and advice. Scholars such as Benjamin Mazar, Nahman Avigad, Ruth Amiran, and others have helped to forestall any possibility of a sharp break.

By this I do not intend to claim that Israeli archaeology is homogeneous and free from dissension. Differences of opinion exist, and we are constantly made aware of them in controversial articles. However, these revolve mainly around disputes (often extremely vocal) as to the manner of solving a particular chronological or archaeological problem or around the interpretation of a specific find in its biblical or historical context but not around the basic essentials. Subjects of contention among Israeli archaeologists, to cite a few recent examples, are the date of the introduction of earthen ramparts, the date and stages of the Israelite conquest, and the stages in the destruction of the Judean kingdom. Aside from obvious differences in temperament, minor differences can also be observed in methods of excavation and recording and, primarily, in interpretation. There is basically, however, a general agreement, and this is readily apparent both by a visit to an Israeli expedition in the field and in published reports.

This continuity is especially noteworthy in the light of the impressive increase in the number of Israeli archaeologists. The single department of archaeology at the Hebrew University in Jerusalem has now been expanded to four (new departments have been established in Tel Aviv, Haifa, and Beer-sheba), and the number of teachers and students has correspondingly grown. Even Bar-Ilan, a religious university which up to now restricted itself to very minor participation in a number of outside projects, recently took on a few archaeologists and began initiating excavations of its own. Active archaeologists in Israel now number about two hundred, and the increasing number of students in the various institutions ensure a solid cadre in future years and an uninterrupted transfer of teaching and experience from one generation to the next.

A further result of the change of generations in Israeli archaeology is the gradual assimilation and introduction of new developments in field techniques which the younger generation was more responsive to and more inclined to implement. New dimensions have thus been added to the *existing* methods but not without thorough investigation and testing. Thus, e.g., every excavator in Israel now employs the vertical method of excavation and the exact recording of sections and layers of soil (following Kenyon) in combination with the older method based on the "architectural excavation" of large horizontal areas (cf. Aharoni 1973; Bar-Yosef and Mazar 1982: 314–18). The cooperation of the various branches of the natural sciences is now taken for granted at Israeli excavations (no less than at others). The participation of geologists, zoologists, paleobotanists, etc., the utilization of the archaeometric laboratory of the Hebrew University, the use of computers for processing statistical data, and all other facets of the "new archaeology" are now intrinsic ingredients in Israeli excavations in contrast to the situation only several years ago. Further innovations include the concept of the regional and environmental excavation, with emphasis on the ecology, and the concentration of effort in a single central site for a more accurate long-term investigation. Parallel with these changes in field work are more refined recording techniques. Due to the adoption of these changes by the majority of Israeli archaeologists, excavations here present a strikingly uniform appearance, as has already been noted (cf. Ussishkin 1982; Bar-Yosef and Mazar 1982: 314–18). From our American colleagues we have learned many new principles of organizing large expeditions and cooperation between institutions. By means of a gradual incorporation of the new field methodology we have reduced the possibility of confusion and held firm to our original aims.

It should be kept in mind that for Israeli archaeology, as opposed to others, biblical archaeology constitutes a more restricted concept in *time and space*. In *time* it relates only to the period of the Old Testament with a possible over-lapping into the preceding period; i.e., from the fourth millennium B.C.E. to the end of the Persian period. It does not include the days of the New Testament, which are considered part of "Jewish archaeology" or archaeology of the "Mishnaic and Talmudic period." Though in no way less important than the former, they are assigned to the field of classical archaeology and are usually dealt with by separate groups of scholars specializing in the literary sources of this period.

The same difference pertains to the *space* concept. Theoretically Al-bright's classic definition of biblical archaeology is still accepted literally; i.e., it includes all the lands and geographic areas mentioned in the Bible, and we have many scholars who specialize in the comparative study of Near Eastern cultures, both near and far. Yet *in practice* the entire area outside Israel's borders has been physically closed to Israeli archaeologists (a single exception is perhaps an excavation carried out by the Hebrew University in Eithemou in Cyprus, an exception which proves the rule). Even excavation results of close neighboring regions reach us in piecemeal form after much delay, and we are in fact practically cut off from them. As a result, Israeli field work is naturally concentrated only in Israel and is much more confined in comparison with other studies. While these special circumstances have obvious disadvantages, they ultimately contain not a few advantages.

For the above reasons most of us closely following the dispute in American journals find it to a great extent to be sterile and unintelligible. For us, Palestinian and biblical archaeology are synonymous terms which it would be unthinkable to separate. At best it has been interpreted as a question of semantics and not as a fundamental argument and, in general, as "much ado about nothing." Some even feel a degree of disparagement towards it. In some circles, however, the matter is taken more seriously, mainly by those of the older generation who fear that the entire question arose as a result of the present political situation and the awakening of the Arab, especially Syrian, "national archaeology," which endeavors to diminish the role of the Bible as much as possible and particularly of the Israelites in the history of the ancient Near East. They also see a connection with the increasing tendency to conduct excavations in the areas of Jordan and Syria instead of Israel and to transfer research centers to these countries.

However, this circle represents a minority view, with the majority opinion being the one mentioned above. This approach apparently stems from the fact that by virtue of education and background most Israeli archaeologists, myself included, do not consider archaeology to be an independent discipline which can be separated from the literary sources. For us it is not a cut-and-dried subject to be described merely in terms of facts, figures, and plans. Our ties with the Bible are direct and emotional. I would even go so far as to say that all of us dealing with this period in the field are motivated by the desire of experiencing the excitement of excavating a building of a biblical settlement and bringing its contents to light as well as by the possibility of clarifying details of everyday life not mentioned in the Bible or, more rarely, of interpreting or supplementing the historical background, even though we are fully aware of the limitations of this material (cf. Dever 1981; Wright 1971).

This feeling of personal involvement is held by all Israeli archaeologists without exception. It is also the reason for the immense popularity of archaeology in Israel and accounts for the constant increase in the number of those engaged in it. It also often finds expression in scholarly publications even by veteran archaeologists for whom it is not a unique experience. Let me quote one of many examples by my teacher, Nahman Avigad, in his publication of the bullae of Berechia, son of Neriah the scribe, and of Jerahmeel the king's son:

> In conclusion I cannot abstain from expressing my own feelings when handling and deciphering these two bullae for the first time. One has the feeling of personal contact with persons who figure prominently in the dramatic events in which the giant figure of Jeremiah and his faithful follower Baruch were involved at a most critical time preceding the downfall of Judah (1978: 56).

This is the essence and the main purpose of archaeology, while the professional aspect is only a more or less efficient *means* of attaining it. Most of us do not believe that these means should be turned into the aims, even though we are prepared to accept all advanced clinical methods. If, because of this, we remain "backward" and rooted in the concepts of former generations, so be it!

Another phenomenon unique to Israeli archaeology is the pressure exerted by the expectations of a wide circle of the local public who form a highly qualified group of amateur archaeologists. Their experience as volunteers in field work and their constant vigilance concerning the excavation results and the significance for biblical studies make all of us aware, either consciously or unconsciously, of a sense of responsibility to this public.

Interestingly enough, this is a *secular* public that is mainly interested in the classical subjects of archaeology, the reconstruction of the historical background and the description of everyday life. This is in sharp contrast to American archaeology whose enthusiasts are motivated mainly by deep religious feelings. The same is true of Israeli *archaeologists* themselves. Try as I will, of the hundreds of local archaeologists known to me, I cannot conjure up a single member of an extreme religious group. At most, some of them are traditionalists. As I noted above, Bar-Ilan, the only religious university in Israel, was the last to take up this study despite its liberal religious tradition, and it has still failed to establish a department called "Archaeology." Paradoxically, the religious extremists oppose all archaeological activities, maintaining that they are contrary to religious principles, since all that should be known of those days is written in the Scriptures. This is the background both of the struggle in Israel in recent years for excavations in the City of David, Beth-shearim, and other sites and of the opposition to the proposed "Archaeological Law" initiated by a party of religious extremists to transfer some of the jurisdiction over archaeological research to the Rabbis. Our close ties with the secular public on the one hand and the hostility of the religious radicals on the other have, again paradoxically, freed the Israeli archaeologist from some of the dilemmas faced by archaeologists in other countries who are sometimes called upon to furnish archaeological interpretations of matters which do not lend themselves to such interpretations.

I turn now to the information explosion described so well by Lance and to the increasingly narrow specialization. This is truly a problem and a danger. As the excavations and their publications become increasingly complex and demand students to possess greater and greater technical and professional proficiency and when students of archaeology in Israel must acquire mastery of the technical sides of the subject, their ability to devote themselves to the literary sources, whether biblical or external, becomes sharply reduced. As in all spheres of research today, more and more is being studied about less and less, but in Israel the need for specialization and greater concentration on field work at the expense of biblical studies is considered a genuine loss. This is certainly nothing to be proud of or to transform into an independent discipline. Furthermore, specialization is an existing evil today even within the limited sphere of Palestinian archaeology itself. Can one person today cope with all the finds from an excavation which can range through widely separated and dissimilar periods? I think not. Is this a reason, however, to divide Palestinian archaeology into a number of different disciplines, each of which will claim autonomy? So far, fortunately, no one has proposed this. Yet, it is basically an inevitable process, and, of the many and varied suggestions for addressing the issue, the chief one is undoubtedly the team effort, as many have already maintained.

In this matter as well, local specialists in Israel enjoy a decided advantage. Because of the small physical area of the country, its relatively few scientific institutions, and the existence of centralized organizations, such as the Israel Exploration Society, we receive (and this holds true for biblical scholars and historians of the ancient Near East, etc.) the latest excavation reports almost at the very time of discovery not only through publications (such as *Hadashot Archeologiyot, Qadmoniot,* etc.) but also orally. Scholars in related fields also visit the various excavations every year to observe, offer advice, and exchange views on interpretations of finds. This information exchange is supplemented by conferences of the Israel Exploration Society, by professional archaeological meetings, and, especially, by advanced seminars which are frequently addressed by guest speakers from other institutions, thus ensuring a constant flow of information.

This is made possible, as was stated above, by the simple geographic concentration of numerous scholars of all branches of research in one or two institutions. It is thus easy to meet scholars of different fields, to inform them of new developments, to turn over to them material for examination, and to receive their advice.

Such large concentrations of specialists in closely related disciplines is a singular phenomenon, especially in comparison with the United States where most of the departments of Near Eastern studies at universities have a single expert in a very broad discipline such as an archaeologist, an Egyptologist, an Assyriologist, a specialist in Hebrew language, etc. If, like many of us, they specialize in much narrower fields within each discipline, this may be one of the main reasons for the feeling of isolation of which Lance has written. Reading and attending annual meetings is not sufficient today to preserve interdisciplinary ties, to maintain schools, and to cultivate future generations of students. Even in this age of team effort the feeling of isolation is known by those who are preparing publication reports of a single excavation, and how much more so by those whose work is ever more detailed and complex.

Israeli archaeology, in summary, suffers neither from a lack of continuity nor from confusion as to its purpose in relation to either biblical studies or the study of the history of the ancient Near East. It has also successfully assimilated the new field methodology and in my opinion has overcome the problems of specialization and of the information explosion.

The greatest deficiency of Israeli archaeology is in its failure to present to the scientific world the complete results of its research. This is its Achilles' heel, and in the last few years it has reached catastrophic proportions. In this matter it is a full partner in the dilemmas facing archaeological study in general, despite the large number of preliminary reports appearing in journals, both Israeli and others, and despite the synthetic works produced here (e.g. Amiran 1969; Avi-Yonah and Stern 1975–78; Dothan 1982; Stern 1982). Almost no final reports of the scores of large excavations carried out in the past few decades have appeared, and only a few will probably be published in the near future. Those which have been published can almost be counted on the fingers of one hand. This sin was begun by the founders of Israeli archaeology, with the second generation following in their footsteps, and there is no reason to anticipate any improvement with the new generation.

The problem is a very grave one, and for some reason it has been totally neglected aside perhaps from repeated complaints (Bar-Yosef and Mazar 1982: 321–22). Anyone, including the present writer, who has attempted to summarize the material culture of a particular period or has done research on a subject connected with a comparative study of the results of several excavations, is well aware that the major part of the material one seeks is lying concealed in the archives of the various excavators from whom one must beg the key. If this is the case with pure archaeological subjects, how much greater are the difficulties when the subject is an archaeological-biblical or another interdisciplinary combination.

There is an absurdity in the situation that is not unique to Israeli archaeology. How many changes has field methodology undergone since the 1930s, how many scores of technical articles have been published on new developments in excavation and recording techniques, and how few, if any, studies are devoted to the method of the publication of the excavation results? The models for such publications have remained the same since the 1930s and 1940s, and reports like *Tell Beit Mirsim* and *Megiddo* continue to be imitated to this day.

The contrast between the advanced excavation and the recording methods of the results of this research is the reason for the intolerable situation today.

In this matter there is indeed true confusion in Israeli archaeology. The root of the problem, in my opinion, is that in this era of teamwork there has been a great increase of material that was previously not dealt with at excavations, and we lack basic guidelines as to what part of this material must be published and what part can be left in the archives for examination by experts requiring additional details. Instead of focusing on the question of whether or not Palestinian archaeology is a discipline distinct from biblical archaeology, it would be more worthwhile if all of us, Americans and Israeli, would tackle the problem of how to ensure that the research results in this field reach all those interested in it, no matter what their starting point or field of interest.

BIBLIOGRAPHY

Aharoni, Y.
  1973   Remarks on the "Israeli" Method of Excavation. *Eretz Israel* 11: 48–53 (Hebrew).

Albright, W. F.
  1966a   *Archaeology, Historical Analogy, and Early Biblical Tradition*. Baton Rouge: Louisiana State University.
  1966b   *New Horizons in Biblical Research*. London: Oxford University.
  1969   The Impact of Archaeology on Biblical Research—1966. Pp. 1–14 in *New Directions in Biblical Archaeology*, eds. D. N. Freedman and J. Greenfield. Garden City, NY: Doubleday.

Amiran, Ruth
  1969   *Ancient Pottery of the Holy Land*. Jerusalem - Ramat - Gan: Massada.

Avigad, N.
  1978   Baruch the Scribe and Jerahmeel the King's Son. *Israel Exploration Journal* 28: 52–56.

Avi-Yonah, M. and Stern, E. (eds.)
  1975–   *Encyclopedia of Archaeological Excavations in the Holy Land*. 4 vols. Jerusalem: Israel Exploration Society and Massada.

Bar-Yosef, O. and Mazar, A.
  1982   Israeli Archaeology. *World Archaeology* 13: 310–25.

Cross, F. M.
  1973   W. F. Albright's View of Biblical Archaeology and its Methodology. *Biblical Archaeologist* 36: 2–5.

Dever, W. G.
  1974   *Archaeology and Biblical Studies: Retrospects and Prospects*. Evanston, IL: Seabury-Western Theological Seminary.
  1981   What Archaeology Can Contribute to the Understanding of the Bible. *Biblical Archaeology Review* 7: 40–41.
  1982   Retrospects and Prospects in Biblical and Syro-Palestinian Archaeology. *Biblical Archaeologist* 45: 103–7.

Dothan, Trude
    1982   *The Philistines and Their Material Culture.* New Haven and London:
              Yale University.
Holland, D. L.
    1974   "Biblical Archaeology": An Onomatic Perplexity. *Biblical Archaeologist*
              37: 19–23.
Lance, H. D.
    1982   American Biblical Archaeology in Perspective. *Biblical Archaeologist* 45:
              97–101.
Rainey, A.
    1975   "In Archaeology Think Square." *Eternity* 26: 56–57, 63.
Stern, E.
    1982   *Material Culture of the Land of the Bible in the Persian Period 538–332*
              B.C.E. Warminster: Avis and Phillips and Israel Exploration Society.
Toombs, L. E.
    1982   The Development of Palestinian Archaeology as a Discipline. *Biblical
              Archaeologist* 45: 89–91.
Ussishkin, D.
    1982   Where is Israeli Archaeology Going (?). *Biblical Archaeologist* 45: 93–95.
Wright, G. E.
    1969   Biblical Archaeology Today. Pp. 149–65 in *New Directions in Biblical
              Archaeology,* eds. D. N. Freedman and J. Greenfield. Garden City, NY:
              Doubleday.
    1970   The Phenomenon of American Archaeology in the Near East. Pp. 3–40 in
              Near Eastern Archaeology in the Twentieth Century, ed. J. A. Sanders.
              Garden City, NY: Doubleday.
    1971   What Archaeology Can and Cannot Do. *Biblical Archaeologist* 34: 70–76.

Chapter 4

A PERSPECTIVE ON THE NEW ARCHAEOLOGY

Lawrence E. Toombs
Wilfrid Laurier University

From its planning stages in 1968–69 through the eight field seasons which
have taken place since that date, the Joint Expedition to Tell el-Hesi has been
committed to an experimental approach to excavation, recording, and interpretation. Its first director, Dr. John Worrell, insisted on the practice of meticulous field techniques and on the development of comprehensive systems of
recording in order to preserve as much data of as wide a variety of types as
possible. Much of the detail included in the *Tell el-Hesi Field Manual* (Blakely
and Toombs 1980) is the direct result of his leadership. Even when working
with limited budgets he brought scientific specialists into the field and saw to it
that they had input not only into the interpretation of data in their specific
areas of specialization but also into the planning of excavation strategy and the
overall interpretation of the stratigraphy of the site. In matters of interpretation he took the position that cultural questions were fully as significant as, if
not more important than, the traditional chronological/historical questions.

Dr. Worrell's successor, Dr. D. Glenn Rose, preserved the interests of his
predecessor but added a further dimension. His studies in the "new archaeology" led him to begin the application of its leading principles to the development of excavation strategy and to the interpretation of the results (Rose
forthcoming). He envisaged a creative interplay between the theoretical task
of hypothesis formation and the field activity of hypothesis testing, the result of
which would be an ongoing process, cumulative in its effect and as accurate in
its conclusions as the nature of the data permitted. The material recovered
from initial excavation would lead to the formulation of an hypothesis or a
series of alternative hypotheses to account for the nature of the data. Digging
strategy would then be designed to test the hypothesis or to discriminate among
the alternative hypotheses. The result would be confirmation, rejection, or

modification of the hypothetical framework or, frequently, the formulation of new hypotheses as new phenomena appeared. In the light of these conclusions the research design of the excavation for subsequent seasons would be adjusted or redeveloped.

Regrettably, events dictated that Dr. Rose could do no more than *begin* the application of these principles to the excavation of Tell el-Hesi. He put in place the theoretical framework for archaeological planning and refined it during three seasons of excavation (1977, 1979, 1981). However, his untimely death, in Jerusalem on August 6, 1981, cut off the possibility of two projects toward which he looked with great enthusiasm: the incorporation of the method into the final publication of the site and an investigation of the Hesi region as a whole in terms of the methodology which he favored.

Dr. Rose's involvement with Tell el-Hesi indicates his insight into the nature of the "new archaeology." He recognized that it was not primarily a revision of methodology but rather a profound reexamination of philosophy and theory. This is not to say that a revolution in theory would not have reflex effects on archaeology at all levels, including field and analytical procedures; it is, rather, to assert that methodological changes are indicated by and derivative from the theoretical framework. The movement is from theory to praxis, not the reverse. Such a conclusion reflects the conviction that refinements in the ways in which data are gathered and sorted do not constitute increases in archaeological knowledge but only provide qualitatively and quantitatively better raw material for the interpretive task which is the main goal of archaeology.

During the decades prior to 1968 a considerable body of literature appeared in which attempts were made to describe the weaknesses of traditional archaeology and to indicate directions in which progress was possible (e.g., Stewart and Seltzer 1938; Willey and Phillips 1958). Several major sources of dissatisfaction surfaced in the discussion. One of these was the almost completely descriptive nature of most archaeological reporting. Many site reports seemed satisfied to describe structures and catalog artifacts systematically, the apparent assumption being that the data thus set forth would, in some measure at least, interpret itself. How the researcher could pass from organized lists of things to a knowledge of the societies which produced them was given little consideration. Where the interest of the excavator did focus on interpretation it did so without an articulated theoretical framework. The intuition of a talented excavator and his or her inferences drawn from the material remains by unsystematized and often unexpressed criteria provided the interpretation. If put forward by archaeologists of stature such interpretations often became accepted as valid generalizations or even as "facts." The only text of the interpretation available to the scholars was their own estimate of its intrinsic probability and of the capability and intellectual honesty of the interpreter (Thompson 1956).

These and other deficiencies in traditional archaeology appeared to stem from a double epistemological failure: on the one hand, a failure of the discipline to understand itself and, on the other, a failure to comprehend the nature of the entities with which it had to deal (Toombs 1982). The "new archaeology" set out to deal with these two epistemological problems.

The complexity of the issues and the number of scholars who have contributed to their discussion preclude the possibility of making this short paper a history of the new archaeology or even a review of the pertinent literature. Summary articles by Robert C. Dunnell in the *American Journal of Archaeology* (1979; 1980; 1981; 1982) and the collection of papers published in the *Bulletin of the American Schools of Oriental Research* (no. 242, 1981) give a historical perspective on the movement and encapsulate its internal debates, the development of its theory, and its potential for the future. The present paper will concentrate on selected theoretical problems central to the new archaeology and attempt a brief assessment of their significance.

Archaeology as Science

In a fundamental paper entitled "Archaeological Perspectives" (1972, a reprint of *New Perspectives in Archaeology,* 1968: 5–32), L. R. Binford assumes as self-evident that archaeology must understand itself as a science and must, consequently, develop its theories and procedures in ways congruent with those of the physical sciences. Without directly saying so the paper excludes archaeology from the realm of humanistic studies. In considering the nature of archaeological reasoning and the character of archaeological proof the authors consistently draw on the principles of scientific explanation.

The authors' argument rests on a multistage view of the process of scientific reasoning: observation, induction, hypothesis formation, deduction, hypothesis testing, and principle (or law). The observation with which the process begins is the material remains recovered by excavation. The inductive reasoning applied to them is a psychological phenomenon subject to no rules. It may be the result of intuition or inference or a pure guess. Whatever its quality, induction produces a tentative explanation of the observed archaeological record; i.e., a hypothesis. A particular hypothesis is one of many competing possibilities and possesses only a greater or lesser, but generally indeterminate, degree of probability.

Traditional archaeology, however it defined its aims, usually stopped its interpretive activity at the point of hypothesis formation, leaving others to judge the degree of probability of the hypothesis and to accept or reject it on the basis of whatever criteria they chose to employ. The thrust of Binford's paper, the feature which he identified as the element of epistemological new-ness in the new archaeology, was its insistence that archaeological reasoning must go beyond induction and hypothesis formation to deduction and hypoth-esis testing (Binford 1978: 90). Deductive reasoning differs from induction in that, granted the truth of the premise, the conclusion is not a probability but a certainty. Assuming the truth of the hypothesis arrived at by induction, the researcher can deduce conclusions which inevitably follow from it. The con-clusions become the basis for testing. A research design can be established which will determine whether the results that were predicted deductively from the hypothesis do in fact occur. If they do not, the hypothesis must either be abandoned or be modified and retested. If they do, the hypothesis may be considered proved and may be given the status of a confirmed generalization or law. Confirmed generalizations arrived at by deductive reasoning and ex-perimental testing constitute archaeological knowledge.

The proposed pattern of archaeological interpretation, simple to state in broad outline, invites debate on each separate element as well as on the validity of the epistemological concept as a whole. Since the publication of Binford's paper, discussion has proceeded on all these fronts.

The Nature of Archaeological Data

The assumption that the material remains recovered by the archaeologist are *direct* evidence for the culture which produced them will not bear scrutiny. What the archaeologist uncovers has passed through a long history from the time of original production to the time of discovery (Daniels 1972; Clarke 1973). At some point the structure and objects were items of use, functioning within the activity patterns of a human community. They have meaning in the context of those activities. They were deposited, presumably intentionally, in a particular context within the living space of that community, or they went out of use and were discarded. Many of the artifacts underwent changes caused by the activity of later settlers on the site. An example from Hesi is the reuse of basalt grinders as capstones for drains and graves. Finally, the sojourn of the material in the earth produces physical and chemical changes resulting in various degrees of modification or even in destruction. The end result of all these processes is the archaeological record as excavated (Sullivan 1978: 195–205).

Before the connection can be made between artifact-as-found and cul-ture-as-lived, the archaeologist must follow out and interpret the traces which remain of each stage or facet of the artifact's history. In effect, he or she must analyze the process of transmission of the artifact from its function in a cultural system to the state in which it was recovered. The necessity of understanding the process of transmission involves three closely related interpretive provinces: retrieval theory, analytical theory, and site-formation theory (Clarke 1973; Hill and Evans 1972; Sullivan 1978: 201-3).

The first of these deals with "sampling theory, field research design, and flexible research strategies" (Clarke 1973: 16) and enables the researcher to estimate the potential interpretive value of archaeological remains and systematically to recover the kinds of material of greatest interpretive significance. The second treats theories of classification and their use in selecting material of interpretive value. The third analyzes the factors which are operative in the formation of sites, so that the material recovered may be interpreted in the light of the processes by which they came to occupy the place where they were found on the site.

The Aims of Archaeology

Moving from the beginning of the schema of archaeological reasoning to its concluding phases (deduction—hypothesis testing—confirmed generalization) raises strongly the questions of what is to be explained and what kind of generalizations are sought.

In reconstructionist archaeology the interpretive route followed is to establish on the basis of the material remains a reconstruction of the culture which produced them. The reconstruction is then the datum to be explained. The new archaeology would insist that this amounts to the explanation of an artificial creation of the investigator whose errors and biases may be included. The proper subject of explanation is not the construct but the variations and similarities in the empirical data itself.

The answer given to the question of the type of generalization to be generated is a basic one. It has repercussions all the way back through the reasoning process to its beginning. The tentative hypothesis, formed by induction, and the generalization, confirmed by testing, are the same proposition with a different epistemological status. The kind of data sought by the investigator and the manner in which it is manipulated will also be influenced by the expectation of the end result of the process.

Binford (1972) described traditional archaeology as having three principal aims. At one level it worked toward the reconstruction of cultural history. At another it aimed at reconstructing the life-ways of the people who left the archaeological record. A third goal, less frequently pursued, was the study of cultural process. In terms of the structure of a tell, the reconstruction of cultural history may be thought of as a grappling with the chronological relationships involved in the vertical dimensions of the excavation. Its archaeological symbol is the stratigraphic trench. Reconstruction of the life-ways of an ancient people involves spatial relationships such as the use of living areas and the function, in relation to that space, of the objects accumulated on the surfaces. Its archaeological symbol is the area exposure of a single level or stratum. Processual theory concerns itself with what happened between the levels, with the processes by which the culture changed from one relatively static stage to the next. Its symbol is the interstices between the levels. The processual aim requires both cultural history and cultural reconstruction, but its intention is to discover the laws of cultural change. The new archaeology in general accepts the processual goal of archaeology.

To be meaningful the study of cultural processes requires an understanding of culture in systemic terms. An artifact or class of artifacts has no cultural significance apart from its place as a functioning element within a cultural system, since it is the system as a whole which determines the function and defines the significance of the artifact or artifact class. The task of archaeology is to determine the laws governing the changes in cultural systems. Out of such an understanding the changing cultural significance of artifacts and artifact groupings would emerge. However, the reasoning cannot be unidirectional from cultural system to artifact significance. The processes of cultural change may have to be inferred from variations in groups of functionally related artifacts through time. This means that a continuous interplay should be maintained between the study of artifact variation and the concept of the cultural system through which the investigator confers meaning on the artifact.

The examples given in the previous paragraph relate to single sites. However, in the study of cultural process a single site can serve only as an exemplar, since the dynamics of cultural process are regional, not site-specific, and the laws of cultural process, if they can be developed, are universal. One practical result of the proposed process of archaeological reasoning is to force the archaeologist, even when working on a single site, to think regionally and to regard the settlements within a region as an interrelated cultural unit; in effect, as a system of cultural systems in interaction with one another and with the ecology of the region.

Regional interest brings with it a battery of theoretical problems. Not least among them is the development of principles for the delineation of the region. In addition, the methodology of regional surveying and the sampling techniques to be used must be worked out. These requirements bring the archaeologist back to retrieval and sampling theory.

The Role of Models

Interpretation, whether it takes the form of hypothesis formation or explanation of observed phenomena, ordinarily implies the existence of a model, sometimes unconsciously present, in the mind of the interpreter. It may be a model of site-formation or a model of the spatial interrelationships of the architectural constituents of an ancient city. The hypotheses which in the mind of the excavator have the highest order of probability will be those derived from the model. Three types of models, with broader interpretive significance than the examples just given, have dominated recent archaeological literature: the ethnographic, the evolutionary, and the ecological. Each of these models has been the subject of intense investigation. The utility, strength, and weakness of each has been probed, and the interpretive value of each for archaeology has been assessed. For the purposes of this paper a brief statement of the characteristics of each model must suffice.

Ethnography/Ethnoarchaeology (cf. Kramer 1979). The employment of an ethnographic model is analogical (Anderson 1969; Ascher 1961; Binford 1967). Its premise is that the behavior of contemporary social groups provide analogies on the basis of which valid (i.e., highly probable) generalizations concerning the relationships between material culture and behavior in the past may be drawn. The level of explanation may be the function of a single artifact or artifact class within the structure of a culture. It may operate also on a broader plain, attempting to elucidate the interrelationships of all the items recovered in terms of human behavior as operative in contemporary cultures. The aim of ethnographic analogy is to establish a correlation between artifact and behavior, for only in the context of such a correlation does the artifact have archaeological meaning.

Ethnoarchaeology has met with varying degrees of approval ranging from enthusiastic acceptance to outright rejection. The claim has even been made that archaeology should inform ethnography rather than the reverse. Nevertheless, ethnography remains a model or tool widely used in current archaeological work.

The Evolutionary Model. This model interprets cultural process in terms of the theory of biological or social evolution. Its premise is that a culture is an adaptive system. Changes in its physical environment and interaction with other societies through such factors as trade, immigration, invasion, or political domination bring about adaptive cultural changes. The attempted adaptations leave their traces in the archaeological record. Successful adaptations survive and their continuance modifies the society and constitutes the processual development of the culture.

The evolutionary model, derived as it is from the natural and social sciences, is subject to the internal debates within the sciences, and evolutionary theory in these sciences is in a state of flux. Consequently, the archaeologist has no commonly accepted model with which to work. E.g., agreement does not exist on so basic a point as whether the theories of biological evolution are directly applicable to culture (Yoffee 1979) or on whether social evolution is sufficiently different to require a distinct set of laws (Trigger 1978).

The Ecological Model (Richardson 1977; Vayda and McCay 1975). The ecological and evolutionary models are closely related. Both view culture as an adaptive system. Whereas evolutionary theory lays out long-range processes of adaptation and development, ecology is more directly attuned to specific situations. It seeks to discover and explain the causes of observed phenomena by investigating the complex influences to which the culture has been exposed and the nature of its reactions to them. The influences may originate in the physical environment (floods, earthquakes, climatic variations), or they may result from interaction with other cultures. The theoretical basis of the model is provided by the sciences of biological and human ecology. Adoption of an evolutionary or ecological model has two implications.

(1) Neither model can be used effectively if the cultural traces gathered in the excavation belong to only a few obvious categories. Both may be described as totality models. For full implementation they require that all the influences impacting on a culture and all its reactions to them be available for study. This ideal can only be approximated in practice but, in order that the approximation be as close as possible, a very large number of variables must be measurable in the archaeological record. This implies the gathering of as wide a range of data as ingenuity can devise. It also requires meticulous control of the quality of the data.

(2) Both models derive from the empirical sciences. Consequently, their application most readily results in materialistic hypotheses to account for cultural phenomena. Social factors, susceptible of measurement, may also be invoked in the hypothesis (Thomas 1978). Explanations capable of statistical expression are preferred by the models. As a result, the role of ideology and, even more clearly, the effect of individual creativity and imagination in producing cultural variability tend to slip through the net of ecological or evolutionary explanation.

General Observations

A gap between the promise of the new archaeology and its performance has often been noted (Schiffer 1978). It has failed to produce a generally accepted body of archaeological theory, a philosophy of archaeology parallel to the philosophy of science. It has not generated general laws of cultural process, and archaeological theory still remains a matter of vigorous debate. One probable reason for these failures is the nature of the hypotheses which can be inferred from the cultural traces surviving in the archaeological record. In most cases they are not the kind of hypotheses from which conclusions of certainty can readily be deduced. It is more likely that even the most carefully crafted hypothesis will contain ambiguities and hidden assumptions which make deductions from it virtually impossible. The alleged deduction will frequently be an inference in disguise.

The enterprise of hypothesis testing in archaeology is beset by difficulties. The physical sciences can test an hypothesis by experiments in which all the variables except one are held constant, and the effect of the single variable can be accurately determined. Biological sciences approximate this ideal but with less rigor. The more uncontrolled variables operative in a test, the less certain its results. As archaeological investigation abundantly illustrates, the number of variables operative within a culture and in its interactions with its environment are almost literally innumerable, and none lie within the control of the investigator. By its nature archaeology may have to be content with hypothesis only imperfectly tested, remaining debatable, and depending upon probability rather than being able to attain confirmation.

Alan P. Sullivan (1978) poses the question of justification in archaeological explanation in a way somewhat different from but not incompatible with Binford's formulation (1978). He argues that a distinction must be made between archaeological remains (which are not archaeological data since they are contemporary, not ancient, phenomena) and the evidence which can be inferred from them (which is the data of archaeology). The drawing of inferences from the known contemporary phenomena to the unknown ancient situation is a psychological activity. The inferences must be made public, and this is done by arguments. These may involve either deductive or inductive reasoning. In either case the validity of the arguments can be assessed by the principles of logic applicable to the type of reasoning employed. In order that the validity of archaeological argumentation may be established, archaeological publication must maintain a distinction among the description of phenomena, explanatory hypotheses, and arguments in support of the hypotheses. Only when this is done can other scholars evaluate the weight of the arguments advanced in justification of the hypothesis.

Although the new archaeology has not yet developed a firm theoretical framework, it has raised basic theoretical questions in every aspect of the discipline and has explored them in detail. Theoretical interest of this kind is relatively new to Syro-Palestinian archaeology, and its impact is just beginning to be felt (Dever 1981). Its influence provides an impetus toward a reorientation of Syro-Palestinian archaeology from merely methodological interests toward a more systematic examination of its theoretical base, particularly in the areas of research design and interpretation theory.

The involvement of Syro-Palestinian archaeology with the new archaeology will, hopefully, not be one-way traffic. The deeply stratified sites of the Syro-Palestinian area provide unique opportunities for devising and testing cultural hypotheses, and the variety of material-culture items recovered provides a broad base for the application of systems theory and for the study of cultural process. In a relatively short time the learners should become contributors to the ongoing development of archaeological theory and its application.

In the context of a volume devoted to "Bible and Archaeology" the present paper, which has nothing to say about Bible, must have the appearance of a fifth wheel. However, it may have more relevance to biblical studies than appears on the surface. Retrieval theory, analytical theory, site-formation theory, and the nature of archaeological reasoning all contribute to an understanding of what archaeology can validly say about the cultures which left their traces in the archaeological record. By presenting biblical scholars with cultural interpretations refined to their highest degree of probability, archaeology in the Bible lands may be performing the greatest possible service to those whose main task is literary interpretation.

BIBLIOGRAPHY

Anderson, K. M.
  1969   Ethnographic Analogy and Archaeological Interpretation. *Science* 163: 133–38.

Ascher, X.
  1961   Analogy in Archaeological Interpretation. *Southwestern Journal of Anthropology* 17: 317–25.

Athens, J. S.
  1977   Theory building and the Study of the Evolutionary Process in Complex Societies. Pp. 353–58 in *For Theory Building in Archaeology*, ed. L. R. Binford. New York: Academic Press.

Binford, L. R.
  1962   Archaeology As Anthropology. *American Antiquity* 28: 217–25.
  1967   Smudge Pits and Hide Smoking: The Use of Analogy in Archaeological Reasoning. *American Antiquity* 32: 1–12.
  1972   *An Archaeological Perspective*. New York: Academic Press.
  1978   *An Archaeological Perspective*. New York: Seminar Press.

Blakely, J. R. and Toombs, L. E.
  1980   *The Tell el-Hesi Field Manual: The Joint Expedition to Tell el-Hesi* Vol. 1. Cambridge: American Schools of Oriental Research.

Clarke, D. L.
  1973   Archaeology: The Loss of Innocence. *Antiquity* 47: 6–18.

Daniels, S. G. H.
  1972   Research Design Models. In *Models in Archaeology*, ed. D. L. Clarke. London: Methuen.

Dever, W. G.
1981   The Impact of the "New Archaeology" on Syro-Palestinian Archaeology. *Bulletin of the American Schools of Oriental Research* 242: 15–30.

Dunnell, R. C.
1979   Current Americanist Archaeology. *American Journal of Archaeology* 83: 437–49.
1980   Americanist Archaeology: The 1979 Contribution. *American Journal of Archaeology* 84: 463–78.
1981   Americanist Archaeology: The 1980 Literature. *American Journal of Archaeology* 85: 429–45.
1982   Americanist Archaeological Literature: 1981. *American Journal of Archaeology* 86: 509–29.

Fritz, J. M. and Plog, F. T.
1970   The Nature of Archaeological Explanation. *American Antiquity* 35: 405–12.

Hardesty, D. L.
1980   The Use of General Ecological Principles in Archaeology. *Advances in Archaeological Method and Theory* 3: 157–87.

Hill, J. N.
1972   The Methodological Debate in Contemporary Archaeology. Pp. 61–108 in *Models in Archaeology*, ed. D. L. Clarke. London: Methuen.

Hill, J. N. and Evans, R. K.
1972   A Model for Classification and Typology. Pp. 231–274 in *Models in Archaeology*, ed. D. L. Clarke. London: Methuen.

Kramer, C. (ed.)
1979   *Ethnoarchaeology: Implications of Ethnography for Archaeology*. New York: Columbia University.

Levine, M. E.
1973   On Explanation in Archaeology. *American Antiquity* 38: 387–95.

Meltzer, D.
1979   Paradigms and the Nature of Change in American Archaeology. *American Antiquity* 44: 644–57.

Redman, C. L.
1974   Archaeological Sampling Strategies. *Addison-Wesley Modular Publications in Archaeology*, No. 55.

Redman, C. L. and Watson, P. J.
1970   Systematic Intensive Surface Collection. *American Antiquity* 35: 279–91.

Richardson, P. J.
1977   Ecology and Human Ecology: A Comparison of Theories in Biological and Social Sciences. *American Ethnologist* 4: 1–26.

Rose, D. G.
forth-   Tell el-Hesi and the New Archaeology. In *Tell el-Hesi: The Site and the*
coming   *Expedition*. Excavation Reports of the American Schools of Oriental Research: Tell el-Hesi 4, eds. B. T. Dahlberg and K. J. O'Connell, S. J. Winston Salem, NC: Wake Forest University.

Ruppe, R. J.
1966   The Archaeological Survey: A Defense. *American Antiquity* 31: 313–33.

Sabloff, J. A.
    1981   When the Rhetoric Fades: A Brief Appraisal of Intellectual Trends in
                American Archaeology During the Past Two Decades. *Bulletin of the
                American Schools of Oriental Research* 242: 1–6.

Schiffer, M. B.
    1978   Taking the Pulse of Method and Theory in American Archaeology.
                American Antiquity 43: 153–58.

Schiffer, M. B., Sullivan, A. P., and Klinger, T. C.
    1978   The Design of Archaeological Surveys. *World Archaeology* 10: 1–28.

Stewart, J. H. and Seltzer, F. M.
    1938   Function and Configuration in Archaeology. *American Antiquity* 4: 4–
                10.

Sullivan, A. P.
    1978   Inference and Evidence in Archaeology: A Discussion of the Conceptual
                Problems. Pp. 183–222 in *Advances in Archaeological Method and
                Theory*. Vol. 1, ed. Michael B. Schiffer. New York: Academic Press.

Thomas, D. H.
    1978   The Awful Truth About Statistics in Archaeology. *American Antiquity*
                43: 231–44.

Thompson, R. H.
    1956   The Subjective Element in Archaeological Inference. *Southwestern Jour-
                nal of Archaeology* 12: 327–32.

Toombs, L. E.
    1982   The Development of Palestinian Archaeology as a Discipline. *Biblical
                Archaeologist* 45: 89–92.

Trigger, B. G.
    1978   *Time and Traditions*. New York: Columbia University.

Tuggle, N. D., Townsend, A., and Riley, T. J.
    1972   Laws, Systems, and Research Design: A Discussion of Explanation in
                Archaeology. *American Antiquity* 37: 3–12.

Vayda, A. P. and McCay, B. J.
    1975   New Directions in Ecology. *Ecological Anthropology* 4: 293–306.

White, L. A.
    1949   *The Science of Culture: A Study of Man and Civilization*. New York:
                Farrar, Strauss, and Giroux, Inc.

Willey, G. R. and Phillips, P.
    1958   *Method and Theory in American Archaeology*. Chicago: University of
                Chicago.

Willey, G. R. and Sabloff, J. A.
    1980   *A History of American Archaeology*, Revised edition. San Francisco: W.
                H. Freeman.

Yoffee, N.
    1979   The Decline and Rise of Mesopotamian Civilization: An Ethnoarchaeo-
                logical Perspective on the Evolution of Social Complexity. *American
                Antiquity* 44: 5–35.

Chapter 5

THE BIBLE AND ARCHAEOLOGY: THE STATE OF THE ART

D. Glenn Rose
The Graduate Seminary,
Phillips University

The predominant approach to the relationship of archaeology to the Bible is the synthesis which grew out of the works of W. F. Albright (1957: 1–3; 1963: 1–9; 1969), G. Ernest Wright (1950: 20–29; 1962: 17), and their students (Bright 1960; 1972: 68–72). This synthesis stressed the general historical reliability of the biblical record and the possibility of its correlation with archaeological data.[1] The historiography involved was largely positivistic and the archaeological method was inductive-scientific. Underlying this approach was a theological or philosophical assumption, more obvious in some than in others, that revelation or value was to be found within the realm of history. This theme was often given a particularistic slant which separated Israel's history and religion from that of other peoples of the ancient Near East.

A major challenge to this basically American synthesis had appeared much earlier in terms of the predominantly German tradition history school represented by Albrecht Alt (1967), Martin Noth (1960: 42–50; 1966: 139–144), Gerhard von Rad (1962: 3–14; 1980: 9–18), and their students. Although the American group at times accused the German school of denying archaeology "the right to speak" in the reconstruction of biblical history and religion (Bright 1960: 87), the real issues were found elsewhere. Both groups actually affirmed the importance of history as the particularistic area of revelational activity; however, the German school had some reservations about the ability of the historian or the historian of religion to recreate the past from the biblical record, at least in terms of the Bible's own story line. They pointed to the cultic modification of the literature reporting historical data and therefore preferred a history of traditions approach to the Bible (Noth 1972: 252–55). Their history was oriented more toward an existentialist historiography and the results were often at variance with those of the American school where the result was more akin to the story line of the Bible. At the same time, Noth in particular was also skeptical of the ability of archaeology to provide corroborating evidence of both such literary modification and the actual events, and thus he appeared to make little use of the discipline, at least in the sense in which it was used by the American school (Noth 1966: 142–44). The point in introducing this older form of the debate is to indicate that both perspectives stressed the historical nature of the biblical literature and the belief that the history could be recaptured, although they differed sharply on the meaning and nature of that history and thus on its relationship to the field of archaeology.

Recently, an internal debate has come to the fore within the American school centering on the question of whether a biblical archaeology is possible. This debate is carried on with a set of common assumptions and a disagreement over the independent nature of archaeological methodology which has become increasingly inductive-scientific (Dever 1982; Lance 1982). Although it is the common assumptions that will be questioned in this paper, it is instructive to examine the background to the internal debate.

Since the beginning of modern scientific archaeology with the work of Sir Flinders Petrie at Tell el-Hesi in 1890, there has been an increasing tension among proponents of Bible and archaeology. Petrie first correlated the layers of soil with the pottery forms contained therein and established a solid base for chronological determination (Petrie 1891). His successor at Hesi, F. J. Bliss, went even further when he published his excavations as a series of stratified cities (Bliss 1894). It remained, however, to W. F. Albright and G. Ernest Wright to put the pottery sequences into a tight typology which is still in use in modern Palestinian archaeology (Albright 1932; 1933; 1938; 1943; Wright 1962). Both of these techniques, i.e., stratigraphy and ceramic typology, stress the chronological development of a site which correlates well with the biblical concern for development within the realms of history and religion. Stratigraphy and pottery typology have been increasingly honed by several generations of ASOR excavations, beginning with those of Shechem (Wright 1965), influenced by the methodological work of Dame Kenyon at Jericho (Kenyon 1960), through Gezer (Dever 1973; Seger 1985), and on to third generation excavations such as Bad edh-Dhra (Rast and Schaub 1980), Lahav (Seger and Borowski 1977), Hesi (O'Connell and Rose 1980), Caesarea (Roller 1980), Meiron (Meyers, Strange, and Meyers 1981), and others. All of the latter take the practice of stratigraphy and pottery typology for granted. The scientific spirit of these excavations which produce objective data has led to a strained relationship with the Bible in the eyes of some because the same kind of "hard" data cannot be produced by biblical scholarship. Thus, some question whether there is such a discipline as biblical archaeology since archaeology has its own method and must be separated from those enterprises whose method is less scientific. For these people, Syro-Palestinian archaeology has become the name of the archaeological discipline (Dever 1982: 103). While the two sides of the internal debate disagree about the status of biblical research, they both agree that archaeology is a scientific enterprise with an inductive method.

Archaeologists of this consensus persuasion, perceiving archaeology as an inductive science, assume that individual items of material culture contain their necessary meaning inherent within themselves. The archaeologist, therefore, excavates the artifacts and inducts their meaning for a historical or religious reconstruction. Although no one item can give meaning to an entire site, the accumulation of these various inducted traits/meanings creates an overall interpretation which can be related to similar interpretations from other excavations or to historical texts, especially the Bible (Hill 1972: 64–68). The relationship between artifact and history is thus rather simple and straightforward. It is this relationship which has led some archaeologists to suggest that circular reasoning is involved in the process. Max Miller, in *The Old Testament and the Historian* (1976: 47), suggests that the Bible is the interpretive context for many who unconsciously use it as a basis to discover the meaning derived from the artifact and who then argue that the artifact "proves" the biblical passage. While this may be an overly simple explanation, it is true that in much archaeology one looks for evidence of Shishak's destruction, e.g., without always considering the many other possibilities for a destruction which are not mentioned in historical texts.

A parallel to this approach occurs within the discipline of anthropology where a history of culture approach yielding chronological sequences is constructed on the basis of cultural traits identified with different cultural and historical groups. This position has been under much attack in recent work in anthropological archaeology and the debate has produced a counterposition referred to as the "new archaeology" (Willey and Sabloff 1974: 183–97; Toombs 1985). It suggests that the inductive-scientific approach is not adequate to deal with archaeological data. Without going into all of the argumentation, the position suggests that every artifact is multimeaningful; i.e., it will supply as many different meanings as there are questions asked. This is another way of saying that the meaning of an object depends upon the context in which it is placed or the type of question which is asked. To place the item into different contexts is to produce different meanings.[2] In terms of excavation strategy, this position generates hypotheses about the material to be excavated and then excavates in order to test the various hypotheses. This is a deductive-scientific approach which extremists claim is the only scientific approach to archaeology (Hill 1972: 68–70).

In the interpretive realm the important dimension is the definition of context for interpretation. In the new archaeology every artifact/cultural item from an excavation has a functional meaning in relation to every other item. They are all part of a cultural system which can be divided into subsystems, such as social, ideational, technological, and economic subsystems. All of these subsystems must be viewed in relationship to the environment, since culture is the product of human adaptation to environmental change. The result of all this is a method which produces only cultural meaning from the archaeological record. History is only a small part of the cultural system and not meaningful in and of itself. Also, culture is the adaptive response of humans to the environment rather than the shaping agent of that environment. At times this approach becomes very deterministic as it is handled through statistics and systems theory (Binford 1965).

This newer approach has affected the archaeological understanding of some third-generation ASOR excavations with the result that some archaeologists feel there is a valid archaeological method of inquiry which is independent of the work of the historian (Dever 1981; Rose forthcoming). Material culture has its own proper cultural context and can yield no historical information per se. To explore the culture historically is a secondary step dependent upon the prior cultural interpretation of the excavated data. Obviously, this approach greatly affects the synthesis understanding of archaeology and Bible by suggesting that there is very little primary relationship between the two; in other words, the two disciplines deal with apples and oranges, respectively.

In the consensus position, the historian often relates the archaeological data to both the Bible and other ancient Near Eastern histories and cultures. Normally one assesses these relationships by a comparative method. When a correlation between a non-text culture and a biblical text is required, a similar culture is often found for which a historical record exists, and the correlation is assumed to be the same in both the non-text and the text cultures. The similarity is usually based upon a list of culture traits common to both groups; however, this assumption overlooks the possibility that similar items may function differently in different cultures. Therefore, what appears to be similar may be radically different when the proper cultural context is established. The historical data associated with one culture does not necessarily apply to the other (Binford 1962).

Archaeology sometimes produces texts, although these are not the normal fare, and they often create spectacular conflicts, as the Dead Sea Scrolls and Ebla witness (Sanders 1973; Matthiae 1976; Freedman 1978). When texts produced by archaeology are involved, the comparative method is again used. While the relationship of biblical text to extra-biblical text seems direct, the recent controversy of the Ebla tablets should make us wary of any simple approach to the issue (Archi 1979; 1981; Pettinato 1980). In the debate which goes on about the patriarchal period, it is suggested that the kinds of historical comparison possible must be limited (Thompson 1974; Van Seters 1975). Only texts of a similar literary type are to be compared and, in the realm of history, only those which exhibit a historiographical intent are valid. This sharply limits the texts available for historical reconstruction. Still, when observing such conditions, the results vary widely, suggesting that other assumptions are at work. In an attempt to control the use of the comparative method, William Hallo has suggested a simple control which he calls the contextual approach (Hallo 1980). According to Hallo, comparisons should be made not only for similarities but also for contrasts. The issue in this is whether an explicit methodological control has been exercised in the comparative method as it is applied to material culture and texts produced by archaeology. The apparent parallelomania in some circles would suggest that this control is not yet present (Sandmel 1962).

The end product of this discussion is that archaeological method and associated methods of interpreting the data are in flux (Hill 1972: 61–62). As a result, the inductive-scientific and comparative approaches of the consensus are under attack or are being eroded by different approaches. The relationship of this changing archaeology to the Bible is thus also in flux.

We can look at this whole issue from another point of view, that of biblical scholarship. The Bible-archaeological consensus has tended to work with a positivistic historiography that recently has come under strong methodological criticism expressed by several new approaches to the Bible (Krentz 1975: 73–88). There are at least four new approaches to the Bible which raise serious questions for the consensus as well as for any attempts to construct a new consensus between Bible and archaeology. These are the literary, the socio-logical/anthropological, the canonical/hermeneutical, and the structuralist approaches. Each of these in its own way sets a limit on the understanding of the biblical text as history. In a sense, they all represent a synchronic approach to the Bible or at least bracket out diachronic concerns, if they do not oppose them; they all deny history as a court of final appeal to which all under-standings must conform.[3]

Who would have thought to compare Exodus 1—15 with *The Bacchae*, yet that is what is done by David Robertson utilizing the new literary approach (1977: 16–32). This approach assumes that the Bible is a collection of pieces of literature whose final level can be read and understood irrespective of later redactions or historical settings. To use Robertson's categories, we are to read the Bible as "pure" literature since that is the form it now has, regardless of the fact that the Bible arose as "applied" literature. As pure literature, the norm for judgment lies not with questions of historical truth or even truth, but it lies in the realm of correspondence between the literature and the world of our own experience (Robertson 1977: 2–15). Robert Polzin's new work on *Moses and the Deuteronomist* (1980) stresses this same general approach and argues that the literary approach takes an operational priority to the historical-critical approach which remains a legitimate method. What this approach suggests for our topic, as a minimum, is that there are legitimate ways of reading the Bible which are outside the historical model.[4] In Robertson's words, the approach represents a paradigm shift and indicates that the historical approach is as much a product of its time as allegorical approaches were a product of the medieval period (1977: 4). Thus one is less sure that the meaning of the text lies in those historical categories which are the stock and trade of the Bible-archaeological consensus.

Another approach is that of the sociological and anthropological analysis, represented by those wishing to study the social world of the Bible or those who wish to look at ethnographic parallels to biblical phenomena. In general, these scholars are demanding that the concept of history, as practiced within the humanistic tradition, be broadened to include the data of the social sciences, especially when that history is construed almost totally in political terms. Norman Gottwald has some rather critical remarks about this humanistic tradition and scholarship in *The Tribes of Yahweh* (1979: 5–7). Robert Wilson points to the inability of history to deal adequately with the relationship between the early and the latter prophets. He suggests that anthropological data offers fruitful material for comparative purposes (1978). J. W. Rogerson suggests that the anthropological assumptions underlying biblical scholarship are inadequate and, in fact, just plain wrong when considered against the body of current anthropological data (1979). The reconstructions of Mendenhall (1962; 1973) and Gottwald (1979) demonstrate something of these changing views in their models of the conquest tradition. I am sure that these perspectives do not represent an ahistorical, much less an antihistorical approach, since they pay close attention to dimensions of biblical history and archaeology. However, while a destruction layer by a political foe can be related to both a biblical text and an archaeological destruction layer, the theory of a peasant's revolt is more difficult to substantiate. Even so, the framework of history resulting from such a theory no longer correlates well with the Bible's own story, and thus it reduces the reliability of the latter as history.

A third approach deals with the canonical/hermeneutical issues in the Bible. We can see this in the work of Brevard Childs (1979) on the one hand and in the Overtures to Biblical Theology Series on the other (eds. Brueggemann and Donahue). In the former the canon serves as an interpretive context, while in the latter it is some issue of the modern age which serves the same purpose. Both of these have the effect of suggesting that something outside the realm of purely descriptive data accessible to history controls the meaning of the text. For Childs, reading the text in terms of its canonical intentionality overrides the concerns and issues of the historical-critical method. Indeed the canon has replaced history as the proper context for studying the Bible as the sacred text produced by believing communities of faith. In some volumes of the Overtures Series, the dialogue with modern issues produces a reading of the text which is quite unlike that produced in literary-historical studies.[5] While one would not call either of these antihistorical, they are at least ahistorical and suggest again that meaning is not beholden to a purely historical view. Likewise, it is obvious that these readings of the text do not rely upon or require any type of archaeological correlation, although they could occur. The end result is an ahistorical meaning which does not need the results of the archaeologist's spade.

The fourth approach is structuralism, which is strictly synchronic in its orientation. Since the breakdown of the medieval theological approach to Scripture, the historical approach has seemed mandatory for recovering the meaning and description of the past. The application of a more scientific precision to the historical realm allowed us to understand a religious text by placing it in its proper historical context. History, with its descriptive approach, became the norm for judging the Bible. The final outcome of this approach, with its particularizing of religion and its relativizing of religious experience, was the use of history to establish positive and negative values among the various religions of the Levant. This approach has magnified the distinctive elements at the expense of the universal in the descriptions of the religions of the ancient Near East. The commonality of the creation motif in Near Eastern religions, however, suggests that ancient humanity was more aware of these universal aspects of existence than are later generations (Brandon 1963).

Structuralism, as inherited from Claude Lévi-Strauss (1963; 1976), suggests there are ways of recovering the universal elements in religion, elements which are akin to the basic structure of mind, if not of reality itself. This approach to religion questions the right of the historical approach to form the final judgment by suggesting a descriptive task which is ahistorical, if not antihistorical. As applied to the Bible by Edmund Leach (1969) and others, historical questions are bracketed by the concern to find the universals which reflect the truth of reality.[6] The deep structures of the Bible are to be the primary concern of scholarship.

When these various approaches to the Bible are put together, they suggest as a minimum that the historical approach is one of several viable approaches to the Bible and thus does not have the ability to act as a court of appeal for the truth of the Bible. As a maximum, these approaches indicate that the historical approach represents only the views of a particular cultural epoch which is now past and which is thus of antiquarian interest but little more. In either of these postures the dominant reasons for relating Bible to archaeology are, for many, undercut. It does not rule out a possible relationship per se, but it does ask for what purpose the relationship is to be established and what it could hope to demonstrate. As an extreme position, it perhaps also questions whether the Bible is of sufficient historical character to allow the correlation in the first place.

The title of this article does not indicate that a new consensus is to be set forth, and I certainly am not prepared to do so. In fact, it may be that we have arrived at the time when each discipline must find its own way and methodology before it will even be possible to think of a consensus. The fruitful work being done at the moment in Bible and archaeology is forcing us to become more explicitly methodological in our endeavors. While this is all very frustrating, it is a sign that creativity is alive and it bodes well for a future we may not see. Therefore, I think we need to free archaeology of the debate over whether there is a biblical archaeology or not and allow it to pursue a method which produces an understanding of the past which is broader than the term "biblical" suggests. This does not mean that a relationship of archaeology to Bible is ruled out, but it does mean that archaeology can have meanings other than biblical.

NOTES

1. Albright and Wright should not be accused of attempting to use archaeology to "prove" the Bible. There are those, however, who do make this attempt and point to the writings of Albright and Wright for support.

2. Thus, "a cooking vessel need not be interpreted solely as a cooking vessel; it may also be interpreted as a status symbol, a product of a specialist, an indication of the size of the group using it, and so forth" (Hill 1972: 69).

3. In structuralist terms, the diachronic method aims at explaining what the author (a creator of significations—ideas, symbols, etc.) meant. The diachronic method is associated with the traditional historical approach to a text. The synchronic method would add that "significations are imposed upon man" through the assimilation of language. Therefore, an author's speech, although aimed at one particular meaning (signification), will reveal certain other assimilated significations within its language. The synchronic approach to a text would assume a plurality of semantic possibilities, the diachronic concern being only one (Patte 1976: 13–15).

4. On the new literary approach cf. Gros Louis (1974); Fokkelman (1975); Licht (1978); Fishbane (1979); Alter (1981); and Miscall (1983).

5. Good examples of this are seen in Brueggemann (1977) and Bailey (1979).

6. In addition to Leach (1969), cf. Funk (1974); Patte (1978; 1983); and Culley (1980).

BIBLIOGRAPHY

Albright, W. F.
   1932   *The Excavation of Tell Beit Mirsim I*. Annual of the American Schools of Oriental Research 12.
   1933   *The Excavation of Tell Beit Mirsim IA*. Annual of the American Schools of Oriental Research 13.
   1938   *The Excavation of Tell Beit Mirsim II*. Annual of the American Schools of Oriental Research 17.

1943   *The Excavation of Tell Beit Mirsim III.* Annual of the American Schools of Oriental Research 21–22.
1957   *From the Stone Age to Christianity.* Garden City: Doubleday.
1963   *The Biblical Period from Abraham to Ezra.* New York: Harper.
1969   *Archaeology and the Religion of Israel.* Garden City: Doubleday.

Alt, Albrecht
1967   *Essays on Old Testament History and Religion.* Trans. R. A. Wilson from German, 1953. Garden City: Doubleday.

Alter, Robert
1981   *The Art of Biblical Narrative.* New York: Basic Books, Inc.

Archi, Alfonso
1979   The Epigraphic Evidence from Ebla and the Old Testament. *Biblica* 60: 556–66.
1981   Further Concerning Ebla and the Bible. *Biblical Archaeologist* 44: 145–54.

Bailey, Lloyd R., Sr.
1979   *Biblical Perspectives on Death.* Overtures to Biblical Theology, edited by Walter Brueggemann and John R. Donahue. Philadelphia: Fortress.

Binford, Lewis R.
1962   Archaeology as Anthropology. *American Antiquity* 28: 217–25.
1965   Archaeological Systematics and the Study of Culture Process. *American Antiquity* 31: 203–10.

Bliss, Frederick J.
1894   *A Mound of Many Cities.* London: Alexander P. Watt.

Brandon, S. G. F.
1963   *Creation Legends of the Ancient Near East.* London: Hodder and Stoughton.

Bright, John
1960   *Early Israel in Recent History Writing.* London: SCM.
1972   *A History of Israel.* Philadelphia: Westminster.

Brueggemann, Walter
1977   *The Land.* Overtures to Biblical Theology, edited by Walter Brueggemann and John R. Donahue. Philadelphia: Fortress.

Brueggemann, Walter, and Donahue, John R. (eds.)
1977   Overtures to Biblical Theology. Philadelphia: Fortress.

Childs, Brevard S.
1979   *Introduction to the Old Testament as Scripture.* London: SCM.

Culley, Robert C.
1980   Action Sequences in Genesis 2—3. *Semeia* 18: 25–33.

Dever, W. G.
1973   The Gezer Fortification and the "High Place": An Illustration of Stratigraphic Methods and Problems. *Palestine Exploration Quarterly* 105: 61–70.
1981   The Impact of the "New Archaeology" on Syro-Palestinian Archaeology. *Bulletin of the American Schools of Oriental Research* 242: 15–29.
1982   Retrospects and Prospects in Biblical and Syro-Palestinian Archaeology. *Biblical Archaeologist* 45: 103–7.

Fishbane, Michael
   1979   *Text and Texture*. New York: Schocken Books.

Fokkelman, J. P.
   1975   *Narrative Art in Genesis*. Amsterdam: van Gorcum.

Freedman, David Noel
   1978   The Real Story of the Ebla Tablets: Ebla and the Cities of the Plain.
               Biblical Archaeologist 41: 143–64.

Funk, Robert W.
   1974   Structure in the Narrative Parables. *Semeia* 2: 57–73.

Gottwald, Norman K.
   1979   *The Tribes of Yahweh*. Maryknoll, NY: Orbis Books.

Gros Louis, Kenneth R. R.
   1974   *Literary Interpretations of Biblical Narratives*. Nashville: Abingdon.

Hallo, William W.
   1980   Biblical History in its Near Eastern Setting: The Contextual Approach.
               Scripture In Context: Essays on the Comparative Method, ed. Carl D.
               Evans, William W. Hallo, and John B. White. Pittsburgh: Pickwick.

Hill, J. N.
   1972   The Methodological Debate in Contemporary Archaeology: A Model.
               Models in Archaeology, ed. David L. Clarke. London: Methuen.

Kenyon, K. M.
   1960   *Excavations at Jericho, I: The Tombs Excavated in 1952–4*. London: The
               British School of Archaeology in Jerusalem.

Krentz, Edgar
   1975   *The Historical-Critical Method*. Guides to Biblical Scholarship, edited by
               Gene M. Tucker. Philadelphia: Fortress.

Lance, H. Darrell
   1982   American Biblical Archaeology in Perspective. *Biblical Archaeologist* 45:
               97–101.

Leach, Edmund Ronald
   1969   *Genesis as Myth*. London: Jonathan Cape.

Lévi-Strauss, Claude
   1963   *Structural Anthropology*. Vol. I. Trans. Claire Jacobson and Brooke
               Grundfest Schoepf from French. New York: Basic Books, Inc.
   1976   *Structural Anthropology*. Vol. II. Trans. Monique Layton from French.
               New York: Basic Books, Inc.

Licht, Jacob
   1978   *Storytelling in the Bible*. Jerusalem: Magnes, Hebrew University.

Matthiae, Paolo
   1976   Ebla in the Late Early Syrian Period: The Royal Palace and the State
               Archives. *Biblical Archaeologist* 39: 94–113.

Mendenhall, G. E.
   1962   The Hebrew Conquest of Palestine. *Biblical Archaeologist* 25: 66–87.
   1973   *The Tenth Generation: The Origins of the Biblical Tradition*. Baltimore:
               Johns Hopkins University.

Meyers, E. M., Strange, J. F., and Meyers, C. L.
1981   *Excavations at Ancient Meiron, Upper Galilee, Israel, 1971–73, 1974– 75, 1977*. Cambridge, MA: American Schools of Oriental Research.

Miller, J. Maxwell
1976   *The Old Testament and the Historian*. Guides to Biblical Scholarship, edited by Gene M. Tucker. Philadelphia: Fortress.

Miscall, Peter D.
1983   *The Workings of Old Testament Narrative*. The Society of Biblical Literature Semeia Studies, edited by Dan O. Via, Jr. Philadelphia: Fortress/Chico, CA: Scholars.

Noth, Martin
1960   *The History of Israel*. Trans. Peter R. Ackroyd from German second edition, 1958. New York: Harper.
1966   *The Old Testament World*. Trans. Victor I. Gruhn from German fourth edition, 1964. Philadelphia: Fortress.
1972   *A History of Pentateuchal Traditions*. Trans. Bernhard W. Anderson from German, 1948. Englewood Cliffs, NJ: Prentice-Hall.

O'Connell, K. G., and Rose, D. G.
1980   Tell el-Hesi, 1979. *Palestine Exploration Quarterly* 112: 73–91.

Patte, Daniel
1976   *What Is Structural Exegesis?* Guides to Biblical Scholarship, edited by Dan O. Via, Jr. Philadelphia: Fortress.
1978   *Structural Exegesis: From Theory to Practice*. Philadelphia: Fortress.
1983   *Paul's Faith and the Power of Gospel*. Philadelphia: Fortress.

Petrie, W. M. Flinders
1891   *Tell el Hesy (Lachish)*. London: Alexander P. Watt.

Pettinato, Giovanni
1980   Ebla and the Bible. *Biblical Archaeologist* 43: 203–16.

Polzin, Robert
1980   *Moses and the Deuteronomist: A Literary Study of the Deuteronomic History*. New York: Seabury.

Rast, W. E. and Schaub, R. T.
1980   Preliminary Report of the 1979 Expedition to the Dead Sea Plain, Jordan. *Bulletin of the American Schools of Oriental Research* 240: 21–61.

Robertson, David
1977   *The Old Testament and the Literary Critic*. Guides to Biblical Scholarship, edited by Gene M. Tucker. Philadelphia: Fortress.

Rogerson, J. W.
1979   *Anthropology and the Old Testament*. Atlanta: John Knox.

Roller, Duane W.
1980   Hellenistic Pottery from Caesarea Maritima: A Preliminary Study. *Bulletin of the American Schools of Oriental Research* 238: 35–42.

Rose, D. Glenn
forth-   The Methodology of the New Archaeology and Its Influence on the Joint
coming   Expedition to Tell el-Hesi. *Tell el-Hesi: The Site and the Expedition*, ed. Kevin G. O'Connell, S.J.

Sanders, James A.
  1973   The Dead Sea Scrolls—A Quarter Century of Study. *The Biblical Archae-
            ologist* 36: 110–48.

Sandmel, Samuel
  1962   Parallelomania. *Journal of Biblical Literature* 81: 1–13.

Seger, J. D.
  1985   Tel Gezer: Phase II Excavations 1972–1974. *Archaeology and Biblical
            Interpretation: Essays in Memory of D. Glenn Rose,* eds. Leo G. Perdue,
            Gary L. Johnson, and Lawrence E. Toombs. Atlanta: John Knox.

Seger, J. D. and Borowski, O.
  1977   The First Two Seasons at Tel Halif. *Biblical Archaeologist* 40: 156–66.

Seters, John Van
  1975   *Abraham in History and Tradition.* New Haven: Yale University.

Thompson, Thomas L.
  1974   *The Historicity of the Patriarchal Narratives.* New York: Walter de
            Gruyter.

Toombs, Lawrence E.
  1985   A Perspective on the New Archaeology. *Archaeology and Biblical Inter-
            pretation: Essays in Memory of D. Glenn Rose,* eds. Leo G. Perdue, Gary
            L. Johnson, and Lawrence E. Toombs. Atlanta: John Knox.

Von Rad, Gerhard
  1962   *Old Testament Theology.* Vol. 1. Trans. D. M. G. Stalker from German,
            1957. New York: Harper.
  1980   *God at Work in Israel.* Trans. John H. Marks from German, 1974.
            Nashville: Abingdon.

Willey, G. R. and Sabloff, J. A.
  1974   *A History of American Archaeology.* San Francisco: Freeman.

Wilson, Robert R.
  1978   Early Israelite Prophecy. *Interpretation* 32: 3–16.

Wright, G. E.
  1950   *The Old Testament Against Its Environment.* London: SCM.
  1962   *Biblical Archaeology.* Philadelphia: Westminster.
  1965   *Shechem. The Biography of a Biblical City.* New York: McGraw-Hill.

II. ARCHAEOLOGICAL EXCAVATIONS AND BIBLICAL INTERPRETATION

Chapter 6

TEL HALIF: PROSPERITY IN A LATE BRONZE AGE CITY ON THE EDGE OF THE NEGEV

Paul F. Jacobs
Lahav Research Project
University of St. Thomas

Introduction[1]

The history and culture of the ancient people of Israel and therefore also of the biblical narrative are deeply involved in the history and culture of the indigenous population of Canaan. Hence, whatever information concerning Canaanite culture and history can be gained through the archaeological processes aids directly in establishing the history of ancient Israel and indirectly in interpreting the theological texts about Israel. This information would appear to be critical with respect to the interaction of Israelites and Canaanites in the southern Shephelah and northern Negev; here the biblical sources are tantalizingly brief and obscure, and the archaeological evidence is just beginning to accumulate. The history and culture of Tel Halif fits precisely into this critical period; excavation here has already added not only confirming but also new and significant information[2] to our knowledge about this period. It is for these reasons that the role of Tel Halif in the Late Bronze and Early Iron Ages is especially significant.

Halif: The Site and the Lahav Project

Tel Halif (Khirbet Khuweilfeh),[3] a site whose history of occupation extends from present-day Kibbutz Lahav to an unnamed village of the EB I–II period,[4] is located on the northeastern tributary to Wadi Gerar, some 45 km. from the coast (fig. 1). The geographical location of Halif is also marked by the fact that it sits at the juncture of three geomorphological zones: the coastal plain, the southern Judean hills, and the Negev. The combined geographical and ecological features of the location make the investigation of Halif intrin-

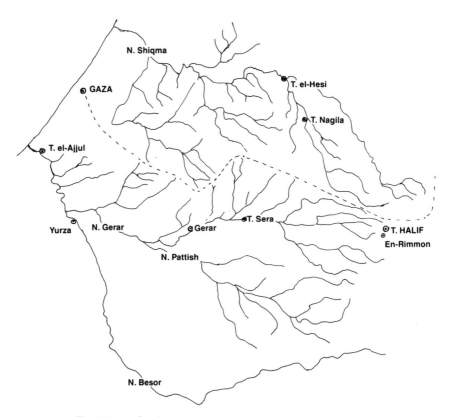

Fig. 1. Map of wadi systems and the route between Gaza and Halif.

sically interesting, requiring not only that the question of the historical reason
for the establishment of Halif be answered but also that the question of the
ecological reasons for such a prolonged use of the site be investigated. Such has
been the task of the Lahav Research Project.

For the interest of this paper in the role of Halif in the northern Negev,
however, only the historical question will be addressed. To that question the
reply must surely be that Halif flourished in the Bronze[5] and Iron Ages in great
part because of its location on the easiest route between Gaza and Hebron and
other cities in the interior (fig. 1). A traveler in ancient times on this route from
Gaza crossed no major wadi system and also enjoyed the gentlest rise in the
land to the Judean hills. The advisability of this route is confirmed by the
modern highway built precisely along this way.

The Archaeological Evidence

Stratum X—MB IIC/LB IA. Occupation of Tel Halif resumed in the Late Bronze Age after a hiatus of centuries, in fact the time of the Middle Bronze Age.[6] The resettlement above the ruins of Stratum XI (EB III) appears to have been little more than an unfortified village. Pottery in association with the architecture places the settlement at the transition to the Late Bronze Age, at MB IIC/LB IA. The buildings of Stratum X were of poor quality construction and of minor size;[7] hence, little needs to be said about this stratum, except that in the mid-sixteenth century a venture occurred to establish a new city at Halif, an attempt that soon proved quite successful.

Stratum IXB—LB IB (fig. 2). The Stratum X village appears to have been short-lived, perhaps no longer than a generation. However, an ambitious building of Stratum IXB blossomed immediately above it, a certain sign of the turn in fortunes of the occupants of Halif. What had begun in Stratum X as a village of thin-walled houses was replaced in Stratum IXB with a large and handsome building, perhaps one qualifying for the term "villa." Yet the newly constructed Stratum IXB town, like its predecessor, was unprotected by fortification.

Deep deposits of fill were set in to raise and extend the area for construction on the eastern slope of the tell, while scavenging for building stones robbed much of the foundations of Stratum X walls. Meter-thick stone and brick walls were set on raised, compacted-clay foundations to form a large, well-constructed building, much in contrast to the flimsy architecture of Stratum X. The new Stratum IXB building, probably domestic in nature, though possibly the residence of an official or of a wealthy family, displays a new affluence that continued to mark Halif in the fifteenth century. The obvious prosperity corresponds, of course, to the renewed interest and control by Egypt in Canaan as part of its new empire, one of the features of the Eighteenth Dynasty generally but especially of Thutmose III and his successors. Indeed the security and prosperity of Canaan under Egyptian control is reflected at Halif not only in the size of the architecture but also in the fact that throughout this stage of its history (through the end of LB) Halif remained unfortified.[8]

The Stratum IXB house (fig. 2) belongs to the "central courtyard" type with rooms opening onto all four sides of the central room, a style paralleled particularly in Syria at Ugarit (Drower 1973: 498) but found in other places in the ancient world as well. Similar houseplans were found as far away as Ur belonging to early second millennium (Woolley 1955: 198; Müller 1940: 179ff.) and at Lagash belonging to late third millennium (Parrot 1961: 226). An example of this style is found as close to Halif as Tel Sharuhen (Yisraeli 1978:

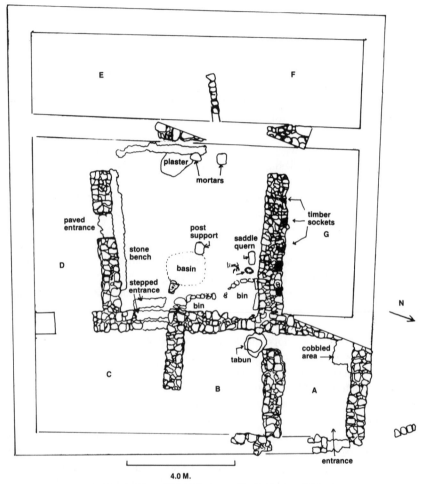

4.0 M.

Fig. 2. Plan of LB IB house at Halif, Stratum IXB.

1077). Two of the clearest examples in Canaan are the free-standing "temple" at Rabbath-ammon (Avi-Yonah and Stern 1978: 990) and the MB "villa" on the slopes of Mt. Gerizim (Boling 1975: 34). In addition, attention has been called to the similar plan of Amarna houses of Egypt (Borchardt and Ricke 1980; Fritz 1981: 66; Smith 1981: 334). The "central courtyard" house appears to have been a widespread and popular style, one apparently adaptable to both arid and moist climates (Beebe 1968: 48–49).

Several writers (Aharoni 1982: 134; Fritz 1981: 66; Oren 1982: 166) have maintained that the "residencies" at Tell esh-Shari'a and Tel Sharuhen imitate the typical Amarna house ("a local version of the Egyptian courtyard house of

Fig. 3. Photograph of the "central room" of LB IB house, viewed from the south.

Fig. 4. Photograph of wall of Room G showing "sockets" for beams, viewed from the north.

the New Kingdom"; Oren 1982: 166). However, this appears unlikely in that the plan (1) is so widespread, (2) appears at much earlier times in Ur and Syria as well as Canaan, and (3) is already used in a house at Tel Halif that had been destroyed well before the Amarna age and the construction of the "residencies" at Shariʿa and Sharuhen. It is therefore more appropriate to suggest that Amarna borrowed a plan already found in common use in Asia. In fact, other "Asiatic" architectural techniques in the Halif Stratum IXB house tend to connect the style to origins in the north rather than in Egypt.

As seen in the plan, the Stratum IXB house consisted of a large (6.5 m. x 6 m.) "courtyard" surrounded by smaller rooms, some of which on the southeast corner have been dismantled or eroded. Entrance to the central room was possible from all four sides, though apparently none of the outer rooms could be closed (no door sockets or the like have been found). The outer, smaller rooms proved to have utilitarian, domestic functions, where identifiable; e.g., at least two of the rooms (B and F) contained remains of tabuns and may therefore have been partially open to the sky.[9] Room A opened to the outside, serving as a "vestibule" with a wooden door;[10] exit from this vestibule led directly to two steps and a path down and along the slope of the tell. The vestibule itself opened to the south, indirectly leading to the central room through Rooms B and C. This "indirect entrance" technique through not only a vestibule but also one or more additional rooms is also fairly well-represented in the examples of the "central courtyard" type (cf. Yisraeli 1978: 1077; Avi-Yonah and Stern 1978: 990; cf. also House P49.2 at Amarna). However, in the final phase of the Stratum IXB house an alteration in the use of the eastern part of the house proves that the vestibule Room A no longer served its original purpose; a tabun was built in the entrance between Rooms A and B, effectively blocking access, while Room A was abandoned to be used for collection of rubbish (fig. 3). Ashes from the firing of the tabun A9007 as well as broken pottery, stone tools, and even discarded bone artifacts and beads were thrown into Room A from Room B. This points out the obvious fact that another entrance, probably through the southern wall of the house, must have been in use in this final phase.

The size and wealth of this Stratum IXB house is seen best in what was likely the main "living quarter" and in the content and makeup of the central courtyard room. Room G, the northernmost one exposed the so-called main living quarter, was entered from an opening in the northwest corner of the central room. Room G itself is unique to the building from several perspectives: its floor had been specially prepared and was neither the typical packed-earth floor of the other rooms nor the partially plastered floor of the central room. Rather, the floor of Room G was a fine, metaled surface, even in its earliest phase. Likewise, the southern wall of Room G displayed the high quality of construction of the house and therefore also the prosperity of its owner.

Remnants of six large beams were found set upright into the face of both stone foundation and brick superstructure of this wall (fig. 4). Such large pieces of wood,[11] not locally available except through trade with Lebanon or Syria, again reflect the expense of construction of this house.

The technique of including wood beams into the walls of houses has been reported in Palestine only from Kuntilat 'Ajrud (Meshel 1979: 29), but there the tamarisk branches were laid horizontally only. In northern locales, however, the use of wood in construction was apparently a standard procedure. Contemporary buildings with wood frame ("half-timbering") for brick walls have been reported in a palace at Alalakh (Woolley 1955: 126, pl. xxvii) as well as in houses and palaces of Anatolia, Syria, Crete, and Mycenae (Macqueen 1975: 64; Drower 1973: 498; Chadwick 1976: 11; Mylonas 1966: 48, 79; Cotterell 1979: 146).

These authors report a technique of a frame of both upright and horizontal beams whose function is to strengthen brick (sometimes also stone, cf. Mycenae) walls. Of particular interest, however, is the technique of including extruding, upright beams (as well as horizontal, hidden ones) in the brick walls of Neolithic Çatal Hüyük in Anatolia (Mellaart 1967: 63, pl. 9, fig. 11). This is not to suggest that Halif is directly influenced by Anatolian, Syrian, or Mycenaean architectural styles. It does suppose, however, that the connection of this style building with its use of either upright beams alone or of wood frames is far more likely to be related to the same techniques to the north than to the (later) "Amarna" building to the south. (Perhaps the architectural technique of using beams in brick or stone walls is not so foreign to Palestinian construction as the lack of examples suggests, for in the later Stratum VI Wall B10017 the same technique appears.)

The central room also bears an architectural relationship to buildings of this type found in the north, particularly in the way the room was probably fully, but at least partially, roofed. A large flat stone in the center of the room served as a base for a column or post, a fact supported by the discovery of large amounts of charred wood (branches and beams) in the destruction debris of the house. Presumably, then, shorter beams and branches stretched to the centered post from the walls to make a frame for a thatch or clay roof. Similar features were found in the houses at Mt. Gerizim (Boling 1975: 34) and Beth-shan (Aharoni 1982: 135), the "temple" at Rabbath-ammon (Avi-Yonah and Stern 1978: 990), and the private house at Ur (Frankfort 1970: 109). It is necessary to suppose that such a roofed central room was provided light by the means of windows high in the walls of the room; in this case the walls (like those of the "Amarna" house frequently pictured) will have been built higher than the roofs of the surrounding rooms. That such is likely is based not simply on the "Amarna" remains but also on the reconstructions of houses at Ischali where windows permit light to enter the central room through higher walls (cf. the reconstruction of Frankfort 1970: 108, fig. 115). In fact, this is the only logical reconstruction of a roofed central courtyard.

Elements of a possible staircase are preserved along the western wall of the central room. Only three ascending steps have been uncovered leading upward toward the roof above the main living quarter, Room G.[12] It would not be surprising to find that the roof was used, especially in the Negev, for sleeping during the summer months, a practice still exercised in nearby villages. However, clear parallels of staircases are found only in the Ur house (Frankfort 1970: 109) and in the "residency" at Sharuhen (Yisraeli 1978: 1077). It is likely that other examples of stairs to rooftops have escaped notice.

Numerous indications of domestic activity in the central room demonstrate the major use; it was a "kitchen" in which food was prepared (evidence was found of grain, wine, lentils), though it was not cooked there. Several bins and a lined pit, several querns, and four "work areas" for food preparation were located in this large room. In addition, a large number of ceramic vessels (store jars, cooking pots, spouted bowls, etc.) were found on the floor of the final phase of the room, again attesting to the domestic-like function of the room. Interestingly, the large store jars, along with a few of the other vessels, had been arranged in roughly two rows between the southern and northern doorways,[13] forming a pathway of sorts across the central room. One of the features of the room worth noting is a sloping, sunken area (c. 1.9 m. x 1.5 m. across) of the floor near the eastern entrance. The "basin" had been carefully maintained through all three phases of the house, and in the final phase its edge had been rimmed by small vessels, particularly bowls and jugs. It can only be surmised (since nothing was detected in the "basin" except a water jug that had apparently rolled into it) that the basin was used in some chore that required the containment of a liquid.

The pottery on the floor of the final phase of the central room proves the house to have been occupied in the LB IB period, the time of the formation of the empire of the Egyptian New Kingdom. A large collection of whole and restorable vessels from this floor alone provides the clue to the termination of the house, a point marked by a violent destruction. The pottery, as seen in the representative samples of fig. 5, is fairly typical of LB IB.[14] Only one type requires brief comment: a krater with a strainer spout and a "basket" handle (fig. 5). Of course, examples of spouted kraters are known from LB I (Amiran 1969: 132, Lachish II), and in fact two examples of spouted cooking pots were found in the destruction phase of the Halif Stratum IXB house, one in the central room itself. However, the closest example of a krater with a base, strainer spout, and basket handle was published in the report on the excavation of Alaca Hüyük (Zübeyrkoşay 1951, pl. lxiv), called a "Hittite" vessel.

The preceding description of the Stratum IXB building has been given in some detail in order to emphasize the obvious prosperity that brought dramatic

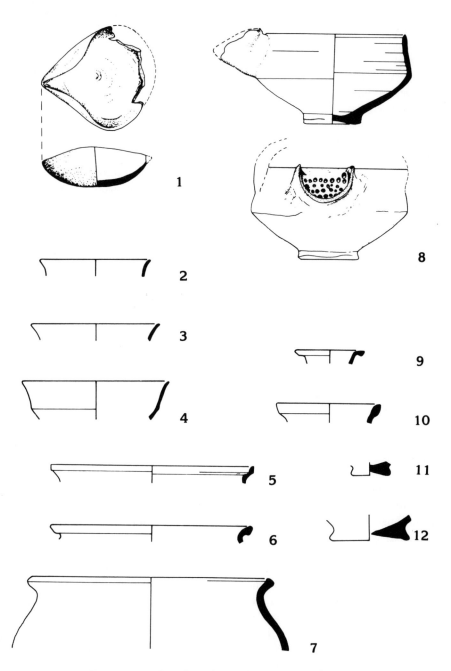

Fig. 5. Pottery from floor of "central room" of LB IB house.

changes to the life of the LB IB town at Halif. Development to a life of prosperity might have been expected as a natural result; i.e., following a time of economic struggle in the formation of a new town (Stratum X) comes, within a generation or two, newer and better conditions of life. At Tel Halif, however, where dry-farming methods necessarily had to be applied[15] in order to produce crops regularly, the only cause sufficient to account for the dramatic, nearly overnight, changes in the prosperity of the town must have been that of a revived economy of the entire region under the urging and for the benefit of Egypt.[16] It is likely that Halif's location on one of the major routes inland to the Judean hills—especially from a town officially belonging to Egyptian royalty (Gaza's epithet was "That-Which-the-Ruler-Seized")—guaranteed its successful and rapid growth.[17] In any case, a healthy town did flourish on the site until a severe destruction by fire reduced the once grand Stratum IXB town to a ruin, a destruction so severe that its immediate reoccupation could not make use of even the broadest of the walls of the "central courtyard" house.

Foundations of the Stratum IXB house were then buried in the collapsed brick walls, the burning so severe that some of the stones of the foundation walls were calcined. Responsibility for the destruction of the LB IB town cannot easily be ascribed to warfare by the Egyptians, to internecine war among the city-states such as that in the later "Amarna" period, or to accident. Nonetheless, it is important to recall that there were frequent military forays into Palestine especially by monarchs of the Eighteenth Dynasty of Egypt; all that can be safely claimed is that the destructions of Strata X, IXB, and IXA (cf. below) are consistent with the sometimes necessary "show of force" by the Eighteenth and Nineteenth Dynasties to maintain control of the empire.

Stratum IXA—LB IIA. The major destruction of Stratum IXB was followed by an immediate rebuilding. In the new building operation there was a general shift of the architecture to the north of the earlier house in Field I. Hence, an attempt to reestablish the life of the city was begun; however, this attempt itself was short-lived, suffering destruction in the so-called "Amarna" period of the fourteenth century. Accordingly, the welfare of the city of Tel Halif once again waned, a fact to be appreciated in the final "squatter's phase" of Stratum IXA occupation following the destruction, a time in which no new buildings were erected.

The meagerness of the Stratum IXA settlement is demonstrated clearly by the roughness and unevenness of the surfaces, virtually following the contours of the rubble where it fell from the destruction of Stratum IXB. Little of the prosperity from the previous settlement survived or was revived in Stratum IXA; only the chance find of a string of faience beads, scarab, and seal, lost at the time of the destruction of Stratum IXA, shows any continuity of prosperity between Strata IXB and IXA.[18] A clear decline in the quality of life overtook Tel Halif by the end of the "Amarna" period.

Stratum VIII—LB II. The final LB Stratum VIII altered completely the nature of the settlement on the eastern slope of the tell. The ruins of the Stratum IXA village and the subsequent "squatter's phase" were buried in yet another deep fill (L.10025) of loose stones in order to provide a relatively even area for the construction of an "industrial site." With the construction of Stratum VIII Tel Halif resumed its status as a relatively important and prosperous site, though no private building equal to the size and quality of the Stratum IXB house has yet been found in Stratum VIII. Rather, excavation has shown the conversion of the area to fulfill another function.

Across the edge of the slope above the fill of stones a raised "platform" (c. 13 m. x 11 m.) was created by the deposition of a thick layer[19] of a wet mixture of clay and loess.[20] This raised "platform," which was used at a level above that of at least two adjacent rooms, created a clean working area and served as a base for several stone-lined pits or silos.[21] The "industrial site" was likely formed for the storage and distribution of grain,[22] since a line of four larger silos and deep, stone-lined pits were set into the western half of the "platform," while five smaller, shallow stone-lined pits were located along the eastern edge. Unfortunately, because of later erosion and disturbance, nearly all direct evidence of function detected from surface remains has been removed. Only the discovery of a four-handled krater set beside lined pit A.10007 points to function: apparently a product was temporarily stored in the shallow lined pit and moved by hand into the waiting krater. Other evidence came from within silo 11024 which, in its final phase, had been filled with soil to be used at a shallower level for the storage of grain jars.[23] At its original depth silo 11024 had been used to store grain (flotation samples produced remains of wheat).

The function of the thick "platform" by itself can be fairly easily surmised: it was to serve as a base for the installation of lined pits and silos and to provide an area easily cleaned and free from rodents. However, whether the entire construction (which includes, as presently known, adjacent rooms whose floors are at levels lower than the platform) was a private concern or a public/government operation cannot be said. Nor can it be said on present evidence whether it is attached to a "palace," public building, or private dwelling.

What does become clear, however, is that in the LB IIB period Tel Halif again became a lively, viable town. If the estimation is correct that the "platform" in Field I is an "industrial site" associated with the collection and distribution of grain, then it becomes necessary to suppose centralization, whether a central government force or local entrepreneur, involved in providing a "permanent" place for this collection from the valley system.[24] Apparently Halif had resumed its place of relative importance among the settlements along the Wadi Gerar. Intensification of Egyptian interest and control of Canaan, particularly southern Canaan, in this period may very well hold the key to understanding the revival of prosperity at Halif (Na'aman 1981: 184–85).

Stratum VII—Iron I. The Iron I period has been located at several places on the summit of Tel Halif, an indication that the settlement was fairly widespread, though also not fortified. Only in Field I in Area B10 has the crucial transition from the Late Bronze Age to the Iron Age been uncovered. The archaeological picture of this transition is far from adequate due to severe erosion in Field I and to other fields just beginning to reach the Iron I levels, but it can be concluded provisionally that the active LB population continued unbroken into the Iron Age. At least the evidence unearthed so far will not permit an interpretation of a destruction of the population and a new arrival. In fact, the architectural history of a single room in Field I (the only architecture associated with the transition to the Iron Age) appears to support a continuity in population. In Stratum VIII LB IIB this room was constructed against the northern limit of the "platform" discussed above and was used through four phases. The fourth phase, however, contained pottery of the transitional LB II/Iron I type, indicating that the Stratum VIII community survived into the beginning of the twelfth century. Beginning with Stratum VII the room in Area B10 was enlarged, the walls being moved further to the north and to the west. Nonetheless, the architecture was aligned with that of Stratum VIII whose walls had been leveled and buried for the sake of the architectural expansion, and, in fact, the connection to the earlier Stratum VIII was completed by the continued use of the northern wall of the Stratum VIII "platform" through all of the phases of Stratum VII. It would appear, then, that Tel Halif is one of those towns which remained outside of the "conquest" by the Israelites and which only eventually was included in that national unity.

Two "cult" objects worthy of note were found in the Iron I levels, one in Field I and the other in Field II. On one of the floors of the Iron I room in Field I was found the head (and also two legs) of a ceramic bull vase figurine.[25] This object does not necessarily reflect a "cult" or "Canaanite" setting, but the bull figure (fig. 6) can scarcely be considered a "neutral" artifact in this setting. It is an artifact that more successfully supports continued "Canaanite" presence than that of a new population. Much the same needs to be said of a ceramic "plaque" representing the human female figure, an artifact found in an Iron I context in Field II. It would not be surprising to find such an object in an "Israelite" Iron I setting, but in this context at Tel Halif it better supports the idea of a continued "Canaanite" population into the Iron Age.

The Role of Halif in the Valley

Besides the critical geographical location of Halif astride the road inland from Gaza, it is also necessary to understand that the city was situated within an ecological system which during the Bronze Age was bound to limit the size of the population and the exploitation of the land. The rainfall of Halif in the

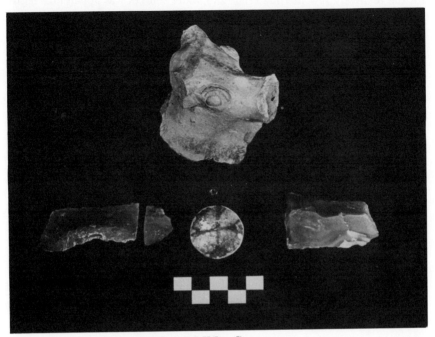

Fig. 6. Objects from Stratum VII floor (LB II/Iron I).

Late Bronze Age could allow only a certain amount of successful exploitation by farming or grazing. Overuse of the land in this ecosystem would surely create a crisis by depleting and eroding the soil. Even the modern farming procedure of Kibbutz Lahav (in those fields where irrigation is possible) is to plow and sow only one out of two or one out of three years. To do otherwise would be to endanger the land's usefulness for a longer period of time afterward. Thus, even in ancient times a balance was required between the needs of people and the use of the land; an overuse would destroy the habitat for human occupation.

During the Late Bronze Age that balance was struck between inhabitants and the Negev. This can be seen, e.g., in the somewhat surprising fact that virtually no site, beyond the tell itself, has been identified with activity of the Late Bronze Age. Not a single farmhouse, industrial site, or even grave belonging to the Late Bronze Age has been found away from the tell by the team which has systematically conducted a survey of the region around Tel Halif.[26] Apparently the life of the people in this northern Negev settlement centered nearly exclusively on the unwalled town itself; i.e., the competition for the relatively few raw materials and water sources was apparently regulated (whether by "natural" means or by "government").

The same balance between inhabitants and their environment is to be seen in the "dovetailing" of the histories of occupation during the Bronze Ages of Tel Halif and of Tell Beit Mirsim. Albright (1971: 80–85) reported that Tell Beit Mirsim was occupied most heavily in the Middle Bronze Age (Strata D–I), less in the Early and Late Bronze Ages (Strata J and C). In fact, there was almost nothing of the EB and LB strata at Tell Beit Mirsim. In contrast, Tel Halif shows heavy occupation during both Early and Late Bronze Ages and no occupation, except a single tomb, in the Middle Bronze Age. Table 1 displays the relationship and interlocking of the occupations at Halif and Tell Beit Mirsim, a fact to be explained in that the valley system in which the two are found cannot have supported large settlements at both simultaneously. It is not until the end of the Late Bronze Age that contemporary settlements begin to appear and shadow each other through the Iron Age, a feature perhaps the direct result of Egyptian policy in the Nineteenth and Twentieth Dynasties (cf. Na'aman 1981: 185).[27]

Table 1. Comparison of Occupation Strata at Tel Halif and Tell Beit Mirsim

	Halif	Beit Mirsim
Early Bronze Age	EB II village on lower slope of tell	- - - - - - - - - -
	EB II–III fortified town, Stratum XIII	- - - - - - - - - -
	EB III domestic, Stratum XII	- - - - - - - - - -
	EB III domestic, Stratum XI	EB IIIB, thin occupation, Stratum J
Middle Bronze Age	- - - - - - - - - -	MB IA, Stratum I
	- - - - - - - - - -	MB IB–C, Stratum H
	- - - - - - - - - -	MB IIA, Strata G and F
	- - - - - - - - - -	MB IIA, Strata E and D
Late Bronze Age	MB IIC/LB IA domestic, Stratum X	- - - - - - - - - -
	LB IB domestic, Stratum IXB	- - - - - - - - - -
	LB IIA domestic, Stratum IXA	- - - - - - - - - -
	LB IIB industrial, Stratum VIII	LB IIB, Stratum C

On the basis of table 1, the suggestion can even be posited that the population of Beit Mirsim probably shifted to Halif at the end of the Middle Bronze Age as the direct result of the punishing destruction of Beit Mirsim by Egyptian forces seeking to reestablish control of Canaan. It is too much to consider a mere coincidence that at the precise moment of the destruction of Beit Mirsim a hastily built settlement (Stratum X) appeared across the valley at Halif. It is more likely that the displaced citizens of Beit Mirsim decided to rebuild at another spot in the valley.

Halif in the Empire of Egypt

The opinion has been widely held that Egyptian interest and control, least of all military campaigns, in the New Kingdom did not push into the north-central Negev. In part, this opinion was based on faulty information; e.g., no evidence of LB settlements in the surveys of the region led some to conclude that there was no Canaanite occupation of the northern Negev, particularly at the time of the biblical conquest. Likewise, the reading of Egyptian topographical lists of the New Kingdom (such as those of Thutmose III's campaigns) has followed unreflectively the idea that Egyptian armies moved nearly exclusively along the coastline of southern Canaan, either failing or not having to subdue this southern region. The campaign of Hatshepsut to take Gaza in LB IA, however, may well have extended into the Negev toward the hill country in order to open the communication lines inland. Likewise, it is only southern Canaan (along with Megiddo) which is explicitly mentioned as suffering military action (Pritchard 1955: 235) in the great campaign of Thutmose III. Furthermore, the topographical lists of this campaign by Thutmose III lists the name n-g-b (57) as a place or site involved in the military campaign, a name which is often taken to be an otherwise unidentified town (Aharoni [1967: 149] suggests it is Gerar) but which on the face of it may just as likely be the name for a region. Since elsewhere in the topographical lists of Thutmose III some names are commonly taken to be regional designations, the same should be extended to the reading of n-g-b as the Negev, particularly in the light of significant LB finds at Halif.[28] Similar considerations of the military activities of Amenhotep II and Thutmose IV need to be made.

The stratigraphical evidence from Tel Halif is sufficient to suggest that the five towns (Strata X–VII) would not have remained isolated from Egyptian scrutiny if only because of the strategic location on the road from Gaza at the entrance to the hills. A town in such a location necessarily had to be assigned to someone loyal to Egypt (perhaps to the governor of Gaza as part of the territory for an increased tax base), lest in the case of revolt the eastern flank of an advancing Egyptian army be open to surprise attack. Also, of course, should the town of Halif join a coalition in defiance of Egyptian control, then one should expect it to be dealt severe punishment so that the entrance to the hill country would again be secured. Such might be the explanation of the severe destruction in Stratum IXB or even Stratum X.

That Halif in the Late Bronze Age enjoyed international contact would not be unexpected in any event; some of the artifacts found in the excavations demonstrate that contact. Faience amulets in the form of the Egyptian Bes, a faience seal, and scarabs, among other objects, prove contact at the level of trade at least. In addition the discovery at Halif of a bulla impressed with a Mittanian-type cylinder seal suggests correspondence from northern regions (Borowski 1982: 60). Although Halif probably remained a town remote from the main flow of Egyptian dignitaries, it must remain a probability that Halif became involved in the politics of the day, particularly as those politics allowed a break from the hold of Egypt.

Yet, it is the rapid appearance of new wealth at Halif which is most convincing that the Egyptian imperial policy of control and taxation was at work here. It can only be imagined that the support of the royal city Gaza was managed through its holdings of farm and grazing land, but, if that is so, then a system of support devised already in the reign of Thutmose III for the region of Megiddo was likely applied to southern Canaan also. Halif, in this proposed reconstruction, is to be seen as part of the supply line for Palestinian royal cities and for the court of Egypt itself during the New Kingdom; for such purposes Halif's continued existence and even resettlement after disaster or destruction were urged and supported by official Egyptian policy.

NOTES

1. The author gratefully acknowledges the assistance of the Faculty Development Committee of the University of St. Thomas for providing a grant through the Constantin Foundation for the completion of the research for this paper. The author also remembers warmly the friendship and interest extended to him by Glenn Rose; it is due in large part to Glenn's leadership that the author has learned to push beyond the mere reporting of architectural details to measured interpretation.

2. Primarily the excavations have shown that there was a significant LB presence at Halif, a fact unknown to historians before excavation. In addition Halif had been considered important by settlers as early as EB II.

3. The ancient name for Halif is unknown. Presently the excavators favor the biblical name Rimmon on geographical considerations. Others suggest Hormah.

4. Salvage excavation by the Department of Antiquities discovered a sprawling EB village northeast of the tell, a fact confirmed by probes of the Lahav Research Project in 1976.

5. The earliest city appeared on the hill already in the twenty-sixth century B.C.E., EB II–III (Seger 1979). This city was defended by walls 3.5 m. thick.

6. The only significant MB find at Halif was a tomb excavated by Dr. J. D. Seger in a salvage operation.

7. Stratum X shows little buildup of debris and, on the basis of presently completed work, only a single phase. Stratum X suffered destruction rather than abandonment.

8. In fact, an exit from the house leads immediately onto a lower set of steps to a path along the side of the tell.

9. Room B contained the remains of two ovens/tabuns, one later than the other. Only if the room were open to allow smoke to escape could they have been used. Indeed the "paving" (broken pottery, all body sherds) of the successive floors suggests that the room had been prepared with an appropriate "outdoor" surface.

10. A stone door "socket" was found in the debris of this room.

11. Dimensions of the "sockets" for the beams are as large as 25 cm. x 33 cm. The height of the beams can only be guessed.

12. Other evidence either of the use of the roof for sleeping or of a second story turned up in the debris within Room G. A whole lamp was found well above the level of the floor, mixed with the fallen bricks and charred wood. It is possible that the lamp fell from the roof/second story.

13. The fact that the jars were found all across the room is another indication that the *entire* room was roofed.

14. An enticing feature of the pottery in the central room is that a number of potter's marks appear on the handles. Several are the typical "†" mark on large store jars; two are simple "–" on store jars. One, however, resembles a kaph (𐤊). Coincidentally, a close parallel in form is found on a handle from Alaca Hüyük (Zübeyrkoşay 1951, pl. lxiv).

15. Cf. below the comments on Halif in the valley.

16. Cf. the comments of Na'aman about the "several signs testifying to the intensification of the Egyptian occupation of Canaan, particularly in southern Palestine, during the time of the 19th and the beginning of the 20th Dynasties" (Na'aman 1981: 185). His conclusion that the building boom in such places as Aphek, Lachish, Tel Sera', Tel Masos, Deir el-Balah and Timnah is to be ascribed to Egyptian involvement and interest in economic development of Palestine is equally applicable to the building boom at Halif and elsewhere after the removal of the Hyksos threat.

17. A curious, as yet unexplained, feature of the LB presence at Tel Halif is that nothing of LB provenance has shown up in the regional survey conducted by the Lahav Research Project. Yet this is perhaps not so surprising in that, prior to excavation on the mound, earlier surveys had also declared that no LB presence was to be found in the region (Aharoni 1976).

18. J. Weinstein, in a preliminary evaluation of the scarab, has said that it belongs to the type of "Hyksos" scarabs; hence, it was already an "heirloom" at the time it was lost.

19. As much as 2.3 m. deep. The deposition of this mixture followed a burning across the foundation fill L.10025, leaving a layer of black ash. The purpose of the burning is not known, though it may have had the function of destroying possible contamination from vegetation and rodents. Subsequent intermittent and limited burning also marked the deposit of the clay and loess mixture; this latter burning may have been to harden the wet mixture.

20. Characteristic vertical cracking of the "platform" as it dried following exposure is typical of loess deposits (Press and Siever 1978). In addition, the use of the "platform" went through several phases of growth which added to the height especially in the western part.

21. The word "silo" will be used only where evidence of grain storage has been found. "Bin" applies to above-ground storage unit; hence, "stone-lined pit" is a descriptive term.

22. Remains of grain were found in the deep fill in silo 11024.

23. A large number of store jars were found, originally set on their rims, inside the silo in its final, rebuilt phase. Since they were placed into the installation rim-side down, they must have been empty at the time.

24. Cf. the reports of Tell Beit Mirsim which at this same time included mainly lined silos.

25. A parallel is found at MB Negila (Amiran and Eitan 1967: 46). Found on the same floor with the bull's head were a number of other interesting objects, including a carved limestone disc painted black on the reverse and with a black cross-like figure with "frond" extensions on all four arms on the obverse.

26. As noted above these "findings" confirm earlier surveys of the region.

27. Note that, like the area of LB IIB exposed at Halif, the excavated LB IIB area of Tell Beit Mirsim shows a great many "silos," perhaps too many to match the needs of the people in the number of houses. This may suggest that both sites were used then for the collection of grain for some other central group.

28. It is remotely possible that the Thutmose III lists hold a reference to the destruction of Halif by the Egyptian army. Aharoni (1967: 149) has posited that name #59 *r-n-m* be read as Hebrew *rmn*. On other grounds we have suggested that Halif is biblical Rimmon. If Aharoni is correct in his reading of name #59—be it noted, two names after *n-g-b* in the lists—then it might be biblical Rimmon which is named in the Thutmose III list.

BIBLIOGRAPHY

Aharoni, Y.
  1967   *The Land of the Bible: A Historical Geography*. London: Burns and Oates.
  1976   Nothing Early and Nothing Late: Rewriting Israel's Conquest. *Biblical Archaeologist* 39: 55–76.
  1982   *The Archaeology of the Land of Israel*. Trans. A. Rainey from Hebrew, 1980. Philadelphia: Westminster Press.

Ahituv, S.
  1978   Economic Factors in the Egyptian Conquest of Canaan. *Israel Exploration Journal* 28: 93–105.

Albright, W. F.
  1971   *The Archaeology of Palestine*. Gloucester, MA: Peter Smith.
  1975   Tell Beit Mirsim. In *EAEHL* I: 171–78. Englewood Cliffs, NJ: Prentice-Hall.

Amiran, R.
1969   *Ancient Pottery of the Holy Land.* Jerusalem: Masada Press.

Amiran, R. and Eitan, E.
1967   A Canaanite-Hyksos City at Tell Negila. Pp. 41–48 in *Archaeological Discoveries in the Holy Land.* New York: Thomas Y. Crowell.

Avi-Yonah, M. and Stern, E.
1978   Rabbath-Ammon. In *EAEHL* IV: 987–93. Englewood Cliffs, NJ: Prentice-Hall.

Beebe, H.
1968   Ancient Palestinian Dwellings. *Biblical Archaeologist* 31: 38–58.

Boling, R.
1975   Excavations at Tananir. In *Bulletin of the American Schools of Oriental Research Supplement Studies* 21: 25–85.

Borchardt, L. and Ricke, H.
1980   *Die Wohnhäuser in Tell el-Amarna.* Wissenschaftliche Veröffentlichung der Deutschen Orient Gesellschaft 91. Berlin.

Borowski, O.
1982   Four Seasons of Excavations at Tel Halif/Lahav. *Qadmoniot* 15: 57–60 (Hebrew).

Chadwick, J.
1976   *The Mycenaean World.* New York: Cambridge University Press.

Cotterell, A.
1979   *The Minoan World.* New York: Charles Scribner's Sons.

Drower, M.
1973   Syria c. 1550–1400 B.C.E. In *Cambridge Ancient History.* Third edition. II.1: 417–525.

Frankfort, H.
1970   *The Art and Architecture of the Ancient Orient.* Baltimore: Penguin.

Fritz, V.
1981   The Israelite "Conquest" in the Light of Recent Excavations at Khirbet el-Meshâsh. *Bulletin of the American Schools of Oriental Research* 241: 61–74.

Macqueen, J.
1975   *The Hittites and Their Contemporaries in Asia Minor.* Boulder, CO: Westview Press.

Mellaart, J.
1967   *Çatal Hüyük: A Neolithic Town in Anatolia.* New York: McGraw-Hill Book Co.

Meshel, Z.
1977   Kuntilat 'Ajrud. 1975–1976. *Israel Exploration Journal* 27: 52–53.
1979   Did Yahweh Have a Consort. *Biblical Archaeology Review* 5: 24–34.

Müller, V.
1940   Types of Mesopotamian Houses. *Journal of the American Oriental Society* 60: 151–80.

Mylonas, G.
1966   *Mycenae and the Mycenaean Age.* Princeton: Princeton University Press.

Na'aman, N.
1981   Economic Aspects of the Egyptian Occupation of Canaan. *Israel Explora-tion Journal* 31: 172–85.

Oren, E.
1978   Tell esh-Shari'a (Tel Sera). In *EAEHL* IV: 1059–69.
1982   Ziglag—A Biblical City on the Edge of the Negev. *Biblical Archaeologist* 45: 155–66.

Parrot, A.
1961   *The Arts of Assyria*. New York: Golden Press.

Press, F. and Siever, R.
1978   *Earth*. Second edition. San Francisco: W. H. Freeman.

Pritchard, J. B.
1955   *Ancient Near Eastern Texts*. Princeton: Princeton University Press.

Seger, J.
1979   Tel Halif (Lahav), 1979. *Israel Exploration Journal* 29: 247–49.

Shea, W.
1979   The Conquests of Sharuhen and Megiddo Reconsidered. *Israel Explora-tion Journal* 29: 1–5.

Smith, W.
1981   *The Art and Architecture of Ancient Egypt*. New York: Penguin.

Weinstein, J.
1981   The Egyptian Empire in Palestine: A Reassessment. *Bulletin of the American Schools of Oriental Research* 241: 1–28.

Woolley, L.
1955   *Alalakh: An Account of the Excavations at Tell Atchana*. Oxford.

Yisraeli, Y.
1978   Tel Sharuhen. In *EAEHL* IV: 1074–82.

Zübeyrkoşay, H.
1951   *Les Fouilles d'Alaca Hüyük*. Ankara: Entreprises par la Société d'Histoire Turque.

Chapter 7

AI (ET-TELL): PROBLEM SITE FOR BIBLICAL ARCHAEOLOGISTS

Joseph A. Callaway
Southern Baptist Seminary

I never had the privilege of working with D. Glenn Rose on an excavation, but I came to appreciate his work through reports and visits to Hesi. His devotion to high academic standards, good excavation methodology, interdisciplinary objectives, and harmonious personal relationships impressed me greatly. It was with momentary disbelief that I learned of Glenn's death in Jerusalem, because there was still so much he wanted to do. Fortunately, he had, perhaps unconsciously, prepared for such an eventuality in the training of staff members who are carrying on all aspects of the Hesi project. His objectives will be reached, which is encouraging to others of us who still have much work laid out to do. I am grateful to be included in the circle of friends who honor his memory with this volume.

If the writer of the book of Job were an archaeologist, he might well begin a sequel to his epic poem as follows:

> Now there was another day when the sons of God came to present themselves before the Lord, and Satan also came among them. The Lord said to Satan, "Whence have you come?" Satan answered the Lord, "From going to and fro upon the earth, and walking up and down on it." And the Lord said to Satan, "Have you considered my servants, the biblical archaeologists, who fear God and prove the Bible?" Then Satan answered the Lord, "Do the archaeologists fear God and prove the Bible for naught? Have you not hedged them in with support from religious institutions on every side and blessed the work of their hands? But now put forth your hand and give them the site of Ai and they will curse you to your face."
> So Satan went forth from the presence of the Lord, and the site of Ai was given to the archaeologists.

It was given first in September 1928 to John Garstang, the British archaeologist who was excavating Jericho at the time. Garstang rather hurriedly opened three "feeler" trenches on the acropolis area of the tell and five trenches against the outer face of the city walls on the south side. The results of this work were never published, although a five-page summary report was submitted to the Department of Antiquities at the conclusion of the soundings (Garstang 1928). He did claim in a later book (Garstang 1931: 356) that LB pottery dating to c. 1400 B.C.E. was found and was left "in the collection of the American School," now the Albright Institute in Jerusalem. This pottery has not been located.

Garstang espoused the traditional 1400 B.C.E. date for the conquest of Canaan, based upon 1 Kings 6:1: "In the four hundred and eightieth year after the people of Israel came out of the land of Egypt, in the fourth year of Solomon's reign over Israel . . . he began to build the house of the LORD." The chronology at the time for Solomon's accession was 970 B.C.E., so the fourth year would be 966 B.C.E. The time of the exodus would be calculated by adding 966 and 480, giving a date of c. 1446 B.C.E. Subtract from this the forty years of wilderness wandering and a date of 1406 B.C.E. or 1400 in round numbers is reached for the conquest. Thus the discovery of a 1400 B.C.E. city at Ai supported the traditional time accepted for the conquest and confirmed the biblical account of the capture of Ai as related in Joshua 7—8, to the satisfaction of Garstang's church-oriented financial backers. At this point it seems that Satan entered the picture and caused the oldest axiom in archaeology to be broken; i.e., when you get your problems solved, stop digging!

Hence the site was given a second time on September 11, 1933, to Judith Krause, a twenty-seven-year-old Palestinian-born Israeli recently graduated from the Sorbonne in Paris and one of the pioneer women archaeologists in the Holy Land. Inspired by the prospect of "resurrecting" the ancient biblical city of Ai from the dust of its ruins, she embarked upon a series of annual campaigns that were abruptly terminated on July 1, 1936, when she died at the age of twenty-nine.

Krause, who in 1934 married Yves Marquet, a promising young French specialist in Arabic studies, is to be credited with the "blockbuster" interpretation of the evidence at Ai that has given the site its distinctive place in biblical archaeology: there was no evidence of a city at Ai from c. 2400 B.C.E. to about 1200 B.C.E. The city dated by Garstang to c. 1400 B.C.E., which confirmed the "biblical" chronology of 1 Kings 6:1, in fact, never existed!

Thus the world of biblical scholars and archaeologists faced a dilemma that would have delighted the writer of the book of Job: a generally accepted "biblical" chronology of the exodus and conquest did not find confirmation in one of the major cities named in the conquest traditions. Nevertheless, as in the case of Job's dilemma, there was no lack of "friendly" solutions to the problem.

One proposal came as a result of Albright's excavations at Bethel, 2 km. from Ai, in 1934. He found that the LB city was terminated sometime between

1250 and 1220 B.C.E. by a disastrous fire that left a heavy layer of ashes over all the ruins which he excavated. This layer paralleled in time similar levels at Tell Beit Mirsim (identified by Albright with biblical Debir), at Lachish, and at Hazor. Since these cities are named in the conquest accounts as captured by Joshua and the Israelite forces, Albright felt "compelled" to attribute the destruction at Bethel also to the Israelites (Albright 1934: 10).

This interpretation was not without its problems, however. The archaeological evidence did seem to fit a general conquest that could be attributed to the Israelites, but the biblical accounts dwelt at length on the taking of Jericho and Ai and said nothing about Bethel. On the other hand, there was no archaeological evidence that cities even existed at Jericho and Ai between 1250 and 1220 B.C.E., the time of the destruction of Bethel by the "Israelites" in Albright's reconstruction. The problem was to account for a "shifting of scene" (Albright 1939: 16) in the biblical traditions from Bethel, which was actually taken, to Ai, which did not exist at the time.

Albright observed that the narrative in Joshua "cannot be based on first-hand tradition throughout, but must have aetiological elements" (Albright 1939: 17) because it seems to reflect an ancient Canaanite tradition of a destruction eight centuries before the time of Joshua. "What was more natural," he asked, "than that this tradition, current for many generations among the Israelite inhabitants of Bethel, should have been attached to the impressive Canaanite ruins of et-Tell, whose destruction actually preceded the foundation of Bethel?" (Albright 1939: 17). Thus, the need to explain the presence of the 27.5 a. ruins at Ai in time shifted the scene of a conquest of Bethel to a conquest of Ai.

Vincent attempted to make this interpretation more credible by proposing that a military outpost of Bethel was hastily constructed on the ruin at Ai to slow the advance on Bethel from Jericho. The conquest of Ai, therefore, was the capture of this outpost, whose remains perished in time and left no material evidence. However, the Iron I village, which was established on the site after 1220 B.C.E., was Israelite (Vincent 1937: 262–66).

A more radical solution to the problem of Ai was proposed by Marquet-Krause and Martin Noth. Marquet-Krause followed the interpretation of her mentor, Dussaud, and concluded that the conquest account in Joshua 7—8 is more legend than history (Marquet-Krause 1935: 341; Dussaud 1935). Martin Noth, following the views of his mentor, A. Alt, recognized the prominence of legend in the conquest account and made its association with history aetiological (Noth 1935; 1958: 149 n. 2). The legends were based upon the historical presence of the ruins at et-Tell, but the destruction was an event which occurred at the end of the Early Bronze Age (c. 2400 B.C.E.) not in the Late Bronze Age. Thus there was no historical Israelite conquest of Ai, but the Iron I village at et-Tell was, to Marquet-Krause and Noth, Israelite or Benjaminite.

Other scholars have speculated that biblical Ai must be found at a site other than et-Tell. Kitchener suggested long ago that Khirbet Hai, southeast of Mukhmas, may be the biblical site. Guerin proposed Khirbet Khudriya, east of et-Tell and on the Wadi el-Jaya route to Jericho. J. M. Grintz of Tel Aviv University revived Dussaud's identification of et-Tell as biblical Beth-aven and suggested that Khirbet Haiyan in the southeast edge of Deir Dibwan and 1 km. from et-Tell may be the site of Ai (Grintz 1961).

I came on the scene in May 1964 when the site was given a third time to archaeologists, and I must admit that I entertained notions of bridging the widening gulf between the biblical accounts in Joshua 7—8 and the actual evidence of the ruin itself. My extension of the areas excavated by Marquet-Krause quickly confirmed her conclusions that the site was abandoned from the end of the Early Bronze Age until the beginning of Iron I; i.e., from about 2400 B.C.E. to 1200 B.C.E. If the gap between the biblical traditions and the evidence at Ai was to be bridged, therefore, a conquest of some sort would have to occur after 1200 B.C.E., not before, as Albright contended.

This view was set forth in a paper read at the Society of Biblical Literature meeting in New York in December 1967 and published in 1968 (Callaway 1968). Four lines of new evidence were presented in support of a proposed conquest of Ai in the twelfth century, at the end of the first Iron I phase rather than in the thirteenth century B.C.E. The first evidence cited was from excavations and soundings at alternate sites proposed for the location of Ai. One way of holding to the view of Garstang that the conquest occurred about 1400 B.C.E. or to the view of Albright that it took place in the mid to late thirteenth century B.C.E. was to posit another location of Ai.

Jehoshua M. Grintz had proposed that Khirbet Haiyan, 1 km. southeast of et-Tell, could be the biblical site (Grintz 1961), and et-Tell was identified as the Beth-aven of Joshua 7:2. A sounding was carried out at Haiyan in 1964 near the tomb of Sheik Ahmed, and the earliest evidence found was Roman coins and pottery on bedrock dating to the first century C.E. (Callaway and Nicol 1966). Structures on the site were later, consisting of a Byzantine church, a house with adjacent animal quarters, and tombs. This clearly eliminated Haiyan as a Late Bronze Age site.

Two other sites had been proposed long ago as locations of Ai, one because of the name and the other because of location. Kitchener suggested that Khirbet Hai, southeast of Mukhmas and a namesake of biblical "Hai," could be the site (Grintz 1961: 201–3). Exploration of the tiny ruin revealed a very shallow deposit of debris with bedrock protruding here and there and nothing earlier than Byzantine visible. Khirbet Khudriya, east of et-Tell and on the Wadi Asas route to Jericho, was suggested by Guerin although it had never been excavated (Grintz 1961: 201–3). Rather extensive excavation there in 1966 and 1968 uncovered a thriving Byzantine settlement, probably a monastery, and more than twenty tombs. The earliest tombs were Jewish dating to the Herodian period and reused by the Byzantine settlement. Nothing earlier was evident. Thus the proposed sites of Khirbet Hai and Khirbet Khudriya were eliminated, and we were left with et-Tell as the site of biblical Ai, as Albright had maintained forty years earlier (Albright 1924).

The second line of evidence is from the Qumran texts of Joshua which tend to support the LXX version of Joshua 7—8. It has long been known that the LXX text of Joshua 7:2–5 and 8:1–29 is a more concise account of the conquest of Ai than is that of MT. It omits redundancies (8:4), extensive involvement of the divine as in 8:5b–8a, technical names such as "Shebarim" in 7:5 or "Beth-aven" in 7:2, the association of the men of Bethel with the defense of Ai in 8:17, and the summarizing statement in 8:26 (Callaway 1968: 319).

There are unpublished fragments of Joshua 8:3–18 from Qumran Cave IV, that Frank M. Cross kindly brought to my attention, which support the LXX texts at certain points. Omitted with the LXX is 8:9b, and 8:10–18 seems to be a very short text, also omitting some of the items noted above. We cannot be sure that the "Men of Bethel" passage is omitted, because that section of the 4Q fragments is missing. Thus, as Cross warned, we cannot rely too heavily on those fragments to support the LXX reading, but taken together with the other evidence presented in this section we cannot dismiss them either. The likelihood is that, in the Palestinian tradition recovered from 4Q as well as in the LXX version, Bethel is not mentioned in the account of the conquest of Ai in Joshua 7—8. This erodes the position of Albright who maintained that the conquest in Joshua 8 was of Bethel and was transferred to the site of Ai by later traditioners. On the contrary, Bethel seems to have been inserted into the account by later traditioners.

The third line of evidence is that there are two closely limited Iron I phases at Ai separated by a rather extensive repair and reorganization of the village. In the second phase some house walls were rebuilt, entrances were blocked and relocated, floors were resurfaced with layers of fine earth packed over flagstone or cobblestone surfaces, streets were resurfaced, and round silos were constructed both in houses and, in some instances, in the narrow streets, suggesting a significant increase in population. In my 1968 presentation I attributed the change in the village of Phase II to a possible conquest by the Israelites.

Finally, the fourth line of new evidence was from the cities associated with the conquest. Places mentioned in the biblical accounts, such as Arad, Dibon, and Gibeon, were occupied in Iron I, but thus far no Late Bronze Age evidence has been reported. If we accept the accounts as essentially historical, these sites would have to be involved in an Iron I conquest along with the site of Ai, rather than in the latter part of LB.

The view of an Iron I conquest presented in 1968 was rather speculative, because it was set forth before all of the evidence from the Iron I village at Ai was in hand. Further research and study of the internal evidence at Ai have introduced new perspectives on both the conquest and the biblical traditions. As J. Max Miller observed, my position was one supported by circular reasoning, and, in retrospect, I suppose it was. In any case, the hypothesis no longer seems viable.

Hence we are back at the drawing board as far as the site of Ai is concerned. Years of excavations and tens of thousands of dollars spent on research have systematically eliminated historical reconstructions of the conquest of Ai that various scholars tried to relate to the biblical account in Joshua 7—8. The fourteenth-century hypothesis of Garstang went first, then the thirteenth-century view of Albright, and now the twelfth-century proposal that I made in 1968 is gone. We must agree that Satan has had a lot of fun with the site of Ai. Is this the end, however? Is this all that archaeology has to contribute?

The answer is no! Actually archaeological research is simply playing out its role. The first thing to admit is that biblical archaeologists do not "fear God and prove the Bible" as Satan accused. They may fear God, but what they seek to prove is their view of the Bible. In the case of Ai it has been the views or hypotheses of archaeologists which have foundered in the face of material evidence from the site. We still have the Bible. Archaeology is pressing us to redirect our thinking into more profitable directions, and that is what I propose to do in the remaining part of this paper.

One problem in studying the conquest has been a reluctance to give up the essential historicity of the conquest traditions. However, it has been recognized since the 1920s that the traditions as we have them come from a much later time and setting than that of the entry of Israel into Canaan. The so-called "deuteronomic" framework superimposed upon the materials actually is a barrier denying access to the early history of Israel (Hayes and Miller 1977: 266ff.). Albrecht Alt was one of the first to accept the implications of this conclusion, and as a result he set out in 1925 to develop a perspective external to the biblical traditions to bypass the redactors' barriers and to control the selection of data (Alt 1925).

Alt's method, summarized by Weippert, was to construct a history of the land's territorial divisions based upon extra-biblical sources contemporary with the time of Israel's settlement at the end of the thirteenth century B.C.E. This history provided the starting point for evaluating tradition relevant to the conquest embedded in the Deuteronomistic History in the Bible. Working from Egyptian sources, Alt concluded that by the end of the Amarna Age, in the fourteenth century B.C.E., Shechem was the only significant city-state in the highlands of Canaan between Jerusalem and the valley of Jezreel (Weippert 1971: 11). A century later, when the authority of the Nineteenth Dynasty collapsed, the city-state system of political organization that had prevailed in Canaan since the Hyksos period began to give way to larger entities such as Moab, Edom, Israel, and Peleseth, but the hill country between Jerusalem and Jezreel still seemed to be relatively free of occupation. This is the region where the biblical traditions place the initial settlements of the Israelites.

Alt's conclusion was that no coordinated military offensive such as that depicted in the capture of Jericho and Ai in Joshua 6—8 ever occurred. Instead, the central hill country was acquired relatively peacefully by infiltration and eventual settlement of the wide unoccupied gaps between the city-states of Jerusalem, Shechem, and Jezreel. Lacking specific evidence of the infiltration and establishment of settlements, however, he worked from historical analogy and conjectured that "nomad" Israelites entered the land from the east and south, pasturing their flocks in the hills year after year until they eventually established villages and became sedentary (Weippert 1971: 18, 41). These are the villages known to be scattered over the central highlands during the Iron I period.

A second phase of the settlement occurred late in Iron I, in Alt's reconstruction, when the Israelites moved aggressively to expand their territory. This was a process that began with battles waged by individual tribes, as reflected in the book of Judges, and culminated with the establishment of the monarchy under David. The original infiltration phase was associated with a wave of immigration by the so-called "Leah" tribes, and the second or expansionist phase was connected with the "Rachel" tribes (Weippert 1971: 41–46).

Alt's reconstruction has been the starting point for scholarly discussion of the settlement in Canaan for more than half a century, and it is, in my opinion, the place to begin a discussion of Ai and the Bible. Certainly, Albright's effort to interface the external evidence from archaeology with the deuteronomic traditions in Joshua 1—12 has proved inadequate. Also, Mendenhall's theory of a peasant's revolt against Canaanite overlords as the substance of the conquest is equally inadequate because it lacks supporting evidence from contemporary inscriptions or the excavated sites in central Canaan. It is an argument from historical analogy which, though attractive, is alien to the evidence of Iron I highland villages in Canaan.

Alt's basic reconstruction of an Iron I settlement of the highlands mainly by peaceful infiltration still stands after many years of excavations, but his argument from historical analogy that the infiltrators were "nomad" Israelites who entered from the east and south is no longer viable. The evidence from Ai, Khirbet Raddana, and numerous other village sites is that the newcomers were primarily farmers and secondarily herders of small cattle, not nomads. These settlers came to the highlands with fixed patterns of village life and established small villages in marginal and inhospitable areas with the aid of two new subsistence technologies: the introduction of bell-shaped rock-cut cisterns for water supplies; and the construction of agricultural terraces which enabled the cultivation of steep hillsides never before planted in crops. Also, the newcomers seem to have migrated from the lowlands and coastal regions north and west of the hill country, instead of east and south as Alt postulated. Furthermore, the migration to the highlands seems to have occurred because of population pressures imposed by more warlike newcomers to the more fertile coastal and lowland areas. Thus the hill country settlers took refuge in their inhospitable mountain villages to escape war and violence rather than, as Joshua 11:12 indicates, to wage holy war upon everything that breathed.

The village at Ai was one of about 90 new sites established at the beginning of Iron I cataloged by Lawrence E. Stager in a recent survey of the region from Hebron to Shechem (Stager 1981: 1). The number of villages in the area of about 4,200 sq. km. had increased from 23 in LB to 114 in Iron I, and the estimated population increased from about 14,000 to more than 38,000. This increase occurred too rapidly to be ascribed to natural growth, Stager observed. Clearly, a significant increment of newcomers had moved into the highlands.

At Ai, closely spaced houses with cobblestone streets were built on the acropolis ruins of the ancient EB city, covering about 10% of the ancient site. The other 90% of the 27.5 a. ruin was terraced and planted in crops, creating a subsistence base for the villagers. Albright characterized the major house type, which was found at Bethel in 1934, as a pier-technique construction. A row of piers, usually four, was located on one side of the long axis to support transverse roofing beams (Kelso 1968: 32). The piers were either squared monoliths, some of which still bear the marks of the stonemason's chisel, or stacks of from two to four large stones in piers comparable in size to the pillars. A typical house consisted of either a single room divided by the pier into two areas, or the "greatroom" of two spaces plus a long narrow room across the back or side (cf. Shiloh 1973 for examples).

This type of house was not confined to the highlands. Several sites in the foothill region to the west and even in the coastal plains have pier-type houses dating to early Iron I. Numerous examples are reported from Tell Beit Mirsim and Beth-shemesh. These are dated to the end of Iron I by Albright and his pupil, Wright, but the wealth of evidence accumulated since the 1930s indicates that the earliest phases should be moved toward the beginning of Iron I. A house with stacked brick piers is reported in Stratum IX (eleventh century B.C.E.) at Tell Qasile by Mazar (Mazar 1951: 138), and houses with squared stone pillars are evident in Stratum IV at Tell Abu Hawam, near Haifa (Hamilton 1934: 8–9, pls. iv, ix, xi). The Central Moab Survey has reported several Iron I sites east of the central highlands with pillar houses still visible in the surface ruins, but they have not been excavated.

Weippert noted in 1975 that the Iron I settlements in Transjordan may be accounted for by "emigration to Transjordan" or "internal colonization," and he seems to prefer the latter. Nomads in the region, he postulates, were "forced to convert to *systematic* agriculture" and thus gradually settled in permanent villages (Weippert 1971: 33–34). When some of the villages are excavated, we may learn that overpopulation in the highlands caused emigration to Transjordan in an expansion of the movement that brought them to the highlands in the first place.

Widespread use of the pier-type house in the highlands, Shephelah, coastal plains, and, even in some instances, Transjordan suggests a cultural pattern that would hardly be consistent with Alt's theory of nomads infiltrating the highlands from the east and gradually becoming sedentary. At Ai and at nearby Khirbet Raddana the builders had bronze chisels which left their mark both on roof-support pillars in houses and in cisterns dug in solid rock underneath the houses. The uniformity of house patterns, cistern form and size, and the availability of metal tools indicate cultural traditions that would associate better with agricultural than with nomadic backgrounds. The village at Ai was clearly an agricultural settlement.

During Iron I the small village of less than five acres was the dominant form of social organization in the highlands. G. Edwin Harmon has noted that, since the small village was the major societal feature of the highland population, it was also a microcosm within the larger context of society (Harmon 1983: 116–19). This is attested by certain shared features of villages throughout the land of Canaan, such as house types, an agricultural subsistence base, and what van Nieuwenhuijze called "isolation" (van Nieuwenhuijze 1962:L 300). The village was an economic entity within itself, independent of other villages and not subject to any market or trade system. Instead, its basic character was that of a subsistence system dependent more upon the vagaries of nature than upon political or economic influences. Consequently, isolationism was enhanced, and dependence upon nature and its deities was reiterated in daily life. Actually, very few imported artifacts are reported from excavated villages, apart from the few bronze tools essential to agricultural life. Thus the predominant characteristics of the hilltop village, such as Ai, were self-sufficiency and pragmatic isolation. This has implications for the larger social structure of the people and their political organization, because the tendency would be to resist political unification and social as well as religious conformity if the integrity of the village unit was threatened in any way.

The foregoing discussion indicates that the settlement at Ai was established as a part of widespread population movements into the land of Canaan in Iron I. Instead of taking the highlands in mass military campaigns, the settlers claimed unoccupied ruins of ancient cities or barren hilltops that had never before supported permanent villages. Indeed, they seem to have fled from conflict in the lowlands and coastal areas to escape more warlike newcomers to those regions. As Stager puts it, "the mountains served as a refuge and redoubt" for the two centuries preceding the founding of the Israelite monarchy (Stager 1981: 3).

To some degree these conclusions are not new. In 1942 Albright noted the loss of much territory over which Canaanite culture had presided at the beginning of Iron I. By attributing the mass settlement of the central highlands to invading Israelites, and the loss of Phoenicia and the coastal plains of Canaan to the Sea Peoples, he estimated that nine-tenths of the Canaanite culture area was lost (Albright 1965: 456ff.). Dispossessed along the Phoenician coast, the Canaanites

> were forced by circumstances and enabled by the march of civilization to exploit their mountainous hinterland of Lebanon to an extent not previously possible. Thanks to the then recent discovery of the uses to which plaster made with slaked lime could be put, they were able to dig cisterns everywhere and to line them with true lime plaster, impervious to water. As in Israelite Palestine, this made it possible not only to develop intensive cultivation of the rich coastal lands of the Lebanese Riviera but also to build villages in the mountains (Albright 1965: 456ff.).

The displaced Canaanites are thus given credit for the development of cisterns which enabled them to move into the mountains of Lebanon and establish villages away from natural sources of water. Noth agreed with Albright's view and noted the decisive influence of this new water source in the distribution of settlements in the highlands, but both Noth and Albright failed to associate the movement into the mountains between Jerusalem and Jezreel with the movement into the mountains of Lebanon. My view is that both were a part of the same population movements and that the development of cisterns and agricultural terracing were common in both areas. In fact, Stager has noted that agricultural terracing was practiced in Canaanite territory near Ugarit in viticulture during the Late Bronze Age. The evidence is in the Ugaritic texts which name "at least two villages, *Bq't* and *Hlb-rpš*, from the mountain district which paid a wine tax to Ugarit" (Stager 1981: 29). He goes on to observe that "these villages must have had hillside vineyards." The earliest references to terraces (*sdmt*) in the Levant are also in the Ugaritic texts: "Mot, the god of death, is seized by vine-dressers who prune, bind, and drop him to the terrace" (Stager 1981: 29). Since Canaanites from the coastal cities south of Tyre carried on trade with Ugarit in the Late Bronze Age and Canaanite merchants from Ashdod and other coastal cities actually lived in Ugarit or its port city of Minet el-Beidah, terracing technology would have been known by people in the lowlands and coastal areas before the settlement of the hill country in Iron I.

My conclusion in the light of these discussions is that the Iron I villagers at Ai had their background in Canaanite culture and religion and that this can be documented extensively with artifacts which have their parallels at lowland and coastal sites. Space does not permit this documentation, but it does appear in another publication now in press (cf. Callaway: Olga Tufnell Festschrift forthcoming). If there was a conquest of Ai, it occurred in the eleventh century B.C.E. when the village was sacked and abandoned near the beginning of the monarchy. This is the time in which Alt placed the expansionist phase of Israel's history, leading to the establishment of the monarchy.

The site of Ai as I have come to know it in nine seasons of excavations would fit in best with the picture of Israel's early history in the book of Judges. Points at which the material evidence of the site is compatible with Israel's backgrounds in the book of Judges are: (1) prominence of small villages; (2) an agricultural subsistence base; (3) the characteristic of isolationism; (4) dominance of fertility religion; and (5) social and family life. The evidence does not support at any point the account of the conquest of Ai in Joshua 7—8.

As I noted earlier, one function of archaeological research is to redirect our thinking about the Bible. The research at Ai compels us, in my opinion, to review and evaluate the Deuteronomistic History's presentation of Israel's origins and to ascertain more realistically its relevance for today's world. Foremost among the items that should be reviewed is the "preaching" of holy war in Joshua 1—12 which, taken literally for centuries by conservative and fundamentalist Christians, has made Bible-belt church members in particular the most militant segment of our population in every war we have fought. Who can conceive of the waste of resources and life, as well as the damage to the social and religious fabric of our society, that wrong interpretation of the conquest of Ai, and of Canaan, have wrought! If we take seriously the redirection of our thinking occasioned by the findings at Ai, then it may be that Satan made another mistake when he gave the site of Ai to the archaeologists.

BIBLIOGRAPHY

Albright, W. F.
  1924   'Ai and Beth-aven. *Annual of the American Schools of Oriental Research* 4: 141–49.
  1934   The Kyle Memorial Excavation at Bethel. *Bulletin of the American Schools of Oriental Research* 56: 2–15.
  1939   The Israelite Conquest of Canaan in the Light of Archaeology. *Bulletin of the American Schools of Oriental Research* 74: 11–23.
  1965   The Role of the Canaanites in the History of Civilization. Pp. 438–87 in *The Bible and the Ancient Near East*, ed. G. E. Wright. Garden City, NY: Doubleday.
Alt, A.
  1925   Die Landnahme der Israeliten in Palästina, 1. Pp. 89–125 in *Kleine*

Schriften zur Geschichte des Volkes Israel. München: C. H. Beck. English translation: *Essays on Old Testament History and Religion* (1968): 175–221.

Callaway, J. A.
1968   New Evidence on the Conquest of Ai. *Journal of Biblical Literature* 87: 312–20.
forth-   A New Perspective on the Hill Country Settlement of Canaan in Iron Age
coming   I. *Palestine in the Bronze and Iron Ages,* ed. Jonathan Tubb. A Festschrift in honor of Olga Tufnell.

Callaway, J. A. and Nicol, M. B.
1966   A Sounding at Khirbet Ḥaiyân. *Bulletin of the American Schools of Oriental Research* 183: 12–19.

Dussaud, M. R.
1935   Note additionnelle. *Syria* 16:346–52.

Garstang, J.
1928   El-Tell: Ai. Report on the 1928 soundings at Ai submitted to the Department of Antiquities, Jerusalem. September 21, 1928. 5 pages. Unpublished.
1931   *Joshua Judges.* London: Constable.

Grintz, J.
1961   'Ai which is Beside Beth-aven: A re-examination of the identity of 'Ai. *Biblica* 42: 201–16.

Hamilton, R. W.
1934   Excavations at Tell Abu Hawâm. *Quarterly of the Department of Antiquities in Palestine* 4: 1–69.

Harmon, G. E.
1983   *Floor Area and Population Determination.* Unpublished Ph.D. dissertation, Southern Baptist Theological Seminary, Louisville, Kentucky.

Hayes, J. H. and Miller, J. M. (eds.)
1977   *Israelite and Judean History.* Philadelphia: Westminster Press.

Kelso, J. L. (ed.)
1968   *The Excavation of Bethel (1934–1960).* Annual of the American Schools of Oriental Research 39. Cambridge: American Schools of Oriental Research.

Marquet-Krause, J.
1935   La deuxième campagne de fouilles à 'Ay (1934). Rapport sommaire. *Syria* 16: 325–45.

Mazar (Maislar), B.
1951   The Excavations at Tell Qasîle. *Israel Exploration Journal* 1: 61–76, 125–40.

Nieuwenhuijze, C. A. O. van
1962   The Near Eastern Village: A Profile. *Middle East Journal* 16:3: 295–300.

Noth, M.
1935   Bethel und 'Ai. Palästinajahrbuch 31: 7–29.

1958 *The History of Israel*. London: Adam and Charles Black.

Shiloh, Y.
 1973 The Four-Room House—the Israelite Type-House? *Eretz Israel* 11: 277–85 (Hebrew).

Stager, L. E.
 1981 Highland Village Life in Palestine Some Three Thousand Years Ago. *The Oriental Institute Notes and News* 69: 1–3.

Vincent, L. H.
 1937 Les Fouilles d'et-Tell = 'Ai. *Revue biblique* 46: 231–66.

Weippert, M.
 1971 *The Settlement of the Israelite Tribes in Palestine*. Studies in Biblical Theology, second series 21. London: SCM.

Chapter 8

DAN

Avraham Biran
Hebrew Union College-Jewish Institute of Religion
Nelson Glueck School of Biblical Archaeology

I

Dan may well serve as a case study for the examination of the synthetic approach to biblical, historical, and archaeological research. Known as Laish in the second millennium B.C.E., Dan is located at the foot of Mt. Hermon by one of the main sources of the river Jordan.[1] No historical or biblical records are known up to the present which attest to the existence of a city earlier than the second millennium. However, archaeological excavations[2] have revealed a settlement of considerable importance already in the third millennium B.C.E. This is not surprising, as an abundant water supply, fertile land, and a junction of international trade routes create suitable conditions for a major settlement. Perhaps evidence for a settlement earlier than the third millennium will still be found in the unexcavated areas to the west and north of the spring.

In the absence of historical or biblical documents, we must rely on the results of archaeological excavations for information about the early history of the site. In practically every basket of excavated material EB sherds were found. Although undisturbed levels of occupation were reached in only three small soundings, these suggest that Dan-Laish was already well established in the second quarter of the third millennium B.C.E. and covered an area of about 50 a. One of these soundings on the southern side of the mound produced an almost complete storage jar, a decorated bone handle of a weapon, and fragments of various vessels, mainly platters, all dated to the EB II–III periods. Early Bronze Age levels were reached also on the eastern part of the mound, and here a complete jar of the EB III period was found standing on a floor, together with platters of EB II.

In the third probe, in the southeastern corner of the excavation, under the

MB steps, remains of structures and a flagstone floor could also be dated by the pottery to the EB II–III periods. The material from these occupation levels and the examination of the pottery collected from all the baskets lead to the conclusion that Dan-Laish was founded c. 2700 B.C.E. We cannot tell what caused the city to be abandoned ca. 2400 B.C.E., but it was not the result of violent destruction by fire. Yet abandoned it was, for the next stage of occupation of the site begins a few centuries later during the MB II period.[3]

There is disagreement among scholars concerning the terminology and dates of the MB II period. In this paper we follow that of the *Encyclopedia of Archaeological Excavations in the Holy Land* (ed. Michael Avi-Yonah, Jerusalem: Massada, 1975), according to which the MB IIA period begins c. 2000 B.C.E. However, it is doubtful whether Dan-Laish was resettled at the very beginning of this period. Three levels of occupation belonging to the MB IIA period were found in the southern part of the tell. Stone-built tombs usually associated with the MB IIA period were found, containing offerings of characteristic pottery vessels of the period. In other areas decorated vessels similar to the so-called Khabur Ware (Amiran 1969: 113) were also found. This is significant, for it suggests cultural connections of Dan-Laish with northern Syria in the early second millennium B.C.E.

The earliest MB IIA city may have been as large as the EB city, and the population could reasonably be estimated at about seven thousand. Whether this city was fortified, or how, we cannot as yet say, but we do know that a formidable defensive system consisting of huge earthen ramparts was erected on these early occupational MB IIA levels. However, before proceeding to discuss other MB II archaeological evidence, we shall examine the historical and biblical references pertinent to this stage of the history of Dan.

The later Execration Texts mention Laish (Posener 1940: 92) and Horonab, its king, who bears a typically West-Semitic name. Perhaps this can be taken as an indication of the ethnic affiliation of the king and possibly the population. The date of these Execration Texts has not been definitely fixed, but a date in the first half of the eighteenth century B.C.E. seems reasonable (Van Seters 1967: 78–80; Mazar 1968; 1974: 66–72).

Another historical reference is in the Mari archives (Malamat 1970a). King Zimri-lim of Mari sends eight and one-third minas (about ten lb.) of tin to Laish (Malamat 1971: 35–36). Tin is an essential alloy in the production of bronze, and a metal industry may have existed in Laish sometime in the eighteenth century B.C.E. A more exact date would depend on the date for the reign of King Zimri-lim (c. 1780–1760 or 1715–1695 B.C.E., according to the middle or to the low chronology, respectively).

There is also a biblical reference to Dan in the narrative of Genesis 14. This is not the place to analyze this narrative or to discuss the historicity of the

Patriarchs. It is sufficient to recognize that sometime in the first half of the second millennium B.C.E. there existed in northern Israel a city of sufficient importance to be mentioned in the story.[4]

The difficulty in synchronizing the historical and biblical references with the archaeological remains stems from the lack of a commonly accepted, absolute dating. Moreover the nomenclature for the archaeological periods covers rather extensive time frames. This is especially significant when we examine the date of the construction of the earthen ramparts. Albright suggested already in 1935 that the mound of Tel Dan is a typical Hyksos site with earthen ramparts and glacis similar to other Hyksos cities. The Hyksos appear on the historical scene in the eighteenth century B.C.E. and conquer Egypt around the second half of that century.

The ramparts at Dan were discovered during the first season of excavation, and their investigation has continued through the following fifteen seasons. With a 50 m. base and a built core in the center, the sloping ramparts rose to a height of well over 10 m.[5] We estimate that some 800,000 tons of material was used in the construction of the ramparts, needing three years for about a thousand workers to complete the task. A gate or gates were, of course, necessary, and these perhaps required the greatest ingenuity of the planners and builders.

A gate of this period was discovered at the southeastern mudbrick corner of the site. It is built of sun-dried mudbrick with stone steps leading up to it from the eastern plain and similar steps leading down into the city on the west. The structure, the northern half of which was excavated, stood 7 m. high. If, as is probable, the gate was of symmetrical design, it consisted of two chambers on each side, with three arches forming the passageway through the gate (Biran 1980b: 89–91; 1981b; 1982a: in press). Since the gate was an integral part of the ramparts, the date of its construction is crucial to the discussion of the date of the ramparts.

We thought that perhaps the discovery of the arches and a vaulted passageway would help in the dating, but vaulting was not unknown in antiquity, and certainly in Mesopotamia vaulted structures were used already in the third millennium (Oates 1973). This method of construction could have been applied to city gates, but we know of only one such gate, at Tell Mumbaqat, and its date is uncertain (Boese and Orthmann 1976: 6–11; Kühne and Steuerwald 1977). We then sought architectural comparisons to other gates of the second millennium B.C.E. However, the gate at Dan is, to the best of our knowledge the only complete gate of the period so far discovered, standing as originally built. Analogies provided by the gates found, e.g., at Qatna (which is the closest in form), Alalakh, Hazor, Akko, and others, are at best inconclusive. Consequently our dating will have to depend on the pottery.

The mudbrick used in the construction of the gate contained sherds, over 90% of which belong to the Early Bronze Age. The remaining sherds belong to MB II, ranging in date from MB IIA to the transitional MB IIA–MB IIB period. The identical results were obtained from the examination of the pottery found on the floor of the gate as well as on and below the steps. The same picture emerged from the examination of the pottery found in the ramparts. The gate was blocked and covered with earth already in antiquity. The pottery in the earth fill, as in the earth which covered the entire structure, was examined and showed similar results.

We shall now turn to examine the pottery from other sections of the excavated ramparts, notably in the southern and eastern parts of the site. Here too most of the sherds belong to the EB period while about 10% belong to MB II. The MB II pottery found both in the layers of earth used in the construction of the ramparts and in the gate area belongs to the same ceramic horizon as that of the MB IIA levels found under the ramparts. Obviously the ramparts are later than the levels they cover, the only remaining question being how much later.

In their construction the builders of the ramparts used reddish virgin soil brought from the surrounding plain as well as occupational debris from the EB and MB IIA periods. Consequently, two possibilities suggest themselves. Sometime towards the end of the MB IIA period, it was decided that the safety of Laish would depend on a new defensive system consisting of earthen ramparts. These then were rapidly built with soil from the surrounding plain as well as with soil from previous levels of occupation. The other possibility is that Laish suffered a military defeat and perhaps had to be abandoned. When the same people or a new population came to resettle the site they decided to erect the ramparts for their protection. In either case, the lapse of a few years would account for any development in the MB IIA pottery. A date in the transitional period between MB IIA and MB IIB, which we proposed in previous publications, is still valid. We would accordingly date the ramparts to about the middle of the eighteenth century B.C.E. They served as the city's defenses till the end of the tenth century B.C.E. when an Israelite city wall and gate were built in the south at the foot of the ramparts.

Following the construction of the ramparts, the city was reduced to about 30–35 a. Here the population lived during the following centuries, and here they buried their dead. Some of the burials were dug into the inner slopes of the ramparts.

According to the present stage of our investigations, the MB II settlement of Laish seems to have lasted from the nineteenth to the sixteenth centuries B.C.E. Such is the nature of archaeological research that new discoveries often require considerable revision of earlier conclusions. However, within that time span Laish of the Execration Texts, of King Zimri-lim, and of Abraham existed at Tel Dan. If the Execration Texts are to be dated to the very beginning of the eighteenth century B.C.E., they would refer to a Laish that existed before the construction of the ramparts. If we accept the lower chronology for dating the reign of Zimri-lim, then the tin from Mari was sent to the city within the ramparts. As for Abraham, that would depend on the date for the campaign of Chedorlaomer and his allies to the Jordan Valley and the Negev.

II

Laish appears next in a historical context in the middle of the fifteenth century in the list of Thutmose III, together with Hazor, Pehel, and Kinnereth. Our archaeological excavations have so far shed no light on this campaign, but two finds at Dan testify to contacts with Egypt. One is a red granite statuette of a man in a sitting position, Nefertem by name, found in secondary use in a wall of the Israelite period. The statuette is of a well-known type used in the ritual of the dead dated to the Nineteenth Dynasty, c. the fourteenth century B.C.E.

Another fragment of an Egyptian statuette was found on the surface. Originally from the Middle Kingdom, it bears a secondary inscription of the Ptolemaic period. That these statuettes are found at Dan is not surprising, considering the geographic location of the site, but in later periods the closer contacts must have been with the Aegean and Phoenician world. The discovery of a very rich tomb, which we named the "Mycenean" tomb because of the large number of Mycenean imported vessels, is just one indication of trade with the west. The reference to Sidon in Judges 18:28 may point to a political relationship that existed between Dan-Laish and the Phoenician coast in the late thirteenth or the early twelfth century B.C.E.

With the beginning of the Iron Age we have to rely solely on the historical references to be found in the Bible and on the results of the archaeological excavations for unraveling the story of Dan. The material culture of the inhabitants of Laish at the end of the Late Bronze Age and the beginning of the Iron Age (our Stratum VII) is no different from any other Canaanite settlement. However, a relatively large number of pits, some stone-lined, in all the areas excavated indicates evidence of a new life-style. The pits or silos are reminiscent of similar constructions in the hill country of Judah and Benjamin, which are termed "settlement pits" and belong to the Israelite period. Now, for the first time at Dan, we also encounter a new type of storage jar, the "collar-rim" jar. This level of occupation (Stratum VI) appears to represent a change in the pattern of settlement or of population.

Judges 18 is the most detailed account of the migration and settlement of a tribe to be found in the Bible. There is no reason to doubt the historicity of the event or the narrative, although the date of this migration is by no means certain. There is extensive literature on the subject and this is not the place to embark on an internal analysis of Judges 18 (Malamat 1970b; Yadin 1968). With the excavation of Tel Dan, however, it is possible to examine the external evidence.

The Bible speaks of the conquest of Laish and its destruction by fire at the hand of the Danites. No such devastation was discovered in the course of excavation in the levels of occupation preceding the construction of the "settlement pits" mentioned above. Here and there evidence of fire is visible, and in some places the pits were built into a sterile layer of pebbles. We suggest that Laish at the beginning of the twelfth century was perhaps a small town feeling "secure" (Judg. 18:10) within the formidable defenses provided by the ramparts. However, these did not withstand the Danite tribesmen who then settled within the perimeter of the ramparts. After a certain time, however, the ramparts once again failed the inhabitants of the site, now the Danites themselves. Sometime in the middle of the eleventh century B.C.E., the city (our Stratum V) was destroyed in a fierce conflagration dated by the ceramic evidence. Who caused the destruction we cannot say. Perhaps it was in the course of the Assyrian attempt to extend their empire westward. The destruction of Dan may not have been an isolated incident. Stratum XIV of Tyre "must have ended before 1070/1050 BC" (Bikai 1978: 66). This may not have been a violent destruction, but the fact that Stratum XIV at Tyre ends at about the same time as our Stratum V is nonetheless noteworthy.

The destruction of Dan may be reflected in Judges 18:27–31. Here reference is made to the fact that the statue (idol?) "made" by Micah lasts as long as the temple of Shiloh is in existence. As is well-known, Shiloh was destroyed by the Philistines about the middle of the eleventh century B.C.E., and this event has left its mark on the historiographers of the age. The destruction of Dan by fire, however, did not mean that it was abandoned. The city was rebuilt almost immediately and some of the walls of Stratum V continued to be used in Stratum IV. New walls were built, dividing the spacious areas of Stratum V into smaller units, indicating perhaps a more intensive settlement. The finds include jars, cooking pots, chalices, pyxides, and oil lamps, but no "collar-rim" jars. Stratum IV may be dated between the eleventh and the early ninth centuries B.C.E. The discovery of clay tuyeres and numerous broken crucibles, containing bronze sediment and slag, indicates an extensive metal industry. The evidence for metallurgical activity appears first in Stratum V and points to extensive development in Stratum VI. The existence of a metal industry at Dan may have prompted Hiram of Tyre to recommend to Solomon an artisan for the temple whose mother was a Danite (2 Chron. 2:13–14).

III

Towards the end of the tenth century B.C.E. an event took place which affected the future history of Dan: Jeroboam established the kingdom of Israel and made Dan the main cult center in the north of the country. He set up a golden calf at Dan which apparently became a more important sacred site than Bethel (1 Kings 12:30). Some one hundred and fifty years later the prophet Amos condemned the people who swore by the "god of Dan" (Amos 8:14).

Dan bore the brunt of an attack by Ben-hadad of Damascus about 885 B.C.E., but not long afterward Ahab defeated the Arameans and obtained trading rights in Damascus (1 Kings 20:34). To ensure his lines of communication, in peace as well as in war, Ahab would have had to fortify Dan, his northern outpost. Jeroboam II must have done the same when he sallied forth on his conquests to the north and the east.

Dan is not mentioned among the cities "taken" by Tiglath-pileser (2 Kings 15:29), but it is unlikely that it escaped the fate of the rest of the Northern Kingdom. Indeed, Judges 18:30 may well echo the Assyrian conquest. The city nevertheless continued in existence, as is attested by the archaeological remains. Some of its inhabitants probably answered the call of Hezekiah to come and celebrate the Passover in Jerusalem (2 Chron. 30:5). The last mention of Dan in the Bible is by Jeremiah (4:15; 8:16), reflecting the impending Babylonian conquest.

Can archaeology paint a wider canvas than the one presented by this meager record spanning over three hundred years? In the northern and southern parts of the mound monumental structures of the Israelite period were uncovered, while in the center the living quarters came to light. A 4 m. thick wall and gate and a flagstone pavement dated to the tenth–ninth centuries B.C.E. were found at the foot of the MB ramparts. Two stages in the construction of the gate and the pavement could be discerned. The first belongs to the late tenth century B.C.E. and the second to the ninth century. Little is known of the first stage of construction, but from the second stage we have an outer gate flanked by two towers and approached from an extensive, beautifully paved piazza, with a bench along the city wall. The threshold is 3.70 m. wide with sockets and a doorstop. Beyond the threshold the stone pavement widens into a square or piazza (19.5 m. x 9.4 m.) which is protected on the north and south by the city walls.[6] The square leads to the main city gate (29.50 m. x 17.80 m.) with its two towers, each having two guard rooms. The pavement continues through the 4 m. wide passageway and on leaving the gate widens to 8 m. and continues westward until it turns northward, rising on a 28° incline to the top of the mound. This magnificently built road probably served also as a royal processional and ceremonial way. A unique feature of the gate complex is the structure built of ashlars with four decorated bases, found at the entrance to the main gates next to the bench running along the outer face of the northeastern tower.

The entire gate complex and city wall should be dated to the ninth century B.C.E. It could only have been built by a king conscious of his own importance as well as of the security needs of the area. Such a king was Ahab. He found at the site remains of a gate and pavement built probably by Jeroboam, who had turned Dan not only into a religious center but also into a military and administrative one as well.

The end of the tenth through the ninth centuries B.C.E. saw great building activities also at the northern end of the site (Biran 1982b). Here a large structure (19 m. x 19 m.) of the Israelite period was uncovered. The fine masonry, laid in headers and stretchers, is similar to the monumental Israelite method of construction found in Samaria and Megiddo. A courtyard of crushed yellowish limestone surrounds the structure on three sides. Two square surfaces of flat ashlars were part of the courtyard. A four-horned altar, one horn of another, much larger altar, and vessels of cultic character were found here. We believe this area to be the location of the sanctuary.

Under this complex, earlier structures were found including two courses of a rectangular platform (7 m. x 19 m.) built of large dressed limestone blocks, which was destroyed by a fire so fierce that it turned the top of the stones a fiery red. Next to this structure parts of large storerooms were uncovered. Two large pithoi with a capacity of 300 l. each, decorated with a snake motif, as well as incense burners, chalices, a bowl with a trident incised on its base, a decorated incense stand, and the broken head of a male figurine, represent an assemblage of a cultic nature dated to the late tenth or early ninth century B.C.E.

Further south an installation consisting of a large sunken basin flanked by two basalt slabs and two plastered jars was uncovered. A number of faience figurines and another pithos with a snake motif were found here. The installation forms a unit 6.7 m. long which we believe was used in a ceremony connected with water libation.[7]

The date of these structures corresponds to the reign of Jeroboam, and it is reasonable to assume that he erected them when he set up the golden calf at Dan. If so, the destruction level found may be the result of Ben-hadad's attack in c. 885 B.C.E. Whether we are correct in assuming that these structures constitute what the Bible calls *bêt bāmôt* and *bāmâ* must await further study and research.[8]

In the eighth century new structures with walls over 30 m. long were erected, but because of the considerable building activities in the hellenistic and Roman periods it is impossible to determine the nature of these buildings. However, this area continued to serve the religious needs of the community through the hellenistic and Roman periods. In this connection mention should be made of the find of an inscription in Greek and Aramaic: "To the god who is in Dan" (Biran 1981a) and a hellenistic basin which may have been used for divination.[9] The Roman fountain house may have also served a cultic function (Biran 1982b: 15–17).

Also in the eighth century B.C.E. changes occurred in the defensive system of Dan. Following the destruction of the main gate at the foot of the mound, a stone wall running east-west was built on the stone pavement halfway up the slope. Here a new gate was built with tower and bench, to provide entrance from the east. A new pavement was laid on top of the original one. An upper two-chambered gate was also built on the edge of the mound. The stone pavement continued to serve as a road leading northward into the city through the 3.70 m. passageway of this new gate. At a later stage, perhaps in the hellenistic period, the upper chambers were blocked and benches were built along the walls. The pavement, however, continued to be in use but for how long it is difficult to say.[10] In the Roman period the entrance to the town must be sought elsewhere, since cisterns and clay pipes as well as burials were found to have been built on top of and into the pavement.

In the center of the mound the last remains found belong to the end of the Iron Age. Well-built houses with flagstone floors and a rich assemblage of vessels indicate that the city referred to by the prophet Jeremiah before the Babylonian conquest was a substantial and prosperous community.

NOTES

1. Tel Dan, called Tell el-Qadi in Arabic (meaning "hill of the judge") was already identified with ancient Dan by Edward Robinson in 1838. Eusebius in the fourth century C.E. refers to Dan as being located 4 m. from Paneas (modern Banias).

2. The excavations at Tel Dan are the major archaeological project of the Nelson Glueck School of Biblical Archaeology of Hebrew Union College-Jewish Institute of Religion since 1974. They were begun as a rescue operation in 1966 by the Department of Antiquities and Museums. Yearly reports have appeared in "Notes and News" of the *Israel Exploration Journal*. Cf. also Biran 1967; 1971; 1974a; 1974b; 1975; 1980a; 1980b; 1981a; 1981b; 1982a: in press; 1982b.

3. It is possible that MB I tombs, similar to those found at Ma'ayan Barukh a few kilometers to the west, exist at Dan. In the 1981 season sherds from a number of MB I vessels were found in the central area of excavations.

4. The geographical location of the city is not affected by the fact that it was then called Laish and not Dan.

5. The base of the core in the south was reached in 1982. The core is preserved to a height of 10.50 m. but must have been higher considering the 40° incline of the slope of the earthen ramparts.

6. Note should be taken of the translation of the Hebrew word $r^e\hat{h}\hat{o}b$. The KJV translates it in Genesis 19:2; Judges 19:15; and 2 Chronicles 32:6 as "street." Even the NEB

translates it in the Genesis and Judges passages as "street," but in 2 Chronicles 32:6 as "square." The Jewish Publication Society of America (1967, 1978, 1982) translates $r^e h\hat{o}b$ as "square" in all three cases.

7. The suggestion made by Stager and Wolff (1981) must be rejected on archaeological grounds (Biran 1982b: 33). It should be remarked in passing that an Iron Age stone slab almost certainly used in oil production was found in the area where the Roman fountain house was excavated.

8. There are earlier remains in this area which correspond to Strata V and VI in other parts of the excavation of Tel Dan. Here too Stratum V was destroyed by fire and Stratum VI is represented by pits. Earlier remains of LB and Early Iron periods have also been found. It is tempting to seek in this area remains of the sanctuary built by the tribe of Dan to house the cultic vessels brought by them from the house of Micah (Judg. 18), but so far no identifiable structures of that period have been found.

9. The basin is plastered inside and out but with no conduit for the water.

10. We suggest that one of the reasons for the construction here of the wall and gates in the Israelite period was due to the existence of a gate already in the MB II period. Remains of such a gate were found in the course of the excavations. In the Roman period the density of settlement was considerably less than in the earlier periods, and the inhabitants lived close to the spring.

BIBLIOGRAPHY

Amiran, R.
   1969   *Ancient Pottery of the Holy Land.* Jerusalem: Massada.

Bikai, P. M.
   1978   *The Pottery of Tyre.* Warminster, England: Aris and Phillips.

Biran, A.
   1967   Howbeit the Name of the City Was Laish at First. Pp. 21–32 in *All the Land of Naphtali,* ed. H. Z. Hirschberg. Jerusalem: Israel Exploration Society (Hebrew).
   1971   Laish-Dan—Secrets of a Canaanite City and an Israelite City. *Qadmoniot* 4: 2–10 (Hebrew).
   1974a   Tell Dan. *Biblical Archaeologist* 37: 26–51.
   1974b   An Israelite Horned Altar at Dan. *Biblical Archaeologist* 37: 106–7.
   1975   Tell Dan. Pp. 313–21 in vol. 1 of *Encyclopedia of Archaeological Excavations in the Holy Land,* ed. M. Avi-Yonah. Jerusalem: Massada.
   1980a   Tell Dan—Five Years Later. *Biblical Archaeologist* 43: 168–82.
   1980b   Two Discoveries at Tell Dan. *Israel Exploration Journal* 30: 89–98.
   1981a   To the God Who Is in Dan. Pp. 142–51 in *Temples and High Places in Biblical Times,* ed. A. Biran. Jerusalem: The Nelson Glueck School of Biblical Archaeology of Hebrew Union College-Jewish Institute of Religion (Hebrew).
   1981b   The Discovery of the Middle Bronze Age Gate at Dan. *Biblical Archaeologist* 44: 139–44.
   1982a   The Gate of Laish at Dan. *Qadmoniot* 15 (Hebrew) in press.
   1982b   The Temenos at Dan. *Eretz-Israel* 16 (The Harry M. Orlinsky Volume) 15–43 (Hebrew).

Boese, J. and Orthmann, W.
1976   *Mumbaqat, Eine 5000 Jahre alte Stadt am Euphrat*. Saarbrucken.

Kühne, H. and Steuerwald, H.
1980   Das nordost Tor von Tell Mumbaqat. Pp. 203–15 in *Le Moyen Euphrate*. Actes du Collogue de Strasburg, ed. J. Cl. Margueron. Strasburg.

Malamat, A.
1970a   Northern Canaan and the Mari Texts. Pp. 164–77 in *Near Eastern Archaeology in the Twentieth Century: Essays in Honor of Nelson Glueck*, ed. J. A. Sanders. Garden City, NY: Doubleday.
1970b   The Danite Migration and the Pan-Israelite Exodus-Conquest. *Biblica* 51: 1–16.
1971   Syro-Palestinian Destinations in a Mari Tin Inventory. *Israel Exploration Journal* 21: 31–8.

Mazar, B.
1968   The Middle Bronze Age in Palestine. *Israel Exploration Journal* 18: 65–97.
1974   The Middle Bronze Age in the Land of Israel. Pp. 48–83 in *Canaan and Israel*, ed. B. Mazar. Jerusalem: Bialik and the Israel Exploration Society (Hebrew).

Oates, E. E. D. M.
1973   Early Vaulting in Mesopotamia. Pp. 183–91 in *Archaeology and Practice*, ed. D. E. Strong. London: Seminar Press.

Posener, G.
1940   *Princes et pays d'Asie et de Nubie*. Brussels: Fondation Egyptologique Reine Elisabeth.

Stager, L. E. and Wolff, R. S.
1981   Production and Commerce in Temple Courtyards: An Olive Press in the Sacred Precinct at Tell Dan. *Bulletin of the American Schools of Oriental Research* 243: 95–102.

Van Seters, J.
1967   *The Hyksos*. New Haven: Yale University.

Yadin, Y.
1968   And Dan, Why Did He Remain in Ships? *Australian Journal of Biblical Archaeology* 1: 9–23.

Chapter 9

TEL GEZER: PHASE II EXCAVATIONS 1972–1974

Joe D. Seger
Cobb Institute of Archaeology
Mississippi State University

After eight very successful seasons of archaeological investigation at Tel Gezer, Dr. W. G. Dever resigned his position as director of the Hebrew Union College Gezer Project at the close of the 1971 season in order to assume new responsibilities as Director of the W. F. Albright Institute of Archaeological Research in Jerusalem. At that time the writer was invited to fill the vacated post of Archaeological Director at Hebrew Union College Biblical and Archaeological School (now the Nelson Glueck School of Biblical Archaeology) and to take up the task of directing continuing field work at Gezer in a second phase. As previously, the Phase II excavations were sponsored by Hebrew Union College with financial support from the Smithsonian Institution. In addition to the writer, who had participated as a Core Staff member during Phase I from 1966, continuity for the project was also provided by the other members of the Phase II Core Staff. These included Seymour Gitin, Karen E. Seger, John R. Osborne, and Janet McClennan, all of whom had also participated extensively in Phase I work. In 1973 Dan P. Cole, another member of the Phase I Core Staff, also returned to serve Phase II work as a Field Consultant.[1]

The principal objectives of the Phase II work (fig. 7) involved concentration on two of the major problems relating to the site's stratigraphic history that still required attention. These involved (1) continuation of the reassessment of the sequence and development of the city's "outer" and "inner" wall systems and (2) the provision of a fresh, broad-scaled examination of strata from the Iron Age through hellenistic periods of occupation on the site (Seger 1972b: 241). To accomplish these goals primary Phase II efforts were focused in two main sections on the south side of the mound: to the west in Field IV, the area of the so-called "southern gate" of Macalister's "inner wall" system; and to the east in Field VII, a new area on the mound's untouched south-central plateau.

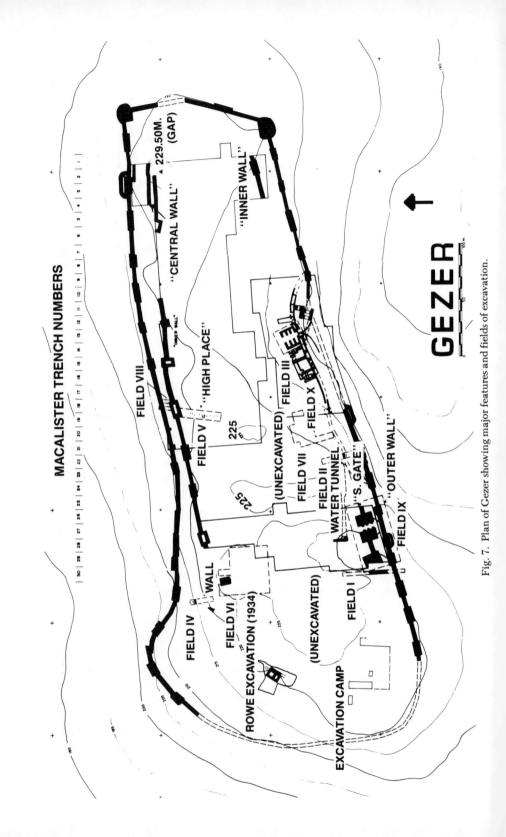

Fig. 7. Plan of Gezer showing major features and fields of excavation.

In 1973 work on the first objective was expanded to include investigations along the "outer wall" in four widespread probe sections: in Field VIII, between the "inner" and "outer" walls just northeast of Field V (the "high place"); in Field IX on the northwest slopes below Field VI; in Area 4 of Phase I Field II, on the south-central slopes; and in Field X just south of Field VII (Seger 1973: 248). With the conclusion of the 1973 field season and a brief spring campaign in April of 1974, both of the main Phase II objectives had been accomplished and they provided substantial new data about the history of the site. What follows is a summary of these Phase II results and their contribution to the stratigraphic and historical profile of ancient Gezer (cf. table 2).

The History of the "Inner Wall" System

The "inner wall" was so named by Macalister early in the century. His workers traced 400 m. or more of the massive fortification line principally along the northern perimeter of the site (1912: Gezer III, pls. ii–iii). His date for the building of the system in the "First Semitic" period (2600–1800 B.C.E.) is clearly too early, but the conclusion that its use ends in the mid-second millennium (during his "Second Semitic" period) is basically correct (1912: Gezer I, 253). Evidence from Phase II work in Field IV shows clearly that the "southern gate" complex was destroyed at the very end of the LB IA period in the late sixteenth or early fifteenth century.

Clearance of the massive dumps with which Macalister had covered the complex began in 1967. However, more deliberate excavation work started only in 1970 and 1971 (Dever and Lance 1971: 101ff.). The first important addition to our understanding of the stratigraphy of the complex came as the result of a probe section that was opened in Areas 3 and 13, which cut across the extender wall, L.13004, which connected the gate with Wall/Tower 5017 to the west (Seger 1975: 39). This work showed that Macalister had seriously misunderstood the nature of the wall structures at this point, taking a 10 m. wide mass of collapsed mudbrick to be the wall. The probe showed the connector to be a more modest, 3 m. wide structure joining the respective foreparts of the 15 m. wide gate and tower, forming a slightly inset linkage. As the brick debris inside of this wall was removed during the 1972–74 seasons, buried elements of a well-preserved series of rooms were revealed. Evidence recovered from these rooms shows that they were employed for storage and other domestic uses. Among the more important finds from the surfaces in these rooms was a large collection of storage vessels with incised letters, very possibly related to the proto-Canaanite alphabet (cf. Seger: forthcoming) and a hoard of gold and silver objects including several foil pendant figurines of the Canaanite goddess Astarte (Seger: 1976b). The ceramic evidence from these

Table 2. Field Phase and City Stratum Correlations

Tel Gezer Phase I and II Excavations

City Stratum	I	II	III	IV	V	VI	VII	VIII	IX	X
-							(1)			
I	1	1		1						
II	2	2A–B	1	2			2A–B/C		1	
III	-	Sub 2	2	Sub 2		1	3		(2)	
IV	-	3A–B	-	-		-	4		(3)	
V	-	4	3	-		2	5A–B		(4)	
VI	-	5A–B	4			3	6A			
VII	-	6A	4			3	6B			
VIII	-	6B	5–6	3		(3)	7A–B			1
IX	-	7A–B		-		4	8			2
X	-	8A–C		-		4	8			2
XI	3	9		-		5A–B	9A–B			3
XII	4	10		-		5C	10			
XIII	4	11A–B		-		6A–C	11			
XIV	5A?	12		-		7	12			
XV	5B–C	13		-		8A–B	12			
XVI	6A–B	14		4	1?	9A–B		1		
	1.10A Upper									
XVII	1.10A Lower			-	-	-		-		
XVIII	7A–B			5A–B	2	10A		2		
XIX	8A–B			6	2	10B				
XX	9			(7)	-	11A				
XXI	10				-	11B				
XXII	-				3	12				
gap	-				-	-				
XXIII	11A–B				4	13				
XXIV	12				4	13				
XXV	13				5	(14)				
	1.3A									
XXVI	14									

Underline, e.g., <u>4</u>, indicates destruction; parenthesis, e.g., (1), indicates ceramic phase.

City Stratum	Cultural Phase	Date
-	Late Roman/Byzantine	4th–7th C. C.E.
I	Early Roman	Late 1st C. B.C.E.
II	Hellenistic	Early 2nd–Mid 1st C. B.C.E.
III	Hellenistic	Late 3rd/Early 2nd C. B.C.E.
IV	Persian	5th–4th C. B.C.E.
V	Iron IIC	Late 8th/Early 6th C. B.C.E.
VI	Iron IIB	Mid–8th C. B.C.E.
VII	Iron IIB	9th C. B.C.E.
VIII	Iron IIA	Mid–Late 10th C. B.C.E.
IX	Iron IC	Early 10th C. B.C.E.
X	Iron IC	Late 11th C. B.C.E.
XI	Iron IB	Early–Mid 11th C. B.C.E.
XII	Philistine	Late 12th C. B.C.E.
XIII	Iron IB	Early–Mid 12th C. B.C.E.
XIV	LB IIB/Iron IA	13th/12th C. B.C.E.
XV	LB IIB	13th C. B.C.E.
XVI	LB IIA	14th C. B.C.E.
XVII	LB IB	Late 15th C. B.C.E.
XVIII	MB IIC/LB IA	16th/Early 15th C. B.C.E.
XIX	MB IIC	Late 17th/Early 16th C. B.C.E.
XX	MB IIB/C	Mid 17th C. B.C.E.
XXI	MB IIB	18th–Early 17th C. B.C.E.
XXII	MB IIA/B	Early–19th C. B.C.E.
gap	(EB III–MB I)	(27th–20th C. B.C.E.)
XXIII	EB IIB	29th–28th C. B.C.E.
XXIV	EB IIA	31st–29th C. B.C.E.
XXV	EB IB	32nd–31st C. B.C.E.
XXVI	Late Chalcolithic	33rd–32nd C. B.C.E.

structures, including the store jar types, cooking pots, and the finer wares, provides a date in the late sixteenth century B.C.E. during the LB IA transition period. Pending more detailed comparative study of the accumulated artifactual evidence, an association with the northern campaigns of either Amenophis I (1546–1525) or of Thutmose I (1525–1512) is posited to explain the massive destruction of MB Gezer and its fortifications.[2]

Beginning in 1972 a determined effort was also launched to explore more fully the stratigraphy remaining above the massive stonework of Tower 5017 to the west, in order to connect with the earlier exposures in Field I (1974: Gezer II, 33ff.). As anticipated from the Field I section, extensive evidence of disturbances by hellenistic and Roman period pitting and robbing operations were discovered (Seger 1973). Particularly destructive were large Roman terrace walls built across the southern two-thirds of the structure. However, some fragmentary remains of late MB–early LB I structures, covered by patches of heavy destruction debris, were detected at the tower's northern edge connecting with the stratigraphy of Field I Areas 4 and 5. This provided a firm tie-in with the basic framework of city strata on the site, relating the latest Field IV MB IIC/LB I occupation to Field I Phase 7 and City Stratum XVIII.

The history of MB occupation as defined by work in Field I included four distinct stratigraphic levels (Phases 10–7, City Strata XXI–XVIII) (1974: Gezer II, 28–30). To these were added an earlier phase (City Stratum XXII), identified in both Field V (Phase 3) and Field VI (Phase 12) (Dever and Lance 1971: 120ff.). This earlier phase is dated from the transitional MB IIA/MB IIB period (c. 1800 B.C.E.) and appears to have had no major fortification walls associated with it. From evidence in Field I and elsewhere the same situation existed until the end of the MB IIB period (City Stratum XXI). Only with City Stratum XX, at the start of the MB IIC period, does the evidence of major fortification building appear. Data from Field IV Areas 3 and 4 supplement that from Field I Area 4 in showing that the massive "inner wall" structures were erected at this time, with deep foundation trenches being cut through Stratum XX floors already in use. Pottery from these foundation trenches in Fields I and IV on the south of the tell, as well as in probes both inside and outside the wall system in Fields V and VIII on the north, uniformly provides an early to mid-sixteenth century (c. 1650 B.C.E.) terminus post quem for the building of the system.

Phase II efforts in Field IV show that the ambition initially demonstrated by these Gezer MB IIC builders did not flag for well over a century. Here the successive Strata XIX and XVII occupation levels are marked by major additional architectural developments (Seger 1975: 40–41). In Area 3, where all Stratum XX occupation traces were removed by the deep foundation trench for Tower 5017, two surface levels of Stratum XIX occupation were identified. These correlated with Field I Phases 8A and 8B. Both were associated with an initial phase of extender wall construction, Wall 3097A, found immediately below but distinct from Wall 13004 (Seger 1973: 250). This lower wall was built of much larger masonry than Wall 13004 and, unlike that upper wall, was bonded to the stones of Wall Tower 5017. Elements of this same early structure were investigated along its outside perimeter in Area 16 in 1973. This area lay just at the junction with the western tower of the gate itself, and, significantly, the Wall 3097A elements discovered there were not bonded to the foundations of the gate. Rather they appeared to pass independently beneath them. This indicates that at least the exposed upper gate structures, like Wall 13004, were part of the subsequent Stratum XVIII construction.[3]

Discovery of this earlier Stratum XIX wall also helps explain apparent discrepancies between Field I pottery dates for the founding of the "inner wall" system and those associated with the adding of the carefully prepared chalk glacis lying outside of it. While the founding of the wall system was dated to early MB IIC, c. 1650 B.C.E., fills under the latter structure included late MB IIC pottery forms (cf. Dever 1973b: 65–68). As Field IV work has now clarified, the glacis was indeed a later feature, being added only in Stratum XVIII in connection with major redevelopment work at that time. This included adding the "southern gate" in its preserved form, supplementing the foundation structures of the wall connection between Tower 5017 and the gate (Wall 13004), and, finally, adding the chalk glacis along the whole face of the complex from the gate entryway west along the foundations of Tower 5017. Additional probes and clearance in the spring of 1974 also showed evidence of a similar chalk glacis flanking the gate to the east in Field IV, as well as in Areas 4 and 14 in Field II (Seger 1974). It was this well-defended city that fell, presumably to the Egyptians, in the late sixteenth century.

Thus, unlike the broad chronological frame proposed by Macalister, the Phase II work shows the history of the construction and use of the "inner wall" structures at Gezer to have been of fairly limited duration, certainly less than one hundred and fifty years, from the mid-seventeenth to the late sixteenth centuries. The political occasion that motivated this massive refortification effort, which is paralleled also at other MB sites,[4] seems clearly to be the consolidation of power in the Egyptian delta by the aggressive Fifteenth Dynasty, Hyksos kings, and especially of its third ruler, Khyan (1653–1620 B.C.E.). This Stratum XVIII redevelopment can, in turn, be seen as a response by Khyan's successor, Aphophis I (1620–1580), to increasing pressures by resurgent Seventeenth Dynasty Theban rulers against the delta strongholds.

The "Outer Wall" Controversy

In addition to the "inner wall" structures, Macalister also traced an "outer wall" system of fortification walls which he attributed, in its initial use phase, to his "Third Semitic" period, 1400–1000 B.C.E. (1912: Gezer I, 253). This system followed a line slightly down slope from that of the "inner wall" and considerably expanded the city's size. Although it was followed for 1100 m., around 80% of the city's circumference, no associated gate structures were found.[5] If Macalister's dates for its founding are correct, the system is unique in being the only known city defense system in the country to have been originally constructed in the Late Bronze Age. This, however, based on accumulated evidence from the HUC Phase I and Phase II excavations, seems to have been precisely the case.

Phase I data from Areas 8 and 9 in Field I provide a strong argument in support of an early LB IIA date (cf. 1974: Gezer II, 36–39). Excavations to bedrock on both sides of the "outer wall" (Field I, Wall 9011) show it to have been laid directly on bedrock and against a scarp left from cutting a deep trench along the lower slopes of the Stratum XVIII glacis. This cutting through the MB glacis provides a *terminus post quem* of not later than 1500 B.C.E. This *terminus* is advanced by about a century by ceramic evidence collected both from within the slender "foundation trench" deposits of looser soils between the inside face of Wall 9011 and the truncated glacis scarp and from the excavation of a later glacis, L.10014, located outside of and related to the use of Wall 9011.

Additional stratigraphic evidence, which offers proof of *pro quem* dating is provided by excavations in Cave 10A, located beneath bedrock at the south end of Field I, Area 10.[6] In this cave two distinct burial phases were identified, the first dating to the LB IB period (1465–1400 B.C.E.) and the second the LB IIA period (1400–1350 B.C.E.). The interruption phase, between these burial levels, is characterized by massive fills deposited through a fault opening in the upper chamber roof. This fault opening is in turn sealed above bedrock by the footing walls (L.10052 and L.10054) for glacis 10014. The interruption phase fills contained ample ceramic evidence with latest materials dating to the LB IB/LB IIA transition. As there seems little doubt that the "interruption" itself was caused by the "outer wall" construction effort, this pottery should mark its date fairly exactly. In turn, the ceramic repertoire of the upper burial phase in the cave, dated firmly within the LB IIA period, provides a secure *terminus pro quem* for completion of the wall building enterprise.

Despite this evidence, skepticism has persisted concerning a LB founding date, especially among Israeli scholars (cf. Kempinski 1972: 185). The main counterarguments center on the presence of a sizable retrenching along the outer face of Wall 9011 which in Field I cuts off completely all connections between the wall and the outlying glacis L.10014. Supported by ceramic and stratigraphic evidence, this L.10012 retrenching has been interpreted by the writer and W. G. Dever as the result of tenth-century, Solomonic period, redevelopment of "outer wall" structures and, specifically, as related to the construction of intermittent towers with ashlar block masonry all along the "outer wall" line (1974: Gezer II, 37). From Macalister's plans, such a tower apparently exists within 5 m. to the east of Field I, and in Field I itself displaced ashlar blocks were found at hellenistic levels above and adjacent to Wall 9011. Phase II work in Fields IV and II has now amplified considerably the data related to this argument and to the overall understanding of the "outer wall" structures and their history (Seger 1973: 248–49; 1974: 134).

During Phase II the inside foundations of the "outer wall" were retested in Areas 13 and 6 in Field IV, in Field VIII, and in Areas 4 and 14 in Field II. Of all the sections tested, Field II on the southern slope yielded the most directly helpful information. In Area 4 the earliest elements reached included a section of the carefully built chalk glacis already familiar from work in Fields I and IV. At the foot of this glacis and cut into it, as in Field I, was a section of the "outer wall." At the area's west balk a slightly expanded foundation trench gave modest additional evidence supporting the early LB IIA date. At the Area 4 east balk, however, the lower courses of the wall were battered tightly against the glacis face. Above this, evidence of a secondary cutting could be noted which was, in turn, associated with an apparent rebuild of the upper two courses of the structure. These courses were built with large, rough-cut rectangular stones, and the uppermost course included several ashlar blocks. Pottery from this later trench and from below and within a small buttressing wall found running north from these upper additions included early Iron Age forms. Subsequent investigations in adjacent Area 14 during the 1974 spring campaign provided additional data showing that these upper courses had, at points, been rebuilt still again in the second century B.C.E. This reconstruction narrowed the width of the wall by over half a meter and added additional stone support structures inside of the wall line. These support walls served to bond the wall to the slope and apparently also provided foundations for building features within the city. Here, as in Area 4, probes below the upper courses, including removal of some of the lower wall stones, provided pottery evidence terminating in early LB II.

The pattern of early LB IIA data from Field II is thus wholly consistent with that in Field I and in several ways supplements the case for an early LB II founding date. Moreover, a similar picture was also provided by 1973 work in Field VIII where evidence was derived from the disassembling of a section of the "outer wall" itself, as well as from the deepest exposures along the continuation of Wall 9011 in Field IV. Field IV work in Area 16 also provided data solidly confirming aspects of the wall system's later periods of use and redevelopment. Here excavations concentrated on one of the ashlar-built rectangular towers with sloping outer bastions that Macalister had pictured and described (1912: Gezer I, 247–48, figs. 128–129). Clearance of a section along the inner line of the ashlar tower foundations revealed pottery of the LB and

Iron I periods, with latest indicators belonging to a late tenth-century horizon. Outside of the wall, work probed the foundations of the tower's sloping stone bastion and subsequently removed a section of the stone facing. This effort revealed the well-formed foundations of ashlar stones of the original tower construction, and, from the fill sealed in by the bastion's stone facing, a small but definitive collection of Persian and early hellenistic ceramic data was recovered.

This Field IV data, together with that provided by other Phase II efforts in Fields II and VIII, thus firmly establishes the history of the three main stages in the history of the use and construction of the "outer wall." These include: (1) its original founding in the early LB II period (City Stratum XVI); (2) its reconstruction by the addition of ashlar-built rectangular towers and other supplements during the Solomonic period in the late tenth century B.C.E. (City Stratum VIII); and (3) its final refurbishing in the early second century B.C.E. (City Stratum III/II) including the addition, at that time, of the sloping bastions to revet the ashlar towers, as well as the repair of wall segments and the addition of needed intramural support structures. Overall, this data correlates well with the major periods of resurgence otherwise demonstrable both in the historical records and in the stratigraphic profile of occupation at the site.

Gezer in the First Millennium B.C.E.

Phase I efforts in Fields I and VI on the western end of the mound provided only scant information about the site after the tenth century B.C.E. (1970: Gezer I, 28–30). Detailed stratigraphic evidence for the first millennium B.C.E. was recovered only from the Field II sounding (1970: Gezer I, 56ff.; 1974: Gezer II, 47ff.) and from the reinvestigation of the Solomonic gate area in Field III (Dever and Lance 1971: 112–20). Between these two fields, on the south-central plateau of the tell, lay a section of the mound untouched by Macalister during his early work. It was here that Phase II Field VII was laid out. The objective of work in this new field was to provide a broad exposure through the latest, Iron II–Roman phases of the site's occupation history. By the close of work in the 1973 summer excavation season, this objective had been fully realized (Seger 1972b; 1973). Overall, twelve major phases of occupation were identified in Field VII, including a fairly tight sequence of levels from the late thirteenth century B.C.E. down to the end of the hellenistic period in the mid-first century B.C.E. and with additional surface evidence of subsequent late Roman/Byzantine presence in the fourth-seventh centuries C.E.[7] Within this stratigraphic frame substantial architectural exposure was provided for Iron II and hellenistic period remains.

Almost immediately below cultivation levels, areas at the western end of the field yielded occupation evidence from the final hellenistic settlement, belonging to Field VII Phase 2 and City Stratum II. Ultimately, the floors and foundation walls of a large, late second century B.C.E. domestic complex were exposed (cf. Seger 1976a). The complex included three separate living units, with associated ovens and storage bins, all clustered around a central courtyard. From the fills over the floors of the rooms came quantities of hellenistic pottery, including lamps of the small folded-over Maccabean type. Moreover, several coins were recovered, one a silver tetradrachma of Demetrius II dated 144 B.C.E., and another a bronze drachma bearing the name of Antiochus VII (138–129 B.C.E.). The latter was found below the latest floor in Area 34 and provides a *terminus post quem* for the latest subphase of the complex. Together the pottery and coin evidence securely date the structures to the last half of the second century B.C.E. and confirm its identification with the Hasmonean settlement at Gezer following the conquest by Simon Maccabeus in 142 B.C.E. (cf. Reich 1981).

The evidence from Field VII suggests that this Maccabean occupation, which followed the siege and capture of the city, involved extensive house cleaning and redevelopment. Removal of the Phase 2 structures in Field VII yielded evidence of extensive redistribution of destruction debris and only modest traces of architecture from the preceding Phase 3. The most dramatic Phase II evidence recovered from levels related to the Stratum III city came from other fields and included the reconstructions along the fortifications in Fields II and IV noted above. In addition, a large collection of lamps and other artifacts from this occupation phase were found during the 1973 spring and summer campaigns in Field IX on the northwest side of the mound (Seger 1973). In this section, downslope from Field VI, several test areas were laid out in an attempt to intersect the "outer wall" as planned by Macalister. While exposures were limited and provided no firm data on the "outer wall" itself, substantial terracing wall elements dating to the late hellenistic, City Stratum II, period were identified. Below the upper courses of this wall and in associated fill levels were located great quantities of early hellenistic pottery. Along with the lamps and vessels mentioned above were two Aramaic ostraca, dated on paleographic grounds to the late third century (Rosenbaum and Seger forthcoming). This debris can thus be associated with the mid-second century Maccabean "cleansing" of the city and accordingly provides a good profile of City Stratum III material culture.

The four easternmost areas of Field VII were specially plotted to extend the field to the east to include a section where Macalister's early work had already exposed the upper level hellenistic strata. Here, already in the spring of 1972, evidence of the deep pitting and robbing that characterized the hellenistic and Persian intrusions into Iron II levels were encountered. Nonetheless, from these and areas subsequently excavated in 1973 to the west, isolated patches of surfaces and structures from Phases 4 and 5 (Persian City Stratum

IV and Iron IIC/City Stratum V) occupation levels were identified. From one of the pits in Area 45 came an ostracon written in a developed Aramaic script that can be associated with Stratum IV occupation (Rosenbaum and Seger forthcoming). Architecturally the most prominent remains of this stratum were sections of a heavy chalk plaster surface found in Areas 43 and 44. Immediately below these plaster remains and identified with Stratum V levels a large stone vat was uncovered. It was similar in type to those found in Iron II houses at Tell Beit Mirsim, which Albright originally associated with a textile dyeing industry (1943: TBM 55–62, pl. 53) but which now seem to belong to olive press installations (Eitam 1979; also cf. below). Use of this Gezer vat originated with Stratum VI occupation.

Below the hellenistic and Persian pits and the remnants of Strata IV–V, a heavy layer of destruction debris was encountered all across the field. This debris surrounded and covered a substantial architectural complex of the Iron II period (Seger 1973: 250–51). Two major building phases (Field VII Phases 7 and 6) and several subphases were identified. Field VII PHases 6A and 6B correlate with City Strata VI and VII, respectively, and Field VII Phases 7A and 7B correlate with City Stratum VIII. Stratum VIII structures include wide, well-founded mudbrick on stone walls and broad flagstone courtyards. Elements of a number of three- and four-room houses, typical of the Iron Age, were identified. In Areas 46 and 47, in the southeast section of the field, part of a pillared building was exposed. Ceramic evidence related to these Stratum VIII structures clearly indicates association with city redevelopment in the Solomonic period connected with the construction of the gate area in nearby Field III and with the addition of the ashlar towers along the "outer wall" fortification system.

Subsequently, in the late tenth or early ninth century, a substantial further rebuilding took place. While Field VII did not provide extensive evidence of Stratum VIII destruction, ceramic evidence and other indications are sufficient to show that Stratum VII changes follow the disruptive campaign of Pharaoh Shishak c. 918 B.C.E. (cf. Lance 1971: 82ff.; Dever and Lance 1971: 117). In Field VII this phase of redevelopment was especially evident along the southern areas of the exposure. Here a series of narrower stone walls were added, subdividing the earlier paved areas into smaller rooms. Several of these Phase 6B Stratum VII rooms remained in use without alteration also through the Phase 6A Stratum VI period of occupation. The heavy destruction debris which marked the end of Stratum VI sealed ample evidence of the domestic and industrial nature of these buildings. During the whole Iron IIB period the pillared house in Area 47 remained in use. From within it and from the adjacent smaller rooms to the west a large collection of ceramic loom weights was recovered. Large numbers were found not only on the floors but also lodged in the debris above collapsed sections of mud roofing plaster. An extensive weaving industry is thus suggested. Immediately to the west (Areas 44–45) elements of another pillared house were located. Here, the latest building elements provided clear evidence of the Phase 6A City Stratum VI stage of redevelopment in the complex. Resting on a midden of dark-brown oily debris in the easternmost courtyard room of this building was a large drilled stone weighing almost 100 lb. Adjacent to it was another large stone with a shallow basin. Analysis of the accumulated midden showed it to be composed largely of olive pits and associated residues indicating conclusively that the heavy drilled stone and basin were parts of an olive press. This in turn was probably related to the larger and more elaborate pressing vat found in adjacent Area 43 (cf. above). Also among the finds from this room area was an inscribed stone "pym" weight.

Apart from the addition of new floors, the rooms along the north side of the field remained unchanged between Phases 7 and 6. In the northwest corner where hellenistic pitting had been especially severe, work did not probe below levels of the final Phase 6A use surfaces. The evidence of massive destruction and related artifact assemblages provides a late eighth-century date for the end of Phase 6A and City Stratum VI. The destruction is almost certainly related to the wave of Assyrian campaigns into Israel and Judah beginning in the third quarter of the eighth century. From evidence on a relief found in the palace of Tiglath-pileser III at Nimrud, which depicts the siege and capture of a city called *ga-za-ru*, it is virtually certain that the destruction of the Iron IIB city at Gezer took place during that monarch's 734/733 B.C.E. campaign through Philistia (Lance 1967: 43–44; 1970: Gezer I, 33).

Only in Areas 37 and 38 at the northeast end of Field VII did probe sections reach beneath the Phase 7 City Stratum VIII, Solomonic period levels. Here, a sequence of occupation levels (Phases 8–12) from the early tenth century back to the LB IB/Iron IA transition were examined. Except for several pits, suspected to represent some industrial use, these phases all seemed to represent routine domestic buildup. A complementary exposure was also provided in Field X (Seger 1973: 251). This field was opened toward the end of the 1973 season in order to test the lines and relationships between Solomonic period and "outer wall" fortifications on the southern slope just south of Field VII.[8] A line of outcropped wall at the crest of the mound quickly proved to be Solomonic in date, and a relationship to the continuation of casemate structures on the west of the Field III gate was established. Below this wall, as in Phase 8 of Field VII, evidence of an early tenth-century occupation level was found. Preceding this were substantial Phase 9 Philistine period remains. Although the overall exposure in Field X was modest, it did allow for the clearance of a wine vat with well-plastered stone sidewalls and of a slab stone base with recessed sump and drainage channels. Vats of this type were also found in Iron I levels in Fields (1970: Gezer I, 26–28, pl. 7B)[9] and VI.

Overall, the excavations in Field VII complement and embellish the picture of first millennium B.C.E. occupation represented in nearby Fields II and III. In addition, the deep stratigraphic sections in Field VII Areas 37 and 38 and in Field X provide a firm linkup with the site's earlier and significant third and second millennium phases so well-documented in Fields I, IV, and VI to the west. Thus, with the conclusion of Phase II efforts and after ten years of the Hebrew Union College excavations at the site, a new, broader, and more detailed perspective on the occupation history of this significant ancient city has been provided.

As if to punctuate this achievement, another of the series of bilingual Gezer boundary inscriptions, identified first in 1873 by Clermont-Ganneau, was found on the day following the official close of the 1973 summer season during final survey work in the ring of hills to the south of the site (Seger 1973: 251). Other new inscriptions of this type had also been discovered just before the beginning of Phase I work in 1964 (1970: Gezer I, 2) and again in the summer of 1972 just at the start of Phase II operations (Seger 1972a). This 1973 discovery brought the total number of such inscriptions, including those found by Macalister (1912: Gezer I, 37ff.), to nine and provided a fitting closure to a very active and productive decade of Hebrew Union College investigations.

NOTES

1. All of the Phase I Core Staff members, including W. G. Dever, H. D. Lance, John S. Holladay, Jr., Anita Walker, and Dan P. Cole, remained as active consultants for Phase II work. Their continuing support is acknowledged with sincere appreciation. For a joint summary of Phase I accomplishments, cf. Dever and Lance 1971.

2. Earlier assessments posited association with the slightly later campaigns of Thutmose III c. 1468 B.C.E. (Dever and Lance 1971: 103; Dever 1976: 438).

3. The recently discovered gate structure in Area K at Tel Dan has many features strikingly similar to those of the "south gate" at Gezer (cf. Biran 1980; 1981; Laughlin 1981). The writer plans to address the comparative relationship of these two structures in a future article.

4. These include Shechem, Megiddo, Hazor, Tell Beit Mirsim, and Lachish, among others (cf. Seger 1975: 42–43).

5. W. G. Dever has argued that the gate for the "outer wall" system most probably lies below the Solomonic gate in Field III (1974: Gezer II, 39; Dever 1976: 439).

6. Preliminary reference to this data is provided in Dever and Lance 1971: 100–101. More detailed presentation of the evidence reviewed here will be provided in my forthcoming volume, *The Field I Caves*, which will be vol. 4 or 5 in the AHUCNGSBA Gezer series.

7. This sequence and its relationships to the ceramic data recovered from associated deposits in Field VII has been studied in detail by S. Gitin. The results are presented in his three-volume doctoral dissertation, *A Ceramic Typology of the Late Iron II,*

Persian and Hellenistic Periods at Tell Gezer, submitted to Hebrew Union College in 1979. An updated version of this report will appear shortly as *Gezer III* in the AHUCNGSBA series. Our understanding of the Field VII stratigraphy and of its correlations with the overall sequence of city strata at Gezer has been refined in significant ways by this study. The writer warmly acknowledges the contribution of Dr. Gitin in this regard.

8. Due to limits of time it was not possible to pursue work in Field X to any final conclusions in regard to this problem. The area from Field X east to Field III remains as the tell section most suited to further exploration in this connection. W. G. Dever is now planning a modest campaign of additional work there.

9. In Field VI, NE Area 15, the writer supervised excavation of a similar vat from field Phase 5 levels in 1969.

BIBLIOGRAPHY

Biran, A.
  1980   Two Discoveries at Tel Dan. *Israel Exploration Journal* 30: 89–98.
  1981   Tel Dan, 1979, 1980. *Israel Exploration Journal* 31: 103–5.

Dever, W. G.
  1967   Excavations at Gezer. *Biblical Archaeologist* 30: 47–61.
  1973a   Tower 5017 at Gezer—A Rejoinder. *Israel Exploration Journal* 23: 23–26.
  1973b   The Gezer Fortifications and the "High Place": An Illustration of Stratigraphic Methods and Problems. *Palestine Exploration Fund Quarterly Statement* 105: 61–70.
  1976   Gezer. Pp. 428–43 in vol. 2 of *Encyclopedia of Archaeological Excavations in the Holy Land,* ed. M. Avi-Yonah and E. Stern. Jerusalem: Israel Exploration Society.

Dever, W. G., Lance, H. D., et al.
  1971   Further Excavations at Gezer, 1967–71. *Biblical Archaeologist* 34: 94–132.

Eitam, D.
  1979   Olive Presses of the Israelite Period. *Tel Aviv* 6: 146–55.

Kempinski, A.
  1972   Review, Gezer I: Preliminary Report of the 1964–66 Seasons. *Israel Exploration Journal* 22: 183–86.

Lance, H. D.
  1967   Gezer in the Land and History. *Biblical Archaeologist* 30: 34–47.
  1971   *Studies in the History of the Ancient City of Gezer.* Ph.D. dissertation, Harvard University, Cambridge.

Laughlin, John C. H.
  1981   The Remarkable Discoveries at Tell Dan. *Biblical Archaeology Review* 7: 20–37.

Reich, R.
  1981   Archaeological Evidence of the Jewish Population at Hasmonean Gezer. *Israel Exploration Journal* 31: 48–52.

Rosenbaum, J. and Seger, J. D.
  forth-   Three Unpublished Ostraca from Gezer. *Bulletin of the American*
  coming   *Schools of Oriental Research.*

Seger, J. D.
  1972a   Gezer (spring 1972). *Israel Exploration Journal* 22: 160–61.
  1972b   Tel Gezer (summer 1972). *Israel Exploration Journal* 22: 240–42.
  1973   Tel Gezer (spring 1973). *Israel Exploration Journal* 23: 247–51.
  1974   Tel Gezer (spring 1973). *Israel Exploration Journal* 24: 134–35.
  1975   The MB II Fortifications at Shechem and Gezer: A Hyksos Retrospective.
            Eretz-Israel 12: 34–45.
  1976a   The Search for Maccabean Gezer. *Biblical Archaeologist* 39: 142–44.
  1976b   Reflections on the Gold Hoard from Gezer. *Bulletin of the American*
            Schools of Oriental Research 221: 133–40.
  1977   The Search for Maccabean Gezer. Pp. 389–95, figs. 1–4 in *Proceedings of*
            the Sixth World Congress of Jewish Studies I, ed. A. Shinan. Jerusalem:
            Academic Press.

Gezer I–III, PEF
  1912   Macalister, R. A. S. *The Excavation of Gezer.* Vol. I–III. London: J.
            Murray.

Gezer I, HUC
  1970   Dever, W. G., Lance, H. D., and Wright, G. E. *Gezer I: Preliminary*
            Report of the 1964–66 Seasons. Annual of the Hebrew Union College
            Biblical and Archaeological School. Vol. I. Jerusalem: Keter.

Gezer II, HUC
  1974   Dever, W. G., Lance, H. D., et al. *Gezer II: Report of the 1967–70*
            Seasons in Fields I and II. Hebrew Union College/Nelson Glueck School
            of Biblical Archaeology. Vol. II. Jerusalem: Keter.

TBM III
  1943   Albright, W. F. *The Excavation of Tell Beit Mirsim.* Vol. III: *The Iron*
            Age. AASOR 21–22. New Haven: Yale University Press.

Chapter 10

ARCHAEOLOGY AND BIBLICAL INTERPRETATION: TELL EL-HESI

Ralph W. Doermann
Trinity Lutheran Seminary

The investigations and excavations at Tell el-Hesi over the past century and a half could well serve as a paradigm for the continuing debate concerning the relationship between archaeology and biblical studies. Dr. D. Glenn Rose, a staff member of the Joint Expedition to Tell el-Hesi from its inception in 1970 and its director from 1975 until his untimely death in 1981, was a vigorous participant in these discussions, and it is to his memory that this brief essay is dedicated.

In the survey which follows, the excavations themselves will not be described fully. More emphasis will be placed on the way in which these results have been interpreted and sometimes reinterpreted.

The Site

Tell el-Hesi (fig. 8) is located on the coastal (Philistine) plain about 26 km. east-northeast of Gaza and 6.5 km. west of the Shephelah in ancient Judah (map reference 124106). The acropolis of the site towers about 38 m. above the Wadi el-Hesi and is 144 m. above sea level (fig. 9). From its summit there is a commanding view to the south and to the east. The tell is composed of 21 m. of occupational debris resting on a large sand dune about 17 m. in height. The area on top of the acropolis is quite small (about 0.7 a. prior to Bliss's excavation in 1891–92; even allowing for considerable erosion to the eastern section of the mound by the changing course of the wadi over the millennia, the original summit was probably not larger than 1.5 a.), while the area at the base is about 4 a. In the Early Bronze Age the tell was part of a 25 a. walled city. In this article discussion will be limited to the interpretation of work on the tell itself, with emphasis on the strata most closely connected with Old Testament history.

Interpretation Without Excavation:
Hesi, Lachish, Eglon

Though Palestine has been visited by pilgrims and travelers throughout the centuries, it was not until the nineteenth century that systematic explorations and geographical studies were undertaken. Napoleon's invasion of Egypt and Palestine in the late eighteenth and early nineteenth centuries focused international attention on the countries of the Near East and served to awaken interest in the "Bible Lands." A number of scholars from Europe and America, motivated by a desire to clarify the background of the Bible, explored the land, described its topography, and attempted to identify biblical sites. In 1865 the Palestine Exploration Fund was founded in London to promote "the accurate and systematic investigation of the archaeology, the topography, the geology and physical geography, the manners and customs of the Holy Land, for biblical illustration." It is important to note that "archaeology," as used here, refers to the location and description of ancient ruins; excavation is not necessarily implied. As far as we know none of the early explorers was aware that tells are made up of strata of occupation debris.

It is in this context of exploration and site identification that Tell el-Hesi, known in the Middle Ages as "Al hassi" (Conder and Kitchener 1883: 261), was visited and described. Edward Robinson, generally recognized as the founder of the study of scientific biblical geography, visited the site in 1838 in connection with his investigation of the ruins at Umm el-Lakis, 5 km. northwest of Hesi, and Khirbet 'Ajlan, 2 km. north-northwest of the tell. He described the tell as a truncated cone similar to Frank Mountain (Herodium) southeast of Bethlehem but reported that he found no trace of walls or other ruins (1841: 388–92).

Robinson identified 'Ajlan as biblical Eglon but wrote that he did not expect to find ancient Lachish at Umm el-Lakis because of "the fallacy of any supposed resemblance in the two names" (1841: 388). Of the remains at Umm el-Lakis he wrote:

> These remains are certainly not those of an ancient fortified city, which could for a time at least brave the assaults of an Assyrian army. . . . [Lachish] lay, according to Eusebius and Jerome, seven Roman miles from Eleutheropolis toward the south. This would seem to imply that it was situated among or near the hills . . . while the present Um Lâkis lies in the middle of the plain west of Beit Jibrin (1841: 388–89).

Robinson thus rejected the identification of Umm el-Lakis as Lachish and did not attempt to identify Tell el-Hesi.

About twenty years later the French geographer Victor Guérin wrote a description of Tell el-Hesi and its environs. He reported seeing walls and ruins at the site. He made no attempt to venture an identification of Hesi, but identified Umm el-Lakis with Lachish (1868: pt. 2, 296).

Capt. C. R. Conder visited the area in connection with the Palestine Exploration Fund's Survey of Western Palestine and was the first to suggest the identification of Tell el-Hesi as Lachish:

> Tell el Hesy . . .—A truncated cone, with a broad flat top, and traces of ruins about its base. There are several springs in the neighborhood, but the water is bad. It is a conspicuous site (1883: 290–91).

> Lachish.—The site of this strong and important town is uncertain. In the 'Onomasticon' it is placed 7 miles from Eleutheropolis towards Daroma; but no important site occurs at this distance. Ten English miles from Beit Jibrîn is the important site of Tell el Hesy, the name of which approaches that of Lachish, with the substitution of a guttoral for the Hebrew Caf, as in the case of Michmash (1883: 261).

Conder thus sought to identify the "el" of the Arabic name with the first consonant of the name Lachish. This was later called a "false etymology" by Bliss (1894: 140) and was not accepted by others, but the site identification was soon to be championed by Petrie and was to become almost universally accepted following his excavations.

I close this section on the period of exploration with the concluding paragraph of Conder and Kitchener's volume on the survey of Judea (1883: 450):

> The study of archaeology in Palestine, by excavation or otherwise, is not likely to bring to light very much of value with respect to the illustration of the Bible. The work which is really of importance is that in which the Fund is now engaged, namely, the examination of the topography of the land.

Identification by Early Excavators Prior to Excavation: Hesi Is Lachish

Flinders Petrie, 1890

Fortunately the Palestine Exploration Fund was not persuaded by Conder's statement in the preceding paragraph. In 1890 W. M. Flinders Petrie, after ten years of excavation in Egypt, was asked by the Fund to conduct an excavation in Palestine. The original plan was to explore "Umm Lakis and Khurbet Ajlan, two sites which were supposed to be Lachish and Eglon; but happily the area asked for included some other ancient sites, and among them Tell el Hesy" (Petrie: 1891: 9). From his work in Egypt, Petrie was acquainted with the formation of tells and with Roman, Greek, and "Phoenician" pottery. He abandoned work at Umm el-Lakis after three days because only late

(Roman) remains were there. Khirbet 'Ajlan he found to be even less impressive and did no digging there at all. He turn turned his attention to Tell el-Hesi because of its height and its "pre-Greek" style of pottery. The top of the tell was cultivated so he dug trenches on the side of the tell and did some tunneling. Concerning this short season of excavation he (modestly?) stated (1891: 10):

> I had six weeks of work there, including the whole of the month of Ramadan, when work is very difficult to the fasting and thirsty Muslims. But in that time, and without disturbing the crops, I succeeded in unravelling the history of the place, and obtaining a long series of pottery approximately dated.

Petrie is rightly praised for being the "father of Palestinian archaeology" because of his recognition of stratigraphy and relative pottery chronology. From his work in Egypt he recognized what he called "Phoenician" pottery (actually LB Cypriot imports and imitations) and correctly reasoned that all pottery forms from lower strata were earlier and those from higher strata were later. Once the pottery sequence is established it becomes a "key" for all other excavations.

It is also important to note, however, that Petrie's interpretation of his excavation at Hesi depended heavily on his prior identification of the site as Lachish. In his report to the annual meeting of the Palestine Exploration Fund in 1890 he wrote concerning Hesi (1890a: 142):

> Topographically, this place and Tell Nejîleh, six miles south, are the most valuable possessions in the low country, as they command the only springs and watercourse which exist in the whole district. From their positions, their early age, and their water supply, it seems almost certain that they are the two Amorite cities of the low country, Lachish and Eglon. The transference of the names in late times to settlements a few miles off, is probably due to the returning Jews not being strong enough to wrest these springs from the Bedawin sheep-masters.

With this identification established, Petrie proceeded to "read" the strata of the east section of the tell which had been eroded by the wadi (1890b: 227):

> On the river face of the Tell I have had the surface all cleared down at the north end, and have spent hours there tracing out the sections of the various brick-wall fortifications of the town. These are far the best source for its history, when combined with the notices in the O.T. of Lachish.

It is not surprising then that in his chronological summary Petrie assigned each structure to a particular biblical reference either to Lachish or to some incident in biblical history. He estimated that debris buildup averaged 5 ft. a century, and that helped him to determine to which "biblical" period each stratum belonged.

One of the most prominent strata noted by Petrie was a heavy ash layer lying over a layer of stones (fig. 10). Beneath it was a massive wall which he assigned to the "Amorite period" (c. 1700 B.C.E., Eighteenth Egyptian Dynasty) when there was a need for protection (1891: 12). The stone stratum he related to the period of the Judges "when there were only rude stone huts" —a barbaric period "between the destruction of the Amorite civilization, and the establishment of Jewish civilization under the Kings" (1891: 17, 16). The site was then deserted and used by alkali burners; this accounts for the heavy layer of wind-deposited ash (1891: 22).

A wall at the 291 ft. level was related to Rehoboam, who is reported to have fortified Lachish. The "pilaster building" (fig. 10) is also dated to this period, but its reused carved stones were probably from a Solomonic building, when fortifications were not needed (1891: 22). Subsequent rebuilding and new structures were dated as follows (1891: 26–29):

(1) The strengthening of the Rehoboam wall was by Jehoshaphat (2 Chron. 17:11) c. 910 B.C.E.

(2) A stump of wall inside the Jehoshaphat wall dates to the building program of Uzziah (2 Chron. 26), but was destroyed by Rezin and Pekah c. 735 B.C.E. (2 Kings 16:5). To this stratum also belongs the "long range of chambers" based at the 319 ft. level (fig. 10).

(3) A wall at the 300–305 ft. level and some stone steps on the south slope are from the time of Ahaz (732 B.C.E.).

(4) The base of a thicker wall in the north at the 303–305 ft. level and a glacis on the south slope with a very small wall at the top of it (333–335 ft. level) belong to a hasty defensive construction by Hezekiah just prior to Sennacherib's invasion in 701 B.C.E. After the destruction the buildings were "largely of rude stones, as in the old barbarism of the Judges" (1891: 28).

(5) The final fortification of the site was a wall at the 310–319 ft. level built by Manasseh c. 660 B.C.E. as part of his defensive buildup (2 Chron. 33:14), probably against Egypt. Petrie claimed to have traced this wall around the tell; on the south slope it was built over the glacis (figs. 10, 11). These were the walls destroyed by Nebuchadrezzar (Jer. 34:7).

Following that destruction

> the place was probably desolate and left the Bedawin and their cattle. Even after the return of the Jews, about 445, Lachish appears to have been hardly reoccupied, as we have seen; at least the surrounding villages were not restored, and before long the settlement was moved to the later site of Umm Lakis. On the top of the city mound is found at the N.W. part some amount of Greek pottery of the Vth cent. B.C.E. But after this was a desolation, and neither Greek nor Roman attempted to occupy the site (1891: 29).

While Petrie's pioneering work in stratigraphy and pottery chronology is widely recognized, the above summary shows how heavily influenced he was by his prior identification of the site with Lachish.

F. J. Bliss, 1891–92

An American archaeologist, Frederick J. Bliss, was asked by the Palestine Exploration Fund to continue the excavations at Tell el-Hesi. After a brief apprenticeship with Petrie in Egypt, he conducted four seasons of work in 1891 and 1892, excavating the northeastern third of the tell to dune sand. Digging down layer by layer he identified eight major cities and three subcities.

In his book, *A Mound of Many Cities,* Bliss mentioned the reasons for Petrie's identification of the site as Lachish (1894: 15–16), but he himself was more cautious. In the preface of his book he emphasized that his purpose in writing was "to present facts with as slight an admixture of theory as is possible" (1894: xi). He gave a description of the walls, buildings, artifacts, and pottery from each stratum without attempting to relate them to biblical events. Even the discovery of a clay tablet, similar to the Tell el-Amarna tablets, which mentioned the name Zimridi, known from the Amarna letters to have been a governor of Lachish, did not convince him that Hesi was Lachish. In one of his reports to the PEF (1892: 113) he wrote:

> I am constantly struck with the smallness of the place. The first Amorite town probably covered an area a quarter of a mile square; but through the subsequent centuries of the Tell's history the towns were hardly 200 feet square. I am inclined to think that in its post-Amorite history the place was hardly more than a fortification to defend the springs. I have shown that the buildings are found on the edge of the Tell, and that the centre was probably an open place. This would be in favour of the fort theory. Any miserable mud village in the vicinity covers ten or twenty times the ground occupied by Tell el Hesy. Perhaps the idea of a fort, rather than of a town, may throw some light on the mysterious lines of stones and walls.

In chap. VI of his book Bliss gave a tentative chronology of the tell. Each layer should be dated only by material found *in situ,* in the following order of importance: (1) the inscribed objects; (2) the figured objects; (3) the metal tools and weapons; (4) the pottery (1894: 129). City III was most securely dated by the clay tablet and Eighteenth Dynasty scarabs to c. 1450 B.C.E. Working backwards and forwards from this level he proposed a date for each stratum, ranging from 1700+ B.C.E. for subcity I to 400 B.C.E. for City III (1894: 137–39).

It was only *after* this that he turned to the problem of site identification and biblical interpretation (1894: 139).

> I regret that my investigations have thrown no new light on the identification of Tell el Hesy with Lachish. Should a more complete inspection of the original

> tablet [up to then studied only from casts] show that the letter was addressed to
> Zimridi, the Governor of Lachish, instead of merely mentioning him, the
> probability of the identification would be greatly strengthened.

Bliss did not find the arguments of Petrie and others concerning name shifts
convincing. He did, however, agree with Petrie's argument for "identifying
Tell el Hesy and Tell el Nejileh with Lachish and Eglon on the ground of
position and importance" (1894: 142). According to Joshua 10:34–35 they were
within easy marching distance and in the Shephelah. That fits the situation of
Hesi and Tell en-Nejileh perfectly: "If these two important mounds are not
these two important cities, what are they? If these two important cities are not
to be found at these two important mounds, where are we to look for them?"
(1894: 142). Yet, for Bliss the question of identification was not nearly as
important as the sequence of occupational layers which had been uncovered:
Canaanite stronghold, Israelite conquest, Judean city, captivity, and return.

A. H. Sayce

Archibald H. Sayce of Queen's College, Oxford, was a member of the
Palestine Exploration Fund and was the first to publish the text and translation
of the clay tablet found in Bliss' City III, included as Appendix A in Bliss 1894:
184–87. A later critique and translation was published by Albright (1942). For
Sayce the tablet was positive proof that Tell el-Hesi was ancient Lachish, and
he had in fact predicted that tablets would be found at the site (1890: 17).

> Mr. Petrie's excavations have further shown what a rich harvest awaits the
> scientific explorer in the Holy Land. There, as in Egypt or Assyria, the soil still
> holds in its bosom the inscriptions and other monuments which are yet to throw
> floods of light on Old Testament history. Among the Tel el-Amarna tablets are
> despatches sent by the governor of Lachish to the Egyptian king in the century
> before the exodus. Lachish, therefore, must have possessed an archive-chamber,
> and there is no reason why the clay tablets of the archive-chamber should not
> yet be found.

When the clay tablet was discovered in 1892, Sayce claimed that Bliss was at
the entrance to the ancient archive chamber of Lachish. In speculating about
what might be found there he articulated a theme which was to become all too
common and which is still stressed in some quarters today; namely, that
archaeology can "prove" the Bible (1892: 22):

> Who knows what is in store for us, during the next few years, if only sufficient
> funds can be provided for carrying on the costly work of excavation? Histories
> of the patriarchs, records of Melchizedek and his dynasty, old hymns and
> religious legends, may be among the archaeological treasures that are about to
> be exhibited to the wondering eyes of the present generation. A few years ago
> such a possibility could not have been dreamed of by the wildest imagination;

now it is not only a possibility, but even a probability. To dig up the sources of Genesis is a better occupation than to spin theories and dissect the scriptural narrative in the name of "higher criticism." A single blow of the excavator's pick has before now shattered the most ingenious conclusions of the Western critic; if the Palestine Exploration Fund is sufficiently supported by the public to enable it to continue the work it has begun, we doubt not that theory will soon be replaced by fact, and that the stories of the Old Testament which we are now being told are but myths and fictions will prove to be based on a solid foundation of truth.

The above statement is certainly extreme, but it illustrates a tendency that still persists—to expect archaeology to substantiate the "truth" of the Bible. This has prompted a number of reactions over the years, two of the more recent being de Vaux's "On Right and Wrong Uses of Archaeology" (1970) and G. Ernest Wright's "What Archaeology Can and Cannot Do" (1971b). In the last-mentioned article Wright states:

> With regard to Biblical events, however, it cannot be overstressed that archaeological data are mute. Fragmentary ruins, preserving only a tiny fraction of the full picture of ancient life, cannot speak without someone asking questions of them. And the kind of questions asked are part and parcel of the answers "heard" because of predispositions on the part of the questioner (1971b: 73).

The last sentence of the above quotation is very important to keep in mind because as archaeological work increased in Palestine the majority of American excavators, at least, came out of a background of biblical studies and this, of course, determined the type of questions which were asked.

Reinterpretation: Hesi Is Not Lachish, But Eglon(?)

Sayce's second prediction did not come true. No archive of tablets was unearthed at Hesi and no "blow of the excavator's pick" was able to silence the literary critics who espoused the "Higher Criticism." The identification of the site as Lachish, however, was generally accepted and most atlases and geographical works reflected this (G. A. Smith 1932 [first edition 1894]). An increasing number of excavations at other sites tended to overshadow Tell el-Hesi which remained memorable chiefly because of its unusual appearance caused by Bliss' cut.

In 1924 W. F. Albright, then director of the American School of Oriental Research in Jerusalem, visited Tell el-Hesi and claimed that the site was far too small to be a significant city of the Late Bronze Age or a major defensive citadel of Judea. Instead, he suggested the site must be identified with biblical Eglon, whose name was preserved in the Roman ruins of Khirbet 'Ajlan (Albright 1924).

A few years later Albright suggested that the site of ancient Lachish was Tell ed-Duweir, a large mound in the Shephelah south of Beit Jibrin, which was at least "four times as large" as Hesi and whose location is more in accord with the "Onomasticon" of Eusebius and Jerome (1929: 2). Excavations at Tell ed-Duweir by J. Starkey from 1932–38 and the discovery of the "Lachish ostraca" confirmed Albright's identification which is now almost universally accepted. Hesi became Eglon(?) almost by default, though M. Noth argued that Tell 'Aitun, located 10 km. south-southwest of Tell ed-Duweir on the route to Hebron, would be most in keeping with the geographical sequence in Joshua 10:34–35 (Rainey 1976: 252).

In 1964–65 G. Ernest Wright visited Tell el-Hesi and was convinced that "this site could never make sense as a defense point, or as an independent city-state, unless it served as an integrated part of a larger whole" (1971a: 77). He went on to postulate that Hesi was one of a series of forts (Tell Bornat, Tell el-'Areini, Tell el-Quneitirah, Tell en-Nejileh, Tell esh-Sharif'ah and possibly Tell Beit Mirsim) surrounding Lachish and built for its protection (1971a: 79–86).

Further Excavation: "Tell Me, Tell el-Hesi, the Secrets of Your Past"

The Joint Expedition to Tell el-Hesi, under the sponsorship of the American Schools of Oriental Research and with the planning and encourage-ment of ASOR's then president, the late G. Ernest Wright, began work on the field in 1970. It has conducted eight seasons of excavations, the first three with John E. Worrell as director, and the next four under D. Glenn Rose. Lawrence E. Toombs has been senior archaeologist for six of the seven seasons. An eighth season occurred in 1983 with Valerie Fargo as Project Director and Ralph Doermann as Archaeological Director.

Methodology

The expedition was planned as an interdisciplinary undertaking with an emphasis on "holistic" archaeology.

> In essence and over-simplification, this means that a shift has taken place from an interest in history *per se* to an interest in the lifeways of man behind the history. However, this does not mean that an interest in history itself is lacking. . . . This emphasis, which examines the whole cultural environment of the site rather than part of it (culture-history) created the Hesi tradition which is in line with what preceded and yet is a new entity (Rose, forthcoming).

From the outset there has been a strong emphasis on the best possible excava-tion and recording techniques (Blakely and Toombs 1980), and there has been

a specialist staff which includes a geologist, a botanist, and cultural and physical anthropologists, with a lithicist and a malecologist as consulting specialists.

In the course of excavation, remains from the Chalcolithic, Early Bronze,
Late Bronze, Iron I and II, Persian, hellenistic, Arabic, and Modern periods
have been encountered. Excavations on the acropolis have now reached the
Iron II period (Stratum VI and Stratum VII), and it is on these remains that
attention will be focused in the following pages.

Personal Reflections

First a subjective note. I have been associated with the Joint Expedition
since the first season in 1970 (our teacher and technical man, Abu Issa, Glenn
Rose, and I were the only three to have been on the site in each of the first seven
seasons), and Tell el-Hesi has become an increasingly important part of my
psyche, not only when I have been working at the site but also in the off-seasons
when it has come back to haunt me in dreams and in a multitude of other ways.
The ghostly voices of previous investigators and excavators keep sounding: "a
truncated cone, like Herodium" (which has since been shown to have been
built up by a deliberate filling operation); "too small to have been a major
city—maybe a fort"; "perhaps one of a series of fortified sites encompassing
Lachish." These voices, in addition to "living with" the site over the past dozen
years, have influenced my interpretation more than my background in biblical
studies or my practical experience in field archaeology. This "instinct" has
caused me to oppose some of the decisions made concerning which fields to
close and which to excavate. One can only hope that such subjective instincts
can be verified by objective archaeological results.

The Iron II Wall/Fill Structure

Stratum VIID is the largest single structure yet encountered at Tell el-
Hesi. In previous seasons some of the features described by Petrie had been
encountered: his "long range of chambers," his "glacis," and his "Manasseh
wall" (fig. 10). He had dated these by their relative levels, based on his estimate
of 5 ft. of debris buildup per century. In addition a large wall system near the
base of the south slope of the tell, not excavated by Petrie, was traced for about
75 m. (Field III, figs. 8, 15). In the 1981 season a stratigraphic connection was
made between Fields I and III, which showed that all of the features mentioned are part of a massive construction program which raised the summit of
the mound by more than 7 m. in the ninth or eighth century B.C.E. (figs. 13, 14,
19). As the structure and function of Stratum VIID are treated more fully in
this volume in a chapter by Valerie Fargo, a very brief summary must suffice
(for the excavation report of the 1981 season cf. Toombs 1983).

Fig. 14 is a schematic section of Stratum VIID, showing the probable steps of construction. One should note that the section extends only to the inner face of the lower wall system, which continues an additional 13 m. to the south. This wall system is shown in plan in fig. 15 and in section in figs. 16 and 17.

On the south slope of the mound a series of steps were cut into the earlier remains to form a rough terrace system (1 in fig. 14; fig. 13). On the summit of the mound a leveling fill was used; e.g., over Petrie's "pilaster building" below his "long range of chambers" (fig. 10). This operation formed a series of construction platforms. At the base of the south slope a large retaining wall (Zone A Wall) with a heavy stone foundation was constructed in a deep foundation trench (2 in figs. 14, 9, 18). It was about 4.5 m. wide and bonded to its inner face was a series of "piers" or subsidiary walls which extended north and stepped up over the earlier material (figs. 12, 15). Fill was thrown between the piers and mudbrick capping was placed over the entire complex. Evidently this Zone A Wall was not substantial enough to support the weight of the fill on the south slope. In rapid succession Zone B, built on a one-layer foundation of wadi stones, and Zone C,[1] founded on a wet-laid layer of plaster, were built as buttresses to keep Zone A from slipping. The relationship between the zones and the different foundation levels are shown in figs. 15, 16, 17, 18.

After the lower retaining wall was built, fill was placed over the terrace platforms, and a consolidation layer and mudbrick capping was laid on top of the fill (3 in fig. 14). At the same time the foundational part of the upper wall system was built and the series of chambers (walls and crosswalls constructed to contain fill) was begun on the mound itself (4 in fig. 14). Filling of the chambers (fig. 20)[2] with material from earlier periods (which makes dating difficult) raised the height of the tell as construction continued. The fill between the chambers and the upper wall system was consolidated by a layer of stones covered with a heavy layer of lime plaster (Petrie's "glacis"; cf. fig. 22). The higher part of the upper wall system was built over the southern section of the construction glacis; then layers of stone and consolidating fills were thrown against the north face of the upper wall, bringing the summit of the tell up to a much higher level (figs. 13, 14, 15, 19).

Occupation Levels of the Iron II Period

(1) *Stratum VII.* Strata VIIC–A are the levels directly above the VIID construction. Little has been preserved of these latter Iron Age strata because most of them were removed by the Persian building program. The foundations of a small courtyard building were delineated in Field I Areas 22 and 32 (figs. 19, 21), and several layers of occupation (VIIC, VIIB, VIIA) were discerned in Areas 41 and 51 (fig. 23) just south of the Persian cut through earlier material.

(2) *Stratum VI.* After the site was destroyed, probably by the Babylonians

in 587/86 B.C.E., a poorly constructed house was built on top of the destruction debris (fig. 23). It has been tentatively dated to c. 550 B.C.E.

Interpretation of the Current Excavations

Interpretation of the Archaeological Data

What was the purpose of such a massive effort to increase the height of the acropolis of Tell el-Hesi? Even with most of the Iron Age occupational material removed by Persian building programs, there can be little doubt that the summit of the mound was raised significantly in order to improve its effectiveness as some kind of a "watch tower" or observation post. With its increased height visibility was improved in all directions, especially to the south and east. The small courtyard building may have been part of a military outpost assigned to keep watch against invading armies or to protect the surrounding villages from brigands.

Lawrence E. Toombs (1982: 23) describes the Stratum VIID construction as follows:

> The building technique is probably a late example of a very old method of construction, appropriately called in Hebrew *millo* ("filling," "earthwork"). The structure built on the fill was called "the house of the earthwork" (*beth millo*). Constructions of this type existed at Jerusalem and Shechem from the Middle and Late Bronze Ages. A closely analogous structure occurs at Lachish, Hesi's more powerful neighbor, in Stratum IV, which, like Hesi, Stratum VIId, belongs to the 9th century B.C. The "Courtyard Building" of Hesi, Stratum VIIc, is one of the best examples of a *beth millo* yet found in Israel.

The hypothesis that Hesi was a military outpost raises the question of whether the upper and lower wall systems were meant to serve a defensive purpose as well as being retaining walls. It was previously thought that there was mudbrick capping covering all the structures on the southern slope, but excavations in 1981 exposed a southern face of the upper wall system with a sloping buttress built against it. At this point on the slope the "mudbrick capping" turned out to be collapsed brick and brick detritus from the upper courses of the wall. It would thus appear that the upper wall system was also defensive. Toombs (1982: 31) argues that the lower wall also served a defensive purpose because the Zone B Wall was battered and faced with plaster to ground level (figs. 17, 18). A look at the section will show that there probably was an exposed face with a dry moat in front of Zone B, but this was soon filled by the construction of Zone C where there is little evidence for an exposed face. Toombs also uses the analogy of the double wall system at Lachish Stratum IV, which has other parallels with Hesi's VIID structure: construction glacis, massive filling operations, etc. At Hesi, however, the lower wall is at the *base* of the tell, hardly a place for a defensive structure. Further, the current director of excavations at Lachish, David Ussishkin, has recently expressed doubt that the lower wall there was meant to be defensive (1980: 191). During the 1983 season, however, excavation revealed that the lower wall system does form a corner at the southwest and then continues northward along the western slope of the tell. This suggests that the wall may have been defensive as well as being part of a retaining system.

In a very thorough study entitled *Judahite Refortification of the Lachish Frontier* (1981), Jeffrey Blakely has summarized excavation results of more than thirty sites in Judah and the Negev and has also made a study of those sites which have been surveyed though not excavated. A number of small sites in the Hesi area have the same cone-shaped appearance (Tell esh-Sheqef, Tell el-Quneitirah, Tell el-'Areini, Tell Bornat) and excavations at Tell el-'Areini have shown the same *bêt millô'* type construction. Blakely's conclusion is that Hesi was one of a number of early warning sites surrounding Lachish, the chief military fortress in the south during the Iron II period.

"Biblical" Interpretation of the Data

I have used quotation marks in the heading because the Bible is not the only source of literary evidence for this period of Judean history. Annals of Assyrian and Babylonian kings have provided a good deal of information from a different perspective and they should be taken just as seriously as the biblical texts.

(1) *The Relationship to Earlier Interpretation.* Though levels of pre-Iron II occupation have been encountered in excavating Stratum VIID, there has not been enough exposure of them to attempt a correlation with Bliss' Cities III, IV, and V (his LB and Iron I cities) or with Petrie's "pilaster building" (LB/Iron I). This means that the proposed sequence of Canaanite city, destruction during the Israelite conquest, and rebuilding by the Israelite tribes has been neither confirmed nor disproved. That question must await further excavation.

(2) *Site Identification.* The almost universal acceptance of the identification of Tell ed-Duweir as Lachish leaves the question of Hesi's identification open. Albright's identification of the site as Eglon is doubtful. Nowhere in Kings or Chronicles is Eglon even mentioned. Even if one accepts the hypothesis, set forth with variations by Alt, Noth, Albright, Wright, Cross, and others, that the city lists in Joshua 12 and 15 belong to the Judean period, Eglon is merely listed and not mentioned as a fortified city. Eglon's identification remains a topographical question and from that perspective Noth's suggested identification of Tell 'Aitun as Eglon is more attractive than positing Eglon as Hesi. It will be suggested below that, because of lack of evidence for an

Assyrian destruction, Hesi may be one of the cities captured by the Philistines during the reign of Ahaz—either Gederoth or Gimzo.

(3) *Date and Purpose of the VIID Construction*. It seems clear that Hesi was one of a series of observation points in the Shephelah and coastal plain which was built and destroyed in the Iron II (Judean) period. The similarity of construction techniques at the various sites would suggest that the construction at Hesi must have been part of an extensive building program. The biblical sources for the period, Kings and Chronicles, mention five Judean kings who carried out building programs in the south, with Chronicles giving greater detail: Rehoboam (932–916 B.C.E.), Asa (913–873 B.C.E.), Jehoshaphat (873–849 B.C.E.), Uzziah (783–742 B.C.E.), and Hezekiah (715–687 B.C.E.). The latest pottery from the fill material of Stratum VIID at Hesi dates from the mid-ninth to the mid-eighth centuries B.C.E., which would make it too late for the reign of Rehoboam and too early for that of Hezekiah.

Of the other three kings it is stated that Asa built fortifications for the cities of Judah (2 Chron. 14:6–8), that Jehoshaphat built fortifications and cities throughout Judah and received tribute from the Philistines (2 Chron. 17:1–13), and that Uzziah tore down the walls of the Philistine cities of Gath, Jamnia, and Ashdod and built fortified cities near Ashdod and in the rest of Philistia (2 Chron. 26:6–8). From these accounts the building program of Uzziah fits Hesi's situation most closely, for Hesi is located in the Philistine plain not far from Ashdod (25 km.). The next most likely period would be during the reign of Jehoshaphat who received tribute from the Philistines and presumably had enough control over them to build fortified cities along their border.

The border between Judah and Philistia fluctuated depending on the strength of the reigning Judean king. During the reign of Jehoram (849–842 B.C.E.), e.g., the Philistines were able to penetrate as far as Jerusalem (2 Chron. 21:16–17), but during the reign of Uzziah most of Philistia was brought under Judean control. A fortress such as Hesi would have been built in an attempt to ensure the containment of the Philistines, to give early warning of approaching armies from Egypt or Edom, and to protect Judean settlements in the farming and pasturelands of the Philistine plain.

(4) *Occupation and Destruction*. The two major invasions of Judah in the late Iron II period for which we have literary evidence were those of the Assyrians under Sennacherib in 701 B.C.E. (2 Kings 18, 2 Chron. 32, and *The Sennacherib Prism* [ANET 287–88]) and of the Babylonians under Nebuchadrezzar in 587/586 B.C.E. (2 Kings 25, 2 Chron. 36, and *The Babylonian Chronicle* [ANET 307]). The Hesi excavation reports ascribe the heavy destruction between Strata VI and VII "probably" to the Babylonian destruction in 587/586 B.C.E. This is supported by ceramic evidence from Stratum VIIA, the last occupation level before the destruction.

What of Sennacherib, though, who boasted that he destroyed forty-six fortified cities and gave control of many of them to the kings of Ashdod, Ekron, and Gaza? One would certainly expect that a fortress such as Hesi would have been destroyed at that time. Yet Blakely, in his study of Judahite fortifications (1981: 144), states that

> no evidence for a destruction by the Assyrians has been found. This is the only site in this study which was occupied during this time period where no evidence of such a destruction has been found.

He then gives the following occupational summary (1981: 145):

STRATUM	STRUCTURE	DATE
VIId	Wall-pier-fill construction	9th century B.C.E.?
VIIc	Two houses	9th to 8th cent. B.C.E.
VIIb	House and pit	8th to 7th cent. B.C.E.
VIIa	House and pits	7th cent. to 588 B.C.E.
	DESTRUCTION	
VI	House	mid 6th century B.C.E.

Blakely's statement is based on negative evidence and should be read with caution. His main argument is that no Royal Judean Store Jars with $l^e melek$ handles have been found at Hesi, while at every other excavated site in Judah associated with Sennacherib's invasion some of these handles have been encountered. Even if his assumption that $l^e melek$ handles are necessary to prove Assyrian destruction is true, it must be remembered that most of the Iron II occupational material was removed by builders in the Persian period. Yet it is also true that in the limited area south of the Persian building platform no debris from an earlier destruction has been found.

The question then arises: how did an important fortress such as Hesi escape the fate of the other fortified sites? One possibility is that Hesi had been brought under Philistine control *before* the Assyrian invasion. In the late Iron II period it is almost impossible to differentiate between Judean and Philistine pottery, except for the distinctive Judean handles which one would not expect to find at a site under Philistine control.

This change of control could have taken place during the reign of Ahaz (737–715 B.C.E.). The Chronicler informs us (2 Chron. 28:16–20):

> At that time King Ahaz sent to the king of Assyria for help. For the Edom-ites had again invaded and defeated Judah, and carried away captives. And the Philistines had made raids on the cities in the Shephelah and the Negeb of Judah, and had taken Beth-shemesh, Aijalon, Gederoth, Soco with its villages, Timnah with its villages, and Gimzo with its villages; and they settled there. For the Lord brought Judah low because of Ahaz king of Israel, for he had dealt wantonly in Judah and had been faithless to the Lord. So Tilgath-pilneser king of Assyria came against him, and afflicted him instead of strengthening him.

In the above passage harassment by the Edomites, the Philistines, and the Assyrians is mentioned, but the Philistines were the ones who settled the conquered Judean towns and villages. Those sites which remained under Philistine control would not have been subject to the punitive wrath of Sennacherib when Hezekiah withheld tribute a generation later. If, as the lack of archaeological evidence for Assyrian destruction suggests, Hesi was one of the sites spared, two possibilities for site identification emerge: Gederoth or Gimzo (all the other cities mentioned have been identified). Little is known about either of these cities except that they were located in the Shephelah or Negev and that Gimzo was surrounded by villages that were also captured by the Philistines.

In this reconstruction Stratum VIIB would be assigned to Philistine occupation. A bulla found in a Stratum VIIA pit, which reads "(belonging) to Mattanyahu (son of) Ishmael" (O'Connell 1977: 197), would suggest Judean occupation at the site at some time after the Assyrian invasion but before Hesi was destroyed by the Babylonians.

Conclusion

The interpretation set forth here is an attempt to correlate archaeological data with historical references in both biblical and extra-biblical texts, but it does not and cannot verify the Chronicler's interpretation that it was the Lord who punished Ahaz for his faithlessness. Such a statement is beyond the scope of archaeology. Any attempt at archaeological and historical interpretation can be no more than a hypothesis which is subject to modification by further investigation and discovery.

NOTES

1. A preliminary analysis of the pottery from the 1983 season indicates that there was a substantial time gap between the construction of the Zone B Wall and the addition of Zone C.
2. Excavation in 1983 revealed two E-W walls, with crosswalls in between, at the northern end of the chamber/fill system. Fig. 20 should thus show a row of chambers in the north parallel to the chambers in the south.

BIBLIOGRAPHY

A. *References in the Article*
Albright, W. F.
    1924   Researches of the School in Western Judea. *Bulletin of the American Schools of Oriental Research* 15: 2–11.

1929   The American Excavations at Tell Beit Mirsim. *Zeitschrift für die alttestamentliche Wissenschaft* 47: 1–18.

1942   A Case of Lèse-Majesté in Pre-Israelite Lachish, with some Remarks on the Israelite Conquest. *Bulletin of the American Schools of Oriental Research* 87: 32–38.

Blakely, J. A.
1981   *Judahite Refortification of the Lachish Frontier.* Unpublished M.A. Thesis. Waterloo: Wilfrid Laurier University.

Blakely, J. A. and Toombs, L. E.
1980   *The Tell el-Hesi Field Manual: The Joint Expedition to Tell el Hesi.* Vol. 1. Cambridge: The American Schools of Oriental Research.

Bliss, F. J
1892   The Excavations at Tell el Hesy. *Palestine Exploration Fund* 24: 95–113.
1894   *A Mound of Many Cities.* London: Palestine Exploration Fund.

Conder, C. R. and Kitchener, H. H.
1883   *The Survey of Western Palestine.* Vol. 3. *Judea.* London: Palestine Exploration Fund.

Guérin, H. V.
1868   *Description Géographique, Historique, et Archéologique de la Palestine.* Vol. 1: *Judea.* Paris: Imprimé par autorisation de l'empereur à l'Impr. impériale.

O'Connell, K. G.
1977   An Israelite Bulla from Tell el-Hesi. *Israel Exploration Journal* 27: 197–99.

Petrie, W. M. F.
1890a   Annual Meeting. *Palestine Exploration Fund* 22: 141–43.
1890b   Journals of Mr. W. M. Flinders Petrie. *Palestine Exploration Fund* 22: 219–46.
1891   *Tell el Hesy (Lachish).* London: Palestine Exploration Fund.

Rainey, A. F.
1976   EGLON (CITY) 1. Tell 'Aiṭûn? P. 252 in *The Interpreter's Dictionary of the Bible*, Supplementary Volume, ed. K. Crim. Nashville: Abingdon.

Robinson, E.
1841   *Biblical Researches in Palestine, Mt. Sinai and Arabia Petrea.* Vol. 2. Boston: Crocker and Brewster.

Rose, D. G.
forth-   The Methodology of the New Archaeology and Its Influence on the Joint
coming   Expedition to Tell el-Hesi. In *Tell el-Hesi: The Site and the Expedition. Excavation Reports of the American Schools of Oriental Research: Tell el-Hesi 4*, eds. B. T. Dahlberg and K. G. O'Connell. Winston-Salem: Wake Forest University.

Sayce, A. H.
1890   Mr. Petrie's Excavation in the South of Judah. *The Sunday School Times* 32: 563.
1892   The Latest Discovery in Palestine. *The Sunday School Times* 34: 546.

Smith, G. A.
  1915   *Atlas of the Historical Geography of the Holy Land*. London: Hodder and Stoughton.
  1932   *The Historical Geography of the Holy Land*. 25th edition. New York: R. Long and R. R. Smith.

Toombs, L. E.
  1982   *Stratum VIId (Late Iron II) at Tell el-Hesi*. Research Paper Series No. 8248. Waterloo: Wilfrid Laurier University.
  1983   Tell el-Hesi, 1981. *Palestine Exploration Quarterly* 115: 23–46.

Ussishkin, D.
  1980   The "Lachish Reliefs" and the City of Lachish. *Israel Exploration Journal* 30: 174–95.

Vaux, R. de
  1970   On Right and Wrong Uses of Archaeology. Pp. 64–80 in *Near Eastern Archaeology in the Twentieth Century: Essays in Honor of Nelson Glueck*, ed. J. A. Sanders. Garden City, NY: Doubleday.

Wright, G. E.
  1971a   A Problem of Ancient Topography: Lachish and Eglon. *Biblical Archaeologist* 34: 76–87.
  1971b   What Archaeology Can and Cannot Do. *Biblical Archaeologist* 34: 70–76.

B. *Excavation Reports Relating to the Iron Age Construction at Tell el-Hesi*
Fargo, V. M. and O'Connell, K. G.
  1978   Five Seasons of Excavation at Tell el-Hesi (1970–77). *Biblical Archaeologist* 41: 165–82.

O'Connell, K. G. and Rose, D. G.
  1980   Tell el-Hesi, 1979. *Palestine Exploration Quarterly* 112: 73–91.

O'Connell, K. G., Rose, D. G., and Toombs, L. E.
  1978   Tell el-Hesi, 1977. *Palestine Exploration Quarterly* 110: 75–90.

Rose, D. G., Toombs, L. E., and O'Connell, K. G.
  1978   Four Seasons of Excavation at Tell el-Hesi: A Preliminary Report. Pp. 109–49 in *Preliminary Excavation Reports: Bâb edh-Dhrâ', Sardis, Meiron, Tell el-Hesi, Carthage (Punic)*, ed. D. N. Freedman. Annual of the American Schools of Oriental Research 43. Cambridge: American Schools of Oriental Research.

Toombs, L. E.
  1982   Cf. sec. A. above.
  1983   Cf. sec. A. above.

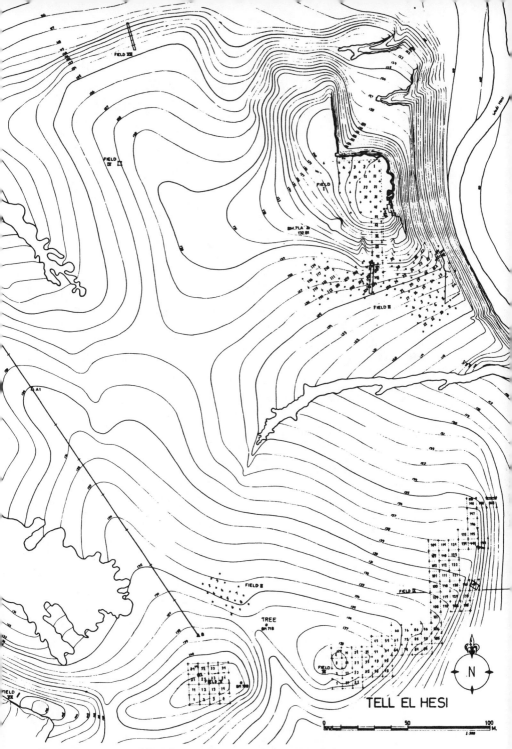

TELL EL HESI

Fig. 8. Contour map of Hesi showing the excavated areas through the 1981 season. Fields I and III, on the acropolis and south slope of the tell respectively, are where the Iron Age structures were excavated. All other fields are in the Early Bronze Age city.

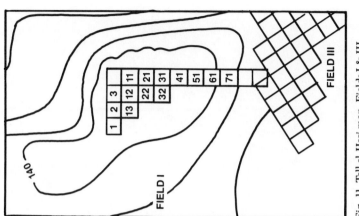

Fig. 11. Tell el-Hesi map, Fields I & III.

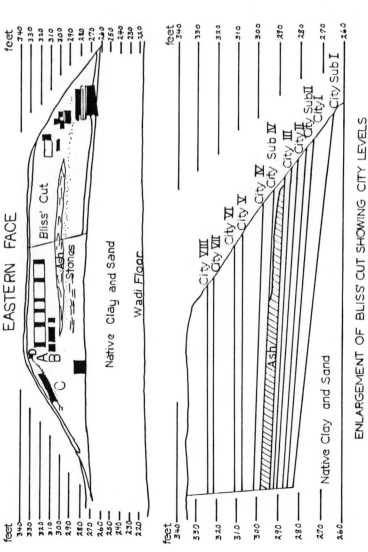

ENLARGEMENT OF BLISS CUT SHOWING CITY LEVELS

Fig. 9. (Above, facing page) Tell el-Hesi during the 1975 season, viewed from the south. Field III is at the base of the tell, Field I on the acropolis (photo by Ralph Doermann).

Fig. 10. Schematic sections of the excavations by Petrie and Bliss. The upper drawing shows the results of Petrie's excavations on the eastern slope. A is his "building with long, narrow chambers," B the "Pilaster Building," C the "Manasseh Wall" with the glacis below, and D the supposed termination of the glacis. The lower drawing gives the levels of the eleven occupational strata identified by F. J. Bliss. Adapted from Bliss (1898: pl. 2).

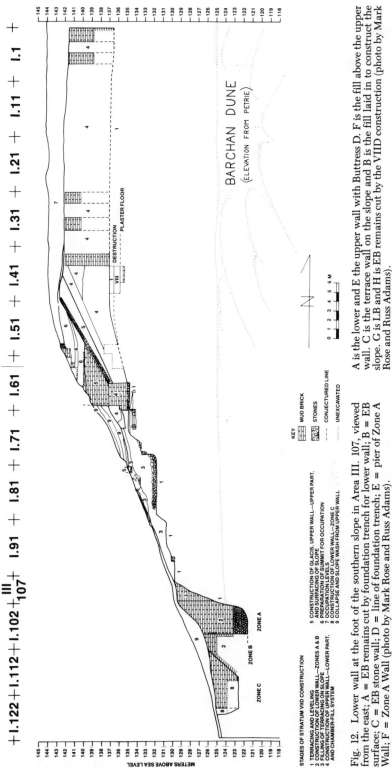

STAGES OF STRATUM VIID CONSTRUCTION

1 TERRACING AND LEVELING	5 CONSTRUCTION OF GLACIS, UPPER WALL—UPPER PART,
2 CONSTRUCTION OF LOWER WALL—ZONES A & B	AND SURFACING OF SLOPE
3 FILLING OF TERRACING ON SLOPE	6 PREPARATION OF SUMMIT FOR OCCUPATION
4 CONSTRUCTION OF UPPER WALL—LOWER PART,	7 OCCUPATION LEVELS
AND CHAMBER-FILL SYSTEM	8 CONSTRUCTION OF LOWER WALL—ZONE C
	9 COLLAPSE AND SLOPE WASH FROM UPPER WALL

KEY

▦ MUD BRICK
▨ STONES
···· CONJECTURED LINE
---- UNEXCAVATED

Fig. 12. Lower wall at the foot of the southern slope in Area III. 107, viewed from the east; A = EB remains cut by foundation trench for lower wall; B = EB surface; C = EB stone wall; D = line of foundation trench; E = pier of Zone A Wall; F = Zone A Wall (photo by Mark Rose and Russ Adams).

Fig. 13. Excavation of the southern slope of Tell el-Hesi, viewed from the south.

A is the lower and E the upper wall with Buttress D. F is the fill above the upper wall. C is the terrace wall on the slope and B is the fill laid in to construct the slope. G is LB and H is EB remains cut by the VIID construction (photo by Mark Rose and Russ Adams).

Fig. 14. Schematic section showing stages of Stratum VIID construction.

METERS ABOVE SEA LEVEL

BARCHAN DUNE
(ELEVATION FROM PETRIE)

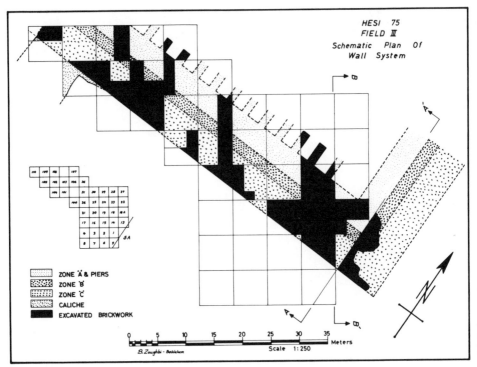

Fig. 15. Schematic plan of lower wall system, Field III (photo by R. Doermann).

Fig. 17. Defensive wall at the foot of the southern slope.

Fig. 16. A closer view of defensive wall.

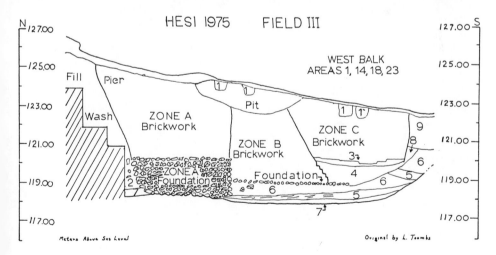

Fig. 18. Simplified section through Field III along the west balks of Areas 1, 14, 18, and 23 showing the three zones of the wall down to foundation level.

1. Persian period graves.
2. Bricky fill through which the Zone A foundation was cut.
3. The plaster foundation of Zone C.
4. Zone B fill in foundation trench 8.

5. Chert filled clay/sand layers.
6. Sand fill.
7. Virgin sand.
8. Zone B foundation trench.
9. Brick detritus.

Fig. 19. Chamber/fill structure, viewed from the east. A = N-S walls; B = E-W walls; C = fills (photo by Mark Rose).

Fig. 22. Glacis on the south slope of the acropolis, viewed from the west; A = southern wall of chamber fill system; B = sloping layer of fill; C = glacis; D = consolidating fill layers above glacis; E = upper wall system (photo by Mark Rose and Russ Adams).

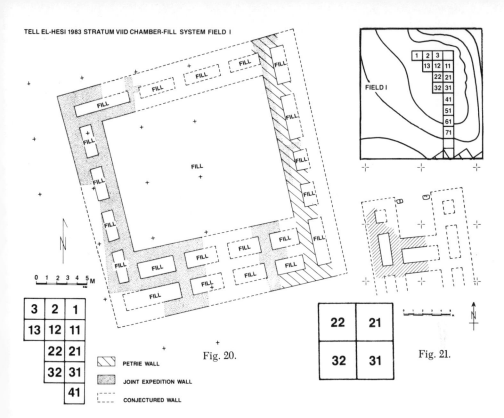

Fig. 20.

Fig. 21.

PETRIE WALL

JOINT EXPEDITION WALL

CONJECTURED WALL

Fig. 20.   Drawing of Stratum VIID chamber/fill system on the acropolis, Field I.

Fig. 21.   Plan of Stratum VIIC courtyard building, Field I.

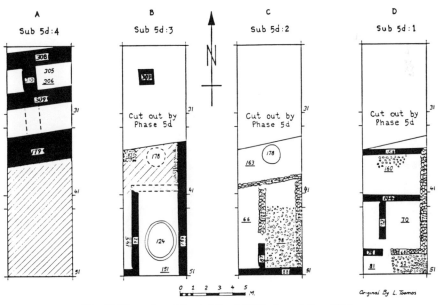

Fig. 23. Phase plan of Strata VI and VII in Areas I.41 and I.51.

Chapter 11

HESI IN THE IRON II PERIOD: A JUDEAN BORDER FORTRESS

Valerie M. Fargo

University of Chicago

When Robinson visited Tell el-Hesi in the early 1800s, he described the site as a truncated cone (1856: 388). This small, conical tell of about 2,700 sq. m. was the focus of continuous occupation from the Chalcolithic through the Hellenistic periods, with a gap only during the Middle Bronze Age (fig. 9). The surrounding 25 a. lower city was in use only during the third millennium B.C.E. (fig. 8). The tell's conical shape was the result of a large-scale building project which can be dated to the Iron II period, specifically the late ninth to early eighth centuries B.C.E. The Iron II builders constructed a platform of crisscross walls and fill (Stratum VIID) which raised the height of the tell 6 m. to 7 m., and on this platform they built a large courtyard building and other installations (Stratum VIIC). The entire complex was surrounded by a double wall system. These structures closely resemble the Iron II constructions of Stratum IV at Lachish (Tell ed-Duweir) and also have more general similarities to a number of other Iron II Judean sites.

The Iron II Construction Phase at Hesi[1]: Stratum VIID

The Stratum VIID structures extended across the southern half of the summit of the tell and down its south slope. The construction process consisted of several stages accomplished more or less simultaneously. The steps in this process can be seen best in the schematic section (fig. 14).

Construction of Lower Wall. The first component to be built was the lower wall (2 in fig. 14) which ran roughly east-west along the base of the slope. The innermost edge of the wall extended southward for 13 m. It was composed of three parts, labeled Zones A, B, and C (figs. 15, 16, 17, 18). Zone A, the

innermost and earliest, was 4.5 m. wide and was placed on a prepared platform
of large irregularly shaped stones. Along its inner face a series of mudbrick
piers extended northward at 2 m. intervals stepping up over earlier remains.
These subsidiary walls served to key the large wall into the slope. The space
between the piers was filled with earth and the entire area was covered with a
capping of mudbrick. Before long, however, this lower wall was found to be too
weak to support the massive constructions farther up the slope, and Zone B was
added. Zone B, about 4 m. wide, was laid directly against the outer face of Zone
A and was founded on a single layer of large stones. In contrast to Zone A,
which had a vertical outer face, Zone B had a batter of 30° and its outer face
was plastered to ground level. Further support was provided by the third and
final southward extension, Zone C, which was built about a century after Zones
A and B. About 4.5 m. wide, Zone C was founded on a layer of bricky material.
Its inner face ran directly against the battered face of Zone B, while its outer
face was vertical. In total, the three zones of the lower wall attained a width of
13 m. and formed the southern base of the Stratum VIID construction. The
entire lower wall system formed a corner at the southwest and extended along
the west side of the acropolis as well.

Filling of Terraces on the Slope. Following the completion of the lower wall,
work continued up the slope. Beginning at the base, the lower terraces were
covered with fill layers (3 in fig. 14). As each terrace was filled, a platform was
produced from which the next terrace could be filled. These fills were held in
place by layers of stone, bricks, or mud. About one-third of the way down the
slope a heavy layer of stones was found, with remains of a mudbrick wall above
it. These were probably remnants of a terrace wall which would have divided
the slope into two sections.

Chamber/Fill System and Lower Courses of Upper Wall. In this part of the
construction process several operations occurred more or less simultaneously.
The first of these was the creation of the chamber and fill system on the summit
(4 in fig. 14; fig. 20). The southern portion of this structure consisted of three
parallel east-west walls connected by cross-walls to form two parallel rows of
chambers. The chamber walls were about 7 m. high and were composed of
large, multicolored bricks. On the west side only two parallel walls with
crosswalls were found. It is likely that there was a third parallel wall here as
well, but it lies outside the excavated area. On the east, most of the walls have
been washed away by erosion, and the only wall fragments encountered here
were parts of Petrie's "long range of chambers" (1891: 29). Along the north
side, the structure's limits were unclear because of the intrusion of several large
pits of the Persian period. However, excavation has shown that the northern
side of the structure consisted of at least two parallel walls.

The entire structure enclosed an area of about 300 sq. m. The corners did not form right angles, and the overall shape was a rhomboid. Both the chambers between the walls and the large central area were completely filled with earth which contained potsherds and other artifacts from earlier periods. The height of the resultant platform was 6.5 m. to 7 m.

While the platform was being built, the lower portion of the upper wall was begun (4 in fig. 14). The lower courses of this mudbrick wall measure about 2.5 m. in height and are about 3.5 m. wide. Heavy fill layers on both the inside and outside of this wall provided support for the upper courses of the wall. The method of construction for both the chamber/fill system and the upper wall was to build a few courses, surround them with supporting fill, and then continue upward. Between the inner face of the upper wall and the south edge of the chamber/fill system the fill layers sloped upward to the north and consisted of many nearly horizontal layers above and more compacted sloping ones beneath (fig. 22). The sloping fill was sealed at the top with a layer of red clay.

Construction of Glacis and Upper Wall. In order to consolidate fully the sloping fill, large wadi stones were driven horizontally into the surface of the fill and were secured in place with smaller stones (fig. 22). This layer of stones was covered with a thick lime plaster and thus formed a "glacis" which extended northward from the base of the upper wall (5 in fig. 14). This glacis was used only for securing the fill layers beneath it. It was never above ground level and did not serve a military purpose. After the glacis was in place, the construction of the upper wall could continue. The inner face of the wall at this point was built over the sloping glacis, so that the wall widened to its top. The outer face extended above ground level for almost 3 m., and this suggests that it did function defensively. Unfortunately, severe erosion at the top of the wall does not allow us to say whether the top of the wall was freestanding.

Leveling Terraces and Fill. The final step in the construction process was to raise the area above the glacis and upper wall to the same level as the chamber/fill system (6 in fig. 14). This served to extend the platform on the summit southward to the upper wall. These fills consisted of alternate layers of earth and stones. In addition, within the fill there were two parallel walls running east-west, connected by crosswalls. These walls probably functioned to support the fills, although severe erosion here has removed most of the evidence.

Date of Stratum VIID. The fill within the chamber/fill system has produced large quantities of pottery from many periods. The latest sherds from the fills date to the ninth-eighth centuries B.C.E. The *terminus post quem* is the eleventh century based on the pottery from the destruction levels of the preceding Stratum VIII. A ninth-eighth century date is also supported by the comparable date of the Stratum VIIC courtyard building constructed immediately above the VIID platform.

The Iron II Construction Phase at Hesi: Stratum VIIC

The major portion of the Stratum VIIC structures had been removed by the building activities of the Persian period. All that remain are the foundations of the large courtyard building, a walking surface to the south, and parts of two walls from a small building (O'Connell, Rose, and Toombs 1978: 80–82; O'Connell and Rose 1980: 77–79). The courtyard building (fig. 21) was placed directly over the Stratum VIID consolidation. The extant remains consist of fragments of chambers around the west and south sides of a courtyard. Probable locations of two doors were suggested by the presence of two door sockets. Two floor surfacings were also identified. The mudbrick walls of the rooms were unusually thick (over 1 m.), which may indicate that the building had more than one story. To the north and east all traces of this structure had been removed by later pitting. Artifactual evidence suggests that the date of the Stratum VIIC phase is very close to that of the preceding Stratum VIID; i.e., ninth-eighth century.

In summary, the evidence from Strata VIIC–D at Hesi indicates that in the late ninth to early eighth centuries B.C.E. a massive construction project was undertaken at this very small site. This effort succeeded in raising the height of the tell's summit by 6 m. to 7 m. and produced a level platform on which the courtyard building was erected. Such a large-scale effort was probably completed by a central authority for a particular purpose, undoubtedly military. Hesi very likely housed a garrison for guarding the southwest border of Judah. Although the facility was not large enough to defend against a full-scale attack, it could effectively deal with raiders, give advance warning of imminent attack, and delay the enemy until other, major sites made preparations for battle.

Judean Border Fortresses in the Iron Age

Archaeological Evidence. Excavations have revealed evidence for close to forty fortified Judean sites in use at various times between the tenth and sixth centuries. There were several basic types of fortifications. Those sites which functioned as fortified cities or towns were enclosed by strong defensive walls and gates with towers. These city walls were both solid walls and casemates. Often the wall was reinforced by an earthen rampart or glacis against its outer face. In addition many of these sites had a citadel within the walls, along with large storehouses. Clearly the cities represented a central authority and functioned both administratively and defensively. In the ninth-eighth centuries a number of sites were fortified in this way: Tell el-Kheleifeh (Ezion-Geber;

Glueck 1965; 1977), Tel Malhata (Kochavi 1967; 1977), Tel Beer-sheba
(Aharoni 1973), Tel Halif (Seger and Borowski 1977), and Tel Lachish (Tufnell
1953; Ussishkin 1978).

The primary function of some sites was defensive. These sites were strategically located near the borders of Judah, and they consisted of isolated
citadels, sometimes with a small settlement nearby. Typical sites in this group
are Khirbet Abu et-Twein, Deir Baghl, and Khirbet Tibneh (Mazar 1982).
These isolated forts served as defensive outposts to give warning of an enemy
advance and to deal with raiders and brigands. The lookout posts were always
in the hills or on high points, which enabled them to signal visually to each
other, probably by means of fire signals. It is likely that these signals enabled
outlying border posts to communicate urgent messages all the way to Jerusalem
(Mazar 1982: 107).

Among the fortified cities Lachish was second in importance to Jerusalem.
The Iron II fortifications at Lachish in the ninth-eighth centuries provide the
closest parallel to the Hesi constructions. Both the 1930s British expedition
(Tufnell 1953) and the current Israeli expedition (Ussishkin 1978) have explored the Lachish fortifications. This complex, although on a much larger
scale than Hesi, contained all of the same elements: double wall system,
constructional fill and glacis, platform, and fortress. The earliest phase of the
construction consisted only of a consolidating platform, Podium A, composed
of crisscross walls and fill, which formed the foundation for the fortress immediately above, Palace A. This tenth century structure (Stratum V) was expanded in the ninth-eighth centuries. Podium B/Palace B (Stratum IV) were
added immediately adjacent to Palace A, and the double wall system was
erected. Between the inner wall and the foundation of Podium B a constructional fill was placed for support. This sloping fill was sealed with a white
plaster facing. This technique is virtually identical to that employed at Hesi.
The similarity of construction and the comparable artifactual evidence argue
for the contemporaneity of these two fortresses. Both sites were undoubtedly
part of the same defensive system to protect the southwestern border of Judah.

Hesi was not the only fortress in its immediate area. In fact, Hesi was the
central site in a chain of fortresses along the southwest border. This group of
sites formed a semicircle beginning at Tell Bornat and ending at Muleihah.
Also included in the chain were Tell el-ʻAreini, Tell esh-Sheqef, and Tell el-
Quneitirah (Toombs 1982: 38–39). All of these sites have the characteristic
conical shape, although most of them have not been excavated. Work at Hesi
and ʻAreini, however, has produced evidence of glacis and fill constructions.
Surface finds suggest that all of these sites were in use at the same time, but
further excavation is necessary to clarify this.

Millo. When publishing the Iron Age strata of Lachish, Tufnell (1953: 80)
commented briefly on the meaning of *millô*ʼ. The biblical references mention

David's *millô* which he built in Jerusalem (2 Sam. 5:9). Solomon also built *millô* (1 Kings 9:15, 24), and two centuries later Hezekiah repaired David's *millô* (2 Chron. 32:5). In addition, Joash was killed by his servants in *bêt millô* (2 Kings 12:20).

The Hebrew *millô* is translated "filling." The biblical references indicate that it was a central part of the city and that other buildings were constructed around it. *Millô* is usually mentioned in connection with the kings' building activities, especially fortifications. *Bêt millô*, "house of the filling," suggests a structure built on the *millô*. The servants of Joash may well have attacked him in his fortress, which had been built on an elevated platform. This evidence suggests that the Iron II platforms and chamber/fill systems at Hesi and Lachish may represent *millô*, and the palaces and courtyard building would then be *bêt millô* (Toombs 1982: 23).

Historical Context. There is considerable biblical evidence for building projects during the reigns of several kings. During the early years of the United Monarchy there was little building. Both Saul and David relied on mobile armies which were gathered together against a particular threat, and they avoided the use of fortified sites which could be besieged or attacked by an enemy. It was not until Solomon that large-scale projects were begun. Solomon's building programs at the four sites of Jerusalem, Megiddo, Gezer, and Hazor (1 Kings 9:15-17) included both public buildings and fortifications. Excavations at Megiddo, Gezer, and Hazor have shown that at all three sites the constructions were very similar. Three other sites were also fortified by Solomon: Lower Beth-horon, Baalath, and Tamar (1 Kings 9:18), but no excavations have been carried out at these sites.

Early in the Divided Monarchy the Egyptian Pharaoh Shishak invaded and defeated a number of Judean sites, with the result that the nation was largely confined to the hill country. At this point Rehoboam refortified a number of sites and established a new network of defensive outposts in the hills (2 Chron. 11:5-12), which protected all possible entrances from the south and west. It was at this time that the important fortress at Lachish was constructed.

The fortification line created by Rehoboam remained in use for several centuries. For the most part succeeding kings merely had to add new outposts as the borders fluctuated. By the ninth century Lachish had assumed a major role as the fortress second in importance next to Jerusalem, and it continued in this role through the eighth century. Thus it was essential that Lachish be protected by a network of outposts and garrisons. The first additions to the system were constructed by Asa (911–873) and Jehoshaphat (873–849) (2 Chron. 14, 17). Uzziah (783–742) expanded the borders into the Philistine plain and added new forts along his border (2 Chron. 26:6-10). This system remained in use through the eighth century when, with the Assyrian conquest of Judah, a systematic defense system came to an end.[2]

Hesi's location at the northern edge of the Negev and in the Philistine plain was strategic for several reasons. First of all, this southern area was a potential entry point for Egyptian, Philistine, and Edomite invaders. The northern Negev then, as today, represented the border of aridity, delineating the region in which there was sufficient rainfall for agricultural production. This area also contained fertile soil for cereal crops, in contrast to the hilly heartland of Judah, and it was adjacent to major trade routes from the south. Thus sites such as Hesi would have functioned in several ways. Not only did they guard against invaders, but also they functioned as commercial and administrative centers. The primary purpose, however, was to defend the country against its enemies.

The Judean kings achieved this protection by establishing lines of defense along all the major roads. Virtually all of the Iron II fortresses were on elevated points which not only provided an excellent view of the approaching enemy but also allowed visual signaling between the fortresses. The system begun by Rehoboam and expanded by Asa, Jehoshaphat, and Uzziah essentially consisted of three lines of fortresses running roughly north-south (Toombs 1982: 35–37). The easternmost line ran southward from Jerusalem to Arad, Malhata, and Beer-sheba and covered the eastern side of the Judean hills. The central line ran from Aijalon to Tell Beit Mirsim and Halif. These sites were located on the western edge of the hills or on isolated high points. The westernmost line ran from Gezer to Lachish and was situated to watch over the coastal plain. An additional group of fortresses ran along the eastern edge of the coastal plain: Bornat, 'Areini, Sheqef, Hesi, Quneitirah, and Muleihah. This line of outposts was located south and west of Lachish and provided a secure line of defense for the protection of this important Judean city. The coherence of this group of sites was first noted by G. Ernest Wright who also emphasized that Hesi "could never make sense as a defense point . . . unless it served as an integrated part of a larger whole" (1971: 437–39). This was indeed the case.

NOTES

1. The author is indebted to Hesi staff members Jeffrey A. Blakely, Ralph W. Doermann, and Lawrence E. Toombs for many conversations which contributed materially to this article. The preliminary reports on the first seven seasons of excavation at Hesi contain further descriptions of the Iron Age strata: cf. articles by L. E. Toombs 1974; 1983; D. G. Rose and L. E. Toombs 1976; K. G. O'Connell, D. G. Rose, and L. E. Toombs 1978; and K. G. O'Connell and D. G. Rose 1980. The article by Ralph W. Doermann in this volume describes the remains identified by earlier excavators and how they have been integrated with the finds of the Joint Expedition.

2. For a thorough treatment of the Iron Age fortification systems in Judah, cf. Jeffrey A. Blakely, *Judahite Refortification of the Lachish Frontier*, unpublished M.A. Thesis, Wilfrid Laurier University, Waterloo, Ontario, 1981.

BIBLIOGRAPHY

Aharoni, Y.
1973   *Beer-Sheba I*. Ramat Gan: Gateway Publishers.

Blakely, J. A.
1981   *Judahite Refortification of the Lachish Frontier*. M. A. Thesis, Wilfrid Laurier University.

Glueck, N.
1965   Ezion-geber. *Biblical Archaeologist* 28: 70–87.
1977   Kheleifeh, Tell el-. Pp. 713–17 in vol. 3 of *Encyclopedia of Archaeological Excavations in the Holy Land*, ed. M. Avi-Yonah. Jerusalem: Massada.

Kochavi, M.
1967   Tel Malhata. *Israel Exploration Journal* 17: 272–73.
1977   Malhata, Tel. Pp. 771–75 in vol. 3 of *Encyclopedia of Archaeological Excavations in the Holy Land*, ed. M. Avi-Yonah. Jerusalem: Massada.

Mazar, A.
1982   Iron Age Fortresses in the Judean Hills. *Palestine Exploration Quarterly* 114: 87–109.

O'Connell, K. G. and Rose, D. G.
1980   Tell el-Hesi, 1979. *Palestine Exploration Quarterly* 112: 73–91.

O'Connell, K. G., Rose, D. G., and Toombs, L. E.
1978   Tell el-Hesi, 1977. *Palestine Exploration Quarterly* 110: 75–90.

Petrie, W. M. F.
1891   *Tell el-Hesy (Lachish)*. London: Palestine Exploration Fund.

Robinson, E.
1856   *Biblical Researches in Palestine and in the Adjacent Regions: A Journal of Travels in the Year 1838*. 3 vols. Boston: Crocker and Brewster.

Rose, D. G. and Toombs, L. E.
1976   Tell el-Hesi, 1973 and 1975. *Palestine Exploration Quarterly* 108: 41–54.

Seger, J. D. and Borowski, O.
1977   The First Two Seasons at Tell Halif. *Biblical Archaeological* 40: 156–66.

Toombs, L. E.
1974   Tell el-Hesi, 1970–71. *Palestine Exploration Quarterly* 106: 19–31.
1982   *Stratum VIId (Late Iron II) at Tell el-Hesi*. Wilfrid Laurier University, Research Paper Series 8248. Waterloo, Ontario.
1983   Tell el-Hesi, 1981. *Palestine Exploration Quarterly* 115: 25–46.

Tufnell, O.
1953   *Lachish III: The Iron Age*. London: Oxford University Press.

Ussishkin, D.
1978   Excavations at Tel Lachish—1973–1977. *Tel Aviv* 5: 1–97.

Wright, G. E.
1971   A Problem of Ancient Topography: Lachish and Eglon. *Harvard Theological Review* 64: 437–50.

Chapter 12

ARAQ EL-EMIR

Nancy L. Lapp
Pittsburgh Theological Seminary

In the summer of 1979 I visited the Tell el-Hesi excavations and was extremely grateful to Glenn Rose for his hospitality and explanations of the field work. Since I had recently come from Transjordan, he was also full of questions about the current archaeological work there. It is fitting that a summary and up-to-date report of a Jordanian site be offered as a tribute to Glenn. It is offered in appreciation for his contributions to archaeological and biblical studies and to a truly helpful and considerate friend and colleague whose passing is a loss to us all.

Earliest Explorations and Evidence

Palestinian explorers have been interested in the ruins of Araq el-Emir since early in the nineteenth century, and by its end a number of travelers had published accounts of their journeys, plans of the ruins, and discussions of the Tobiah inscriptions (Irby and Mangles 1868; de Vogüé 1864; de Saulcy 1865; Conder 1889). Situated on nearly a direct line between Jericho and Amman, Araq el-Emir lies on the heights above the west bank of the Wadi Sir 17 km. west of Amman.

The early explorers and travelers could reach Araq el-Emir only by horseback, and even when excavations were undertaken in the 1960s a roadbed had to be cleared and bridges constructed over the wadi, and a Landrover was needed to go all the way into the site. Today a modern road has brought prosperity to the valley, and one approaches from the north, winding around near the wadi floor where a spring, 'Ain Deir, supports a number of agricultural villages. As one nears the ruins, on the right are the high cliffs (cf. fig. 24) with the Tobiah inscriptions on the facades of the caves which attracted the

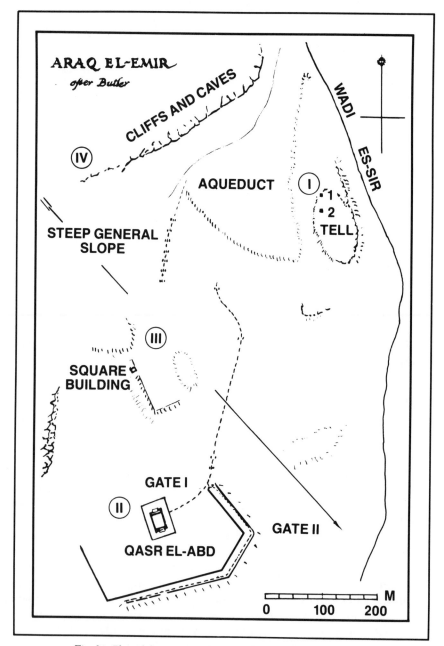

Fig. 24. Plan of the environs of Araq el-Emir adapted from Butler.

explorers. To the left is the modern village situated near ancient ruins, and as the road curves around it ends directly in front of the east wall of the Qasr el-Abd, parts of which have remained standing since their construction, with a defaced lion frieze on its top course.

The identification of Araq el-Emir with the description of the Tyros of Hyrcanus by Josephus has never been seriously contested. The Qasr el-Abd is certainly identified with the "strong fortress" (*baris*) which Hyrcanus "constructed entirely of white marble up to the very roof, and had beasts of gigantic size carved on it, and he enclosed it with a wide and deep moat" (*Ant.* XII.4.11 §230). The Tobiah inscriptions are still seen where

> he also cut through the projecting rock opposite the mountain, and made caves many stades in length; then he made chambers in it, some for banqueting and others for sleeping and living. . . . The entrances of the caves, however, he made narrower, so that only one person and no more could enter at one time (*Ant.* XII.4.11 §§231–32).

The Iron Age identification of the site is less certain, but it should probably be identified with Ramath-mizpeh of the Bible. Of the other sites which have been proposed for Ramath-mizpeh (Khirbet Jel'âad, Khirbet es-Sâr, Khirbet es-Sîreh), only Araq el-Emir has both a geographically satisfactory position and evidence of Iron I occupation (P. Lapp 1962a: 24; 1963: 37). Araq el-Emir is usually considered to be the Birta of the Ammonites in the land of Tobiah mentioned in the Zenon papyri.[1] As yet there is little archaeological evidence to indicate substantial occupation from the eleventh century until about 200 B.C.E. (the time of Hyrcanus). A few coins and sherds of the early third century B.C.E. found in the area may indicate the site was a Tobiad center, and perhaps it is with this that the cave inscriptions can be associated.[2]

Early in the century the Princeton Expedition to Syria under the direction of Howard Crosby Butler spent six days at the site. His study resulted in plans and concise descriptions of the ruins, detailed drawings of capitals and other decorative elements from the Qasr el-Abd and surroundings, and reconstructions which attempted to illustrate the original facades of the collapsed Qasr (Butler 1919). Considering the state of archaeological and comparative architectural studies of the time his results were amazing, and little was added to his work before the excavations of the 1960s.

Butler and others had recognized extensive remains in the area in addition to the monumental building itself (cf. fig. 24). Retaining walls and gates surround the Qasr, and an aqueduct can be traced through the area and northward to the base of the cliffs and a source beyond. A "square building" was located between the cliffs and Qasr, and architectural fragments have been widely dispersed. Equally important are the ruins where the modern village now stands, which command a view of the terraced slopes to the south and southwest toward the Qasr and the precipitous descent to the floor of the Wadi Sir nearly 300 m. below to the east.

The 1961–62 Excavations[3]

The hope for more extensive investigation of the ruins had long been expressed (Butler 1919: 1; McCown 1957: 74), and it was the quest for information concerning a relatively dark period of Palestinian history which led to the work of Paul W. Lapp and the American Schools of Oriental Research. Lapp undertook his first soundings at Araq el-Emir in 1961 in an attempt to determine the stratigraphical history of the site and to date the construction and subsequent history of the monumental building, the Qasr el-Abd (P. Lapp 1962a: 16). In the second and third campaigns more extensive areas were uncovered to clarify the stratigraphical history and gain an understanding of the structures in the village; the origins of the Qasr still needed confirmation, and an effort was made to obtain evidence for its reconstruction (P. Lapp 1963: 8, 20).

In investigations near the modern village (the "village" excavations) six strata of occupation were distinguished. In the northwest, where excavations were undertaken, accumulated debris is represented by 3 m. to 3.5 m. lying upon the rocky outcrop. The earliest, Stratum VI, belongs to EB IA, and although EB pottery was found rather extensively in the lower levels of excavation, there were only small patches of undisturbed debris and EB floors. The repertory of forms and decorative elements on the handmade assortment of jar, bowl, and crater sherds is closest to that found at Tell el-Far'ah (north) in de Vaux's "Chalcolithique Supérieur" material (de Vaux 1961: 572, fig. 2).[4]

The next occupation, Stratum V, belongs to Iron I, and this may be the town that can be associated with Ramath-mizpeh of Joshua 13. It dates to the eleventh century B.C.E., and to it belongs a 17 m. segment of a 1.5 m. wide defensive wall, possibly part of a fort, abandoned at the end of the eleventh century when Ammon is presumed to have eliminated the Gadites from the area.

Stratum IV follows after a long gap in occupation and belongs in the early second century B.C.E., the period of Hyrcanus' building activity at Tyros. No earlier hellenistic stratum can yet be isolated, though scattered evidence of occupation in the third century B.C.E., a period preceding Hyrcanus' activity, may yet be uncovered. At the beginning of the Stratum IV occupation the whole area was leveled off, including the scraping away of Stratum V debris and the chipping off of bedrock in some areas, in order to lay a thick plaster floor. A drain and remnants of a few other Stratum IV installations were oriented differently than were earlier or later constructions. Otherwise later hellenistic occupants had cleared out most of Hyrcanus' major construction

except for what became known as the "plaster building." This building consisted of an area 19 m. x 22 m.; its outer wall was plastered on the interior, and a
second wall, placed concentrically within the area, was plastered on its surfaces. The corridor between the walls was 2.5 m. to 3 m. wide and had a hard-
packed floor. The inner wall had several doorways to a courtyard with a hard-
packed floor of poorer quality. Pottery evidence beneath the court floor and
wall foundations date the building's construction to the early second century
B.C.E. It is possible that this is one of the *aulai* Josephus describes when he says
that Hyrcanus "built enclosures remarkable for their size, and adorned them
with vast parks" (*Ant*. XII.4.11 §233; P. Lapp 1963: 20).[5]

After Hyrcanus' death c. 175 B.C.E. there was probably a break in occupation until the end of the century. Major rebuilding took place c. 100 B.C.E.,
Stratum IIIB. Walls on the east and north sides of the excavated area form a
wide corridor with partitions, perhaps a type of second-century Greek house in
which living quarters were arranged around a central courtyard.[6] Occupants
from c. 50 C.E., Stratum IIIA, reused the IIIB walls with few alterations,
clearing out earlier domestic installations and artifacts but in most places
reusing the IIIB floors.

The Stratum II occupants of c. 100 C.E. reused the Stratum III walls but
added a parallel north-south wall in the corridor and partition walls to make
smaller rooms. Living quarters were extended into the open courtyard and new
rooms were added in the south corridor. Remnants of plaster floors, thresholds,
ovens, and water channels were preserved along with large homogeneous
pottery groups.

In the final village occupation, Stratum I, the Stratum II walls were reused
with minor alterations. Surviving evidence was limited to a broken plaster
floor, several thresholds, and oven remains. Typological considerations date the
final occupation of the ancient village to c. 200 C.E.

When evidence concerning the origin of the Qasr was inconclusive after
the first campaign, excavation was undertaken in the fall of 1961 at the "square
building" where visible architectural fragments indicated construction contemporary with the Qasr. It was hoped that indirect evidence from the square
building might help date the Qasr. Occupation and stratification were indeed
similar; the same pottery horizons and periods of occupation were present at
both the megalithic and the smaller monumental buildings. Details supplement one another, so the stratification of the Qasr and square building, Strata
I–IV, can be presented together.

In the massive fills which form the platform for the Qasr, small quantities
of EB IA and EB IV pottery were consistently present. Some of the main
foundations were laid on at least a small outcropping of rock, and although no
occupation levels were found there must have been a settlement here during
parts of the Early Bronze Age (P. Lapp 1962b: 82). However, at the square

building only EB sherds were found in the layer of green clay on bedrock, evidently an occupational layer left by EB inhabitants. Stratum IV then represents the earliest occupation in the area of the monumental buildings, dating to the EB IA and the EB IV periods.

The construction of the Qasr el-Abd is associated with Stratum III. The determination after the 1961 and 1962 campaigns that the Qasr was of hellenistic construction was due to its architectural style, the historical references, and the scattered hellenistic sherds rather than to decisive stratigraphical evidence. Detailed study of the pottery has shown that layers associated with the Qasr's construction consisted of fills which contained a few hellenistic as well as EB sherds (cf. P. Lapp 1963: 22; and final publication of the hellenistic pottery, N. Lapp 1983: 63–74). Pottery evidence and the stratigraphy thus corroborate the laying of the Qasr foundations in the early second century B.C.E. At the square building Stratum III represents the small monumental building with affinities to the Qasr. Inside the later "square" building well-finished slabs below the Byzantine floors may have served as part of a Stratum III floor. Outside the building a sandy layer separated later remains from a system of terraced walls associated with the Stratum III construction. Stratum III at the Qasr and square building thus represents the monumental building operations of Hyrcanus in the first quarter of the second century B.C.E.

Following the construction of the Qasr, left unfinished by the hellenistic builders, the monumental buildings were not used for sedentary occupation until early in the Byzantine period. Stratum II represents reoccupation by the Byzantines when they made use of the internal Qasr wall foundations, added walls to support their roofs, especially outside the east and west Qasr walls, and laid soil and plaster floors. Two floors of Stratum II were distinguished at a number of places in and around the Qasr, with the earliest at the level of the hellenistic pavement either replacing the hellenistic pavement or providing one where the early builders had never done so. Stratum II at the square building is the period of construction of the "square" building which was the distinguishing feature before the 1962 excavations took place. One floor of Stratum II was delineated there.

Fourth century C.E. pottery is characteristic of Stratum II both at the Qasr and in the square building. At the Qasr the tumbled megaliths of the walls on the Stratum II floors separate Stratum II from the one above. A Theodosius I coin dating to 393–395 C.E. from the fill for the second floor above the destruction debris provides a *terminus ante quem* for the catastrophic event, probably an earthquake. A major earthquake is known to have taken place in Transjordan in 365 C.E. (Kallner-Amiran 1950–51: 225). At the square building a Constantine II coin, dated 335–337 C.E., was found in the Stratum II floor east of the building, so a *terminus post quem* is provided. The dates 335–365, Early

Byzantine I (according to Sauer's terminology, 1973: 4), may tentatively be assigned Stratum II, though a detailed study of the pottery may refine these dates.

Following the earthquake it was necessary at the Qasr to level off the standing remains and sometimes import a massive fill. In the Stratum I rebuilding the main line of the Stratum III Qasr walls continued to be followed with only slight deviations. Two floors of Stratum I were distinguished inside some rooms and outside the Qasr on the west. On the porches fallen debris precluded occupation. A series of piers and fine plaster in a room south of the north porch witness to an occupation of some importance (cf. Groot 1983: 80–81; also cf. fig. 25). At the square building almost a meter of debris and three floors were associated with Stratum I, but no earthquake destruction separated Stratum I from Stratum II. The floors were distinguished both inside and outside the square building and some of the Stratum II building features were reused.

The Byzantine pottery of Stratum I is typologically later than that of Stratum II, and more absolute dates can be assigned the stratum by some coins. The Theodosius I coin (393–395) was in the fill for the IA floor; i.e., the second floor above the earthquake debris. Thus a period of time, perhaps about thirty years, can be allowed for the first phase of occupation in Stratum I. At the square building a coin of Arcadius, dated 383–408 c.e., was found laying on the earliest Stratum I floor. In the fill above the latest floor inside the Qasr was a coin of Zeno, 476–491 c.e., suggesting occupation to the end of the fifth century, and the pottery indicates heavy occupation in the latter half of this century. Stratum I can tentatively be dated 365–450 Early Byzantine II–IV (according to Sauer's terminology, 1973: 4).

Some sixth-century Byzantine pottery has been found in the disturbed debris in and around the Qasr, so squatter occupation probably continued for quite a while.[7] Other surface remains are dated by Mandate coins and World War I artifacts. A relatively modern burial amidst fallen Qasr megaliths included a necklace of beads with two German Rechenpfennigs probably of the sixteenth or seventeenth century (Cooke and Lapp 1983: 37).

A little exploration was carried out up in the cliffs at the mouths of the caves with the Tobiah inscriptions. Architectural fragments were found there similar to those at the Qasr, but only Mamluk pottery was uncovered.

The Animal Fountain. The finest discovery of the excavations of 1961 and 1962, perhaps the most striking sculptural monument in all Transjordan, was the feline in high relief carved out of a large block of mottled red and white dolomite (fig. 26).[8] It was discovered near the end of the third campaign when work was about to cease along the outer east Qasr wall. The sculptured block,

Fig. 25. Byzantine occupation within Qasr walls where fine painted plaster was found in this room with piers.

Fig. 26. Feline fountain in east Qasr wall discovered in 1962.

shorter and thinner than the space provided for, fits into the lowest dressed course. It was surmounted by a lintel resting on the adjacent blocks, and, inside, carelessly laid smaller stones filled out the thickness of the wall.

The feline functioned as a fountain. A hole in the animal's mouth leads through a constricted opening to a plastered channel, and a basin for storing water for the fountain existed just inside the wall. Several channel stones were found in Byzantine debris, and a drain near the cat's right forepaw indicates that a pool to receive the water stream from the mouth must have been planned. Whether such a pool ever existed could not be determined, for Byzantine occupation layers occurred to a considerable depth below the fountain megalith which rests on the upper surface of the hellenistic Qasr foundations. A Byzantine wall, set against the outer face of the Qasr east wall and carefully built around the sculptured block, contributed to the fine state of preservation and concealment of the fountain before the modern excavations.

The sculptured block's maximum dimensions are 2.05 m. by 1.50 m. capped by a stone cut around the animal's head to level with the 1.75 m. height on the lowest course into which the block is set. The 2.05 m. length is unique for megaliths of the lowest course of the east wall, so the placement of the fountain seems to have been part of the original building plan; yet, its crude insertion suggests that it was probably placed after the wall had been erected. It is possible that the relief had been used in another setting or was available when the Qasr architects made their plans for the Qasr, but it seems most likely that its inclusion was planned and then inserted after the hazards from erecting the megalithic walls had passed. The red and white dolomite breccia is available locally.

Artistically there is nothing against its execution in the second century B.C.E. when the Qasr was constructed. There is little evidence of works of art in the second century in Syria-Palestine and the entire Near East. Whole lions or leopards as fountains were rare in the Greek world though the heads of lions were commonly used as spouts. Lion spouts seem to be unknown outside the Greek world. The unequal lengths of the legs is a Greek means of portraying action, and an animal with an extended paw is a common Greek stance of the hellenistic period. Her study led Dorothy Hill to the conclusion that the fountain was a "provincial Greek work of the period 182–175 B.C. (1963: 55).

Qasr Function. The function of the Qasr has been a much debated issue and continues to be today (cf. below). Scholars have interpreted it as a fortress, a temple, a palace, and a mausoleum.[9] Architectural studies of the third campaign drew attention to the stairwell east of the north porch leading to a tower above the frieze course, which presumably gave access to a terrace roof. These three features—stairway, tower, and terrace roof—have been associated with a temple-cult function by R. Amy (1950), and there are other features which find their best parallels in temples (P. Lapp 1963: 27–32). The Qasr is then seen as a thus-far-unique and indigenous example of an old Syrian temple type in the hellenistic period, providing a link between the stair temples of Ugarit and Jerusalem and those characteristic of the Roman East.[10] A possible contemporary parallel was the temple of Onias IV at Leontopolis in Egypt, mentioned by Josephus but not located with certainty. E. Campbell suggests that perhaps these were meant to be centers for an alternative-to-Jerusalem Judaism, not only politically but also theologically motivated (1979: 165).

In any case, Hyrcanus' plans were frustrated when political events turned against him and Antiochus Epiphanes took over Seleucid leadership. Hyrcanus committed suicide (*Ant.* XII.4.11 §236), and his extravagant intentions were not realized to completion. The archaeological evidence of the Qasr's unfinished state was clear: no evidence of any second floor or roof or internally laid floors; unfinished bosses, columns, and other decorative elements; and especially the discovery of one lion stone of the frieze course only partially roughed out.

The Recent Soundings and Qasr Restoration

Paul Lapp would have liked to return to Araq el-Emir for continuing work, to explore further the occupational history of the village, and especially to consider reconstruction of the Qasr. He had contacted a classical architect, but his plans could not see fruition because of his untimely death in 1970. However, the Jordanian Department of Antiquities realized Araq el-Emir's potential for tourism and for Jordan's understanding of its own history and culture. Thus, when Ernest Will of the Institut français d'archéologie du Proche Orient could not return to work in Lebanon in 1976, his participation in work at Araq el-Emir was most welcome.

E. Will, an architect, has been most interested in the Qasr—its hellenistic history, its function, and, ultimately, its reconstruction. Architecturally, his conclusions, like those of the excavators who preceded him, leave no doubt that it is the hellenistic building of Hyrcanus' construction left unfinished at the beginning of the second century B.C.E. In several seasons of work and with the use of heavy equipment, he and his assistant, F. Marché, have been able to uncover, theoretically to reconstruct, and to analyze its architectural elements, and now they have been able in actuality to reconstruct in part the probable structure planned and partially carried out by Hyrcanus (Will 1977; 1982; Marché 1981). Plans can be presented in detail for both the north facade with evidence for the lion frieze continuing from the sides and reconstruction of the corner towers recognized by Lapp and others (Will 1977: 72–74). Clearing on the west side uncovered walls lying face down the way they had collapsed outward. Long slabs of the first main course laid horizontally held second course blocks set vertically, leaving spaces for the windows with smaller blocks serving as sills between. Some lintel course and cornice blocks above have been reconstructed (cf. fig. 27 and Marché 1981). Corrections were made in Butler's earlier plan, most notably in the elimination of the semicolumns, which he thought had filled the spaces between the blocks, that were probably meant to be windows. The accuracy of the reconstruction is much more certain for the lower courses revealed through excavation than for the top courses with the lion frieze and what may have been above (Will 1979a: 139).

Especially significant was the discovery of a pair to the feline fountain placed symmetrically in the west Qasr wall. Unfortunately it has been greatly mutilated, and from appearance alone it is impossible to determine how close a parallel it is to the one in the east Qasr wall (fig. 28).[11] Adding greatly to our knowledge of the lion frieze was one block which was found face down, which had fallen before the defacing, and weathering, and which has altered the appearance of those blocks still standing. The feline is carved in high relief and a small cub is found between her forelegs and hindlegs (cf. Will 1982, fig. 11). Will concluded, as Lapp had before him, that inside the Qasr the hellenistic foundations can be determined though they were reused and added to by the Byzantines (Will 1979a: 139; 1983: 152; P. Lapp 1963: 21). Stratigraphical excavations with the Department of Antiquities uncovered the hellenistic level in at least one place but, as Lapp had concluded, in most places, although the hellenistic level could be determined, the floor had been removed by the Byzantines or had never been completed (Will 1979b: 119; P. Lapp 1963: 21–22). Though Will's reconstruction of the hellenistic building differs considerably from Butler's (who did little or no stratigraphical digging), Will's internal reconstruction is close to that of Lapp's (P. Lapp 1963: 21; contrast Will 1979a: 140; 1982: 17).[12]

Excavation of the remains of the "monumental gateway" were undertaken in 1976 in the hope it would throw light on the Qasr, much as excavations had been undertaken at the "square building" in 1961 (Dentzer, Villeneuve, and Larché 1983: 133). Its architectural affinities with the Qasr did become clear, including decorative eagles and felines. Its orientation is not toward the Qasr or cave area but rather toward a road which, together with the dam, contained the artificial lake.

Will's work has led him to strong convictions as to the purpose of the Qasr to the extent that he believes other considerations should never have been taken seriously (cf. Will 1982: 16–17; 1983). Interpreting Josephus' *baris* as a palatial estate, a chateau or manor, Will considers the interior Qasr rooms on the lower floor to have been used for storage while the incompleted upper story would have been meant for living—as is still seen today in some Near Eastern village

Fig. 27. Reconstruction of the west Qasr wall in 1982.

Fig. 28. Pair found in east Qasr wall.

homes. The high bays were to allow light into the interior and the decorative elements would have been worthy of only someone of Hyrcanus' status—or dreams.

The French investigators consider the Qasr only one part of a huge country estate planned and partially executed by Hyrcanus. Evident throughout the area, obvious even to the early explorers, are the irrigation canals and ancient terraces (cf. fig. 24). Today the wadi flourishes with vegetation, and the natural surroundings make it ideal for gardens and parks now as well as in antiquity. Investigations point to a *lake* (sacred?) rather than to a *moat*, as Josephus describes, held back by an earth dam (cf. further, Dentzer, Villeneuve, and Larché 1983). Continual study of the environs—the "estate" of Hyrcanus, including the village—is a part of the excavation plans of the Institut français d'archéologie du Proche Orient and the Jordanian Department of Antiquities.

Yet, E. Will's assertions concerning the function of the Qasr are not without difficulties, and such assuredness can hardly be justified. Is it likely that such a "palatial" structure, if that is what it was, would have given such prominence to storage or animal keeping? In common village homes it may be expected, but it would seem out of place for the rich unless needed for protection.[13] If they must be viewed as storage rooms, then it must be said that temples with provisions for storage are not unknown. Stairwell tower parallels cannot be disregarded; the lion as a cultic feature is not unusual and other temple decorative elements are present (P. Lapp 1963: 30; Will 1977: 81–82). The Qasr, better known now more than ever as to its hellenistic construction and plan, is also more unique and problematical than ever. The open bays, the lion frieze, the enigmatic inner rooms (with certain hellenistic foundations— but were they to support a solid ceiling or a more open system? [P. Lapp 1963: 21]), all unfinished even in antiquity, have no parallels and little comparative material to aid us. There are still the problems as to whether Josephus understood the function himself and what he meant to describe by Hyrcanus' construction of a *baris* at Tyros.

Scientific survey, stratigraphical excavation, and comparative architectural, archaeological, and historical studies must continue at Araq el-Emir. Contributions of past and future investigations will slowly reveal some of the secrets of the earliest EB site, the Israelite settlement, the Tobiads' activities, Hyrcanus' Tyros, Roman occupation, and the Byzantine inhabitants of this site on the banks of the Wadi Sir.

NOTES

1. But cf. Mittmann 1970: 202–9 who thinks the administrative center of the Tobiads should be at Rabbath-ammon (modern Amman).

2. Cross (1961: 191, n. 13 and 195, n. 75) dates the cave inscriptions to the early third century B.C.E.

3. For more detailed presentation of the following summary cf. the preliminary reports of the first campaign (P. Lapp 1962a) and the second and third campaigns (P. Lapp 1963). The final publications are being edited by myself and the first volume is presently in the press (N. Lapp 1983).

4. For a discussion of the beginning of the Early Bronze Age and the correlation of de Vaux's, Kenyon's, and Lapp's terminology, cf. P. Lapp 1970: 102–6.

5. To be noted is that E. Will also thought the *aulai* should be found on the village mound, but apparently he has overlooked Lapp's identification (Will 1982: 16).

6. For a discussion of this house and the "plaster building" cf. the study of wall decorations by J. Groot (1983).

7. But not until the Arab conquest (Will 1982: 18). Note also Will's disparagement of this important Byzantine occupation and his lack of concern for the Byzantine stratification (Will 1979a: 142 and n. 12 below).

8. A detailed study of this feline fountain has been presented by Dorothy Hill, and it is from her that much of our understanding of this unique sculpture has come (Hill 1963).

9. For a summary of earlier views cf. Plöger 1955.

10. Interestingly E. Will, who vigorously denies the temple function of the Qasr, finds the only parallels to be to an open gallery between corner towers in several early churches of northern Syria (1982: 18).

11. I do not know of any geological analysis or artistic study that has been made which could help in determining its relation to the other, well-preserved fountain. The animal can by no means be described as a panther (Will 1982: 18), as it has features of a lion, leopard (or panther), and paws resembling a bird. Cf. Hill's study (1963: 48).

12. In an effort to find the "hellenistic level" E. Will undertook some soundings within the Qasr walls (Will 1979a). Unfortunately he has shown little interest in the later Byzantine use of the Qasr and oversimplified the Byzantine occupation and constructions. Obviously, more by observation and wishful thinking than by stratigraphical excavation, Will simplifies the Byzantine occupation to one main operation—a leveling of the interior of the monument and a laying of the "fill" above the "hellenistic level" (1979a: 143). Lapp's data is reinterpreted and inaccurately restated. Contrary to Will's analysis (cf. 1979a: 140), Lapp did not interpret the Qasr plan as a basilica with three naves; Lapp cleared between the Qasr outer walls and partition walls in more than one place (cf. plan, P. Lapp 1963: 7; cf. Will 1979a: 142); Lapp recognized the different hellenistic and Byzantine wall constructions (P. Lapp 1962a: 30); he considered the internal Qasr foundations as of hellenistic construction (P. Lapp 1963: 21; 1962b: 83; cf. Will 1979b: 119); and, moreover, it is very doubtful that Will's levels can be equated with Lapp's sections (P. Lapp 1963: 22). Will's soundings were toward the south end of the Qasr where, if he has interpreted his stratigraphical and ceramic data correctly, a different situation is represented in debris deposits. To correlate the work, an area south of Lapp's section (i.e., south of II.2) should be checked stratigraphically; this is impossible due to the reconstruction and cement reinforcement now completed in the west wall.

In any case, Lapp would agree that the hellenistic floor, intended to be paved, would have been at Will's level 85 (Will 1979a: 145, figs. 2–4; cf. P. Lapp 1963: 21–22). However, excavation of at least ten places inside the Qasr and eight outside the Qasr against the outer walls led him to the definitive conclusion that the Byzantines cleared out and had occupational floors at least down to the hellenistic floor level and at places below (note N. Lapp 1979, pl. 1:2, where the Byzantine floor in the upper right is below the lowest dressed wall of the Qasr). The evidence was plentiful: the pottery in the floors and below (P. Lapp 1963: 22); the rough Byzantine walls against and up to the hellenistic walls (P. Lapp 1962a: 31–33; 1963: 32, 36, fig. 1); doorways, sometimes with plaster turning into them (P. Lapp 1962a: 30); and occupational debris (P. Lapp 1963: 32–33).

The Byzantine occupation at Araq el-Emir needs further consideration for the contribution it can make to our knowledge of Palestinian and Transjordanian history and archaeology. In addition to the publication of the decorative plaster of this period by J. Groot (1983) and the Byzantine pottery published from an American Schools of Oriental Research sounding in 1976 (Brown 1979; 1983), Lapp's Byzantine pottery and the anthropological and cultural studies of the Byzantine occupation are the subject of research now in progress by Robin Brown.

13. Will would look for the fortress and the defenses of the site on the village mound rather than to the *baris* Josephus describes (1982: 16). Cf. also P. Lapp 1962b: 80.

BIBLIOGRAPHY

Amy, R.
  1950   Temples à escaliers. *Syria* 27: 82–136.

Brown, R. M.
  1979   Excavations at 'Iraq el-Emir. *Annual of the Department of Antiquities of Jordan* 23: 17–30.
  1983   The 1976 Soundings. Pp. 105–32 in *The Excavations at Araq el-Emir*, vol. 1, ed. N. L. Lapp. Annual of the American Schools of Oriental Research 47. Philadelphia: American Schools of Oriental Research.

Butler, H. C.
  1919   *Syria*, Division II, Section A. Publications of the Princeton University Archaeological Expeditions to Syria in 1904–5 and 1909. Leiden: Brill.

Campbell, E. F.
  1979   Jewish Shrines of the Hellenistic and Persian Periods. Pp. 159–67 in *Symposia*, ed. F. M. Cross. Cambridge: American Schools of Oriental Research.

Conder, C. R.
  1889   *The Survey of Eastern Palestine*. London: Palestine Exploration Fund.

Cooke, G. and Lapp, N. L.
  1983   Beads. Pp. 37–41 in *The Excavations at Araq, el-Emir*. Vol. 1, ed. N. L. Lapp. Annual of the American Schools of Oriental Research 47. Philadelphia: American Schools of Oriental Research.

Cross, F. M.
  1961   The Development of the Jewish Scripts. Pp. 133–202 in *The Bible and the Ancient Near East: Essays in Honor of W. F. Albright*, ed. G. E. Wright. Garden City, NY: Doubleday.

Dentzer, J.-M., Villeneuve, F., and Larché, F.
1983   The Monumental Gateway and the Princely Estate of Araq el-Emir. Pp. 133–48 in *The Excavations at Araq el-Emir*. Vol. 1, ed. N. L. Lapp. Annual of the American Schools of Oriental Research 47. Philadelphia: American Schools of Oriental Research.

Groot, J.
1983   Wall Decoration. Pp. 75–86 in *The Excavations at Araq el-Emir*. Vol. 1, ed. N. L. Lapp. Annual of the American Schools of Oriental Research 47. Philadelphia: American Schools of Oriental Research.

Hill, D. K.
1963   The Animal Fountain of ʻArâq el-Emîr. *Bulletin of the American Schools of Oriental Research* 171: 45–55.

Irby, C. L. and Mangles, J.
1868   *Travels in Egypt and Nubia, Syria, and the Holy Land*. London: Murray.

Josephus
Ant.   *Jewish Antiquities*. Trans. Ralph Marcus from Greek. Loeb Classical Library. London: Heinemann, 1943.

Kallner-Amiran, D. H.
1950–51 A Revised Earthquake-Catalogue of Palestine. *Israel Exploration Journal* 1: 223–46.

Lapp, N. L.
1979   The Hellenistic Pottery from the 1961 and 1962 Excavations at ʻIraq el-Emir. *Annual of the Department of Antiquities of Jordan* 23: 5–15.

1983   *The Excavations at Araq el-Emir*. Vol. 1, ed. N. L. Lapp. Annual of the American Schools of Oriental Research 47. Philadelphia: American Schools of Oriental Research.

Lapp, P. W.
1962a   Soundings at ʻArâq el-Emîr (Jordan). *Bulletin of the American Schools of Oriental Research* 165: 16–34.

1962b   The 1961 Excavations at ʻAraq el-Emir. *Annual of the Department of Antiquities of Jordan* 6–7: 80–89.

1963   The Second and Third Campaigns at ʻArâq el-Emîr. *Bulletin of the American Schools of Oriental Research* 171: 8–39.

1970   Palestine in the Early Bronze Age. Pp. 101–32 in *Near Eastern Archaeology in the Twentieth Century. Essays in Honor of Nelson Glueck*, ed. J. A. Sanders. Garden City, NY: Doubleday.

Marché, F.
1981   Reconstruction of the West Wall of the Qasr il-ʻAbd at Iraq-el-Emir. *Annual of the Department of Antiquities of Jordan* 25: 327–30.

McCown, C. C.
1957   The ʻAraq el-Emir and the Tobiads. *Biblical Archaeologist* 20: 63—80.

Mittmann, S.
1970   Zenon im Ostjordanland. Pp. 199–210 in *Archäologie und Altes Testament: Festschrift für Kurt Galling*, eds. A. Kuschke and E. Kutsch. Tübingen: J. C. B. Mohr.

Plöger, O.
1955   Hyrkan im Ostjordanland. *Zeitschrift des Deutschen Palästina-Vereins* 71: 70–81.

Sauer, J. A.
  1973   *Hesbon Pottery 1971.* Andrews University Monographs 7. Berrien
            Springs, MI: Andrews University.

Saulcy, L. F. de
  1865   *Voyage en Terre Sainte.* Paris: Didier.

Vaux, R. de
  1961   Les fouilles de Tell El-Far'ah: Rapport préliminaire sur les 7e, 8e, 9e
            campagnes, 1958–1960. *Revue Biblique* 68: 557–92.

Vogüé, C. J. M. de
  1864   Ruines d'Araq el-Emir. *Revue Archeologique* 10: 52–62.

Will, E.
  1977   L'édifice dit Qasr el Abd à 'Iraq al Amir (Jordanie). *Comptes rendus de
            l'Académie des Inscriptions & Belles-Lettres* 1977: 69–85.
  1979a   Recherches au Qasr el-'Abd à 'Iraq al-Amir. *Annual of the Department
            of Antiquities of Jordan* 23: 139–49.
  1979b   Araq al-Amir (1976–1978). Chronique Archéologique, *Revue Biblique* 86:
            117–19.
  1982   Iraq el Amir. *Le Monde de la Bible* 22: 12–19.
  1983   The Recent French Work at Araq el-Emir: The Qasr el-Abd Redis-
            covered. Pp. 149–54 in *The Excavations at Araq el-Emir.* Vol. 1, ed. N. L.
            Lapp. Annual of the American Schools of Oriental Research 47. Phila-
            delphia: American Schools of Oriental Research.

III. SELECTED TOPICS IN ARCHAEOLOGY AND BIBLICAL INTERPRETATION

Chapter 13

BAB EDH-DHRA AND THE ORIGIN OF THE SODOM SAGA

Walter E. Rast

Valparaiso University

Introduction

At least from the time of Kraetzschmar's article (1897) Old Testament scholarship has reckoned with the possibility that aspects of the Sodom tradition considerably predate the age of Israel and that they were taken over by the latter only at a later time. Kraetzschmar's study made clear that any consideration of Sodom and the related site of Gomorrah runs up against the difficulties of the texts about these cities. Alongside this is the further problem of what degree of reality (*Wirklichkeit*), if any, may be suggested by this distant tradition. These two problems—the classification of the accounts and the type of reality reflected—are the main ones around which discussion has revolved.

The present article, dedicated to the memory of Glenn Rose, who was himself very interested in issues relating to biblical texts and archaeology, tries to attack the subject in something of a fresh way by dealing with the double-sided cluster of biblical texts and archaeological materials from the Dead Sea region. Because these two differing sets of data are employed, a small part of the discussion below deals with a methodology of interrelationships. At the outset it should be stated that the perspective on the texts adopted here rejects an understanding which overlooks their sagalike representation (Gunkel 1917: 78). The theme of Sodom's destruction was a popular, floating one which came into the Old Testament in different forms—by means of narrative (Gen. 13, cont. in 19, and Gen. 14) and as an element in the judgments of the prophets (references below). What was represented was often not historical but rather theological or social in its intent. On the other hand, it will be proposed below that encapsuled in the formula of two cities experiencing memorable destruction was a fragment of local recollection of great importance for the history of the occupation in the Dead Sea region.

Views on the Impossibility of Locating the Cities

Although commentators often seem to assume a degree of clarity behind the texts about Sodom, a common presupposition which appears to be present is that any traces of sites with which the tradition may be associated are beyond hope of being established. Consequently, it is important to look first at a number of approaches to the texts, which seem to end up at a similar conclusion on this problem.

One way of dealing with these texts is to view them as creations of storytellers. Depending on the amount of creativity attributed to the storyteller, interpreters may differ on the degree of reality which they may take to be presupposed. In assigning Genesis 19 to his category of *Märchen*, Gunkel seems to have envisioned little that was real behind this particular text (Gunkel 1917: 80). Irvin has introduced the term "tale" and has described the narrative account of Sodom as a "remarkable origin-story" (Irvin 1978: 23), but she does imply some remote reality behind the account by arguing that it emanated from the wasteland on the north side of the Dead Sea. Gaster saw the main motif as being the submergence of the cities and cited parallels from many other contexts in coming to his conclusion that it is a "purely mythical tale" (Gaster 1961: 157–58, 161). Yet it has to be asked whether the acknowledged features of story wholly eliminate an intersection with experienced reality at some points, a matter to be taken up below.

A second approach attempts to coordinate the texts about Sodom with conclusions regarding the geology of the Dead Sea basin. According to this view, the cities may have existed at one time but were buried, either gradually through a rising water level or by major cataclysm. The inundation theory (Blanckenhorn 1896: 51–59; Albright 1935: 135–36; Neev and Emery 1967: 30) would suggest that remnants of the destroyed cities are submerged below the Dead Sea and, for that reason, are probably mostly irrecoverable. One underwater expedition was devoted to exploring below the surface of the southern basin but failed to produce substantive data (Baney 1962).

A different version of the geologically influenced disappearance of the cities is that they were the victims of massive tectonic activity which left them forever concealed from view. Wallis (1966: 145) has written recently of Sodom: "Already in the dim, distant past the city had completely disappeared from the face of the earth, its precise location being known no more." Some of the geologic interpretations imply a burial below the present land surface, although it is not always clear whether those holding to a cataclysmic interpretation are thinking of deposition beneath the sea or the land or both (Clapp 1936: 339–43).

A third approach can be said to be based on the theological assertions of the texts. According to this view, traces of the cities are beyond recovery, not

because such cities may never have existed but because they were so successfully exterminated that even entertaining the possibility that something of
them may have survived is, in a sense, to assault the biblical texts and their
message. The geologist Blanckenhorn, although devoting himself to the problem where the cities might once have been located, could nevertheless conclude: "For these accursed cities, according to the book of Genesis, should have
been so totally destroyed that not the slightest trace would have remained,
only a place of horror" (Blanckenhorn 1896: 56). An editorial in the *New York
Times*, following the claims of the 1924 expedition to have solved the problems
of Sodom and Gomorrah (Albright 1935: 134–37), also expressed this
viewpoint:

> According to the only accounts we have of those cities, they well deserved the
> destruction that came upon them, and, having been punished adequately for
> their sins, they well might be allowed to remain in the forgetfulness into which
> they fell. There is no chance that their remains, if any, would make for
> edification or light (*New York Times*, March 29, 1924, p. 14, col. 6).

These different approaches converge on the question of the possibility of
establishing specific connections for the ancient sites and thus also of locating
the texts. The more or less negative result in that respect, however, stands in
tension with speculations by various interpreters on where the cities once
were—north or south of the Dead Sea, buried below the sea or beneath massive
earth convulsions. Even those whose approach is mostly restricted to a literary
study of the texts nonetheless tend to express their preferences for a general
location for the cities. Thus Van Seters, whose contribution falls into the
category of a literary treatment, notes his acceptance of a northerly location for
Admah and Zeboiim and a southerly one for Sodom and Gomorrah (1975: 117).
It seems therefore that, despite the skepticism which arises as a result of all
these approaches and which, it should be said, needs to be taken seriously, there
remains a natural interest in the genesis of this unusual tradition.

A Methodology for Relating Texts and Sites

In order to move the discussion toward the main proposals of this study, it
is necessary to state several preliminaries on the approach assumed here and
the methodology employed. First, it should be evident that proof in an absolute
sense is not being claimed in the discussions below. The position taken here is
the impossibility of absolute proof in any area of investigation and human
reasoning. (This essay has profited greatly from the issues on proof raised by
Douglas R. Hofstadter [1979: esp. 192–193]). One "proves" something by means
of a string of reasoning which has its own inner consistency of moving from
prior statement through argument to conclusion. In the case here, the matter to
be "proved" is the juxtaposition of the texts under discussion and newly

acquired data from the southeastern Dead Sea plain as indicating the same reality.

Methodologically, the proposals made in this study are based on a principle important for the texts under consideration but which could well be applied to other cases. This is that texts, rather than being seen as a different set of material evidence over against archaeological data, are themselves archaeologically contexted. This is no less so for biblical texts despite the fact that they have survived through a complicated transmission process which also involves their status in religious communities. Indeed most ancient texts we possess today have been dug from the earth. The fact that biblical texts, apart from examples like the Qumran scrolls, have not come from such a primary context is due to such contingencies as the perishable material on which they were written. Were we to discover fragments or larger sections of biblical texts in original context, we would no doubt become more conscious of this dimension of the copies we now possess and would probably go at the problem of the relation of archaeology and biblical texts in a different manner.

If biblical texts are so understood, this would mean that they reflect the same spectrum of social, political, economic, and religious forces as other sets of evidence. The unique feature in the case of biblical texts as we now have them, however, is that they are out of primary context, distanced from the site, region, or location with which they are concerned. This can be accounted for by the fact that people who record texts have the freedom to move, so that the process of recording or reflecting can be done away from the site of primary context both in a spatial and in a temporal sense.

An important example of displacement from original location is what is commonly called oral tradition. Although the ramifications cannot be entered into here, it is useful to ask in what manner oral tradition too derives from archaeological context. If, e.g., a text has determinative features of oral literature, then an archaeological approach would have two tasks. One would be to attempt to seek to explain its original locus along with other features of that context; the other would be to trace the processes by which it migrated from there to one or more locations in which its theme was expanded or modified. It seems that much of the discussion about Sodom has groped after these problems but has not been able to sharpen them in respect to procedure and method.

The Sodom Tradition as Non- and Pre-Israelite

The documented form of the Sodom story as we now have it is available in the narratives of the book of Genesis and in the prophets. The first of these has become the object of the largest amount of debate, since it is tied up with the problems of the Israelite patriarchs. Elsewhere I hope to deal with what seems to be evidence that the tradition about Sodom entered Israel during the second part of the Iron Age, quite possibly during the eighth century B.C.E. This means that the secondary context in which it is now found is quite late. The focus of this essay, however, is on what is taken to be an earlier piece of oral tradition about Sodom which had its primary locus in the lower areas of ancient Moab bordering on the Dead Sea.

As was noted previously, it was Kraetzschmar who made the programmatic study which concluded that the Sodom tradition was originally non-Israelite. His conclusion is worth noting:

> From all of this it follows that neither in the case of the narrative of Sodom's termination nor in that of the remaining myths associated with Yahweh are we dealing with basically Hebraic material; rather, these all go back to local Canaanite sagas (Kraetzschmar 1897: 88).

Gunkel (1901: xliii) followed soon after in basically agreeing with this point, stating that "non-Israelite popular sagas from Canaanite locals were available," such as "the saga about the destroyed cities."

More recently several scholars employing history of tradition methods have reached similar conclusions. Noth referred to the fact that among the non-Israelite material taken up into the Pentateuch was "the fundamentally non-Israelite story of Sodom" (Noth 1948: 208). Von Rad did not remark explicitly that the story was non-Israelite, but he did state: "That in the case of the story of Sodom we are dealing with an originally independent saga has long been recognized" (von Rad 1952: 184). Westermann also, while not being specific, implied a non-Israelite origin in commenting that the Sodom story derived from a "local tradition from the region of the Dead Sea" (Westermann 1981: 366). Wallis was explicit in recording that "at the heart of the narrative certainly lies a very old pre-Israelite tradition about the destruction of a city called Sodom" (Wallis 1966: 145). Finally, de Vaux proposed that "there are some traditions originating in Transjordan which have been integrated into the history of Abraham" (de Vaux 1971: 164).

What can be taken as an exception to this consensus was set forth by Van Seters in his study of the Lot-Sodom tradition (1975: 209–26). Van Seters questioned that a pre-Israelite form of the "three heavenly visitors" theme could be established, and he also challenged the general tradition history conclusions of Noth (1948: 167–70) and Kilian (1970), holding that the Sodom narrative was the product of late Israelite crafting. Although Van Seters' date in the exilic period seems extreme, the range of the key word גפרית, "brimstone," elsewhere in the Old Testament does suggest the latter half of the Iron Age, and there also seems to be little to quarrel with in his view that the Lot-Sodom tradition was fundamentally the creation of a single artisan. The only objectionable point is one made on the periphery of his discussion, that the

Israelite author may have used the three visitors theme "to fill out a purely Israelite tradition about divine destruction of Sodom and Gomorrah" (Van Seters 1975: 210). That the theme of the destruction of the cities was a purely Israelite one is put under question by Van Seters' own statement that "it is very unlikely that any of the other references to Sodom and Gomorrah outside of Genesis are in any way dependent on the pentateuchal form of the tradition" (Van Seters 1975: 210 n. 3), since this would make it possible that the prophets and pentateuchal narrative were both dependent on a previously existent form of the tradition.

The non-Israelite provenance of that tradition was reinforced when Kraetzschmar noticed that the formulaic prophetic usages (Amos 4:11; Isa. 13:19; Jer. 49:18; 50:40) were in fact fossilized (*versteinert*) in the texts in which they are found, with the name אלהים tensing the Yahwistic context in which the formulae occur (Kraetzschmar 1897: 87–88). The garbled text of Genesis 19:24, with its double phrases מאת־יהוה and מן־השמים, betrays a similar feature of a Yahwistic writer adapting a fundamentally non-Yahwistic tradition into a new context. On the basis of the emphasis on morning and daylight in Genesis 19, Keel has even made the suggestion that the deity originally involved may have been Shamash (1979).

There is also plausible evidence that the prophetic formulae were taken over in oral form, which might support the pre-Israelite derivation of the tradition. In the first place is the phenomenon of the pair of cities, Sodom and Gomorrah, which constitutes the main element of parallelism in almost all of the prophetic references (Isa. 1:9–10; Jer. 23:14; 49:18; 50:40; Amos 4:11; Zeph. 2:9; cf. Deut. 32:32), the exceptions being Isaiah 3:9, Lamentations 4:6, and Ezekiel 16:46 where only Sodom is mentioned. This phenomenon of paired place names in the Old Testament (2 Sam. 1:20; Isa. 15:2, 4; Joel 3:4) may indicate a feature of oral poetry. Important also is the formula כמהפכת אלהים את־סדם ואת־עמרה ("as when God overthrew Sodom and Gomorrah") which occurs five times in approximately this form (Deut. 29:23; Isa. 13:19; Jer. 49:18; 50:40; Amos 4:11). Its frequent appearance is noteworthy since recurrence has been cited as a piece of "circumstantial evidence" in favor of the oral nature of a formula (Coote 1976: 57). Finally, simile has been noted as a device of oral poetry (Finnegan 1977: 112), and it is interesting that it is in just this manner that the cities are employed in the prophetic threats and judgments.

The Dead Sea Region and Its Remains

When scholarship has turned to the problem of a locus for this tradition, it has usually set its sight on the area around the Dead Sea. There has been little deviation from this, apart from Meyer's curious interpretation that, since the Sodom saga with its description of "brimstone and fire" reflected volcanic activity, its origin must have been Arabia, being only subsequently transferred to the Dead Sea (1906: 71; cf. Keel 1979: 15). For most scholars, however, it has been a question of whether the Dead Sea subarea involved was the north, southwest, south, or southeast (Simons 1959: 222–29; Harland 1942; 1943; Abel 1929). There are strong reasons for connecting the tradition with the Dead Sea, including the reference to this area in Genesis 14:3, the description of the boundaries of Canaan in Genesis 10:19, which suggests a southern perimeter from Gaza due east intersecting with the Dead Sea, and the manner in which the prophetic references are connected with a wasteland suggestive of the Dead Sea area (Westermann 1981: 365). While it is possible that the pair, Admah and Zeboiim, may be related to the region north of the Dead Sea, the view here is that the popular Sodom and Gomorrah couplet sprang from the southeastern end of the Dead Sea basin.

Although the Dead Sea region is recognized as the location with which the basic representations are associated, the common conclusion referred to above, that more specific evidence is beyond possibility of being established, has dominated interpretation. The lack of success of the 1924 expedition to the Dead Sea plain along the southeast (Mallon 1924; Kyle 1924; Albright 1926) seemed to support such a conclusion. Before assessing the data along with Dead Sea which are presently known, however, it is important to ask whether such a conclusion did not result from either a misreading or an overreading of the language and description of the texts.

A term in the Sodom texts which served as a *terminus technicus* in this tradition, but which also seems to have given rise to considerable overinterpretation, is the root הפך ("overthrow"). This word is found in the formulaic utterances of the prophets (Deut. 29:23; Isa. 13:19; Jer. 49:18; 50:40; Amos 4:11), and it also appears in the pentateuchal narrative (Gen. 19:21, 25, 29) where it is coupled with שחת ("destroy") and associated with the motif of "brimstone and fire." A great deal of recent interpretation has rested on this word, and from it have stemmed the various theories of convulsion. Examination of this word shows, however, that it was at home in the language of treaty texts, particularly Neo-Assyrian examples of the eighth and seventh centuries B.C.E., and that it was used with the descriptions of brimstone and fire and of the salting of cities to connote retribution against treaty infringements (Weinfeld 1972: 109–12; Hillers 1964: 74–76). As examples, it appears in a curse in a text from Sefîre in the form of כן יהפכו אלהן אש, "so may the gods overturn that man" (Fitzmyer 1967: 20–21), and again in a curse on the sarcophagus of Ahiram, which reads תהתפך כסאמלכה, "his royal throne shall be overturned" (Donner and Röllig 1966: 1; 1968: 2). We consequently seem to be dealing with the common parlance of treaty curses, which in the case of Genesis 19 is transmuted into story.

The analysis of the language as conventional treaty language thus raises questions about how far the descriptions of Genesis 19 should be pushed in the direction of cataclysmic interpretations. Keel may be correct in comparing such a hybridization of the texts and theories of geologic upheaval to recent attempts to explain biblical events by means of extraterrestrial visits (1979: 11 n. 3). The inclination to introduce accounts of lost or buried cities from other cultures as parallels to the story of Genesis 19 also seems to be based on the misunderstandings of cataclysmic interpretation. Actually, when the language and description are considered more soberly, the closest parallel remains that found in the Old Testament itself, in Judges 19—20. When the question is asked why the theme of the destruction of these cities became so memorable, while that of other cities passed into oblivion, the answer seems to be that representations of the overthrow of Sodom and Gomorrah helped to explain a degenerating environment around the Dead Sea, which became serious in the latter quarter of the third millennium B.C.E. (Harlan 1981: 160).

In considering the work of recent survey and excavation, it can be noted that the last three decades have witnessed an intense activity in almost all the subregions of the Dead Sea. It will be useful to examine the results briefly and to assess their relevance to the problems of explaining the tradition about Sodom.

Beginning with the western shore of the Dead Sea, there are the buildings and caves associated with the discoveries at Qumran dating to the Roman period. To the south of this the 'En Gedi region includes Tel Goren, with an occupation from the very late Iron Age and following (Mazar, Dothan, and Dunayevski 1966: 38), a synagogue dating to the sixth century, and possibly an earlier one from the third century C.E. (Barag, Porat, and Netzer 1981), and the Late Chalcolithic temple complex near Nahal David (Ussishkin 1971; 1980). Again to the south are the ruins of Masada, with primary use in Roman and Byzantine times, and the various cave sites which produced remains from the Roman and Chalcolithic periods (Avigad et al. 1961; 1962). Herodian and Byzantine finds have also appeared at 'En Boqeq (Keel and Küchler 1982: 401). The main periods represented on the western side of the Dead Sea are consequently Late Chalcolithic, Late Iron Age, Persian, Hellenistic, Roman, and Byzantine (Bar-Adon 1972). None of these ruins or the periods they represent helps to explain the Sodom tradition, or offers a primary location for it.

The eastern coastal area of the Dead Sea from the Lisan northward is extremely sparse in any sites whatsoever due to the fact that the mountains here drop almost directly to the sea. Around the hot springs of Wadi Zerqa Ma'in, Herod the Great built the baths of Callirhoe, but very few remains are left (Harding 1959: 77). This is the only site of substantial activity on the eastern side north of Wadi Mojib, while south of Wadi Mojib (Nahal Arnon) evidence for occupation sites appears only from the Lisan southward, with the possible exception of some Byzantine waterworks noted in several wadis just

north of Wadi Ibn Hamad by the recent expedition to the southeastern plain.
The survey of central Moab has recorded many sites of EB and some of MB
date on the east side of the Dead Sea, but their locations all belong to the
plateau and not to the Dead Sea region proper (Miller 1979; oral communication, G. L. Mattingly).

As far as the south end of the Dead Sea and its shallow basin are concerned, it should be noted again that the postulation of ancient remains
indicating that cities once existed where the southern Dead Sea trough now
stands is based on speculation rather than on material evidence. Even assuming
the evidence for the beginning of the infilling of the southern basin "only a few
hundred years ago" (Neev and Hall 1977: 4), the delineation of settlement
patterns by the recent expedition to the southeastern plain has shown that the
natural sites chosen for occupation in antiquity were not in the flat plain itself
but were on flanking, slightly elevated areas (Rast and Schaub 1974: 6–13).
These patternings also suggest that, if the southern basin was an area of open
flatbed in ancient times, it would have served mostly for cultivation rather than
for settlement, with small satellite farmsteads being occasionally in the fan
areas themselves (McConaughy 1981: 190). Regarding the problem of changes
in the southern level, Klein's research has suggested a minimal impact from
tectonic activity during historical times, with any shifts being attributable
rather to climatological changes (Klein 1965: 27). Thus the popular tendency to
theorize about ancient cities being buried beneath the southern basin lacks
either archaeological or geologic support.

As has long been known, the southeastern basin, beginning at the northern
end of the Lisan peninsula and continuing south to the Wadi Hasa (Nahal
Zered), offered highly suitable conditions for settlement. Its alluvial fans and
resources for irrigation (Donahue 1981: 140–41; Harlan 1981: 155–59) encouraged heavy occupation during a number of archaeological periods. Survey
and excavation have shown that, corresponding to the western shoreline, there
was settlement during the Late Chalcolithic period (McCreery 1977–78: 157–
61), while the Early Bronze Age, as will be seen, witnessed some of the most
intensive use of the region. Although occasional MB sherds have been discovered at Tell es-Safi (Sauer 1982: 81), and one sherd of this period was found
at Bab edh-Dhra, the MB period was not one of expansive settlement in the
southeastern plain. Evidence suggests rather a mostly unsettled area between
the end of the Early Bronze Age and the second part of the Iron Age (Rast and
Schaub 1974: 16–17). Finally, the Late Roman, Byzantine, Arabic, and Cru-
sader periods all experienced substantial occupation of the region, the most
prominent being during the Byzantine period (McCreery 1977–78: 159).

The period which stands out in this survey of the Dead Sea region as a
whole is that of the Early Bronze Age, so well-attested along the southeast but
entirely absent on the western side. This fact may not be without importance in

light of the earlier discussion of the originally non-Israelite character of the Sodom tradition. The EB period suggests itself in relation to the latter not only because all other periods represented in the Dead Sea region are either too early or too late for consideration but also because the ruins and remains from these other periods lack any features for a compelling correlation. It is thus to the Early Bronze Age that we must look in attempting to identify the primary locus for the Sodom tradition.

EB III and the Sodom Tradition

In the recent excavations which have taken place along the southeastern Dead Sea plain (Lapp 1968; 1970; Rast and Schaub 1978: 1980; 1981), two EB III walled settlements have been uncovered. Known at present only by their Arabic names of Bab edh-Dhra and Numeira, neither of which seems to be of great age, these two sites are closely interrelated by means of a linear pattern of site location along the southeastern edge of the Dead Sea, Numeira being approximately 15 km. south of Bab edh-Dhra. Of the two settlements, Bab edh-Dhra was the larger, and cross-connections between the two, as are being established by study of apparently shared artifacts, suggest that Numeira may have been colonized at some point in EB III by settlers from the older site of Bab edh-Dhra. The time during which these towns coexisted is fixed by the short-lived occupation at Numeira, which lasted probably not much longer than a century and a half during the latter part of EB III. Bab edh-Dhra, on the other hand, was occupied continuously from the beginning of the Early Bronze Age into the phase which followed the demise of the town, that is, EB IV. Thus for a period of about one hundred and fifty years, from c. 2500 to 2350 B.C.E., the southeastern plain witnessed a thriving civilization with Bab edh-Dhra being, no doubt, the dominant town.

These two towns also seem to have participated in a common fate, since ceramic evidence from carbon-14 tests have shown that they were terminated at approximately the same time toward the end of EB III (Rast and Schaub 1980: 46–47). At Numeira the evidence is extensive that the town was burned during its last major phase, while the destruction of the EB III walled town at Bab edh-Dhra is attested by ruined and abandoned structures and by the demolished upper part of the town wall, the superstructure of which, made of mudbrick in some cases, had suffered exposure to fire (Rast and Schaub 1981: 16–18).

The destruction of these towns in the southeastern plain did not occur in isolation but must be viewed in relation to the broader conditions of the latter part of EB III in the whole of ancient Palestine. Evidence of a pattern of widespread destruction and abandonment is present at a large number of EB III sites. Research on this period is still at work in attempting to explain the different factors, but environmental degeneration, local natural disturbances, and attacks against the towns by hostile forces all seem to be implicated in one way or another. From an archaeological point of view this period witnessed one of the most sweeping disruptions in the history of ancient Palestine (Kenyon 1960: 134; Wright 1961: 86).

Given the large and apparently thriving population of ancient Palestine in EB III, the breakdown of the EB civilization must have had a memorable impact. On the one hand, it seems that, had the population of this period possessed the means for doing so, it may have left written evidence of these events, as happened in the case of similar crises in Mesopotamia and Egypt in roughly the same time period. On the other hand, although the absence of a writing system made such documentation impossible, it is probable that some ties with events of such proportion were secured by oral tradition. The south-eastern plain and areas flanking it on the eastern side would have been a prime location in which visitors to the mostly abandoned area could have maintained some relation to these increasingly distanced events. Even when the particulars were no longer remembered, the visible ruins of the sites, still present in our own century, stood there to evoke an explanation.

When the archaeological data along the southeastern Dead Sea are placed next to the textual material discussed above, a noteworthy isomorphism appears. A pair of destroyed cities emerges in an area distinctly non-Israelite and belonging to a period considerably before the time of ancient Israel. If this isomorphism is taken as the key, it suggests an alternative explanation for the origin of the Sodom saga. This would be that the biblical representations belong to the last bit of fallout from one of the most serious disturbances experienced by the populations of this region. Neither the non-Israelite transmitters who passed on this tradition to the israelites nor the Israelites themselves were in firm possession of details about that destruction, so that, in Israel, the events could be simultaneously attributed to a rain of "brimstone and fire" (Gen. 19) and an onslaught by a league of foreign kings (Gen. 14:1–11) or referred to simply as an "overthrow" in the prophetic form of the tradition. Integral to the tradition, however, was the interpretation that the cities were destroyed at the behest of the divine world and that in the process the entire area became devastated.

A significant feature of the tradition, as it was transmitted, was the names of the two cities, Sodom and Gomorrah, the meanings of which have remained obscure despite attempts to explain them (Borée 1930: 27, 39). The recent discovery that the first of these names may be approximated in the texts from Tell Mardikh (Ebla) is important as a possible piece of relevant evidence, apart from whether the location mentioned there has anything to do with Trans-jordan to the south (Archi 1979: 562–64; Dahood 1981: 287). As a third mil-lennium B.C.E. place name, it provides some support for the proposal here that the name Sodom was at one time connected with the EB III town which existed at Bab edh-Dhra, while the name Gomorrah was associated with the related walled settlement of Numeira in the same period. The importance of this is that it would be from these two specific sites, still partly visible today and uncovered in part by excavation, that the tradition arose which passed into the Old Testament.

Conclusions

Westermann has noted that, if the Sodom tradition is to be properly understood, its central element must be seen to be a catastrophe involving cities presumably by the Dead Sea. He made the point against Gunkel's interpretation of Genesis 19 as an aetiology for the wasteland of the Dead Sea region (Westermann 1981: 362; cf. Rudin-O'Brasky 1982: 128). In other words, the harsh environment of the Dead Sea did not bring about the creation of stories of destroyed cities, but rather a tradition of destroyed cities led to further interpretation regarding the general environment of the Dead Sea. This point puts under question an interpretation which would view the basic theme of the destruction of the cities as a fiction.

The results of the present study are in agreement with this point, and to it can be added that we may now know something rather specific about the cities which suffered catastrophe and the conditions out of which this tradition emerged. The conclusion here is that, from a primary locus of two EB III sites along the southeastern Dead Sea plain in Transjordan, a tradition of a pair of destroyed cities was generated. In the course of time this tradition migrated westward to become the possession of Israelites for whom it served as a paradigm mostly of divine judgment. Its main theme of the destruction of two cities was fluid enough to be used in a variety of contexts.

In connection with this broad availability of the theme in ancient Israel, the results of this study also support the interpretation that the expansion of the number of cities represented from two to four (Deut. 29:23) or five (Gen. 14:2) characterizes the latest and not the earliest development (Schatz 1972: 175–77, 267; Freedman 1978: 152–55; Van Hattem 1981: 90), so that the notion of a pentapolis does not belong to the original form of the tradition. The most recent visits to the sites of Tell es-Safi, Feifeh, and Khanazir in the southeastern plain seem to support this, since it is doubtful that correlative EB III data are present, although material remains from EB I are abundant at es-Safi and Feifeh (Rast and Schaub 1974: 15–18). In making several helpful suggestions for the present article, my colleague, Thomas Schaub, commented that only excavation can really settle the question of phases at these sites, and with that point, of course, I agree. At the same time, it should be said that even though

Genesis 14 is apparently a late document, its composers showed their awareness of the antiquity of the Sodom tradition in situating their narrative in an archaic setting, one which uncannily suggests the third millennium B.C.E.

In sum, then, the parallel sets of texts and site-based remains which have been considered here are enough to suggest that the Sodom tradition may well be a palimpsest through which is refracted a remnant of experience from the latter part of the Early Bronze Age. If this is so, such results are illuminating alike for biblical studies and the archaeological history of the land.

BIBLIOGRAPHY

Abel, F. M.
1929   Notes complémentaires sur la Mer Morte. *Revue Biblique* 38: 237–60.

Albright, W. F.
1926   The Jordan Valley in the Bronze Age. *Annual of the American Schools of Oriental Research* 6: 13–74.
1935   *The Archaeology of Palestine and the Bible.* Third edition. New York: Fleming H. Revell.

Archi, A.
1979   The Epigraphic Evidence from Ebla and the Old Testament. *Biblica* 60: 555–66.

Avigad, N. et al.
1961   The Expedition to the Judean Desert, 1960. *Israel Exploration Journal* 11: 3–52.
1962   The Expedition to the Judean Desert, 1961. *Israel Exploration Journal* 12: 167–262.

Baney, R. E.
1962   *Search for Sodom and Gomorrah.* Kansas City: CAM.

Bar-Adon, P.
1972   Survey of the Judaean Wilderness and the Jericho Plain. Pp. 91–149 in *Judaea, Samaria and the Golan: Archaeological Survey 1967–1968,* ed. M. Kochavi. Jerusalem: Carta (Hebrew).

Barag, D., Porat, Y., and Netzer, E.
1981   The Synagogue at 'En-Gedi. Pp. 116–19 in *Ancient Synagogues Revealed,* ed. L. I. Levine. Jerusalem: Israel Exploration Society.

Blanckenhorn, M.
1896   Entstehung und Geschichte des Todten Meeres. *Zeitschrift des Deutschen Palästina-Vereins* 19: 1–59.

Borée, W.
1930   *Die Alten Ortsnamen Palästinas.* Staatliche Forschungsinstitute bei Universität Leipzig. Leipzig: Eduard Pfeiffer.

Clapp, F. G.
1936   The Site of Sodom and Gomorrah. *American Journal of Archaeology* 40: 323–44.

Coote, R. B.
1976   The Application of the Oral Theory to Biblical Hebrew Literature. *Semeia* 5: 51–64.

Dahood, M.
1981   Ebla, Ugarit, and the Bible. Pp. 271–302 in G. Pettinato, *The Archives of Ebla: An Empire Inscribed in Clay.* Garden City, NY: Doubleday.

Donahue, J.
1981   Geologic Investigations at Early Bronze Sites. *Annual of the American Schools of Oriental Research* 46: 137–54.

Donner, H., and Röllig, W.
1966   *Kanaanäische und Aramäische Inschriften* 1. Texte. Second edition. Wiesbaden: Harrassowitz.
1968   *Kanaanäische und Aramäische Inschriften* 1. Kommentar. Second edition. Wiesbaden: Harrassowitz.

Finnegan, R. H.
1977   *Oral Poetry: Its Nature, Significance and Social Context.* Cambridge: Cambridge University.

Fitzmyer, J. A.
1967   *The Aramaic Inscriptions of Sefîre.* Biblica et Orientalia 19. Rome: Pontifical Biblical Institute.

Freedman, D. N.
1978   The Real Story of the Ebla Tablets: Ebla and the Cities of the Plain. *Biblical Archaeologist* 41: 143–64.

Gaster, T. H.
1969   *Myth, Legend, and Custom in the Old Testament.* New York: Harper & Row.

Gunkel, H.
1901   *Genesis.* Handkommentar zum Alten Testament I/1. Göttingen: Vandenhoeck & Ruprecht.
1917   *Das Märchen im Alten Testament.* Religionsgeschichtliche Volksbücher. Tübingen: J. C. B. Mohr.

Harding, G. L.
1959   *The Antiquities of Jordan.* London: Lutterworth.

Harlan, J. R.
1981   Natural Resources of the Southern Ghor. *Annual of the American Schools of Oriental Research* 46: 155–64.

Harland, J. P.
1942   Sodom and Gomorrah: The Location of the cities of the Plain. *Biblical Archaeologist* 5: 17–32.
1943   Sodom and Gomorrah: II. The Destruction of the Cities of the Plain. *Biblical Archaeologist* 6: 41–54.

Hillers, D. R.
1964   *Treaty-Curses and the Old Testament Prophets.* Biblica et Orientalia 16. Rome: Pontifical Biblical Institute.

Hofstadter, D. R.
    1979   *Gödel, Escher, Bach: An Eternal Golden Braid.* Vintage Books. New York: Random House.

Irvin, D.
    1978   *Mytharion: The Comparison of Tales from the Old Testament and the Ancient Near East.* Alter Orient und Altes Testament 32. Neukirchen-Vluyn: Neukirchener.

Keel, O.
    1979   Wer Zerstörte Sodom? *Theologische Zeitschrift* 35: 10–17.

Keel, O., and Küchler, M.
    1982   *Orte und Landschaften der Bibel: Ein Handbuch und Studienreiseführer zum Heiligen Land* 2. Der Süden. Zürich: Benziger.

Kenyon, K. M.
    1960   *Archaeology in the Holy Land.* New York: Praeger.

Kilian, R.
    1970   Zur Überlieferungsgeschichte Lots. *Biblische Zeitschrift* 14: 23–37.

Klein, C.
    1965   *On the Fluctuations of the Level of the Dead Sea Since the Beginning of the 19th Century.* Hydrological Paper No. 7. Jerusalem: Ministry of Agriculture-Water Commission, Hydrological Service.

Kraetzschmar, R.
    1897   Der Mythus von Sodoms Ende. *Zeitschrift für die alttestamentliche Wissenschaft* 17: 81–92.

Kyle, M. G.
    1924   The Story of Ancient Sodom in the Light of Modern Science. *Bibliotheca Sacra* 81: 262–91.

Lapp, P. W.
    1968   Bâb edh-Dhrâ', Perizzites and Emim. Pp. 1–25 in *Jerusalem Through the Ages: The Twenty-fifth Archaeological Convention,* October 1967. Jerusalem: Israel Exploration Society.
    1970   Palestine in the Early Bronze Age. Pp. 101–31 in *Near Eastern Archaeology in the Twentieth Century: Essays in Honor of Nelson Glueck,* ed. J. A. Sanders. Garden City, NY: Doubleday.

McConaughy, M. A.
    1981   A Preliminary Report on the Bab edh-Dhra Site Survey. *Annual of the American Schools of Oriental Research* 46: 187–90.

McCreery, D. W.
    1977–78   Preliminary Report of the A. P. C. Township Archaeological Survey. *Annual of the Department of Antiquities of Jordan* 22: 150–62.

Mallon, A.
    1924   Voyage d'exploration au sud-est de la Mer Morte. *Biblica* 5: 413–55.

Mazar, B., Dothan, T., and Dunayevski, I.
    1966   *En-Gedi: The First and Second Seasons of Excavations 1961–1962.* 'Atiqot 5 (English Series). Jerusalem: Department of Antiquities.

Meyer, E.
1906   *Die Israeliten und ihre Nachbarstämme.* Halle: Max Niemeyer.

Miller, J. M.
1979   Archaeological Survey of Central Moab: 1978. *Bulletin of the American Schools of Oriental Research* 234: 43–52.

Neev, D. and Emery, K. O.
1967   *The Dead Sea: Depositional Processes and Environments of Evaporites.* Ministry of Development-Geological Survey, Bulletin No. 41. Jerusalem: Geological Survey of Israel.

Neev, D. and Hall, J. K.
1977   *Climactic Fluctuations During the Holocene as Reflected by the Dead Sea Levels.* Preprint International Conference on Terminal Lakes, Weber State College, Ogden, Utah. Jerusalem: Geological Survey of Israel.

Noth, M.
1948   *Überlieferungsgeschichte des Pentateuch.* Second edition. Stuttgart: W. Kohlhammer.

Rad, G. von
1952   *Das Erste Buch Mose.* Das Alte Testament Deutsch, Teilband 3. Göttingen: Vandenhoeck & Ruprecht.

Rast, W. E. and Schaub, R. T.
1974   Survey of the Southeastern Plain of the Dead Sea, 1973. *Annual of the Department of Antiquities of Jordan* 19: 5–53.
1978   A Preliminary Report of Excavations at Bâb edh-Dhrâ', 1975. *Annual of the American Schools of Oriental Research* 43: 1–32.

Rast, W. E. and Schaub, R. T., eds.
1980   Preliminary Report of the 1979 Expedition to the Dead Sea Plain, Jordan. *Bulletin of the American Schools of Oriental Research* 240: 21–61.
1981   *The Southeastern Dead Sea Plain Expedition: An Interim Report of the 1977 Season.* Annual of the American Schools of Oriental Research 46.

Rudin-O'Brasky, T.
1982   *The Patriarchs in Hebron and Sodom (Genesis 18—19): A Study of the Structure and Composition of a Biblical Story.* Jerusalem: Simor (Hebrew).

Sauer, J. A.
1982   Prospects for Archaeology in Jordan and Syria. *Biblical Archaeologist* 45: 73–84.

Schatz, J. A.
1972   *Genesis 14: Eine Untersuchung.* Europäische Hochschulschriften, Series 23: Theology 2. Bern: Herbert Lang.

Simons, J.
1959   *The Geographical and Topographical Texts of the Old Testament.* Studia Fransisci Scholten memoriae dicata 2. Leiden: E. J. Brill.

Ussishkin, D.
1971   The "Ghassulian" Temple in Ein Gedi and the Origin of the Hoard from Nahal Mishmar. *Biblical Archaeologist* 34: 23–29.
1980   The Ghassulian Shrine at En-Gedi. *Tel Aviv* 7: 1–44.

Van Hattem, W. C.
1981   Once Again: Sodom and Gomorrah. *Biblical Archaeologist* 44: 87–92.

Van Seters, J.
1975   *Abraham in History and Tradition*. New Haven: Yale University.

Vaux, R. de
1971   *Histoire ancienne d'Israël: des origines à l'installation en Canaan.*
            Etudes Bibliques. Paris: J. Gabalda.

Wallis, G.
1966   Die Stadt in den Überlieferungen der Genesis. *Zeitschrift für die alttesta-*
            mentliche Wissenschaft 78: 133–48.

Weinfeld, M.
1972   *Deuteronomy and the Deuteronomic School*. Oxford: Clarendon.

Westermann, C.
1981   *Genesis. Biblischer Kommentar Altes Testament* I/2. Neukirchen-
            Vluyn: Neukirchener.

Wright, G. E.
1961   The Archaeology of Palestine. Pp. 73–112 in *The Bible and the Ancient*
            Near East: Essays in Honor of W. F. Albright, ed. G. E. Wright. London:
            Routledge & Kegan Paul.

Chapter 14

UNDERGROUND WATER SYSTEMS IN ERETZ-ISRAEL IN THE IRON AGE

Yigal Shiloh
Institute of Archaeology
Hebrew University

The regular supply of water, whether in days of peace or in time of war, has always presented a primary challenge to the planners and builders of royal centers in the Near East. The proper exploitation of water sources—their catchment, storage, and distribution—determines the standard of living of the populace in this generally semiarid region. The more water resources are developed, the more developed and productive is agriculture. The developing of water resources leads in turn to a strengthening of commerce and the economy and to an increase in population. Such development was especially essential in bolstering settlements and, particularly, royal centers in preparation for war and siege. In a survey of the utilization of water sources in Eretz-Israel, clear evidence was found that an active approach toward development typifies those cultures which led to flourishing periods: the Iron Age, the Early Roman period, the Byzantine period, and recent times. In other periods, when there was a decided drop in settlement and in central authority, there was also a rather passive attitude toward development of water resources, with a corresponding total reliance upon available sources and no special engineering efforts in that direction.

One of the most important factors dictating the situation of large settlements in Eretz-Israel, beginning with urbanization in the third millennium B.C.E., was the proximity of a water source. During the course of the Bronze Age we find evidence of the construction of reservoirs (some subterranean) and pools for rain water within the fortified areas of towns. Such are found at Arad (Amiran 1977: 239–40; 1978: 13–14; 1980: 34), Ai (Callaway 1970: 29–30), Hazor, and Taanach.[1] These water systems were an efficient public development of the method of storing water in cisterns, common in Eretz-Israel but outside the scope of our present discussion. The water systems discovered at the royal centers and in the settlements of the Iron Age II in Eretz-Israel are the earliest example of positive engineering activity within the framework of overall urban planning, serving therein as an essential component.

In the Bible there is considerable evidence of the practical knowledge amassed by the inhabitants of Eretz-Israel and of their ability to distinguish among the various types of water sources and to utilize them: e.g., the basic difference between a regular supply—fed by flowing streams, such as those in Mesopotamia (Isa. 8:7), or from seasonal flooding of the Nile in Egypt (Exod. 7:19, 24; Isa. 19:5-9)—and dependence upon the quantity of rainfall as a guarantee of a successful crop (Lev. 26:4-5; Deut. 11:10-11, 14, 17; 1 Kings 8:35; Isa. 30:23); streams (Deut. 8:7); floods (2 Kings 3:17); pools (gēbîm; 2 Kings 3:16); dew (Gen. 27:28); springs (Deut. 8:7); wells (Gen. 21:25); and cisterns (Deut. 6:11; 2 Sam. 2:13; 1 Kings 22:38; 2 Kings 18:31; Isa. 22:9, 11). Several artificial underground water systems also find mention in the Bible, particularly those in Jerusalem (2 Kings 20:20; 2 Chron. 32:30; Isa. 22:9, 11). These constructed water systems, much in evidence among the archaeological discoveries, are the subject of our present discussion.

Though these water systems are quite impressive in their planning and execution, till now they have been the subject of very few comprehensive reviews. The water systems themselves have been treated by their excavators on the various sites—Megiddo, Hazor, Gezer, Ibleam, Gibeon, Beer-sheba and Jerusalem. The summary by Ruth Amiran (1951) was the first to treat the group as a whole, and it has only recently been superseded by the work of the present author (Shiloh 1972) and that of D. Cole (1980; cf. Pritchard 1961: 12-14).

Review of the Remains (cf. tables 3,4,5)

Megiddo (fig. 29)

There are two springs adjacent to Megiddo: the northern spring, 'Ain el-Qubi (Lamon 1935: 1-2), and the spring at the southwestern corner of the mound, to which the city's water system was connected (L. 925). The investigation of another water installation (L. 2153) adjacent to the city gate began in 1967 (cf. Yadin 1967: 121; 1972: 164).

The schematic plans accompanying this article were drawn by Gary Lipowitz (Lipton), except no. 35 by Wolfgang Schleicher, and were prepared on the basis of the excavators' plans so as to show all the components of the water systems, though this has occasionally led to slight graphic inaccuracies. The legend to all the plans is as follows: (1) City Fortifications, (2) Entrance Structure, (3) Supporting Walls, (4) Shaft, (5) Stepped Tunnel, (6) Horizontal Tunnel, (7) Vertical Shaft, (8) Water Chamber, (9) Spring, (10) Gathering and Feeder Conduit, and (11) Tunnel/Channel, and (12) Reservoir.

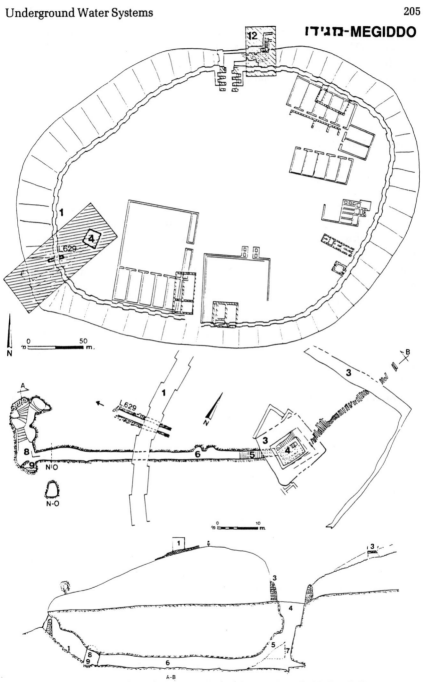

Fig. 29. Megiddo (after Yadin 1972: 221; and Lamon 1935, figs. 2–3).

The Water System (L. 925). The principal water system of Megiddo was investigated by the Chicago Oriental Institute expedition (Lamon 1935) and by the Hebrew University expedition in 1960–70 (Yadin 1972: 161–164). These investigators noted several stages in its functioning:

(1) The spring served in the ordinary manner as a source of water at the base of the mound beyond the fortified area.

(2) The earliest water system, Gallery 629, was constructed by fine ashlar masonry (Lamon 1935: 10–12, fig. 8) and was integrated into the city fortifications of Strata VA–IVB. From its passage through the defenses, it continued along a stairway to the spring. This system was unsatisfactory for securing the water source in time of war.

(3) The major change in the planning of the water system of Megiddo came about in Stratum IVA. Gallery 629 was blocked by the construction of the inset-and-offset wall (325), and a shaft protected by supporting walls was driven down through earlier strata and then hewn to a total depth of 36 m. below the level of the mound's surface. Steps were hewn around the walls of the shaft, leading to the opening of a stepped tunnel and in turn giving access to a horizontal tunnel running about 50 m. to the spring. The natural, external opening to the spring was then blocked up with a massive wall.

(4) At this stage the water system was further improved: the level of the tunnel at its inner end was lowered and the stepped section was removed up to the base of the shaft. Now the water could flow freely from the spring inward to the very base of the shaft where it could be drawn up directly by the inhabitants rather than having to be hauled up through the long tunnel, as in stage (3).

(5) For reasons unclear to us, this phase reverted to the original method of stage (3). Steps were built down to the base of the shift on a new fill.

(6) It can be assumed that the water system served the royal Israelite center at Megiddo up to the destruction of the Northern Kingdom by the Assyrians in the eighth century B.C.E. The large depression formed on its site after its neglect—after it had partially filled with debris—served as a reservoir for runoff, providing water for the city in its final stages.[2]

The Water System and the City Plan. Gallery 629 was well integrated into the new town plan of Strata VA–IVB. It is integrated into the casemate wall like the other public structures built in the peripheral belt of the mound, Palaces 6000 and 1729 and Gate 2156, and, like them, is made of ashlar construction (Shiloh 1979b: 52–55).

The principal water system of Megiddo is one of the new components in the overall planning of Megiddo in Stratum IVA. Its construction necessitated the confiscation of considerable private dwelling areas for public use, as did construction of the northern and southern stables (Shiloh 1979b, figs. 72,73).

Dating. The relative sequence of the several phases of the water system was determined by the Chicago Expedition (Lamon 1935: 36–37). The Hebrew University expedition reexamined the stratigraphical aspect and was able to determine the proper stratigraphical-architectural sequence of the Iron Age on the site, including that of the water system (Yadin 1972: 150–64).

Phase (2), Gallery 629, belongs to Strata VA–IVB, of the tenth century B.C.E. (i.e., Solomon). Phase (3) was part of the replanning of the city in Stratum IVA, the ninth century B.C.E. (i.e., Ahab). There is insufficient data for the dating of phases (4)–(5), though it can be assumed that they were in use sometime during Iron II. The final "reservoir" served the settlement of Stratum I in the Persian period and possibly also the preceding Stratum II (Lamon 1935, fig. 29).

The Northern Water System: The Reservoir on the North of the Mound (L. 2153). During the investigations of the Hebrew University expedition in 1967 (Yadin 1972: 164; 1967: 121), it became evident that structure 2153, previously defined by the Chicago expedition as a pedestrian passageway alongside the city gate (Loud 1948: 57), was actually a stairway leading apparently to a large reservoir built within the lower terrace of the city.

Hazor (fig. 30)

The Water System. The water system of Hazor was uncovered in 1968 by the Hebrew University expedition under Y. Yadin and the present author (Yadin 1969b: 14–19; 1972: 177–78; 1975: 233–47). The water source is visible south of the upper mound in Nahal Hazor. During clearance of the water system special attention was paid to the planning details and the stratigraphic relationship between its various components and the town-planning around it in an attempt to determine its precise date. The water system in Area L was hewn alongside the wall of the upper city above the region of the springs. Four components could be distinguished: (1) an entrance structure; (2) a rock-hewn shaft; (3) a stepped tunnel; and (4) a water chamber.

The builders of this water system initially dug through the accumulation of earlier strata, from the Bronze Age to Stratum X, down to bedrock. The entrance structure consisted of two elongated spaces connecting the occupation level of the Israelite city and the beginning of the stairway descending around the rock-hewn shaft down to the beginning of the stepped tunnel. The latter tunnel, 22 m. long, was hewn in the soft conglomerate bedrock and is of impressive dimensions—about 4 m. wide and 4.5 m. high. It descended to a depth of 36 m. beneath the surface of the mound. At the bottom was a water chamber, the floor of which was on the level of the water table, as at the base of the mound. This level rises or descends in accord with the season and the

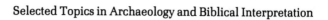

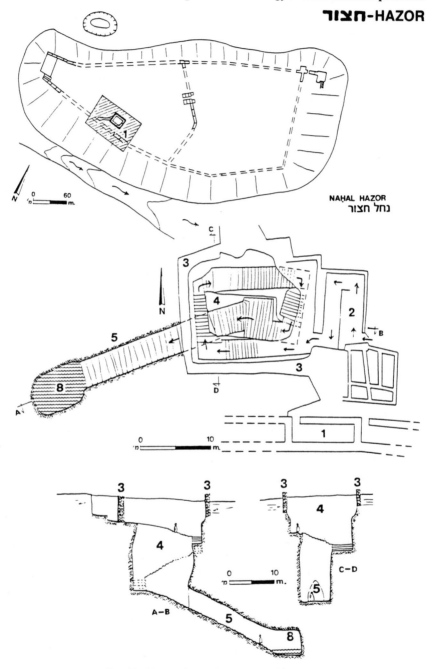

Fig. 30. Hazor (after Yadin 1972, figs. 27, 46–47)

quantity of rains in a given year. This water system was destroyed with the destruction of Stratum V. The tunnel and the shaft became filled as a result of the neglect to the upper supporting walls. Later, the deep depression left in its upper part served in secondary use, in two phases, as an upper reservoir for rainwater.

The Water System and the City Plan. In contrast to initial expectations which held that the water system was connected directly with the springs outside the walled city, it transpired that the planners of the system in Stratum VIII directed it inward, toward the center of the mound, in the assumption (and knowledge) that they would reach the water table. At Hazor, the entrance structure and the four-room house adjacent to it, between it and the city wall, was a complex apparently related to the maintenance and running of this royal project.

Dating. The fact that the builders of the water system penetrated the earlier strata (till Stratum X) and the integration of the walls of the water system within the plan of Stratum VIII enable the ascription of its construction to Stratum VIII; i.e., to the ninth century B.C.E. Its blockage is ascribed to the destruction phase of the city in Stratum V; i.e., the Assyrian conquest of 732 B.C.E. In the clearance of the late reservoir here, at least two main phases of use were distinguished and ascribed to the sparse settlement of the Assyrian and Persian-Hellenist periods, Strata IV–I, which required little water.

Gezer (fig. 31)

The Water System. The water system, excavated and published by Macalister (1912), was adjacent to the line of fortifications on the eastern edge of the mound (Macalister 1912: 256–65; Dever 1969). The water system has three components: an entrance area; a stepped tunnel; and a water chamber. The builders dug through earlier strata, which they apparently shored up with supporting walls,[3] till bedrock was reached. Here they hewed obliquely into the rock, without a vertical shaft, and continuued this stepped tunnel for 41 m., reaching a depth of 43 m. beneath the surface of the bedrock. At that level they encountered the water table. The water chamber was not entirely cleared by Macalister; its dimensions (32 m. long!) indicate that it was originally a natural cavern.

Macalister made several suggestions concerning the role of this large water chamber ("subterranean temple," sewage system, secret tunnel), but he found it difficult to assume that this rock-hewn tunnel was preplanned as a means of assuring a steady supply of water for the city directly from the water table. In his opinion, "the discovery of the spring was a happy accident, made

גזר-GEZER

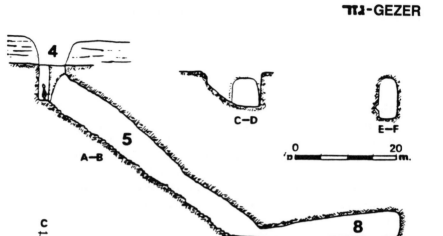

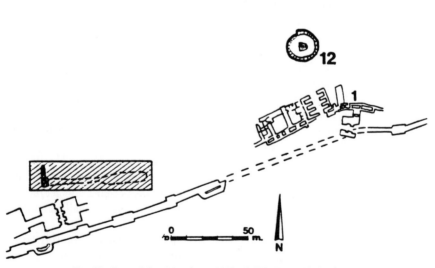

Fig. 31. Gezer (after Macalister 1912, pl. III; Dever 1970, pl. I).

in the course of quarrying the tunnel for some entirely different purpose—
most probably to serve as an exit from the city in time of siege" (Macalister
1912: 263).

Dating. The extant data are insufficient to determine clearly the precise date
of the Gezer water system. In our perusal of the various relative finds within
the fills in the tunnel, we have come to the conclusion that they are unreliable
as indicators for dating (this includes, e.g., the Mycenean cup found there; cf.
Amiran 1951: 36). Macalister ascribed it to his "Second Semitic" period, now
ascribed to the MB II period. Other scholars have ascribed the water system to
LB (for detailed bibliography of the various opinions, cf. Amiran 1951: 36 nn.
12–14; Dever 1969). Yadin's opinion seems most acceptable to us. He notes the
typological, architectural, and hydro-geological similarities (cf. below pp.226–
34; and Yadin 1973: 143) between the water systems at Hazor and Gezer and
thus ascribes the latter to Iron II. It would then have served as part of the new
urban system of Gezer, beginning in the tenth century B.C.E., details of which
have been clarified in the recent excavations of the Hebrew Union College.[4]

The Reservoir (?). A further water installation was uncovered by Macalister
north of the Israelite city gate (Macalister 1912: 265–268). This was an oval
pool 14 m. to 17 m. in diameter, hewn into the bedrock to a depth of 18 m. A
stairway descends along its outer wall to the floor. The walls were crudely
plastered. We possess insufficient data to date this installation or to understand
its precise function—whether it was a huge reservoir or possibly the initial
stage of a projected water system, like the round shaft at Gibeon (Pritchard
1961: 12–13), is hard to determine.

Gibeon (fig. 32)

During Pritchard's excavations in 1956–57, two adjacent water systems
were discovered: the tunnel and the "pool" at the top of the eastern slope of the
mound, above 'Ain el-Balad. Both were fed by the same spring and its water
table which still serve the inhabitants of the village of el-Jib (Pritchard 1961:
12–13; 1962: 53–78).

Gibeon A—The Tunnel. The components of this water system are clear:
entrance structure, stepped tunnel, water chamber, and feed channel. Above
the spring, alongside the line of Iron Age fortifications, a small entrance
chamber was built leading to an oblique, stepped tunnel hewn into the
bedrock. The tunnel is 48 m. long and descends to a depth of 24 m. to a water
chamber. A part of the ceiling of the tunnel, in the upper part, was open and
roofed with stone slabs. In the lower part the tunnel was entirely rock-hewn.

גבעון-GIBEON

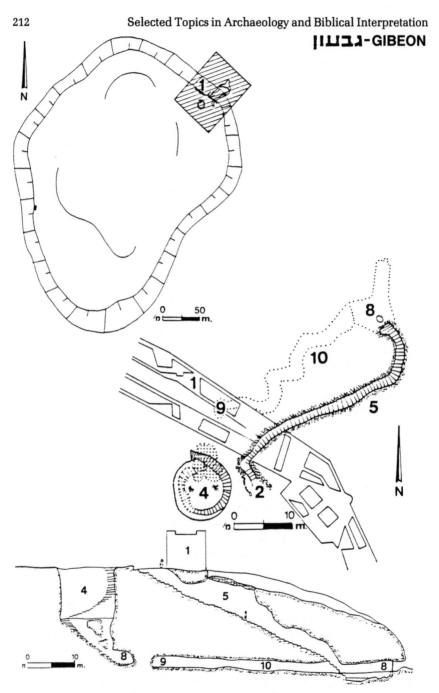

Fig. 32. Gibeon (after Pritchard 1961, figs. 1–3).

The water was collected in the chamber by means of a feeder conduit stemming from the spring proper and hewn alongside the aquifer feeding it. (In the opinion of the geologist, Dan Gil, the feeder conduit, of irregular form, is an artificial expansion of a natural tunnel which was formed by dissolution of the limestone bedrock and then utilized by the builders of the Gibeon water system.)

Gibeon B—The "Pool". In contrast to the tunnel, which was previously known, Pritchard's discovery of the "pool" came as a complete surprise even to the local villagers. It includes a round shaft, a stepped tunnel, and a water chamber. The hewing of the shaft, 11 m. in diameter, began very close to the surface. The hewers left a hewn stairway with a railing descending around the walls down to the floor of the shaft which was 11.8 m. deep. At the bottom a stepped tunnel led down to a water chamber at a depth of 24 m. beneath the surface, and two small vertical shafts served to air and light it. The water chamber is at the same level as the water chamber of "Gibeon A" and is only about 5 m. away from the spring at the head of the feeder conduit. Thus, the two systems are fed by one and the same source.

Location, Function, and Dating. Cole (1980: 28–29) has proposed that the "pool" at Gibeon was initially a round reservoir which was subsequently expanded into a more sophisticated system reaching down to the water table. Pritchard proposed two other alternatives (Pritchard 1961: 9–10). In our opinion (cf. below p. 233) the entire water system should be regarded as an organic unit of uniform planning and execution (cf. Wright 1963). Pritchard held that the "pool" was built alongside the line of fortifications during Iron I. He identified it with the pool at Gibeon mentioned in 2 Samuel 2:13. After the supply of water to this installation diminished, he holds, the second system was hewn—the stepped tunnel (Pritchard 1961: 10), which dates from the same time as the second phase of the fortifications; i.e., the tenth century B.C.E. (Pritchard 1961: 22–23). Though outwardly there is no connection between the two water systems, their water chambers, only 6 m. apart, are on the same level (745 m.) and are fed from the same water table. Thus, Pritchard's suggestion can be set aside chiefly on hydro-geological grounds. Better, in our opinion, is Wright's view that the identification of this installation with the biblical pool is not "necessarily so" (Wright 1963).[5] This, when coupled with typological parallels, makes it preferable to reverse the order of hewing of the two installations: the "pool" was added as an improvement during Iron II sometime after the stepped tunnel had been hewn in the tenth century B.C.E.[6] The two installations may have served the city down to the end of the Iron Age (cf. Jer. 41:12). Here, too, the contents of the fill blocking the round shaft, including pottery and inscribed sherds from the end of this period, are of little chrono-

יבלעם-IBLEAM

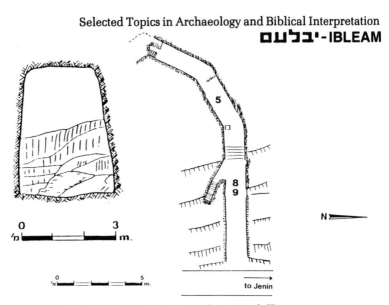

Fig. 33. Ibleam (after Schumacher 1910, pl. II).

logical significance (Pritchard 1959; 1961: 15–21). These articles may have been washed into the shaft during the destruction of the settlement when the water system was abandoned.

Ibleam (fig. 33)

The Water System. The water system at Tell Bal'amah was surveyed by Schumacher (1910). There is a source of water at 'Ain Sinjil on the eastern flank of the mound. It is possible to penetrate into a stepped tunnel at its lower end and ascend for 30 m. The tunnel's dimensions are impressive: 3 m. wide with a vaulted ceiling 4.2 m. high. There are numerous traces of secondary use since the tunnel was originally hewn (as noted already by Schumacher and recently confirmed by Z. Yeivin in trial excavations near the lower end of the stepped tunnel).

Dating. This water system can be ascribed to Iron II on the basis of circumstantial evidence, foremost of which are typological and architectural data: the manner of planning and hewing and the function match well the water systems datable to the Iron Age, as noted already by Schumacher. Secondarily, there is also the geographical-historical grounds: Ibleam was one of the urban centers on the border of Samaria and the Jezreel Valley. It is logical to assume that its town plan in the Iron Age included a subterranean system to assure a regular supply of water.

Jerusalem (fig. 34) [cf. Hecker 1957; Amiran 1951: 35–36; 1975; Vincent 1954: 260–97; Simons 1952: 157–94]

The Gihon Spring at the base of the eastern slope of the City of David has served the inhabitants of Jerusalem since its foundation at the beginning of the Early Bronze Age. The water systems stemming from this spring include Warren's Shaft, the Siloam Channel, and Hezekiah's [or the Siloam] Tunnel. The City of David expedition, currently being directed by the author on behalf of the Hebrew University, has been engaged since 1978 in the reinvestigation of these systems.

Warren's Shaft. This system was discovered by Charles Warren in 1867 (Wilson and Warren 1871: 248–55). It was examined in detail by the Parker expedition, the results of which were published by Vincent (1911). Since 1979 archaeological excavations have been conducted here by the City of David expedition (Shiloh 1981a), and a hydro-geological survey has been carried out by Dan Gil (cf. Gil and Shiloh 1982). The system contains several components: an entrance area, a stepped tunnel, a horizontal tunnel, a vertical shaft, a connecting tunnel, and the spring.

The entrance is hewn into the rock at the head of the stepped tunnel which descends to a depth of 8 m. to the beginning of the horizontal tunnel. (Several parts of the water system have not yet been examined fully, and thus there may still be changes in the dimensions given here.) The latter is 28 m. long and slightly oblique, descending to the head of the vertical shaft. This shaft, oval in section, descends 12.3 m. down to the level at which water is met coming from the spring 22 m. away through the connecting tunnel.

Other secondary features include the following: in the upper entrance area, a later building phase is evident with the "vaulted chamber" protecting the entrance from silting and debris from the eastern slope. An entry tunnel was built within it connecting this later phase with the surface. The additional shaft—the "trial shaft" and the blocked entrance to the cave at the lower end of the horizontal tunnel—can now be understood in the light of the hydro-geological survey: the additional shaft, the cave, and the vertical shaft, as well as the lower part of the horizontal tunnel, are all natural karst clefts and shafts which were utilized and integrated into the water system. This serves to explain the anomaly and irregularity of the plan and dimensions of some of these components. We discovered, inter alia, that the bottom of Warren's Shaft in its natural form continues to a depth of 3 m. beneath the known levels of the spring, of Hezekiah's Tunnel, and of the bottom of the vertical shaft known to date. Further karst shafts were discovered in 1981 in the Cenomanian rock during the course of excavations in Area E.1 in the City of David.

Location and Function. The water flowed from the spring through the connecting tunnel to the base of the vertical shaft whence it could be drawn, as in a well, by anyone having come down the upper tunnels to the head of the shaft. Here we see a unique exploitation of a series of natural tunnels and shafts which were integrated to form a continuous water system. Its planners utilized the vertical shaft and the steep step, 2.7 m. high, which separate the horizontal tunnel from the stepped tunnel, as a means of breaking direct access between the external spring and the interior of the city and hence ready penetration into the city. This integration of artificial and natural components, as we have noted, serves to explain the peculiar form of this system and supersedes all previous explanations (cf. the various opinions in the literature noted at the beginning of this section).[7]

The discovery of the line of the city wall by Kenyon (1974: 144–51) and Shiloh (1981b) indicates that the entrance area known to us today was indeed within the fortifications at a spot apparently adjacent to the "Water Gate." The continuation of this system should possibly be sought higher up, near the additional gate discovered by Parker in 1909 at the top of the slope above the spring (though this gate, in the light of its location, might be from Second Temple times; cf. Vincent 1911: 29, pl. VI).

עיר דוד - CITY OF DAVID

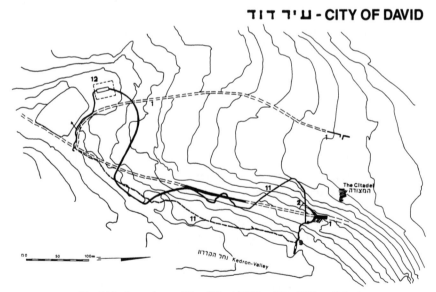

Fig. 34A. Jerusalem—City of David (City of David Expedition).

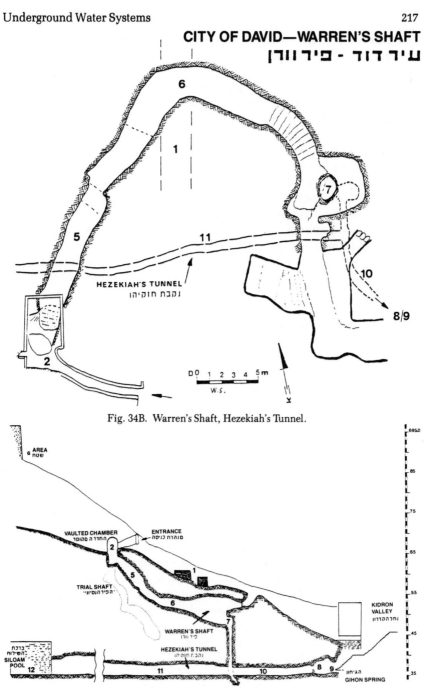

CITY OF DAVID—WARREN'S SHAFT
עיר דוד - פיר וורן

6

1

7

5

11

HEZEKIAH'S TUNNEL
נקבת חזקיהו

10

8/9

2

D0 1 2 3 4 5 m
W.S.

Fig. 34B. Warren's Shaft, Hezekiah's Tunnel.

AREA
שטח

VAULTED CHAMBER
החדר הסגור

ENTRANCE
פתח כניסה

2

1

5

TRIAL SHAFT
"הפיר הנסיוני"

6

7

WARREN'S SHAFT
פיר וורן

HEZEKIAH'S TUNNEL
נקבת חזקיהו

SILOAM
POOL
בריכת
השילוח

12

11

10

8 **9**

KIDRON
VALLEY
נחל הקדרון

הגיחון
GIHON SPRING

695.0

85

75

65

55

45

35

Fig. 34C. Jerusalem underground water system.

The Siloam Channel. Various segments of this water system have been investigated by Meistermann, Schick, Bliss, and Dickie (1898: 115, pl. XIII), Weill (1947: 57–96), and Shiloh (1979a: 168). The City of David expedition has uncovered three segments totaling a length of 120 m. (out of an overall length of about 400 m.). It differs basically from the other water systems reviewed here in that it served to carry water partly in a rock-hewn and stone-covered channel and partly in a rock-hewn tunnel. Its use was threefold: it conducted the waters of the Gihon spring along the Kedron Valley to the region of reservoirs at the lower end of the "Central Valley," at the southwestern tip of the City of David; in the eastern wall of the channel, facing the valley, there are window-like openings through which the flow of water could be diverted for irrigation of agricultural plots in the valley; the upper openings along the channel could be utilized for gathering the runoff from the rock surface outside the city walls on the slope above, thus diverting them to the above noted reservoirs. The major disadvantage of this system was its vulnerability, its entire course being outside the fortified area of the city. Thus, it was necessarily a peacetime system.

The inauguration of Hezekiah's Tunnel (cf. below) actually affected only the first of the three functions of this channel. The new tunnel superseded the Siloam Channel in its first function, but the southern end of the channel (in Area A.1 of the current excavations; Shiloh 1979a: 168) was integrated into the new system as an overflow channel to the Siloam Pool. By lowering the level of its bottom, the direction of flow in this part of the channel was reversed, and the water now ran from west to east.

Hezekiah's Tunnel. Hezekiah's Tunnel has occupied the attention of various scholars since the very beginning of modern archaeological research in Jerusalem (cf. the literature cited at the beginning of this section). This water system solved the special problems of water supply in the City of David in a sophisticated though simple manner. Its components are the spring, the tunnel, the Siloam Pool, and an overflow channel.

From the spring, the tunnel continues for 533 m. under the spur of the City of David till it reaches the Siloam Pool. The survey of the current archaeological expedition revealed that, in contrast to all that has previously been published, the difference in height between the beginning of the channel at the spring and the end of the tunnel is only about 30 cm. (a gradient of only 0.06%). The average height of the tunnel is around 2 m.; at its southern end the height reaches 5 m. The remains of the reservoirs and parts of the fortifications which were uncovered at the bottom of the Central Valley by Guthe, Bliss, Weill, and Shiloh are no earlier than Second Temple times (cf. the references cited above). The reservoirs of First Temple times were (most probably) on the same site, originally fed by the Siloam Channel. We also should place here the beginning of the new line of defenses from the days of Hezekiah, ascending westward and encompassing the Western Hill (Avigad 1983: 24–29, 46–60; Geva 1979). According to this view, the site of the main reservoir is not to be sought beyond the line of the dam to the east, in the Kedron Valley (for the various opinions, cf. Kenyon 1974: 152–59; Ussishkin 1976; Wilkinson 1978; Shaheen 1979; Adan 1979). The overflow channel of the Siloam Pool, which utilized the southernmost part of the Siloam Channel, led the surplus water into the Kedron streambed in a controlled manner. Here, too, the water could be gathered in additional reservoirs, though these could be of value only in times of peace, their location being far outside the line of fortifications. The overflow channel was blocked up by a stone wall in Second Temple times (cf. Shiloh 1979a; Weill 1947, pls. V–VI).

Function and Dating of the Three Jerusalem Water Systems. There is general agreement among scholars as to the relative chronology of these three water systems. Warren's Shaft is certainly the oldest; the Siloam Channel, if not contemporaneous with it, is only slightly later; Hezekiah's Tunnel is the latest of the three, built at the end of the eighth century B.C.E.

The ascription of the hewing of Hezekiah's Tunnel to the reign of that king, late in the eighth century B.C.E., is based on specific evidence in the Bible (2 Kings 20:20; 2 Chron 32:30) and the Apocrypha (Ecclus. 48:17), as well as on paleographic analysis of the Siloam Inscription discovered near the southern terminus of the tunnel in 1880. At its upper end Hezekiah's Tunnel utilizes the connecting tunnel running between the spring and the bottom of Warren's Shaft. The southern end of the Siloam Channel was utilized as an overflow channel for the Hezekiah's Tunnel water system, which also included the redesigned Siloam Pool. Hence, the dates of the Siloam Channel (generally identified with the "waters of Shiloah that flow gently" of Isa. 8:6) and of Warren's Shaft must be prior to the late eighth century B.C.E.; i.e. the period of Hezekiah's Tunnel. In other words, these two earlier systems are from the tenth-ninth centuries B.C.E.

After the discovery of Warren's Shaft, Birch (1878; 1885), followed by Vincent (1911: 33–35; 1912: 146–61), suggested identifying it with the ṣinnôr mentioned in the account of David's conquest of Jebus and the exploits of Joab ben Zeruiah (2 Sam. 5:6–9; 1 Chron. 11:4–7; in the latter narrative, the ṣinnôr is no longer mentioned, apparently the difficulty of this expression already having been felt). This suggestion has been rejected on various grounds, and rightly so, by such scholars as Dalman, Albright (1922), Yadin (1963: 267–70), Mazar (1975: 168–69), Aharoni (1982: 234–35), and Braslavi (1970). If such an ascription were accepted, this water system in Jerusalem would have already been built by the Canaanites and would thus comprise a basic precedent, typologically and chronologically. On another occasion (Shiloh 1972; cf.

below), we noted *ex omnibus disce unum* that examples such as Warren's Shaft, which lack direct chronological and stratigraphical criteria, can be dated on the basis of their analogs to Iron II (tenth-ninth centuries B.C.E.).

Thus, in Jerusalem a complex picture of the water system emerges. The source of water in this city, the Gihon, is a cyclic or pulsating spring quite different in hydrological character from the ordinary sources on other sites, which generally are fed by regular springs or by the water table. In order to utilize efficiently the great quantities of water gushing forth from the Gihon spring, the inhabitants necessarily had to gather them in reservoirs. The most suitable location for such pools, as far as both topography and planning were concerned, was at the foot of the Central Valley. The gathering of the waters at this spot, whether via the Siloam Channel or through Hezekiah's Tunnel, enabled the full, controlled exploitation of almost the entire yield of water.

The Siloam Channel was the initial means of conveying the waters of the Gihon to reservoirs to the south; at the same time, it also enabled utilization of the waters for irrigation in the Kedron Valley. The major disadvantage of this early system was that, as noted, all its components—spring, channel, and pool—were situated outside the walls of the city. Hezekiah's Tunnel provided a sophisticated remedy: not only was the entire conduit concealed beneath the rock surface but also the area of the reservoirs was not brought into the fortified area of the city, the walls having been extended to include the Western Hill.[8]

Warren's Shaft was built according to the usual formula for underground water systems at royal centers in the tenth-ninth centuries B.C.E. It connected the northern part of the City of David (and perhaps even its citadel) with the water source. In the late eighth-sixth centuries B.C.E., the three systems could have functioned simultaneously, all fed from the single source, and the flow of water through them could have been controlled. Hezekiah's Tunnel has continuously conveyed water to the Siloam Pool ever since. Water could also reach the base of Warren's Shaft, from whence it could be drawn for use in the city directly above.

The late phase in the entrance chamber of Warren's Shaft, the vault and the entrance tunnel, indicates that in the first century B.C.E. this installation was still being maintained, whether as a water system per se or for some other use of the extensive subterranean chambers in its upper parts (Shiloh 1981a: 36). (The connection between these parts of the water system, from Second Temple times, and the "First Wall" of the same period, situated atop the eastern slope, is still unclear. It is even uncertain that there was any such connection, though it might be conjectured on the basis of the gate discovered by Parker; cf. Vincent 1911: 29, pl. VI.) The Siloam Channel went out of use as the main conduit of water at the time of the construction of Hezekiah's Tunnel which

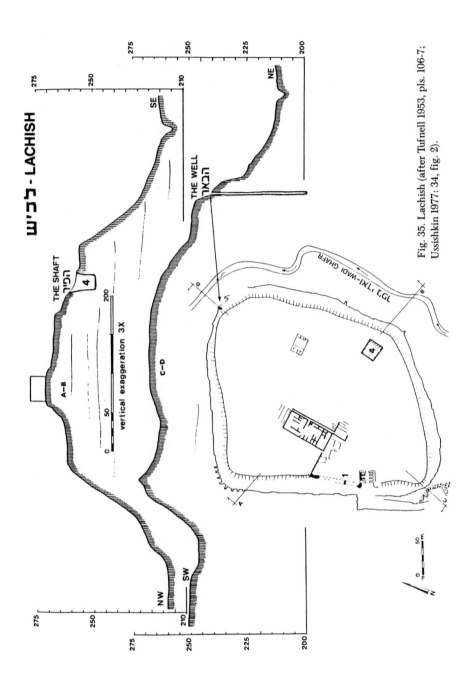

כ'יש - LACHISH

THE SHAFT
הפיר

THE WELL
הבאר

A–B

C–D

NW

SW

SE

NE

vertical exaggeration 3X

275   250   210

275   250   210

275   250   225   200

275   250   225   200

0   50   200

נחל ואדי-ע'אפר WADI-EL GHAFR

0   50 m

N

Fig. 35. Lachish (after Tufnell 1953, pls. 106-7; Ussishkin 1977: 34, fig. 2).

cut the channel off from direct contact with the spring. The channel could have continued in use, however, till the end of the First Temple period as a regular means of both distributing irrigation water in the upper Kedron Valley and feeding various reservoirs there. We still lack all data on the supply of water to the uppermost and most important parts of Jerusalem in this period—the Temple Mount and the adjacent palace complex.

Lachish (fig. 35)

The Water System. The "Great Shaft" at Lachish, investigated by Starkey in 1935–37, remains one of the enigmas of this site (Tufnell 1953: 158–63). It was hewn adjacent to the line of fortifications at the southeastern corner of the settlement. Starkey examined it by tunneling along its walls and found that it measured 22 m. x 25 m. and is about 25 m. deep. Since no tunnel was found at its bottom, the excavator assumed that its hewing was never completed (Tufnell 1953: 162, fig. 14). It can be assumed that the hewers intended the shaft to reach down to the level of the water table, 40 m. to 50 m. below the present surface (this level was known on the basis of the level of the ground water in the well mentioned immediately below).

The well uncovered at the northeastern corner of the mound is one of the few examples of deep wells found in an Israelite city (Tufnell 1953: 92–93; cf. the deep, pre-Iron Age well at Beer-sheba, pp. 222–24 below). In concept it resembles the other water systems: it was hewn to a depth of 44 m. at the lowest point on the mound's surface but still within the line of fortifications, which slightly deviates here to accommodate it (Tufnell 1953, pl. 108).

Dating. The sole chronological datum concerning the well is the fact that it is integrated within the fortification system of the Iron II city. Tufnell thought that it was hewn already in MB II. The "Great Shaft" was hewn, in the excavator's opinion, during the construction of Stratum III in the days of Hezekiah, the late eighth century b.c.e. (Tufnell 1953: 161). It can be assumed that the large shaft was abandoned after the destruction of Stratum III (701 b.c.e.). The layers of stone discovered at the top of the depression, which remained on the site of the shaft after it had become filled with debris from the destruction of the city, indicate a later, secondary use as an open reservoir for rainwater in Stratum I of the Persian-Hellenist periods.

Beer-sheba (fig. 36)

The plan of Stratum II at Beer-sheba (Aharoni 1973: 9–18; Herzog 1978) shows one of the most complete examples of town planning in this period, with all the requisite components (Shiloh 1978: 41–43). At the northeastern corner

Fig. 36. Beer-sheba (after Aharoni 1976: 62, fig. 9).

of the mound, the top of a flight of stairs came to light, along with supporting walls built around the top of a shaft (Aharoni 1973: 16, pls. 84, 89–90). The excavator quite reasonably assumed that these elements belonged to a water system which, as yet, remains to be cleared. Aharoni thought that the shaft led to a series of subterranean cisterns hewn beneath; the water, floodwaters from the adjacent Nahal Beer-sheba, would somehow have been diverted into them. If this were indeed the case, it would be an interesting integration of the engineering methods noted in the parts of the country to the north and the specific conditions of water supply in the semiarid Negev (cf. below the water systems of Arad and Kadesh-barnea). On the basis of this reconstruction we would expect the shaft and the cisterns to be located closer to the streambed at the southeastern corner of the city. Another reconstruction can, however, be made for the functioning of this water system: the level of the water table was surely well-known to the local populace, on the basis of the ancient deep well situated outside the city gate. The hewing of the above noted shaft, at the northern corner of the city, was a planned effort to reach this level in the manner seen at the other royal centers in the north. Stratum II has been ascribed to the eighth century B.C.E.

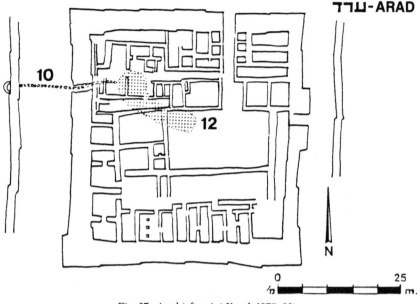

Fig. 37. Arad (after Avi-Yonah 1975: 83).

Arad (fig. 37)

The inhabitants of Arad in the Iron Age utilized the ancient well located at the base of the citadel, at the center of the depression within the walled area of the EB II city (Amiran 1978: 13–14; 1980: 34). (In time of necessity, of course, water could be brought from sources even farther afield.) A large underground reservoir was hewn into the soft limestone bedrock beneath the center of the citadel as an integral component of the initial plan in Stratum X (Aharoni 1968: 6–7, fig. 5). This cistern was fed by a rock-hewn channel entering the citadel from the west. At the point of entry the walls of the channel were integrated into and covered by the solid structure of the wall of Stratum X. (Besides the engineering feat of building an outer feeder channel to the inner cistern, this arrangement precluded the need for bringing beasts, carrying water containers, and their drivers into the fortress, most of which was densely built.) The 32 m. long channel was covered over by stone slabs. The channel was fed with water brought in containers from some outside source, and it was poured into the channel through which it flowed into the cistern beneath the citadel. When the cistern was filled, the water supply for the garrison was assured for a given period. This freed it from dependency upon the well and other outside sources of water in time of war and improved the standard of living in time of peace. The water system served the Arad citadel in Strata X–VI, in the ninth–sixth centuries B.C.E.

Kadesh-barnea

In R. Cohen's 1981–82 excavations at Kadesh-barnea a water system was uncovered resembling that at Arad (Cohen 1981; 1983: xi, fig. 13). The Israelite fortress was built adjacent to a streambed in which the waters of 'Ain Qudeis regularly flow. These waters had been diverted into a well-constructed channel leading through the southern wall of the fortress into a large cistern within. In the part excavated, a broad stairway was revealed descending into the cistern. The excavator ascribed the use of this cistern to Iron Age II, like that at Arad with which it is typologically identical.

Tell es-Sa'idiyeh

In 1964, while seeking a connecting path between the fortified settlement at the top of Tell es-Sa'idiyeh and the spring at the base of its northern slope, Pritchard discovered a built ascent, defined by him as a "secret tunnel" (Pritchard 1964). The ascent was stepped, each of the 98 steps being 2 m. wide. During its construction a channel was dug and its walls lined with stone. The ascent was divided down its length by a central wall; in the excavator's opinion it had been roofed and covered over with earth to conceal it from the view of an enemy (though in our opinion the invulnerability of such a water system is doubtful).

At the top of the mound a well-planned settlement was revealed with a street system and structures of the four-room type (Pritchard 1964: 6). The settlement has been ascribed to the tenth century B.C.E. Its identification as the biblical Zarethan, a center of bronze manufacture where some of the vessels for Solomon's Temple were made, would point to its importance (cf. 1 Kings 7:45–46). Pritchard ascribed the water system to 1200–900 B.C.E.; we assume that it should be ascribed to the principal occupational phase of the planned settlement on the site, i.e., the tenth century B.C.E.

General Discussion

Two factors, a perennial source of water and a rising hill or mound suitable for town planning and military defense, were most significant in determining the choice of location of settlement sites during the process of urbanization in Eretz-Israel since the Bronze Age. During the construction of the royal centers and settlements of Iron II, the subject of exploitation of water sources was a major element in planning for times of both war and peace. The water source, whether a spring or the water table, was generally situated at the base of the hill.[9] The water systems were intended to overcome two problems:

first, a problem of civil engineering—the daily inconvenience of water supply from a source relatively distant from the residential area; second, a problem of military engineering—the securing of an adequate source of water normally outside the fortified area and comprising a weak point in the ability of the settlement to withstand a siege. The technical solution to these two problems was quite clear: a subterranean and thus protected means of linking the source to the interior of the fortified city, providing ready access to the water and yet not visible to the enemy without. An alternative was to lead the waters from the source to reservoirs or cisterns within the fortified area.

The mode of execution taken would thus be determined by various engineering, architectural, and hydro-geological considerations: type of source (water table, perennial spring, gushing spring, abundant supply), geological nature of the bedrock (hard/soft strata, durability and permeability of rock), morphology of surface (slopes, possibilities for gravitational flow, location of reservoirs), and location of source in relationship to line of fortifications (distance, approaches, gradient of slope of mound). The optimal solution, as far as planning was concerned, would be to locate an abundant, perennial source of water at some relatively high spot close to the city's defenses. The bedrock in which the water system would be hewn should be soft enough to be readily quarried but sufficiently hard to preclude collapse. The inner terminal of the system and the reservoirs or cisterns must be within the fortified area of the city at a spot sufficiently large enough to accommodate them and convenient for conveying water to them. In reality, the planners of the various water systems described above had to compromise with local conditions. This led to several variations observed among different types as far as components and mode of function are concerned.

Typological Classification of the Water Systems (fig. 38; table 5)

Shaft and Tunnel Leading to a Source Outside the City (A in fig. 38).

Megiddo — third and fifth phases   Ibleam
Gibeon A — the tunnel

This type is simple in conception and components. Its major fault is that the source is located outside the city and thus the entire system is vulnerable upon discovery, enabling an enemy to penetrate it and hence the city.

Shaft and Tunnel Leading to the Water Table at the Base of the Mound (B in fig. 38).

Hazor   Gibeon B — the pool
Gezer   Lachish — the shaft (?)

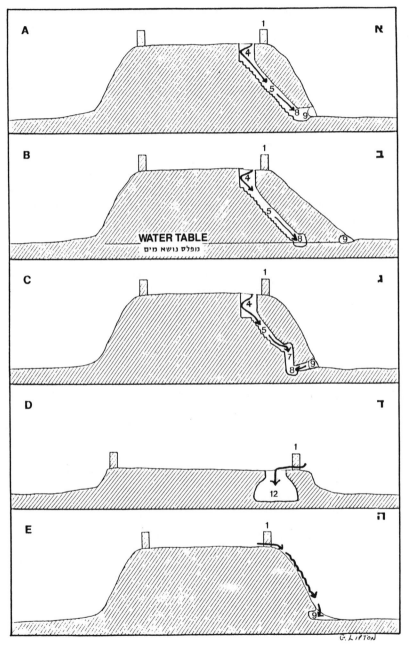

Fig. 38. Typological classification of underground water systems in the Iron Age in Eretz-Israel.

Here, the components of type A in fig. 38 have been combined with the hewing of a subterranean well, often in the form of a stepped tunnel the base of which reaches the level of the water table. In this method, unlike type A, the system is invulnerable to direct enemy action from without.

Shaft and Tunnel Leading from an External Source to the Base of a Vertical Shaft (C in fig. 38).

> Jerusalem — Warren's Shaft
> Megiddo — fourth phase

This type is a combination, so to speak, of the two previous types: water is brought from an external source to the base of a shaft and thence is drawn up, as in a subterranean well. The vertical shaft precluded enemy penetration even if the system were discovered.

Tunnels and Feeder Channels Supplying Large Reservoirs (D in fig. 38).

> Jerusalem — Siloam Channel, Hezekiah's Tunnel, and Siloam Pool
> Megiddo — northern water system (?)
> Arad
> Kadesh-barnea
> Beer-sheba (?)
> Gezer — the reservoir (?)[10]

The main component of this type is the reservoir located within the fortified area of the city. Its location was necessarily at a low-lying spot to which water could be conveyed from a perennial source. Peculiar to this type are the channels and tunnels conveying the water. Several of its components are also seen in the other types (such as shafts and stepped descents).

External Approaches to Sources at the Base of the Mound (E in fig. 38).

> Megiddo — Gallery 629
> Tell es-Sa'idiyeh

The components of this type are not necessarily subterranean. Here emphasis is upon the construction of an external though protected means of ready access to the source. Such water systems are planned for the daily convenience of the inhabitants rather than for their military value, for they are exposed to the enemy by being beyond the fortified area of the city for most of their length.

The Structure of the Subterranean Water Systems (tables 3,4)

In the corpus of water systems full or partial use of several consistent components is found:

> *Entrance Structure:* connecting the occupational level of the city with the upper part of the water system;
>
> *Shaft:* the uppermost part of which is dug through earlier strata and is maintained by supporting walls, while most of its depth is rock hewn;
>
> *Stepped Tunnel:* connecting the base of the shaft and the water source;
>
> *Water Chamber:* located at the end of the tunnel, gathering the waters for drawing;
>
> *Feeder Conduit:* bringing the waters to the water chamber in instances where the latter is not located directly at the source or where greater quantities of water are to be gathered.

In tables 3,4 technical data is presented on the various components of the water systems. The destruction and collapse of most of these systems, as well as irregular methods of excavation in modern times, have denied us much accurate data on the construction of the supporting walls at the heads of such systems. In recent decades excavations at Hazor, Beer-sheba, Gibeon, and, now, Jerusalem (including the reexamination of Warren's Shaft) have provided accurate data on this component.

The upper part of the water system was the shaft. The larger its dimensions, the smaller its gradient could be and the greater the depth it could attain. The restricted dimensions of the shaft at Megiddo, 5 m. x 6.5 m. and 16 m. deep, are surprising in comparison with the other shafts, and thus the gradient at Megiddo is so great—57% compared to 43% at Hazor (at Gibeon B the gradient is 70%!).

The lengths of the stepped tunnels vary between 13 m. (Warren's Shaft) and 48 m. (Gibeon A). Their dimensions are often quite impressive (3 m. to 4 m. wide and up to 7 m. high), facilitating convenient passage and providing sufficient light and air, though it is clear that at sites such as Gibeon, Megiddo, and Jerusalem artificial lighting was required.

The water chambers in many instances were extensions of natural caverns formed around the water sources, as at Megiddo, Gibeon, Gezer, Ibleam, and Jerusalem. The feeder conduits were connected to this component.

The gradient of the ascent/descent in these water systems was relatively steeper than was usual for stairways because of the need to shorten the route of the subterranean tunnels as much as practicable and because of considerable differences in height between the top of the mound and the spring. Table 4 presents the various gradients, from the 26° (55%) at Gibeon A to the 45° (100%) in Warren's Shaft. The overall distance of the descent from the top of

Table 3. Dimensions of the Components in the Water Systems

Site	Water System	Overall Descent		Shaft			Stairs			Stepped Tunnel				
		L	D	L	W	D	W	L	%	L	W	H	D	%
Megiddo	Gallery 629	49	34											
	Water System 925	127	36	6.5	5	16	1.2	28	57	*14.5* 18	?	2–3.5	10	69
	Northern Water System 2153	22+									*15* 22+	1.5–2.6		11	50
Hazor	Water System	80	36	16	13	19	2–6	44	43	*19* 22	4	4.5	11	58
Gezer	Water System	52	29							*34* 41	3–3.5	4.5–7	23	67
	Reservoir (?)	73?	18	17/ 14		18		73?						
Gibeon	A, Tunnel	48	24.6							*45* 48	1.2	2–5	24.6	55
	B, "Pool"	38	24.4	10.3/ 12.3		10.8	1.5	*15.5* 19	70	*14* 19	1	2+	13.6	97
Ibleam	Tunnel	30+								30	3+	4.2+		
Jerusalem	Warren's Shaft	69	41							*8* 13	2	2.8–3.8	8?	100
	Siloam Channel	400?												
	Hezekiah's Tunnel	533												
Tell es-Sa'idiyeh	Stepped Ascent													
Lachish	Great Shaft		40–50?	25.2	22	25								
Beer-sheba	Shaft		35+	17?	17?		3.3							
Arad	Cistern													
Kadesh-barnea	Cistern													

LEGEND: L = Length (m); W = Width (m); H = Height (m); D = Depth/difference in height (m); % = Gradient; italics = level measurement of oblique component

Horizontal Tunnel				Water Chamber			Feeder Conduits			Remarks
L	W	H	D	L	W	H	L	W	H	
15	1.3	2	1							Descent to cave, 20 + 14 to spring
50	2	3	1	4	4	7				Approach 925, 31 28, D 10
										Stairway only
				5	5	5				Entrance structure: L 14, W 3, D 6
			32	3–8	5+					Entrance stairway: L 10.5, W 2.5, D6
				7	5	3	34	2+	1–2+	Lower part of tunnel: L 13.5 8,
				6.8	3.4	2.5				D 6.5, % 81.5
28	2–2.3	2–6	5?	4.8	1.2–1.8	2.8–5.8	22	0.5–0.7	1.6–2.4	Vertical shaft: D 12.3
							400	0.4–0.6	1.4–1.8	
							533	0.65	1.5–5	D 0.3, % 0.06
							32	0.5		L 11,W 4
										Unpublished

Table 4. Slopes of Various Tunnels
(According to Excavators' Plans)

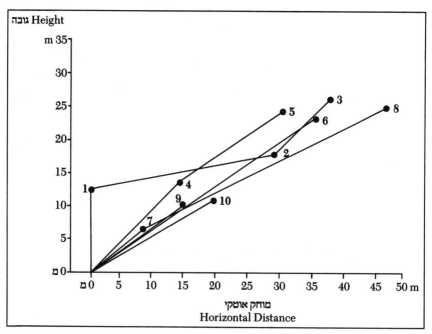

1. Warren's Shaft, vertical shaft	90°
2. Warren's Shaft, horizontal tunnel	9°
3. Warren's Shaft, stepped tunnel	45°
4. Gibeon B, stepped tunnel	43°
5. Gibeon B, steps of round shaft	36°
6. Gezer, stepped tunnel	36°
7. Gibeon A, stepped tunnel, lower part	41°
8. Gibeon A, stepped tunnel, upper part	26°
9. Megiddo, stepped tunnel	35°
10. Hazor, stepped tunnel	29°

the mound down to the source, including all the components of the water system, ranges between 38 m. and 127 m. The spring/water table is located at depths ranging between 25 m. (Gibeon A, B) to 36 m. (Hazor, Megiddo) from the occupation level or upper surface of the mound. On the basis of the measurements in general, it can be determined that the water system at Hazor represents the mean and most convenient dimensions. The nature of the bedrock there, a readily quarried conglomerate, certainly contributed toward the broad dimensions and easy gradients of that system.

The Hydro-Geological Structure and the
Functioning of the Water Systems

In the light of the data accumulated in recent years concerning hydro-geology, it can be recognized that the planners of the water systems utilized the abundant practical knowledge at hand on the nature of bedrock, the location of water sources and water table levels, and the efficient modes of exploiting them (cf., e.g., the preliminary summary of the hydro-geological survey in the City of David in Gil and Shiloh 1982). For lack of data, we have not discussed the matter of rate of flow of the sources. The concept of the utilization of an ordinary spring as a source of water was of the simplest sort (Megiddo, Ibleam, Gibeon A). This was improved by means of feeder conduits (a method which also served for the development of the water supply near various springs in the Judaean hills; cf. Issar 1976: 136). Type B in fig. 38, as at Hazor, Gezer, and Gibeon B, was more sophisticated; here, the planners, on the basis of their practical knowledge, were able to predetermine their route toward the water table deep within the bowels of the mound. The modern theories of "accidental" arrival at the water level at Gezer (Macalister 1912: 263) and Gibeon B (Cole 1980: 27, 29) and of the possibility that Gibeon B evolved in two phases (initial "reservoir" supplemented hurriedly at a later stage by a stepped tunnel; cf. Cole 1980: 28–29; Pritchard 1961: 9–10) are contrary to the very concept and thus are to be rejected.

The water source unique to Jerusalem, the Gihon (literally, a "gushing" spring), dictated particular conditions for its waters gush forth regularly every few hours. If its waters were not gathered and diverted to a reservoir, they would continue to flow into the Kedron brook. When a system for gathering water in large reservoirs developed, the local inhabitants were freed from their dependence upon the gushes of the spring. The drawing of water from the reservoirs could be controlled according to need. We have found that the planners of Warren's Shaft utilized a series of karst tunnels and dolines as parts of their water system. The vertical shaft enabled access to the water at its base but precluded penetration into the city. Most of the waters of the Gihon still flowed into the Kedron brook. The Siloam Channel answered a functional, engineering problem—the conveying of the water to reservoirs. In this phase, still, the entire system was outside the fortified city. Hezekiah's Tunnel was the sophisticated remedy for this fault: it gathered the entire yield of the spring and conveyed it in an entirely secluded manner to the region of the Siloam Pool which, in the period of the hewing of the tunnel, was already included within the fortified area.

In general plan, Warren's Shaft serves as an intermediate model between types A and B, specifically in its successful integration of a vertical shaft of natural form. The plan of this water system (in Jerusalem the capital) may well have served as the prototype both for the first modification of the water system

at Megiddo (transition from the third phase to the fourth phase) and for the
even more sophisticated development finding expression in the systems of type
B. (This is in contrast to Cole 1980: 27, where it is suggested that Gibeon B was
a prototype which influenced the development of types B and C at other sites.)

A Hydro-Geological-Climactic Note: the locations of the early water
systems are, of course, indicative of the levels of the water table and of the
springs in Iron II, for they were planned to tap the sources at those levels. In
light of the clear evidence at Megiddo, Gibeon, Jerusalem, Hazor, Ibleam,
Gezer, and Tell es-Sa'idiyeh the present levels are obviously identical with
those existing in the tenth-ninth centuries B.C.E., the date of these systems.
Thus, we can reasonably assume that the rainfall, too, in the tenth-ninth
centuries B.C.E. was nearly identical to that of modern times.

The Dating of the Water Systems (table 5)

The dating of the water systems, like that of any archaeological find,
must be based upon the entire body of evidence stemming from several
factors: stratigraphic relationship of architectural components to both the
encompassing series of strata and the general town plan; typological comparison; the nature of the small finds discovered within the system; and
historical documentation.

The dating of these water systems has undergone various metamorphoses
largely because of only partial utilization or ignorance of the available data.
Ruth Amiran, in her pioneer study published in 1951, ascribed five (out of six)
of the water systems then known to the end of the Late Bronze Age (Amiran
1951: 37; this ascription was based on stratigraphic-chronological data which
were later corrected for most of the sites concerned). Various scholars often
relied on sparse pottery evidence from one part or another of a water system in
order to date it (Amiran 1951: 36; Lamon 1935: 8–10; Kenyon 1960: 243). Our
experience in clearing the water systems at Hazor and Jerusalem has shown
that, as a rule, such finds are not to be relied upon solely for they may well have
been deposited at the find-spots in various manners and at various times. In the
main they actually stem from the debris and structures surrounding the water
systems. At most, they can comprise auxiliary, supporting evidence for the
dating of the destruction or abandonment of the installations. (Thus, e.g., a
large quantity of finds from the Early Bronze Age till the end of the Iron Age
came to light in the fill of the shaft at Hazor; they clearly found their way there
from the buildings adjacent to the edge of the shaft, after its destruction.)

Despite the difficulty of relating the components of the water systems to
the surrounding stratigraphic series, this relationship indeed holds the major
key to accurate dating. At Hazor this was the basis for ascribing the water
system to Stratum VIII in the ninth century B.C.E. At Megiddo Gallery 629

Table 5. Typological and Chronological Classification of Iron Age Water Systems

Site	Water System	A	B	C	D	E	Excavator's Dating	Modified Ascription	Century B.C.E.
		Typological Classification					Dating of Construction and Use		
Megiddo	Gallery 629					°	Iron I	VA–IVB	10th
	Water System								
	Phase 1	°					Iron I	IVA	9th–8th
	Phase 2		°				Iron I–II	IVA	9th–8th
	Phase 3	°					Iron II	IV/III	9th–8th
	Northern Water System					°	10th	IVA	9th–8th
Hazor	Water System		°				V–III	--	9th–8th
Gezer	Water System		°				Middle-Bronze or Late Bronze	Iron II	10th–8th
	Reservoir (?)				°		?	?	--
Gibeon	A, Tunnel	°					Iron II	--	10th–6th
	B, "Pool"		°				Iron I	Iron II	9th–6th
Ibleam	Tunnel	°					Late Bronze	Iron II	--
Jerusalem	Warren's Shaft			°			Middle Bronze or Iron I	Iron II	10th on
	Siloam Channel				°		Iron II	--	10th(?)
	Hezekiah's Tunnel				°		Late 8th	--	--
Tell es-Sa'idiyeh	Stepped Ascent					°	10th	--	--
Lachish	Great Shaft		°(?)				III	--	--
Beer-sheba	Shaft	°(?)			°(?)		10th–8th	--	--
Arad	Cistern				°		Iron II	--	--
Kadesh-barnea	Cistern				°		Iron II	--	--

served Strata VA–IVB in the tenth century B.C.E., and the two major water systems at Gibeon also began in the tenth century B.C.E. (cf. above p. 213). Those at Beer-sheba, Kadesh-barnea, Arad, Tell es-Sa'idiyeh, and Lachish (?) can be ascribed more generally but definitely to Iron II. For Jerusalem, chronology is based on the sure historical date of Hezekiah's Tunnel; i.e., the late eighth century B.C.E. We have proposed a dating both for the Siloam Channel, which is earlier than the tunnel, and for Warren's Shaft in the tenth-ninth centuries B.C.E. (cf. above pp. 219–22).

The picture which emerges from an analysis of the body of chronological evidence (table 5) reveals that underground water systems in Eretz-Israel first made their appearance in the tenth century B.C.E. as one of the components in the building complexes of the United Monarchy. We can also see further considerable efforts to improve upon them in the ninth century B.C.E., apparently as part of the overall program to develop royal centers in Judah and especially in the Northern Kingdom of Israel in the days of Ahab. In most instances these systems continued in use down to the destruction of the two kingdoms. In Jerusalem, we have found that Warren's Shaft was maintained through Second Temple times and, of course, Hezekiah's Tunnel is still in active use today.

The process of destruction of the water systems is identical at most sites: quantities of debris fell into them blocking the tunnels and shafts. The depressions remaining at the head of the blocked shafts continued to be utilized (at Megiddo, Hazor, and Lachish even after the destruction of these royal centers and as long as they were occupied) as convenient spots for storing rainwater and floodwater atop the mounds, just as there are pools adjacent to most Arab villages today.

Dating and Typology of the Water Systems (table 5)

The chronological data are still insufficient to determine whether there is a correspondence with the typological development of the water systems. Even if outwardly type C appears to be a development of type A and type B is the final, developed form, it is still difficult to prove this because of lack of precise chronological data for the tenth-ninth centuries B.C.E. It should be emphasized that the water systems themselves were planned and adapted to suit local natural conditions and the existing urban plan on the respective sites. Thus, in each instance, a similar overall concept can be seen in both planning and execution as can an identical functioning of the respective components, though each is suited to its respective local system. Moreover, we should note that general analysis reveals the extent of practical knowledge available to the planners concerning the location of underground water sources and the modes of exploiting them. At both Hazor and Gibeon the entire systems were planned so that the ends of the respective tunnels would precisely reach the aquifer, lying immediately over an impermeable layer. This was achieved, in our opinion, purposely and with the prior knowledge that the tunnel would arrive at the right spot, the existence of which was known, just as geologists today know of such matters, through the flows of external springs connected with the same aquifer at the base of the slope of the hill. Water systems of this type, of known date, are no earlier than the tenth century B.C.E. On the basis of comparative typological study we can thus compare the systems at Hazor and Gibeon B (both of known date) and that at Gezer (as already suggested by Yadin 1969a: 70). By the same means we can determine that the date of the Ibleam water system given by Schumacher as MB II is far too early and that it should be lowered to Iron II. Warren's Shaft has also been dated, in the same manner (analogous with the fourth phase of the system at Megiddo) and in accord with its relative position among the other water systems in the City of David, to the tenth-ninth centuries B.C.E. despite the popular appeal of ascribing it to the tradition of the conquest of Jebus in the days of David.

Water Systems in Neighboring Cultures

Earlier studies have raised the question of the origin of this method of building a water system: was it developed in Eretz-Israel in the Iron Age, or did it stem from the engineering concepts of some neighboring culture (cf. Amiran 1951: 37–38; Pritchard 1961: 14)? Our present discussion is too brief to allow for more than a short treatment, for this is a subject worthy of a special study in itself. A priori, we can eliminate urban water systems at centers in both Mesopotamia and Egypt, which were fed in most instances by the major rivers flowing through them (cf., e.g., Jacobsen and Lloyd 1935). Illuminating examples of constructed or hewn tunnels serving as subterranean passageways, secret passages, reservoirs, and water systems are known from the second millennium B.C.E. onward in Syria, Anatolia, and the Mycenean fortresses.

The major problem in discussing the examples in Syria, Anatolia, and Persia is that no detailed information is available concerning their age and function, though some of them certainly served as water systems (cf. Naumann 1971: 190–97, 302–4; Mecquenem 1911: 72–73; Vincent 1914: 377 n. 1; Van Loon 1966: 38–41). The picture is somewhat clearer in regard to water installations in Anatolia toward the end of the Iron Age, especially in Phrygia. Several interesting examples in central Anatolia have been described by von der Osten (1929: 12–34), and in the city of Midas by Gabriel (1965: 27–28). Haspels (1971: 36–40, 144) holds that these are no earlier than the Phrygian period; i.e., the end of the eighth century B.C.E. and possibly even from the sixth century B.C.E.—the golden age of monumental architecture in this city in the Lydian period.

Better examples for comparison are to be found in the Aegean sphere where they served the fortresses of the Mycenean III period, mainly of the thirteenth and early twelfth centuries B.C.E. (Scoufopoulos 1971: passim). At Mycenae a built and hewn tunnel was discovered beneath the foundations of the city wall leading to a small reservoir from the bottom of the slope. The water was conveyed to the reservoir from a far-off spring by means of a segmented pottery pipe (Karo 1934; Wace 1948: 99–100). A similar installation with two parallel tunnels was discovered integrated into the fortifications of Tiryns (Müller 1930: 176; Mylonas 1966: 14–15). At the Acropolis in Athens a built passage was integrated into the fortifications of the thirteenth century B.C.E., utilizing a geological cleft in the rock, and it descended acutely to a natural, hidden cave. This cave is located 34 m. lower down at the bottom of the northern slope of the hill (Broneer 1939; Travelos 1971: 52, 72).

There is certainly a similarity between the water systems of Mycenean Greece and those hewn in Eretz-Israel in the Iron Age. In both instances they were intended to assure the regular supply of water to cities in time of war and in peace. Would it be correct, however, to suggest that the water systems in Eretz-Israel were inspired by those existing in the Mycenean sphere? If so, we would have to prove a typological, chronological, and cultural tie—a contemporaneous link—between the two cultures. The water systems in Eretz-Israel, mainly those of types B and C, are much more developed typologically than those in the Mycenean sphere, and the Aegean water systems are not rock-hewn in the form of shafts and tunnels leading to ground water. If it could definitely be proved that there did exist such subterranean water systems in the Late Bronze Age, as seemed to be the picture when Ruth Amiran wrote her review of this subject (1951: 37–38), there would be good reason to seek actual contacts between the two groups. We may add that there is a decided geological-cultural cleft between the two cultural spheres, which comes to expression in all realms of archaeological finds. The Phrygian water systems, in contrast, are some two hundred years later than the group under consideration here. This fact leads us, at least for the present, to doubt possible influences from the West upon the planners of the water systems in the royal centers of Judah and Israel.

Summary

The water systems discussed in the present study served as organic components within the town plan of the important centers of the kingdoms of Judah and Israel (Shiloh 1978: 46–50; 1979b: 84–86; Kenyon 1971: passim; Yadin 1972: 135–78). With the beginning of the development of these centers in the days of Solomon in the tenth century B.C.E. and with renewed vigor on a broader scale in the days of Ahab in the ninth century B.C.E., the planners also showed their regard for the matter of water supply. It was one of the important factors in the Israelite city both in its military aspect and in the civil engineering aspect concerning ancient town planning, which took into account convenience for private daily life. The improvement of means of protected access to the water sources, the efficient maximal exploitation of the various sources by means of auxiliary installations for tapping the principal sources, the gathering of waters in central reservoirs at which the use of the water could be controlled, and proper maintenance of the various facilities assured a regular supply of water in time of both peace and war. To this end, considerable areas within the fortified cities were allotted to these water systems, as can be seen at Hazor, Megiddo, Beer-sheba, and the City of David. There was much variety in the water systems and in their modes of functioning, according to their local role, local conditions, and type of water source, as can be learned from the models of Jerusalem and Gibeon.

The Bible informs us mainly of reservoirs (at Jerusalem, Hebron, Samaria, Gibeon, and Heshbon). Only in connection with the building activities of King Hezekiah do we learn from a firsthand source of Hezekiah's Tunnel project. The mention of the hewing of an 'ăšûaḥ in the Mesha Stele apparently refers to the execution of a similar type of water system in Moab by King Mesha in the ninth century B.C.E. (as suggested by Yadin). Could the technical knowledge for this project in Moab have come from Judah and Israel (Yadin 1969a: 70; 1969b: 18 n. 18)?[11]

The subterranean water systems, with their several types, are further evidence of the broad architectural initiative which finds expression in the development of the Israelite town plan with all its components—fortifications, public and religious structures, residential quarters, and various urban installations (such as a water system). These underground water systems find maximal expression in the complex town planning, engineering know-how, and fine ability of the builders of these centers. They are a further example of the outstanding cultural differences between the Bronze Age cultures and those of the Iron Age: the inhabitants of the Bronze Age cities were passive in their reliance upon existing water sources and storage of rain and floodwaters. The approach of the town planners of the Iron Age was much more active: seeking out and locating water sources and improving water yields and their storage in a controlled manner. These installations were built and maintained for times of war and of peace. Water utilization, in several instances, was achieved in a controlled manner in accord with the season of the year and the complex demands of the settlement. After the destruction of these urban centers at the end of the First Temple period, the entire subject was neglected. The next phase in the development of improved water systems for major urban centers in Eretz-Israel came only at the end of the hellenistic period and during the Early Roman period.

NOTES

1. An extensive network of tunnels and drainage channels of the MB II period has been revealed in the lower city of Hazor, mainly in Area F, as well as in the fields to the east near the local museum. Cf. Yadin 1972: 43–44, 65–66. A large subterranean cistern was also found hewn into bedrock beneath the LB II palace in Area A (Yadin 1972: 126–28). The latter resembles a similar LB I system discovered at Taanach; cf. Lapp 1969: 31–33. The large depression at the southeastern corner of the enclosure at Hazor served, in our opinion, as a large reservoir for rainwater (cf. Yadin 1959: 2, pls. I–II; Yadin 1969a: 63–71).

2. The excavators hesitated in their chronological and stratigraphical ascriptions of the later parts of the water system, such as the later stairway (L.951); cf. Lamon 1935: 31, 37, fig. 29.

3. On the basis of the single photograph from the top of the Gezer water system, it is difficult to determine which of the walls were the original ones; cf. Macalister 1912, fig. 132.

4. The main basis for this opinion is surely the typological similarity. It should be noted that the water system at Hazor, which serves as the basis for this model, has been dated to the days of Ahab (above, p. 209), whereas the bulk of the royal construction at Gezer is from the days of Solomon in the tenth century B.C.E.; cf. Dever 1971: 112–17.

5. From the biblical description it would seem that the encounter between Joab's men and Abner occurred near a reservoir adjacent to but outside the settlement, like the pool near the modern Arab village. Thus, caution must be taken in accepting Wright's interpretation of the biblical story and the identification it entails as a chronological basis for an early date (eleventh century B.C.E.) for the "pool" (Gibeon B).

6. We cannot accept Pritchard's interpretation that the location of the entrance room to the stepped tunnel (Gibeon A), adjacent to the city wall, seems squeezed in and thus later in date. In general, the builders of such water systems sought to place the entrance rooms to the tunnels as close as possible to the line of the city walls. Thus, this datum can have no special chronological significance for the water systems at Gibeon.

7. For an initial attempt to outline the possibility that some of the elements of the system were natural clefts, cf. Issar 1976. But some of the definitions and esp. the conclusions concerning Warren's Shaft do not find support in the conclusions of the hydro-geological survey of the City of David expedition (Gil and Shiloh 1982).

8. This tallies with the conclusion derived from the excavations in the Jewish Quarter (Avigad 1983), in contrast to the various opinions mentioned above. It is inconceivable that the tunnel was hewn solely to bring water to a new reservoir which, according to this view, was also outside the line of the new city defenses.

9. At Tel Dan, an important royal center in northern Israel, the planners were relieved of the problem of water supply. Abundant springs were located within the defended area of the city already in the Middle Bronze Age.

10. Besides the pools in Jerusalem, the Bible mentions reservoirs adjacent to towns at Gibeon (2 Sam. 2:13–14), Samaria (1 Kings 22:38), Hebron (2 Sam. 4:12), and Heshbon (Song of Sol. 7: 4).

11. The same term also appears in the Tell Siran bottle inscription; cf. Thompson and Zayadine 1973: 10. In this connection it is regretted that no clearer details are available concerning the nature and date of the underground water system at Kerak in Moab; cf. Albright 1924: 11.

BIBLIOGRAPHY

Adan, D.
1979   The Fountain of Siloam and "Solomon's Pool" in First-Century c.e. Jerusalem. *Israel Exploration Journal* 29: 92–100.

Aharoni, Y.
1968   Arad: Its Inscriptions and Temple. *Biblical Archaeologist* 31: 2–32.
1973   *Beer-Sheba I. Excavations at Tel Beer-Sheba 1969–1971 Seasons.* Tel Aviv: Tel Aviv University.
1976   Nothing Early and Nothing Late: Rewriting of Israel's Conquest. *Biblical Archaeologist* 39: 55–76.
1982   *The Archaeology of Eretz-Israel.* Philadelphia: Westminster.

Albright, W. F.
1922   The *Sinnor* in the Story of David's Capture of Jerusalem. *Journal of the Palestine Oriental Society* 2: 286–90.
1924   The Archaeological Results of an Expedition to Moab and the Dead Sea. *Bulletin of the American Schools of Oriental Research* 14: 2–12.

Amiran, R.
1951   Water Supply Tunnels. *Eretz-Israel* 1: 35–38 (Hebrew).
1975   The Water Supply of Israelite Jerusalem. Pp. 75–78 in *Jerusalem Revealed*, ed. Y. Yadin. Jerusalem: Israel Exploration Society.
1977   Notes and News: Arad. *Israel Exploration Journal* 27: 238–41.
1978   *Early Arad: The Chalcolithic Settlement and Early Bronze City. First— Fifth Seasons of Excavations, 1962–1966.* Jerusalem: Israel Exploration Society.
1980   Arad. *Hadashot Arkheologiyot* 74–75: 4 (Hebrew).

Avigad, N.
1980   *Jerusalem. Discovery of the Upper City.* Jerusalem: Skimona (Hebrew). = *Discovering Jerusalem.* Nashville: Nelson, 1983.

Avi-Yonah, M. (ed.)
1975   *Encyclopedia of Archaeological Excavations in the Holy Land* I–IV. Jerusalem: Israel Exploration Society.

Birch, W. B.
1878   Zion, The City of David. *Palestine Exploration Fund* 11: 178–89.
1885   Zion, The City of David. *Palestine Exploration Fund* 18: 61–65.

Bliss, F. J. and Dickie, A. C.
1898   *Excavations at Jerusalem, 1894–1897.* London: Palestine Exploration Fund.

Braslavi, J.
1970   'Vayiga Basinnor,' the Blind and the Lame. *Beth-Miqra* 14: 3–16 (Hebrew).

Broneer, O.
1939 A Mycenaean Fountain on the Athenian Acropolis. *Hesperia* 8: 317–433.

Callaway, J. A.
1970 The 1968–1969 'Ai (Et-Tell) Excavations. *Bulletin of the American Schools of Oriental Research* 198: 7–31.

Cohen, R.
1981 Kadesh Barnea. *Hadashot Arkheologiyot* 77: 47 (Hebrew).
1983 *Kadesh Barnea*. Jerusalem: The Israel Museum.

Cole, D.
1980 How Water Tunnels Worked. *Biblical Archaeology Review* 6: 8–29.

Dever, W. G.
1969 The Water Systems at Hazor and Gezer. *Biblical Archaeologist* 32: 71–78.
1970 *Gezer I*. Jerusalem: Hebrew Union College.
1971 Further Excavations at Gezer, 1967–71. *Biblical Archaeologist* 34: 94–132.

Gabriel, A.
1965 *Phrygie IV. La cité de Midas*. Paris: E. de Boccard.

Geva, H.
1979 The Western Boundary of Jerusalem at the End of the Monarchy. *Israel Exploration Journal* 29: 84–91.

Gil, D. and Shiloh, Y.
1982 Subterranean Water Supply Systems of the City of David: Utilization of a Natural Karstic System. Pp. 32–34 in *Annual Meeting 1982. Elat and Eastern Sinai*. Elat: Israel Geological Society.

Haspels, C. H. E.
1971 *The Highlands of Phrygia* I. Princeton: Princeton University.

Hecker, M.
1957 Pp. 191–207, 427 in *Sefer Yerushalayim*, ed. M. Avi-Yonah. Jerusalem: Bialik Institut (Hebrew).

Herzog, Z.
1978 Israelite City Planning Seen in the Light of the Beersheva and Arad Excavations. *Expedition* 20: 38–43.

Issar, A.
1976 The Evolution of the Ancient Water Supply System in the Region of Jerusalem. *Israel Exploration Journal* 26: 130–36.

Jacobsen, T. and Lloyd, S.
1935 *Sennacherib's Aqueduct at Jerwan*. Chicago: University of Chicago.

Karo, G.
1934 Die Perseia von Mykenai. *American Journal of Archaeology* 38: 123–27.

Kenyon, K. M.
1960 *Archaeology in the Holy Land*. London: Benn.
1971 *Royal Cities of the Old Testament*. New York: Schocken.
1974 *Digging Up Jerusalem*. New York: Praeger.

Lamon, R. S.
1935 *The Megiddo Water System*. Oriental Institute Publications 32. Chicago: University of Chicago Press.

Lapp, P. W.
1969   The 1968 Excavations at Tell Ta'annek. *Bulletin of the American Schools of Oriental Research* 195: 2–49.

Loud, G.
1948   *Megiddo II: Seasons of 1935–39.* Oriental Institute Publications 62. Chicago: University of Chicago.

Macalister, R. A. S.
1912   *The Excavations of Gezer* I. London: John Murray.

Mazar, B.
1975   *The Mountain of the Lord.* New York: Doubleday.

Mecquenem, R. de
1911   Constructions Elamites. *Mémoires, Délégation en Perse* XII. Paris: Leroux.

Müller, K.
1930   *Tiryns* III. Augsburg: Filser.

Mylonas, G. E.
1966   *Mycenae and the Mycenean Age.* Princeton: Princeton University.

Naumann, R.
1971   *Architektur Kleinasiens.* Tübingen: Wasmuth.

Osten, H. H. von der
1929   *Explorations in Central Anatolia, 1926.* Chicago: University of Chicago.

Pritchard, J. B.
1959   *Hebrew Inscriptions and Stamps from Gibeon.* Philadelphia: University of Pennsylvania.
1961   *The Water System of Gibeon.* Philadelphia: University of Pennsylvania.
1962   *Gibeon.* Princeton: Princeton University.
1964   Two Tombs and a Tunnel in the Jordan Valley. *Expedition* 6: 3–9.

Schumacher, G.
1910   The Great Water Passage of Khirbet Bel'Ameh. *Palestine Exploration Fund* 43: 107–12.

Scoufopoulos, N. C.
1971   *Mycenean Citadels.* Studies in Mediterranean Archaeology 22. Goteborg.

Shaheen, N.
1977   The Siloam End of Hezekiah's Tunnel. *Palestine Exploration Quarterly* 109: 107–12.
1979   The Sinuous Shape of Hezekiah's Tunnel. *Palestine Exploration Quarterly* 111: 103–8.

Shiloh, Y.
1972   The Ancient Water Systems in Eretz-Israel, their Date and Typological Classification. Second Archaeological Congress. Jerusalem (unpublished).
1978   Elements in the Development and Town Planning in the Israelite City. *Israel Exploration Journal* 28: 36–51.
1979a   City of David Excavations—1978. *Biblical Archaeologist* 42: 165–71.
1979b   *The Proto-Aeolic Capital and Israelite Ashlar Masonry.* Qedem 11. Jerusalem: The Hebrew University of Jerusalem.
1981a   Jerusalem's Water Supply During Siege. The Rediscovery of Warren's Shaft. *Biblical Archaeology Review* 7: 24–39.

1981b The City of David Archaeological Project: The Third Season—1980. *Biblical Archaeologist* 44: 161–70.

Simons, J.
1952 *Jerusalem in the Old Testament*. Leiden: Brill.

Thompson, H. O. and Zayadine, F.
1973 The Tell Siran Inscription. *Bulletin of the American Schools of Oriental Research* 212: 5–11.

Travelos, J.
1971 *Pictorial Dictionary of Ancient Athens*. London: Thames and Hudson.

Tufnell, O.
1953 *Lachish III. The Iron Age*. London: Oxford University.

Ussishkin, D.
1976 The Original Length of the Siloam Tunnel in Jerusalem. *Levant* 8: 82–95.
1977 The Destruction of Lachish by Sennacherib and the Dating of the Royal Storage Jars. *Tel Aviv* 4: 28–60.

Van Loon, M. M.
1966 *Urartian Art*. Istanbul: Nederlands Historisch-Archaeologisch Instituut.

Vincent, L.-H.
1911 *Underground Jerusalem*. London: Cox.
1912 *Jérusalem antique*. Paris: J. Gabalda.
1914 Gezer et l'archéologie Palestinienne après six ans de fouilles. *Revue Biblique* 23: 373–91, 504–22.
1954 *Jérusalem de l'ancien Testament*. Paris: J. Gabalda.

Wace, A. J. B.
1948 *Mycenae*. Princeton: Princeton University.

Weill, R.
1947 *La cité de David* II. Paris: Paul Geuthner.

Wilkinson, J.
1978 The Pool of Siloam. *Levant* 10: 116–25.

Wilson, C. and Warren, Ch.
1871 *The Recovery of Jerusalem*. London: Richard Bently and Son.

Wright, G. E.
1963 The Water System of Gibeon by James B. Pritchard. *Journal of Near Eastern Studies* 22: 210–11.

Yadin, Y.
1959 *Hazor* I. Jerusalem: Israel Exploration Society.
1963 *The Art of Warfare in Biblical Lands in the Light of Archaeological Study*. New York: McGraw-Hill.
1967 Notes and News: Megiddo. *Israel Exploration Journal* 17: 119–21.
1969a The Fifth Season of Excavations at Hazor, 1968–69. *Biblical Archaeologist* 32: 50–71.
1969b Excavations at Hazor, 1968–1969. *Israel Exploration Journal* 19: 1–19.
1972 *Hazor* (Schweich Lectures). London: Oxford University.
1973 The 1968–69 Seasons of Excavations at Hazor. *Eretz-Israel* 11: 134–43 (Hebrew).
1975 *Hazor*. Jerusalem: Weidenfeld & Nicolson.

Chapter 15

ISRAELITE STATE FORMATION IN IRON I

Frank S. Frick
Albion College

A current concern in American anthropological archaeology and one of interest here is the evolution of complex societies. In a review of Y. Aharoni's *The Archaeology of the Land of Israel* (1982), M. Coogan criticizes that work for its attribution of new cultural elements to new groups of people when movement has been away from explaining every change as a result of migration.

> Cultural change is a complex process which needs to be analyzed with subtlety, taking into account local factors and human creativity and individuality. For too long we have stressed the new and discontinuous in comparing one archaeological period with another, and we have had to fabricate invasions from sparsely populated desert regions to explain the differences between successive eras. It is clear now that the similarities are as important and often more important than the differences; continuity rather than sudden change should occupy our attention (Coogan 1982: 8).

Investigation of cultural change is concerned with elucidating processes that account for general similarities in independent sequences of cultural evolution. The distinction between general and specific evolution is an important one. General evolution is "concerned with structural-functional differences in order of appearance no matter what their relationship or the line of descent to which they pertain" (Service 1962: 5). Specific evolution is concerned with adaptive changes in particular lines. As archaeological evidence has accumulated, it has become increasingly evident that an emphasis on general processes and general unilineal evolution is inadequate for explaining obvious variability present in specific sequences of complex societal evolution.

It is beyond the scope of this essay to attempt a review of specific or neo-evolutionary theory. H. Wright (1978) and K. Flannery (1972) have written summaries of the lines of thought of such theory together with its main proponents. A brief word is needed, however, about the work of two dominant theorists in this area, M. Fried and E. Service, since it is their work which has brought into widespread use the taxonomy of band, tribe, chiefdom, and state to classify and compare human societies. Although there are some significant differences between the evolutionary schemes of Fried and Service, they are both basically unilineal in that cultural evolution is seen as moving through several broad organizational stages. While expressing overtly evolutionary concerns, they are in actuality more concerned with elaborating a taxonomy in a descriptive and typological approach than with classifying types of change and addressing processes of evolutionary transformation in any detailed way.

Models presented in unilineal evolutionary approaches have been developed, by and large, through the utilization of comparative ethnographic material rather than by employing a diachronic approach (Frick 1979; 1983) which has as one of its aims the integration of ethnographic and archaeological data. This essay can only suggest the main lines of this approach, the starting point for which is the idea of "ecological succession," a descriptive term referring to the classification of ecological systems in terms of increasing complexity over time (Gall and Saxe 1977: 257). The concept of ecological succession brings together the concepts of energy, information, and structure in a systemic matrix. It also opens the way, in the analysis of ancient Israel, to the notion of "predatory expansion" (Sahlins 1967), in which one sociocultural form is in some circumstances better adapted than and prevails over alternative adjustments within a particular ecological niche or niches. It also assists in bringing about the lines to a solution of the vexing problem of comparability in the use of archaeological and ethnographic parallels on the part of biblical scholars. Those adopting such an approach observe that there are multiple trajectories to statehood and that whatever sets off the process tends as well to set off other changes. After the tendency to centralized control has been triggered, the hierarchical structure itself becomes a selective determinant that feeds back to all sociocultural features.

This approach also applies in cases of secondary state formation; i.e., cases in which one of the significant variables is cultural contact of a non-state entity with a state. The secondary nature of the state in ancient Israel is evident in the demand of the elders, "Now appoint for us a king to govern us like all the nations" (1 Sam. 8:4). This approach maintains that pristine and secondary states may differ in the way they are set in motion but that the internal interactions which are necessary to transform a non-state society into one recognizable as a state do not vary significantly.

The model of secondary state formation applied to Israel (Frick 1983), which is but briefly outlined here, was developed by W. Sanders and D.

Webster (1978). Their essay sets forth a modified multilineal paradigm in which different evolutionary trajectories relate to variations in agricultural risk, diversity, productivity, and the size and character of the environment. A hierarchy is proposed, with the first-order factors being the degree of agricultural risk and diversity and the second-order factors being those related to the environmental niche. Such factors are not seen as independent variables or prime movers but as functions of one another. Neither are they simply declared as environmental "givens"; rather, full recognition is made of the fact that they may well be conditioned by transformation in the sociocultural system itself. Thus a valuable feature of this model is that it overcomes any dichotomy between ecological variables on the one hand and societal variables on the other and enables the integration of archaeological and comparative ethnographic data.

The first-order factor of risk is defined as "any essential environmental parameters essential to production of energy (e.g., moisture, temperature) with wide, relatively frequent, and unpredictable variations" (Sanders and Webster 1978: 253). Insofar as risk affects diverse ecological niches in different ways, one would expect corresponding productive diversity. This factor operates primarily on the process of centralization, as the attempt is made to buffer the risk factor of any one niche through some form of centralized management. Once such centralization is established, a society is on the way to statehood.

The other first-order factor is diversity. "By diversity we mean the closeness and pattern of spacing of contrasting environmental conditions significant in terms of human exploitation" (Sanders and Webster 1978: 253). While the concept of diversity includes both subsistence and non-subsistence resources, the primary focus is on subsistence diversity, with the insistence that any measures proposed be closely related to basic human needs. One measure of this factor for an agrarian society is variability in soil types. While a quantitative scale for measuring this variable is beyond the scope of this essay, elsewhere (Frick 1983), through the use of soil maps of the area, an attempt has been made to analyze those regions comprising Iron I Israel in terms of both risk and diversity (cf. table 8).

Productivity is a second-order factor included in the model. "By productivity we mean the potential of the landscape to produce energy in the form of subsistence products for the support of human populations" (Sanders and Webster 1978: 261). While there are ecological constraints to the level of production, what is emphasized here is the role of cultural factors such as levels of technology, social organization, and information flow. The fundamental role of agricultural productivity is quite simply to provide adequate energy supplies. There are several ways to assess productivity, but two basic measures are input-output ratios, i.e., the ratio between energy expenditure and energy return, and land-use factor, i.e., how much cultivated land is needed to maintain year-after-year production. When these are combined, the geographical area in which the Israelite state came into being constitutes an example of what Sanders and Webster term "type A" productivity, in which agricultural intensification results in an increase in the input-output ratio of demographic capacity. This kind of productivity typically occurs in arid or semiarid areas like Palestine, where intensification involves technological innovations that have a measurable effect on agricultural yields and crop security. Elsewhere I have examined in some detail the role of technological innovations in Iron I Palestine such as the introduction and spread of iron tools and weapons, of water systems, and of terracing and other measures aimed at making agriculture both possible and profitable in the various regions (Frick 1983).

Having taken the above factors into consideration, a systemic multilineal model discards the notion of a single unilinear evolutionary trajectory, in which there is automatic and invariable progression through a sequence of stages, and proposes several possible trajectories, each of which is conditioned by a particular permutation of factors. These trajectories are represented in tables 6 and 7, adapted from Sanders and Webster (1978: 282).

Table 6

(1)   hr/hd
                         :
→   egal. soc. --- strat. soc. --- state
pop.

(2)   hr/ld
                          :
→   egal. soc. ----- strat. soc. ----- state
pop.

(3)   lr/hd   mr/hd
               :   :
→   egal. soc. ----- chiefdom ------------ state
pop.

(4)   lr/ld   hr/hd
               :   :
→   egal. soc. ---------- chiefdom ------- state
pop.

(5)
→   egal. soc. --------- strat. soc. ------ state
pop.

--------------> TIME ------------>

Multilineal systemic model with ecological variables controlling various evolutionary trajectories. Population growth is assumed throughout each sequence but is not itself necessarily directly deterministic of tempos or limits of evolution; its importance is greater in some trajectories than in others. [l=low; h=high; m=medium; r=risk; d=diversity]

It should be observed that each of these trajectories is characterized by different tempos of transformation as well as by different population sizes and densities and different sequences of organizational forms. There are also potential variations within trajectories which can appear when a wide comparative perspective is taken.

The trajectories which are applicable in the case of ancient Israel are (3) and (4) in table 6 and (1) in table 7. With respect to risk and diversity, early Israel can be characterized as including medium- and high-risk and medium-diversity environments with type A productivity. With this permutation of factors the model predicts the following: high-risk environments should be settled by agricultural societies later than regions where risk is low, assuming choices are available. The stimulus to intensive methods of cultivation is high and such techniques should appear early. Assuming that the relationship between population growth and agricultural system is mutual-causal rather than linear, population growth should be rapid once the area is settled. Population distribution should also be uneven, reflecting adaptation to lower-risk zones and zones available for intensification (Sanders and Webster 1978:

Table 7. Evolutionary Trajectories

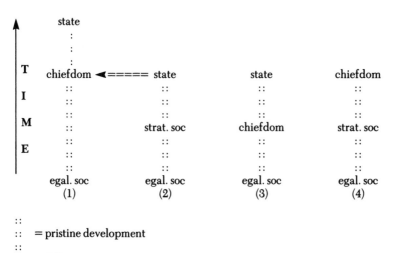

```
     state
      :
      :
 T    :
      chiefdom ◄===== state        state           chiefdom
 I    ::            ::              ::              ::
      ::            ::              ::              ::
 M    ::            ::              ::              ::
      ::          strat. soc       chiefdom        strat. soc
 E    ::            ::              ::              ::
      ::            ::              ::              ::
      ::            ::              ::              ::
      egal. soc    egal. soc       egal. soc       egal. soc
       (1)          (2)             (3)             (4)
```

```
::
::   = pristine development
::

◄    = diffusion

:
:    = secondary development
:
```

298). While the model does not specifically deal with this instance, I would propose that, when the other principal factor of medium diversity is added in, the trajectory should be one of sustained growth from a segmentary society to a chiefdom to a small urban state. Evolution to a large urban state would be retarded by topographical fragmentation. Such a factor was operative in the relatively short-lived "large urban state" of the era of David and Solomon, and its dissolution upon the death of Solomon derives, at least in part, from the topographical fragmentation that is certainly evident in a region which is more topographically suited to separate southern and northern sociopolitical entities. During the early phases of settlement the stimulus toward competition, segmentation, and centralization would be low, and that toward cooperation, moderate; during the middle phase, stimulus to cooperation would be high, with the other processes moderate; during the final state, the stimulus would be high for all four processes.

This model, which combines controlling ecological variables and multilineal trajectories of change with an overtly systemic evolutionary approach, is one which in my estimation lends itself well to application to the situation in ancient israel, and the predictions made on the basis of the model need to be tested against relevant textual and archaeological data pertaining to the agricultural base of Israelite society. In the space that remains I can only suggest the outlines of what such testing might involve, using data from the two highland sites of Ai (et-Tell) and Khirbet Raddana.

In what follows attention is given to both ecological and subsistence variables that were operative in ancient Israel. It should be clear that the position here is not one which seeks to establish a set of techno-environmental factors as determinants of sociopolitical change; rather, this set of factors is viewed as allowing a greater range of small local group adaptations some of which, because of their more stabilized economies and sociocultural patterns, were more susceptible to the centralizing tendencies inherent in a chiefdom. Building upon a model of early Israel as a segmentary society (Frick 1983), the perspective here is of a larger sociopolitical organism composed of such segments which are continually changing and which are tied together politically by a variety of elastic sociocultural bonds.

Utilizing Leon Marfoe's study of sociopolitical organization in southern Syria (1980), the focus here is on particular patterns that characterize the kind of "integrative transformation" which can occur within the context of highland agriculture engaged in by a segmentary society in the type of specific environmental niche or niches that are found in the areas in which Israel had its early development.

What is agriculture and what does it do? First, agriculture is the deliberate caring for, manipulation of, or cultivation of plants so as to enhance their utility for human consumption or use. Its immediate and most far-reaching effect is that it concentrates usable productivity, increasing consumable yield per unit area of land. Second, agriculture involves human intervention in the ecosystem process; i.e., the maintenance of an artificial ecosystem (Athens 1977: 362).

On the basis of such a functional definition of agriculture it is obvious that both techno-environmental and societal concerns are involved. What is needed is an analysis of the way in which the differential constraints imposed by the internal functioning of varying levels of agricultural intensification in the highland areas, together with the extent of agricultural risk and diversity, provide a setting for the mechanisms and processes of centralization to operate as strategies for dealing with the particular kinds of problems that arise in such an environment—in other words, the ways in which ecological opportunity is translated into sociopolitical change.

It is now an established fact, no matter what historical position one may subscribe to, whether of the "conquest," the "settlement," or the "revolt" tendency, that ancient Israel first became established as a recognizable sociopolitical entity in the hill country of Palestine. The political movements that ultimately led to unification, the events that surrounded the formative stages of chiefdom, and then the state at the time of Samuel, Saul, and David were all focused on the central highlands. Subsequent movements (due in part to population growth) onto the lowlands, into the plains of Jezreel and Esdraelon, to the Huleh basin, onto the coastal plain of Philistia and the western Shephelah, into the Transjordan, and finally into the Negev were secondary expansions following upon the success of Israel's having become established in the central highlands. What then are the environmental parameters of this region and how are they to be related to the variables of agricultural risk and diversity?

While Denis Baly (1974: 54–68) has made significant contributions in this area, so far as I know there has not yet been assembled a comprehensive body of such data for the central highlands that can be used in testing archaeologically derived hypotheses concerning subsistence patterns and social organization. There does, however, exist a model for the analysis of such data in the work of Lawrence Stager (1972; 1975; 1976). Stager suggests that the two most important determinants of desert agriculture (and, although of somewhat different dimensions, of semiarid highland agriculture as well) are the dispositions of water and of soil. What is offered here then is a preliminary analysis of these two variables in the central highlands.

With respect to soil fertility in the western highlands it should be noted that generalizations based on soil maps illustrate only in a gross way major patterns of diversity over very large areas and do not take into account the significant microdiversity particularly found in highland areas. The patterning of the larger units of analysis, however, almost certainly reflects differences in the microdiversity within the respective units as well. A useful study that takes microdiversity into account is that of D. Webley (1972). His hypothesis is that distribution of sites is related to the distribution of soil types, with emphasis on the controlling role that soils play in the exploitation of an area. In order to bring together the various factors of land capability, each soil type is assessed for its ability to support pasture and arable crops.

Webley analyzes soil series and their agricultural potential within the catchments of 222 archaeological sites which he examined, an adaptation of which appears below, including only those soil types present in the highlands (cf. Webley 1972: 170).

Table 8. Distribution of Archaeological Sites with Soil Types and Their Agricultural Potential

Soil type	Drainage	Agricultural Class		No. of sites
		Arable	Pasture	
Terra rossa	Good	1b	1	22
Mediterranean brown	Good	1b	1	15
Rendzina	Good	2	2	29
Basaltic	Poor	2	2	6
Alluvial	Poor	2	2	37
Colluvial-alluvial	Good	1a	1a	9
Brown skeletal desert	Good	2c	(1)	10
Stony desert land	Excess	2c	(1)	7
Loess raw	Good	(2)	(2)	7

(Parentheses denote seasonal use)

From this table it can be observed that for arable agriculture terra rossa, Mediterranean brown, and colluvial-alluvial soils provide the most productive natural situations, while the addition of rendzina and basaltic soils permit pastoralism in addition to farming. While a minimum of two different soils per site is the norm, a characteristic distributional feature of sites with a long settlement history is that they have a maximum diversity of soil types in their catchment. In most cases the pattern is similar: sites are located on freely drained land with at least two soil types nearby and, in some cases, three or more. Successful sites thus maximize agricultural diversity by being able to exploit alternate resources should one fail. This kind of analysis does not discount the more often cited political and strategic reasons for site location; it instead emphasizes the fact that sites emerge as political centers because they can be economically viable given the kind of agricultural risks characteristic of the area.

Having considered the relationships between site locations and their economic potentials on a general level, Webley tests his hypothesis at the site level by an analysis of the site of Gezer. Since Gezer comes under Israelite control after the formation of the state, the data are not relevant here, but the method is. For site catchment analysis, Webley made six two-hour walks along chosen compass points, keeping notes on the topography, soil, and agriculture. Visits and interviews with producers within the radius completed the land utilization picture (1972: 172). While Webley's method cannot be duplicated here, it is adapted for application to the analysis of two representative Iron I sites which have been excavated, Khirbet Raddana and Ai, both of which lie on the northern border of the tribal area of Benjamin. In order roughly to duplicate Webley's site catchment analysis, soil maps were examined using a circle with radii of 5 km. as the limit of a site's arable exploitation area and 10 km. as the limit of grazing range (cf. Vita-Finzi 1978: 23–31). Archaeological reports furnish additional data and a land utilization map from the second half of the sixteenth century (*Tübinger Atlas des Vorderen Orients* 1980: A X 8) was analyzed in place of interviews with producers.

Ai is situated on the south side of the Wadi el-Jaya which leads eastward toward Jericho. The foundation of the Iron I village settlement has been dated by its excavator, J. Callaway, to c. 1220 B.C.E., after the site's having been abandoned since c. 2400 B.C.E. (Callaway 1976: 29). The reestablishment of a settlement at Ai is thus roughly contemporaneous with the reoccupation of Tell en-Nasbeh (Mizpah) and el-Jib (Gibeon), together with the establishment of such new sites in the central highlands as Mukhmas (Michmas), Rammun (Rimmon), et-Taiyibeh (Ophrah?), Tell el-Ful (Gibeah), and Khirbet Raddana (Ataroth-Adar?). The Iron IA phase at Ai, c. 1220–1125 B.C.E., is agrarian in nature. Dry farming was practiced, since the only spring in the area is one in the Wadi el-Jaya with a scant flow of 17.5 gal. per hour, which, even if more copious in the Iron I period, would still have had a flow dependent upon the vagaries of rainfall. Numerous food processing tools were in evidence together with an agricultural terrace (Callaway 1976: 29). Bones of sheep and goats were found in every house, pointing to a risk-buffering mixed-subsistence strategy of cereal agriculture and pastoralism. This phase was followed by the Iron IB phase, c. 1125–1050 B.C.E., in which some degree of agricultural intensification is evidenced together with accompanying sociopolitical change. Numerous silo granaries were built in the open spaces near houses or over the cobblestone streets of the previous phase, and large round silos were constructed in the ruins of the EB temple ruin on the acropolis. While the collar-rim type of large store jar was prevalent in the Iron IA phase and continued in use during the Iron IB phase, the prevalence of the above-ground stone granary structures suggests that they became the major storage facilities during the second phase. Callaway, commenting on this change in agricultural storage methods says,

> The sudden transition in the method of storing grain indicates an infusion of people who brought the custom with them, and the manner in which the streets, court areas and temple ruin were converted into *ad hoc* granaries and shelter-type living areas suggests that these people lacked the orderliness and experience in village life of their predecessors (1976: 30).

Thus, even though he observes internal change and cites evidence for population increase on the site, in his explanation he still resorts to the influx of a new ethnic group (of Israelites with a nomadic background no less!) rather than seeking an explanation in the process of agricultural intensification and accompanying changes in sociopolitical structure.

The site of Khirbet Raddana is situated on the northern limits of el-Bireh to the east of Ramallah. Like Ai, Khirbet Raddana has an Iron IA phase, which was established c. 1220–1200 B.C.E., and an Iron IB phase beginning c. 1125, which was a remodeling of the Iron IA phase. This village occupation terminated c. 1050 B.C.E. (Cooley 1976: 7). Thus, in the case of both Ai and Raddana the termination of occupation coincides with sociopolitical changes involving a degree of centralization in which such small sites were vacated. Such changes were thus already in progress before the ascendancy of Saul. The Khirbet Raddana evidence for an agrarian economy virtually duplicates that at Ai, with the exception that no large oval granaries were found at Raddana which could be compared with such structures at Ai. There is also a similar alteration of house plans in the Iron IB phase, and the evidence again suggests an increase in population density with additions to houses and the rearrangement of rooms into smaller units (Cooley 1976: 10). While Cooley, like Callaway, interprets such changes as due to "newcomers who lacked experience in village life or in any case the sophistication of their . . . predecessors" (Cooley 1976: 10), he appears to undermine his own interpretation by citing the fact that there is considerable evidence of metallurgical activity in the Iron IB phase, including not only numerous bronze objects and iron plowshares, knives, and projectile points but also evidence for an on-site metalworking industry. The existence of such an industry is based upon the discovery of crucible fragments with copper slag adhering to them, along with pieces of tuyeres or tips for bellows used for the raising of the temperature in a charcoal fire (Cooley 1976: 11). The place of such metallurgical activity in the society of early Israel and especially in the development of iron technology is an important one which I have detailed elsewhere (Frick 1983). Here I can only say that there appears to be a direct and striking correlation between such metallurgical developments and agricultural intensification in Israel in Iron IA–IC.

Within Ai's area of arable exploitation (a circle with a radius of 5 km.) there are four soil types: terra rossa predominates, with smaller areas of colluvial-alluvial, terra rossa-alluvial complex with terra rossa as dominant, and rendzina-Mediterranean brown complex with rendzina as dominant. A circle with a radius of 10 km. includes, in addition to the above soil types, several areas with plain rendzina, plain Mediterranean brown, plain alluvial, and brown desert soils. When this complex of soil types is compared with the soil types in table 8, it can be seen that there exists around Ai those soil types which support both agriculture and pastoralism, which coordinates with the archaeological evidence.

For Khirbet Raddana a 5 km. circle includes mixed soil types similar to Ai's but with less terra rossa, more Mediterranean brown either by itself or as the secondary soil type in a terra rossa-Mediterranean brown complex, and some alluvial soil. Within a 10 km. radius, which overlaps both the 5 km. and 10 km. areas around Ai, there are, in the area not in that overlap, sizable areas of Mediterranean brown soils either as the dominant or as the secondary type in a complex. This site, like Ai, is situated in an area with a variety of soil types which would in turn support some degree of agricultural diversity.

Such gross data, drawn as they are from soil maps rather than from on-site inspection, need to be supplemented by details regarding soil depth, drainage, etc., before the areas around these two sites could be classified in terms of Webley's land capability classifications, but they are sufficient for the general conclusions drawn here. It is also important to note that there are differences in the way soils lend themselves to cultivation. Mediterranean brown, e.g., is a heavy soil that requires careful and constant working in order to obtain the best tilth for sowing; failure to do this reduces yields considerably. Webley observes that it was only with the metal implements of the Late Bronze Age that Mediterranean brown soils could have been cultivated and that before this they could only successfully have been used for pasture (1972: 173–74).

Data from the late sixteenth century c.e. land utilization map (*Tübinger Atlas des Vorderen Orients* 1980: A X 8) support the above conclusions regarding the relationship between soil types and agricultural diversity. This map shows the money equivalent of the crops and animals raised in specific areas. The areas of Ai and Khirbet Raddana show a comparable figure for total agricultural production in the range of 15,000 to 20,000 aqja. In terms of specific products, the area around Ai produced the following, expressed in terms of approximate percentage of the total: olives, 70%; wheat, 10%; fruit trees (including grapes), 8%; barley, 6%; and goats and sheep, 6%. Although Raddana is only about 6 km. from Ai, the difference in their produce illustrates well the microdiversity in the highland setting. The area around Khirbet Raddana produced the following: wheat, 51%; barley, 8%; olives, 25%; fruit trees (including grapes), 8%; and goats and sheep, 8%.

These two sets of figures are only a very small sample, both representing the tribal area of Benjamin. From the same land utilization map it can be seen that few sites in the central highlands to the north of Ai have more than 10% to 15% of their produce as barley, whereas almost all sites south of there have 15% to 25% in barley; in the area of Philistia, however, most sites have 25% to 40% in barley. Also, from just north of Ai to about 10 km. north of Nablus (Shechem) many sites have as much as 40% to 60% or more in olives. The area of Bethlehem, which might be taken as representative of sites in the highland area of Judah, produced the following: wheat, 40%; fruit trees (including grapes), 30%; ;barley, 15%; and goats and sheep, 15%. One might conclude from these data that the tribal area of Benjamin, which produced the first paramount chief, constituted a distinct ecological niche which had a micro-diversity within it but which had even more significant differences from its neighbors both north and south. While more needs to be done with agricultural technology and social change in early Israel than space allows here (cf. Frick 1983), it is hoped that the above considerations at least show the lines along which such a case might be developed utilizing the model of Sanders and Webster.

In the kind of environments included in Iron I Israel there was a great deal of pressure to use labor efficiently through technological and sociological means. Regarding the latter, it could be anticipated that under conditions of agricultural intensification there was increasing specialization in the kinds of tasks performed for purposes of labor efficiency. When labor needs require a level of efficiency beyond that which can be supplied by productive specialization in the local household or residential group, an organizing principle based on the hierarchical partitioning of society may arise. This hierarchy, concerned with administration, serves to organize and direct energy exchanges between the segments of the society. In addition, the power and authority that usually accompany hierarchical systems make it possible for those holding such positions to require that work critical to agricultural production be completed within the time constraints allowed by environmental factors in a semiarid climate such as that of Israel, thereby ensuring stability of production. In addition, the hierarchical organization of the cultural system is the most effective way in which to monitor matter and energy exchanges and deviations in relevant variables over a large area. Thus, agricultural intensification, discernible through archaeological remains, appears to be a significant contributory factor in ancient Israel's trajectory to statehood.

BIBLIOGRAPHY

Aharoni, Yohanan
      1982   *The Archaeology of the Land of Israel.* Trans. A. F. Rainey from Hebrew, 1978. Philadelphia: Westminster Press.

Athens, J. Stephen
  1977   Theory Building and the Study of Evolutionary Process in Complex
            Societies. Pp. 353–84 in *For Theory Building in Archaeology*, ed. L. R.
            Binford. New York: Academic Press.

Baly, Denis
  1974   *The Geography of the Bible.* Revised ed. New York: Harper and Row.

Callaway, Joseph
  1976   Excavating Ai (Et-Tell): 1964–1972. *Biblical Archaeologist* 39: 18–30.

Coogan, Michael D.
  1982   Review of Y. Aharoni, *The Archaeology of the Land of Israel. Biblical
            Archaeology Review* 8:3:8.

Cooley, Robert E.
  1976   Four Seasons of Excavation at Khirbet Raddana. Privately published
            manuscript.

Flannery, Kent V.
  1972   The Cultural Evolution of Civilizations. *Annual Review of Ecology and
            Systematics* 3: 399–426.

Frick, Frank S.
  1979   Religion and Sociopolitical Structure in Early Israel: An Ethno-Archaeo-
            logical Approach. Pp. 233–53 in vol. 2 of *Society of Biblical Literature
            1979 Seminar Papers,* ed. Paul J. Achtemeier. Missoula, MT: Scholars
            Press.
  1983   *The Formation of the State in Ancient Israel.* Sheffield, England:
            Almond Press.

Gall, Patricia L. and Saxe, A. A.
  1977   The Ecological Evolution of Culture: The State as Predator in Succession
            Theory. Pp. 255–68 in *Exchange Systems in Prehistory,* eds. T. K. Earle
            and J. E. Ericson. New York: Academic Press.

Marfoe, Leon
  1980   The Integrative Transformation: Patterns of Sociopolitical Organization
            in Southern Syria. *Bulletin of the American Schools of Oriental Research*
            234: 1–42.

Sahlins, M. D.
  1967   The Segmentary Lineage: An Organization of Predatory Expansion. Pp.
            89–119 in *Comparative Political Systems,* eds. R. Cohen and J. Middle-
            ton. Garden City, NY: Doubleday.

Sanders, William T. and Webster, David
  1978   Unilinealism, Multilinealism, and the Evolution of Complex Societies. Pp.
            249–302 in *Social Archaeology: Beyond Subsistence and Dating,* eds. C.
            L. Redman et al. New York: Academic Press.

Service, Elman R.
  1962   *Primitive Social Organization.* Second edition. New York: Random
            House.

Stager, Lawrence E.
  1972   Ancient Irrigation Agriculture in the Buqei'ah Valley. American Schools
            of Oriental Research *Newsletter* 1972–73: 2: 1–4.

1975   Ancient Agriculture in the Judean Desert: A Case Study of the Buqeiʻah Valley. Unpublished Ph.D. dissertation, Harvard.

1976   Farming in the Judean Desert during the Iron Age. *Bulletin of the American Schools of Oriental Research* 221: 145–58.

Tübinger Atlas des Vorderen Orients der Universität Tübingen.
1980   Wiesbaden: Dr. Ludwig Reichert Verlag.

Vita-Finzi, Claudio
1978   *Archaeological Sites in Their Setting.* London: Thames and Hudson.

Webley, D.
1972   Soils and Site Location in Prehistoric Palestine. Pp. 169–211 in *Papers in Economic Prehistory*, ed. E. S. Higgs. Cambridge: University Press.

Wright, Henry T.
1978   Toward an Explanation of the Origin of the State. Pp. 49–68 in *Origins of the State: The Anthropology of Political Evolution*, eds. R. Cohen and E. R. Service. Philadelphia: Institute for the Study of Human Issues.

Chapter 16

JEROBOAM AND REHOBOAM AT SHECHEM

Robert G. Boling and
Edward F. Campbell, Jr.
McCormick Theological Seminary

Such an important moment in the life of ancient Israel as the decision to divide the monarchy is presented for us only in an intriguing, tantalizingly partial, at times even comic story in Kings and Chronicles. What is going on here at Shechem, when Rehoboam ignores the wise old heads and follows the advice of the brightest and best of the younger generation? Was Jeroboam present for the negotiations from the start, or did he only arrive in time to capitalize on preceding decisions? At 1 Kings 11:40, all our sources agree that Jeroboam had fled to the court of Pharaoh Shishak; they do not easily harmonize on the point of his return. Speaking of Shishak, what part did his attack upon Israel play in the overall course of events? When and under what circumstances did Jeroboam "build" Shechem (1 Kings 12:25)? We propose here to offer some suggestions about the text of 1 Kings 12, to sketch the picture at Shechem so far as religious and literary associations are concerned, and to bring the archaeology of the site to bear upon the whole picture.

The Texts

The texts and their tendencies in 1 Kings 12 have lately received considerable attention thanks especially to a series of essays and notes by D. W. Gooding and R. Klein. The discussion was launched by the former in a study of the two LXX accounts of how Jeroboam came to power (Gooding 1967). The first LXX account, verses 1–24 (hereafter G[1]), corresponds for the most part to MT but with some very significant differences. According to G[1], Jeroboam returned from Egypt to participate at Shechem only *after* the murder of Adoram (vss. 20–21). Earlier in the chapter where MT vs. 12 has "Jeroboam and

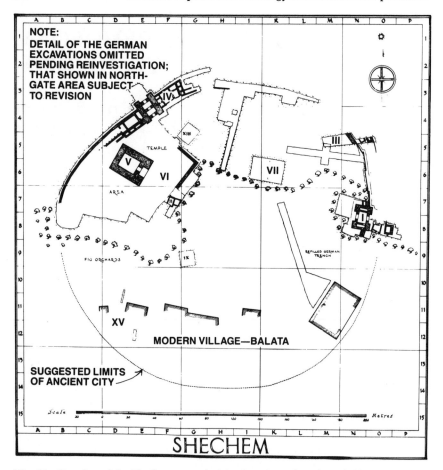

Fig. 39. Site plan of the Shechem mound giving locations of working fields; prepared by G.R.H. Wright; copyright, The Joint Expedition to Shechem.

all the people" going to the second round of negotiations with Rehoboam, G¹ simply has "all Israel" doing so. Still earlier in the chapter, where MT verses 2–3a says that Jeroboam "remained in" (*wayyēšeb . . . bᵉ*) Egypt when, in order to make sense of MT vs. 12, he should have "returned from" (*wayyāšob . . . min*), as indeed he does in the parallel text of 2 Chronicles 10:2, G¹ in LXXᴬ has nothing. The first account in LXXᴬ is the smoothest of the rival versions in 1 Kings 12, for LXXᴮ has a longer parallel to MT vss. 2–31 but puts it *after 11:43*; i.e., according to LXX at 11:43 Jeroboam returned to his hometown and, by implication, remained there in the background, not directly involved in the negotiations with Rehoboam at Shechem.

Although many commentators have concluded from the evidence of LXX that MT verses 2–3a are a secondary reflex of the later account in 2 Chronicles (Klein 1970: 217), Gooding sought instead to explain the differences in terms of a "pedantic timetabling" characteristic of LXX in Kings (Gooding 1969). G^1 thus impressed him as displaying a distinct tendency to whitewash Jeroboam, in contrast to the second LXX account which has no counterpart in MT.

In the second LXX account, verses 24^a–24^z (hereafter G^2), Gooding observed the opposite tendency. This account begins with Jeroboam's return to "sarira," as in LXX^B 11:43, but further specifies that Jeroboam as head of the corvée had built Sarira for Solomon and that he took the initiative in assembling the tribes at Shechem. Gooding observed that, in this account, the "vilifying of Jeroboam is not a superimposed addition; it is the very substance and the basic design" (Gooding 1967: 188). Analysis thus led to three versions of the events, each displaying a different *tendency* toward Jeroboam. As the most moderate of the three, MT was judged to be the earliest, with G^1 and G^2 as two contrasting "Rabbinic, homiletic variations on it" (Gooding 1967: 189). Subsequent studies of G^2 have weakened the charge of "villification" (Aberbach and Smolar 1969) but have further reinforced the low estimate of G^2 as a historical source (Gordon 1975).

Considering "LXX^B's inclusions of material similar in content and length to vss. 2–3a in 11:43" as a "misplaced correction" by a later copyist, R. Klein (1970: 217) has argued that otherwise G^1 is a superior text, as in fact commentators have often concluded from the absence of Jeroboam in LXX vs. 12. For Klein the telling evidence is the cluster of readings in 2 Chronicles 10:3a, which parallel 1 Kings 12:3a and in the MT of which there is no mention of the "assembly." The MT and LXX readings in 2 Chronicles 10:3a are as follows:

MT: וכל־ישראל וידברו

LXX^B: καὶ πᾶσα ἡ ἐκκλησία ἦλθον

LXX^A: καὶ πᾶσα ἐκκλησία Ισραηλ

If the *Vorlage* of LXX^B was $w^ekol\text{-}haqqāhāl\ bā'û$, "the reading in LXX^A can be interpreted as a partial correction" (Klein 1970: 218) containing translations for $qāhāl$ and MT's $yiśrā'ēl$, though, like LXX^B, lacking any word for $wydbbrw$. Consequently the Kings MT reading, $w^ekol\text{-}q^ehal\ yiśrā'ēl$, is a conflation of synonymous variants—attested separately in Chronicles texts. "The secondary character of 1 Kings 12:3a MT is reasonably certain" (Klein 1970: 218).

In response to this reconstruction of textual history, Gooding collected a number of phrases in 1 Kings 12 involving "all Israel" (vss. 1, 16, 20 bis), $kl\text{-}qhl$ (vs. 3), and $kl\text{-}h'm$ (vs. 12), noting the variety of renderings in LXX, as examples of "a common phrase in which variations . . . are synonymous and do not alter the meanings" (Gooding 1972: 530). Further, he took issue with the assumption that the *Vorlage* of 2 Chronicles 20:3a in LXX^B was $wkl\ hqhl\ b'w$ (Gooding 1972: 532).

In response, Klein has demonstrated in detail that the differences noted in the five verses cited above in fact offer "no support for the alleged arbitrariness of the Greek evidence" (Klein 1973: 583). We would add that it is also pertinent to ask, as Gooding apparently did not, whether any or all of these terms have specific referents that are important to the ancient author. Clearly the word that in this respect sticks out like a sore thumb is *qhl* in MT vs. 3, concerning which Klein renews his argument that the most likely source for it is a different Hebrew *Vorlage* to LXX 2 Chron. 10:3.

We suggest that further search for the referent of *qhl* in vs. 3 will indicate that Klein was on the right track. As is well-known, the root *qhl* (both verb and noun forms) is a favorite of Deuteronomy, and it is also ubiquitous in Ezekiel, "P," and the Chronicler's work. *Qhl* words are extremely rare, by comparison, in the books of Joshua—2 Kings. In all of 1 and 2 Samuel the noun is used once (1 Sam. 17:47) and the verb once (2 Sam. 20:14), both in the old premonarchical military sense. However, the distribution of these relatively infrequent words in the deuteronomistic historical books correlates closely with the earlier and later editions of Joshua—Judges, where Boling uses the sigla Dtr[1] (Josianic) and Dtr[2] (post-Josianic, possibly early exilic). In the earlier stratum (Dtr[1]), the *qhl* words are totally absent, while they reappear in the later stratum (Dtr[2]). Moreover, they reappear in close association with another word, *'ēdâ*, that is totally absent from the books of Deuteronomy and Samuel but is characteristic of "P" in material referring to both the prestatehood and post-monarchy eras. It appears clear enough from the distribution that the final edition of Joshua—Judges makes a statement about the post-monarchy "congregation" in the diaspora as a true and legitimate descendant of the prestatehood "assembly," when the latter was no longer possible as a gathering of either the tribes or their representatives. With the *qhl* words, from Deuteronomy to Dtr[2] in Joshua—Judges, we see a semantic shift under way. The shift is complete in Chronicles where the events of 598–587 had made *qāhāl* (deliberative assembly) and *'ēdâ* (worshiping congregation) virtually synonymous. This conclusion is supported by the very scanty use of *'ēdâ* and *qhl* words in Samuel—Kings.

In Kings the words in question occur only in chaps. 8 and 12 (the roster in Boling 1983: 246 is incomplete). The former chapter, recounting Solomon's dedication of the Jerusalem Temple, uses *qhl* words in verses 1, 2, 14 bis, 22, and 65, each of which is an introductory or framework passage. Solomon's speech itself always refers to "your people," "people of Yahweh," or "people of Israel." The sole occurrence of *'adat yiśrā 'ēl*, in 8:5, also narrative framework, shows that the semantic shift described above is under way. The post-monarchy reader is to make no mistake about it—Solomon's prayer continues to express reliable theology for the *qāhāl/'ēdâ* long after the Temple had been destroyed.

The one remaining occurrence of *qhl* in Kings, apart from the problematical use in 1 Kings 12:3a, comes later in the same chapter at 12:21. There we read that Rehoboam returned to Jerusalem and mustered (*wyyqhl*) "all the house of Judah, and the tribe of Benjamin . . . to fight against the house of Israel." This sounds like the older deuteronomic usage, except that it is qualified by context in two ways. First, Rehoboam's action counters the move made by "all Israel" in the immediately preceding verse where "they" called Jeroboam to the '*ēdâ* (second and last use of this word in Kings) and made him king of "all Israel." These two passages juxtaposing a northern '*ēdâ* and a southern *qāhāl* display an incongruity which verges on the comic. Which of the two gatherings is *the real thing*? Which is legitimate, in whose eyes? It is probably safe to say that, for the later edition, Rehoboam's muster could be called a *qāhāl* because there *the king and the people obey* the oracle given by Shemaiah and do not take the field for a civil war but instead go home (vss. 22–25). Here a disastrous internecine war is narrowly averted, as in Josh. 22 where the "congregation of Israel" ('*adat-yiśrā'ēl*) had "assembled" (*wyyqhlw*) and internecine violence was averted by protracted negotiation. That story is clearly a redactional companion piece to the story of the Benjaminite war and its aftermath (Judg. 19—21) where the same clustering of *qhl* words and '*ēdâ* occurs. In this case a resolution is discovered only *after* the violence, in clever diplomacy.

While 1 Kings 12 ends with Solomon's "people of Yahweh" still intact but subject to rival kings, the concluding segment of the chapter is all about Jeroboam. In at least one respect all three accounts (MT, G[1], G[2]) agree in their evaluation of Jeroboam: his provision for a northern '*ēdâ* and therefore his contribution to Levitical history were not good. Now it is generally recognized by critical scholars that the early history of Shechem (a Levitical city assigned to the Qohathite families in Josh. 21:21) must be researched through the haze of a very strong southern bias. At the same time, continued study of Israelite origins points increasingly to early Levitical families, primary carriers of the Exodus-Sinai tradition, as background to the early importance of Shechem, remembered at some length in Joshua 24 but also in brief at Joshua 8:30–35. The dispersion of such families throughout the territories which were redefined at the beginning of the Iron Age, as now given over to the children of Israel, and the reorganizing of old cultic centers to become in one way or another "Israelite" make plausible both a *system* of Levitical centers and the evidence of splits and rivalries within the Levitical cadre. These developments can be only partially but nonetheless convincingly mapped (Boling 1983).

A clear precedent for the *system* (not the extant list) has long been recognized in Egypt's LB domestic administration where "cities had been confiscated, . . . turned into royal Egyptian estates and dedicated by Pharaoh to the great gods of the Egyptians" (Mazar 1960: 205). Building on this hypothesis, N. Allan has suggested that Jeroboam encountered a Levitical presence at

Shechem "acting as an agent of the royal government at Jerusalem" (1974: 356), but must one assume, especially at Shechem in light of its previous significance, a *uniform* Levitical presence? The problem with the monarchical-administrative approach to the Levitical cities, which posits that they originated in the tenth century, is that it fails to account for subsequent Levitical history which was very different in the north than it was in the south. That history is reflected both in the priestly genealogies and in the fluctuating fortunes of rival cult centers some of which were "reformed" holy sites while others were new Israelite foundations. One key to the complex history is the recognition of the name Gershom/n (first son of Levi in the standard genealogy of Exod. 6:16–19) as a major division of Levi alternatively called Mushites in the fragmentary genealogy of Numbers 26:58a (Cross 1973: 197–98). Both genealogy and redactional history point clearly to Shiloh and Dan as having a predominantly Mushite presence at an early period, in contrast to Bethel and probably Hebron where the priesthoods were Aaronite (Cross 1973; Boling 1983; Boling and Wright 1982).

If it is a reliable memory (and it is increasingly difficult to counter this) that Shiloh (newly founded) succeeded Shechem as the place of assembly late in the era of Joshua (Josh. 18:1; Boling 1983; Boling and Wright 1982) because of movements apparently underway at Shechem which would eventuate in Abimelek's destruction of the city and temple (c. 1150–1125), then it is very likely that many of the Levites there, with whom Rehoboam and Jeroboam would have to deal after the recovery of Shechem, were Mushite. Thus it would be among the alienated heirs to the Levitical presence at Shechem, both after Jeroboam's early move of the northern capital away from Shechem (1 Kings 12:25b; 15:21; cf. 14:17) and his non-Levitical appointments at the high places and at Bethel (1 Kings 12:31–32) and after Rehoboam was able, for three years, to exploit a new-found support among the victims of Jeroboam's priestly arrangements (2 Chron. 11:13–14), that we should look for the originators of Deuteronomy. Without the regulation of kingship in Deuteronomy 17:14–20, Deuteronomy is thoroughly amonarchical. Its origins are therefore most likely premonarchical and, in a fair sense, Mosaic.

Archaeology

Can the archaeological record of the Shechem mound and region be brought into conversation with this reading of 1 Kings 12? Such conversation is what is to be hoped for with archaeological results; only rarely will archaeology settle an issue and only rarely is it of total irrelevance. Here are some of the implications of our reading of 1 Kings 12 for Shechem during the tenth century B.C.E.:

(1) Our reading claims that the population in and around Shechem maintained continuity of religious tradition from Israel's formative period, represented by the nucleus of Joshua 24 and the provision for a sacred site and covenantal ritual in Joshua 8:30–35 and Deuteronomy 27.

(2) Our reading of 1 Kings 12 proposes that an element in the population bearing this tradition was Mushite-Levitic. This element kept the old "amonarchic" perspective of the early confederation alive and can readily be expected to have harbored resentment at the style of Solomon's administration. It may have instigated the invitation to Jeroboam to bear rule (somewhat in the Jephthah manner in Judg. 11?) in a political entity conceived as an alternative to the Solomonic establishment.

(3) Our reading implies that the reason Jeroboam left Shechem for other locations of his capital was due less to Shishak's attack upon Israel c. 918 B.C.E. than to disgruntlement at Shechem over Jeroboam's decision to install Aaronite-Levitic priests at Bethel as sanctuary center and illegitimate priests at other sacred sites (1 Kings 12:31). This in turn encourages the thought that Jeroboam "built Shechem" (vs. 25) after the Shishak rampage and left Shechem for Tirzah (by way of Penuel?) at a point early in his reign but enough into it to have experienced the opposition of his Mushite-oriented subjects.

(4) A related question, not raised by 1 Kings 12 but clearly to be faced if we are to sketch Shechem's history at the inception of the monarchic period, is whether Shechem was provincial center for the Mt. Ephraim district (1 Kings 4:8) of Solomon, as proposed by Abel (1938: 81, 460) and plausibly maintained by G. E. Wright, Shechem's excavator (1967a: 60°ff.). What would such a center show in the way of official buildings, fortifications, and population spread?

The archaeological information from Shechem for the tenth century comes from Strata X and IX on the mound and from the regional survey's evidence for outlying settlement.[1] The pottery characterizing Strata X and IX at Shechem is closely comparable to that in the layers representing the Shishak destructions at Gezer and Taanach.[2] Stratum IX pottery continues the forms of Stratum X pottery, although with a change in surface treatment. All the indications are that the change from one to the other represents a relatively short period of time. However, there is a clear break in both form and ware between the tenth-century pottery and that characterizing the end of Stratum XI, the Iron IA occupation terminating about 1125. Here a substantial gap in time is justifiably proposed.

What about the nature of the site during Strata X and IX times? First, a look at fortifications. There is a distinct possibility that the first tenth-century settlement had no fortifications as such; only the rubble and ruins of the LB–Iron I fortifications stood at the perimeter of the site (fig. 39). At Shechem it has proved particularly frustrating to find fortifications of the monarchic period.

Earlier excavation had cleared soil away from some of the walls; besides that, dating of monumental constructions is notoriously problematic even under the best of circumstances, but we should not ignore what evidence there is.

A double wall, resembling the so-called casemate style of the Iron Age, is preserved on either side of the northwest gate at Shechem. Dubbed Wall E, it was assigned to Stratum IX on the basis of a few pieces of IX-period pottery found when a segment was dismantled in 1962. It is now clear that Wall E was first built in MB IIC times just before the final destructive blow of the Egyptians about 1540 B.C.E. Using the exposed tops of the two lines of walling as a base, builders, who had Stratum IX pottery as their own or, equally possibly, who had brought in some fill soil from nearby that had sherds of such pottery in it, evened up the wall stumps with a cushioning layer of soil and built a new top to it. This scrap of evidence is quite lonely in the fortification remains at Shechem. There *may have been* a rebuilding of a lateral wall within the gate towers at Shechem's east gate at this time, although the only surface preserved with this wall has seventh-century pottery on it (Wright 1965: 165, fig. 30; cf. 1957: 30).

Now it is true that hellenistic builders probably removed Iron Age evidence in their zeal to anchor their own fortifications upon the ancient MB IIC ruins and that erosion has done its part in carrying away Iron Age evidence. Nevertheless, in the expedition's work in Field III, where a fresh cut was made across undisturbed remains of fortifications, no Iron Age walls were found, only Iron Age pottery in the screes and fills. With due allowance for the perils of arguments from silence, Shechem X may well have been a site without defense walls; even Stratum IX presents us with little evidence of fortification, but there is at least that stretch of rebuilt Wall E.

One other set of information may pertain to the kind of place Shechem was in the mid-tenth century. The regional survey carried out by Shechem staff gives us a rather comprehensive picture of the settlement patterns in villages, outposts, and guard stations in the Shechem vale (fig. 40). In the LB–Iron I period, i.e., the time of Strata XIV–XI on the mound, there are seventeen known locations of occupation elsewhere in the plain, fourteen of which flank the seven access routes. The distinct impression gained from the map of their locations (Campbell 1983: 267) is one of strategic defense and control.

By contrast, twenty-seven sites of Iron II are to be found, a number of which yielded specifically Shechem X and IX pottery. These are spread all over the hilly flanks of the valley, suggesting that people now chose to live closer to their agricultural lands and felt safe in doing so. The impression is one of a greater sense of security. An unwalled town at Shechem would point in the same direction.

Returning to the mound, it is also the case that we have no public buildings in the excavated portion of the mound which can be connected with

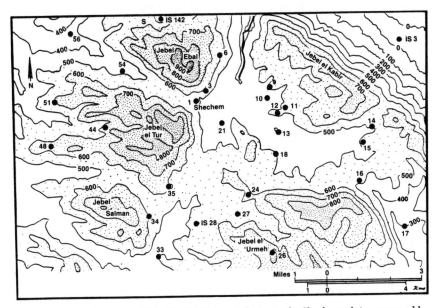

Fig. 40. Spread of Iron II (1000–587 B.C.E.) period sites in the Shechem plain; prepared by
G.R.H. Wright; copyright, The Joint Expedition to Shechem.

royal administration in the tenth century. The well-known 5900 Granary, a
large building made of boulders robbed from the top of Shechem's "Cyclopean
Wall," boulders which were set into a plaster matrix that may have helped to
keep vermin out, appears to have been built in the eighth century, although
again we are dependent upon stray sherds of Iron II ware under the wall stones
(estimates of their date have usually been stated in terms of Shechem Strata
IXA–VII = ninth-eighth centuries). Nothing earlier separates the granary from
the twelfth-century ruin below it.

One further lack. Mention was made above of a temporary misdating of
Strata XII and XI, corrected in 1965. The misconstrual had allowed the west
wall and part of the interior of an inner-city sanctuary in Field IX to be
assigned to the tenth century. Jaroš proposed that it was a private chapel, part
of the residence of Jeroboam I (1976: 122). The sanctuary, however, does not
continue past the Abimelek destruction around 1125 and indeed is contemporary with the final phase of the famous and salient temple complex in the
northwest quadrant of Shechem. We have no sanctuary at the famous temple
location in the periods of Strata X and IX at Shechem nor at any other place
where excavation has reached tenth-century levels (only, it is true, a fraction of
the mound). Just where the sacred *topos* at Shechem was during this period is a

mystery, possibly simply at the ruins of the old temples, possibly outside the city elsewhere, possibly up on Mt. Ebal (Campbell 1983).

What *do* we have then? We have plenty of evidence that people lived on the Shechem mound in the tenth century. What they found on the site when they returned was the destroyed ruins of Stratum XI with debris heaps around the exposed tops of substantial walls. What they did in relation to these Stratum XI ruins narrates something of their story. A wall segment and several connected surfaces belonging to Stratum X were found inside the east gate close to a ruined Strata XII–XI gate tower there. It had the typical dimensions of a house wall and is poorly preserved. It rode only slightly lower than the tops of the ruined tower gate. A similar wall with surface lay nearby but not superimposed; it represents Stratum IX. It appears, then, that dwellings lay this close to the ruins of the old defenses (Toombs, in Bull and Campbell 1968), and it seems that reinforcement of the defense lines did not shelter them in such a manner as to hold in place destruction debris created by their own demise. Again the suspicion is this: dwellings and use; erosion and little debris buildup; perhaps no fortification.

Over near the temple precinct, in Field II, below hellenistic remains and remains of a solid Stratum VIII or VII house, another house wall with a floor reaching it came to light at the conclusion of excavation in 1968 (Ross, in Campbell, Ross, and Toombs 1971: 4–5). Here a Stratum X building lies nearly level with the top of the ruins of the temple precinct wall, founded directly on MB IIC debris. The earlier German excavations at Shechem cleared all hellenistic, Iron Age, and LB remains that lay between Field II and the portion of Wall E mentioned earlier. Such ruins did exist, but we shall never know what precise periods were represented in what way.

Deeper inside town, in Fields VII and IX where stratigraphic cuts were made through domestic housing back to Shechem's earliest periods, there was clear attestation of Strata X and IX. In Field VII, Stratum X had two phases. The first consisted of quite well-built walls—two parallel rows of stone with rubble interior. At a number of points they were founded on the lines of Stratum XI walls beneath, which served as foundation and probably as a readily available supply of building material. The distance between the Stratum X walls was too wide, 5 m. to 7 m., to have been spanned by roofing beams, and there were ovens and work installations throughout. Only in the second phase were two small wall complexes built that looked like dwellings—mere huts—among the work areas (Bull et al. 1965: 9–15, 19–21). In Field IX the circumstances differ only in that there were several of the hut-sized structures and no open areas. The huts give the impressions of careless construction, covered over with mud plaster, and of general poverty.

Stratum X in both fields showed evidence of destruction by fire, a fire so hot that it calcined the limestone rocks in the walls. There will, then, have been a good bit of wood and brush used in these buildings, and there will have been a devastating conflagration.

Stratum IX in both locations represents rebuilding on very much better lines. The foundations of the Stratum X walls were sought as base for new walls. Where the Stratum X walls were rubble core and wider, the Stratum IX walls tended to have single stones chosen and, to some extent, shaped to fit across the width of the wall in rather uniform style ("headers"). Lime plaster gave better strength and a better look to the walls. Both fields now show clusters of rooms into what can really be called houses, one or more of them with a second story, and there is evidence of repair and renovation at various places.

Out of all this data what sense can be made? The archaeological data, incomplete as it is for Strata X and IX, suggests the following:

(1) Shechem began to come back from little or no occupation in the period c. 1125–1000 by way of a gradual settling over the mound, with much open space for work areas given to subsistence matters, during the time covered by Stratum X. The site was probably unwalled. Population at the town itself was probably sparse, but people were living in villages throughout the Shechem vale. The eroded ruins of Stratum XI houses had served as foundations on which to anchor Stratum X walls, but major structures of Stratum XI were not recovered or put back into use. If Shechem was the administrative center for the first Solomonic district, as 1 Kings 4 suggests, we should not think of such a center as a fortified, bustling town. Such meagerness does not preclude the possibility of Shechem being the district's center, but it tells against this identification and may shift our attention toward Tirzah, 12 km. to the northeast, as a viable candidate; at Tirzah there is strong tenth-century occupation (de Vaux 1967: 376–77).

(2) While Shechem was not a flourishing city in Stratum X, that by no means negates its status as a famous central sanctuary location from the early confederacy period, to which Rehoboam would appropriately come in anticipation of being crowned king of "all Israel." What he came to was a *location* in the narrow valley between Mts. Gerizim and Ebal, which was redolent with covenantal associations. For all we know, the people resettling the site in the mid-tenth century were indeed Levitical families, filtering back, who had long been associated with the site. Indeed, to us that seems quite likely.

(3) When Shishak ranged through Palestine in 918 B.C.E., he claims in his topographic list at Karnak to have destroyed a line of locations (57–65) which, poorly preserved as the names are, outlines a route of march northward from Gibeon to "the valley," doubtless the Esdraelon plain. One of his victims was apparently Tirzah (59); just preceding Tirzah comes what is generally read as Migdol, which many see as referring to Shechem, recalling Migdal-Shechem in Judges 9:46–49. Others suspect that Shechem occurred as one of the lost cluster in 61–63 (Kitchen 1973: 293–300, 432–47; Aharoni 1979: 323–30).

The archaeological evidence supports a destruction of the settlement of Stratum X. People and structures were there, and the location was old and famous as well as strategic. As we have suggested, it may not have taken much to destroy the settlement; it was defenseless. The roofs and upper walls would have provided excellent fuel for fire, hot enough to calcine the stones. To see Shishak as the agent is a plausible historical reconstruction. His list of conquests then goes on to suggest that a detachment of his force went from Tirzah down the Wadi Far'ah to Adamah, Succoth, and Penuel in Transjordan, quite possibly in pursuit of a fleeing Jeroboam.

(4) Yet that need not have been the end of Jeroboam's connection to Shechem. Stratum IX represents something more substantial than Stratum X. The inhabitants routed by Shishak probably returned to build at once. Debris was cleared away and pushed into old storage pits or cast broadly over the site. Stratum X foundation walls were used as base for new building on a much better scale. Our claim would be that this substantial improvement indicates the type of impulse and organization that Jeroboam's governmental establishment would have meant. Stratum IX, as "Jeroboam's rebuild," moved toward a substantial town once more, spreading out toward the limits of the old Bronze Age city. With the recognition that the evidence is not compelling, it is probably that the town was fortified and that there began a short period of reign for Jeroboam at the great old covenantal center—a period ending with Jeroboam's departure to a place where making adjustments to the necessities of pragmatic governance would be more readily acceptable and where old idealisms would be less constricting. From that time on, within the Israelite period, Shechem's role would be much the same as many another hill-country town, with a continuing religious history we can only guess at (Hos. 6:9)!

NOTES

1. Strata XII and XI were assigned to the time of David and Solomon for a period of eight months during and after the 1964 campaign at the site; the dates were then corrected to LB IIB and Iron IA, c. 1350–1125. In that brief eight-month period the interim report was written, and three crucial summations of the Shechem archaeological story were readied for publication; namely, Wright (1965: 145 with footnote), Wright (1978: 1093, written in the winter of 1964 and unrevised in the light of clarifications made soon thereafter), and Horn (1965: 304–6). Correction was made in Bull (1965: 11–15) and in Wright (1967b: 366), and the revision is basic to Toombs' presentation of the overall site stratigraphy (1972; 1976). Regrettably, the misinterpretation influenced the most comprehensive and detailed study of Shechem, based on both archaeology and text, available in German (Jaroš 1976: 121ff., cf. 42–44, 86–98) and resulted in erroneous proposals about Jeroboam's city.

2. Thanks are due Mr. Daniel Katz, graduate student at the Oriental Institute, for

preliminary comparative studies on these three corpora done for a seminar at the University of Chicago in the spring of 1978.

BIBLIOGRAPHY

Abel, F.-M.
1938   *Géographie de la Palestine.* Vol. 2. Third edition. Paris: Libraire Le-coffre, J. Gabalda.

Aberbach, M. and Smolar, L.
1969   Jeroboam's Rise to Power. *Journal of Biblical Literature* 88: 69–72.

Aharoni, Y.
1979   *The Land of the Bible.* Revised edition. Trans. and ed. A. F. Rainey. Philadelphia: Westminster.

Allan, N.
1974   Jeroboam and Shechem. *Vetus Testamentum* 24: 353–57.

Boling, R. G.
1975   *Judges.* Anchor Bible 6A. Garden City: Doubleday.
1983   Levitical History and the Role of Joshua. Pp. 241–61 in *The Word of the Lord Shall Go Forth: Essays in Honor of David Noel Freedman in Celebration of His Sixtieth Birthday,* ed. C. L. Meyers and M. O'Connor. Winona Lake: Eisenbrauns.

Boling, R. G. and Wright, G. E.
1982   *Joshua.* Anchor Bible 6. Garden City: Doubleday.

Bull, R. J., Callaway, J. A., Campbell, E. F., Ross, J. F., and Wright, G. E.
1965   The Fifth Campaign at Balâṭah (Shechem). *Bulletin of the American Schools of Oriental Research* 180: 7–40.

Bull, R. J. and Campbell, E. F.
1968   The Sixth Campaign at Balâṭah (Shechem). *Bulletin of the American Schools of Oriental Research* 190: 2–41.

Campbell, E. F.
1983   Judges 9 and Biblical Archaeology. Pp. 263–71 in *The Word of the Lord Shall Go Forth: Essays in Honor of David Noel Freedman in Celebration of His Sixtieth Birthday,* ed. C. L. Meyers and M. O'Connor. Winona Lake: Eisenbrauns.

Campbell, E. F., Ross, J. F., and Toombs, L. E.
1971   The Eighth Campaign at Balâṭah (Shechem). *Bulletin of the American Schools of Oriental Research* 204: 2–17.

Cross, F. M.
1973   *Canaanite Myth and Hebrew Epic.* Cambridge, MA: Harvard.

Gooding, D. W.
1967   The Septuagint's Rival Versions of Jeroboam's Rise to Power. *Vetus Testamentum* 17: 173–89.
1969   Problems of Text and Midrash in the Third Book of Reigns. *Textus* 7: 1–29.
1972   Jeroboam's Rise to Power: A Rejoinder. *Journal of Biblical Literature* 91: 529–33.

Gordon, R. P.
1975   The Second Septuagint Account of Jeroboam: History or Midrash? *Vetus Testamentum* 25: 368–93.

Horn, S. H.
1965   Shechem. History and Excavations of a Palestinian City. *Jaarbericht: Ex Oriente Lux* 18: 284–306.

Jaroš, K.
1976   *Sichem: Eine archäologische und religiongeschichtliche Studie mit besonderer Berücksichtigung von Jos 24.* Orbis Biblicus et Orientalis 11. Göttingen: Vandenhoeck and Ruprecht.

Kitchen, K. A.
1973   *The Third Intermediate Period in Egypt (1100–650 B.C.E.).* Warminster: Aris and Phillips.

Klein, R. W.
1970   Jeroboam's Rise to Power. *Journal of Biblical Literature* 89: 217–19.
1973   Once More: "Jeroboam's Rise to Power." *Journal of Biblical Literature* 92: 582–84.

Mazar, B.
1960   The Cities of the Priests and the Levites. *Vetus Testamentum Supplement* 7: 193–205.

Toombs, L. E.
1972   The Stratigraphy of Tell Balata (Ancient Shechem). *Annual of the Department of Antiquities of Jordan* 17: 99–110, 173–85.
1976   The Stratification of Tell Balâṭah (Shechem). *Bulletin of the American Schools of Oriental Research* 223: 57–59.

Vaux, R. de
1967   Tirzah. Pp. 371–83 in *Archaeology and Old Testament Study: Jubilee Volume of the Society for Old Testament Study 1917–1967,* ed. D. Winton Thomas. Oxford: Clarendon.

Wright, G. E.
1957   Shechem, "Navel of the Land": Part III. The Archaeology of the City. *Biblical Archaeologist* 20: 19–32.
1965   *Shechem: The Biography of a Biblical City.* New York and Toronto: McGraw-Hill.
1967a   The Provinces of Solomon. *Eretz-Israel* 8 (= Sukenik Memorial Volume): 58°–68°.
1967b   Shechem. Pp. 355–70 in *Archaeology and Old Testament Study: Jubilee Volume of the Society for Old Testament Study 1917–1967,* ed. D. Winton Thomas. Oxford: Clarendon.
1978   Shechem. Pp. 1083–94 in vol. 4 of *Encyclopedia of Archaeological Excavations in the Holy Land,* ed. M. Avi-Yonah and E. Stern. Jerusalem: Massada.

Chapter 17

REHOBOAM'S CITIES OF DEFENSE AND THE LEVITICAL CITY LIST

J. Maxwell Miller

Candler School of Theology
Emory University

It would be difficult to overestimate the impact of archaeological research on biblical studies. Definitions of the term "archaeology" vary of course. If one's definition is broad enough to include topographical studies, then a major contribution of Palestinian archaeology is our increased knowledge of biblical topography. This paper will focus on two passages whose interpretation depends to a large degree on topographical information, the list of Rehoboam's "cities of defense" (*'ārîm lemāṣôr*) in 2 Chronicles 11:5–12 and the Levitical city list in Joshua 21:8–42 (par. 1 Chron. 6:39–66 [RSV 6:54–81]).

The first observation to be made about the list of Rehoboam's fortified cities is that it appears in the context of a longer passage (2 Chron. 11:5–23) with which the Chronicler expanded the Kings presentation of Rehoboam's reign (cf. 1 Kings 12:1–24; 14:21–31 with 2 Chron. 10–12). Beginning with Saul's death on Mt. Gilboa (1 Sam. 31:1–13; 1 Chron. 10), the Chronicler's account follows very closely that of Samuel—Kings, often reproducing lengthy pericopes almost verbatim. Apparently the Chronicler had access to the Samuel—Kings material in essentially its present form and relied heavily upon it. The Chronicler had different interests and concerns than did the editors of Samuel—Kings, however, which led to abbreviation of their materials in some places, to expansion in others, and in some places to major revision. This obviously tendentious way in which the Chronicler used the Samuel—Kings materials raises questions, therefore, about the trustworthiness of the extra information which is supplied without parallels in Samuel—Kings. What other sources did the Chronicler have at hand, and to what extent were the materials derived from these other sources also abbreviated, expanded, or revised?

In the full passage designated above, 2 Chronicles 11:5–23, the Chronicler introduces the following new information about Rehoboam; i.e., in addition to what one reads already in 1 Kings 12–14:

(1) Rehoboam built "cities in defense of Judah," fifteen of which are listed by name (vss. 5–12).

(2) Priests and Levites who found themselves at odds with Jeroboam's cultic measures immigrated to Judah and Jerusalem. There they supported Rehoboam in some special way for three years (vss. 13–17). "They strengthened the kingdom of Judah, and for three years they made Rehoboam the son of Solomon secure, for they walked for three years in the way of David and Solomon."

(3) Rehoboam took wives who were themselves related to the royal family. His favorite wife was Maacah, the daughter of Absalom. Her son, Abijah, was appointed chief prince and heir apparent. There were also eighteen more wives and sixty concubines who brought the total of Rehoboam's children to twenty-eight sons and sixty daughters (vss. 18–22).

(4) Rehoboam "distributed some of his sons through all the districts of Judah and Benjamin, in all the fortified cities; and he gave them abundant provisions, and procured wives for them" (vs. 23).

Even the most cautious commentators generally agree that the city list in verses 5–12 represents authentic historical information which the Chronicler derived from some ancient source. A detailed list of this sort is not likely to have been produced fictitiously. Neither does it support in any obvious way the Chronicler's particular interests or concerns. Yet, essentially the same thing may be said of the longer passage, in my opinion. Verses 13–23 also include some rather specific details which neither sound like pure fiction nor can be explained in terms of the Chronicler's particular interests. Why would the Chronicler have specified that the priests and Levites supported Rehoboam "three years," e.g., unless there was information (accurate or not) to that effect. Also, is there any reason to suppose that the Chronicler would have dreamed up the rather specific details about Rehoboam's wives, concubines, and children?

While scholars generally agree that the list is authentic in that it represents an actual fortification program undertaken at some point during the period of the Judean monarchy, there has been less unanimity of opinion as to whether the Chronicler placed the list in proper historical context. Was it perhaps some other Judean king rather than Rehoboam who fortified these cities? At this point the debate moves beyond literary-critical issues into matters of historical interpretation. Given what we otherwise know about Rehoboam's reign, is it reasonable to suppose that he would have undertaken an extensive fortification program? It is also at this point that topography enters the discussion. Is there any noticeable pattern in the location of the defense cities which corresponds to (or conflicts with) other known circumstances of Rehoboam's reign?

Except for Gath and Lachish, the names of all the cities in the list are preserved in modern Arabic place names of the region south of Jerusalem; i.e., the territory of ancient Judah. To be sure, the modern Arabic name does not always mark the exact spot of the ancient settlement, the name of which it preserves. Usually, however, one can assume that the corresponding ancient settlement was somewhere in the same immediate vicinity. The names of the fifteen cities of the list with their modern Arabic equivalents are in table 9 (cf. fig. 41).

One might assume that "cities of defense" would have been associated with the frontier of the kingdom of Judah, regardless of whether the list is assigned to Rehoboam's reign or to some later period. When the cities are plotted on the map, however, it turns out that they were scattered throughout the interior of Judah. Naturally this raises a question about their intended role in the defense of the land. The explanation usually given is that the cities selected for fortification were all strategically situated along routes by which an enemy army would approach Jerusalem from the west or the south (first proposed by G. Beyer 1931). This is true, of course, but not an entirely satisfying explanation since it is difficult to think of any city in the kingdom which was not situated along a route leading eventually to Jerusalem. Also, if protecting the approaches to Jerusalem was the intention of the fortification program, why was there no concern about the northern and eastern approaches, and why were there no fortifications in the extreme southern part of the kingdom?

Returning attention now to the question of the historical context of the list, most scholars have seen no real problem in associating it with Rehoboam's reign (e.g., Beyer 1931; Noth 1957: 140–41; Rudolph 1955: 227–30; Aharoni 1967: 290–94; Welten 1969: 167–71). The main issue for them is whether Rehoboam would have undertaken this fortification program before (and perhaps in anticipation of) Shishak's raid or whether he did so after Shishak's raid. E. Junge (1937: 73–80) and A. Alt (1953) insisted that the fortification program presupposed by the list does not fit the picture of Rehoboam's reign, however, and have proposed Josiah's reign instead. Recently this position has been argued again by V. Fritz (1981) on the following grounds:

(1) It would not have been necessary for Rehoboam to fortify cities since he inherited a good fortification system from Solomon. Although Shishak may have damaged the Solomonic system somewhat, his campaign seems to have bypassed the area where most of the cities of the list were located.

(2) Sennacherib, however, did destroy cities in the area represented by the list. In fact, the list presupposes a strategic concept which might reasonably have emerged in the aftermath of Sennacherib's 701

Table 9. Ancient Hebrew Place Names and Related Arabic Names.

Hebrew	Arabic	Comment
Bethlehem	Beit Lahm	
Etam	'Ain 'Atan	Khirbet el-Khokh nearby probably is the site of ancient Etam.
Tekoa	Khirbet Tequ'	
Beth-zur	Beit Sur	Khirbet et-Tubeiqeh nearby probably is the site of ancient Beth-zur.
Soco	Shuweikeh	Khirbet 'Abbad nearby is probably the site of ancient Soco.
Adullam	Khirbet 'Id el-Ma	Also called Khirbet el-Mi'ah. Tell esh-Sheikh Madhkur nearby probably is the site of ancient Adullam.
Gath		"Gath" is an appellative name which means something like "winepuss" (cf. Rainey 1966: 36 n. 2). Several different Gaths are mentioned in the biblical materials, therefore, and probably there were still others that failed to receive mention. Of the known Gaths, the one that comes into first consideration as the Gath of this list, because of its proximity to other cities in the list, is Moresheth-gath (i.e., the Gath of Mareshah). Remembered as the home of the prophet Micah (Jer. 26:18; Mic. 1:1) and included in the wordplay section of Micah 1, Moresheth-gath generally is identified with Tell el-Judeideh. While this identification remains open to question, we can be certain that Moresheth-gath would have been located somewhere in the general vicinity of Mareshah.
Mareshah	Khirbet Mer'ash	Tell Sandahannah nearby probably is the site of ancient Mareshah.
Ziph	Tell Zif	
Adoraim	Dura	
Lachish		Location uncertain. Most scholars favor Tell ed-Duweir, first proposed by W. F. Albright in 1929. The alternate candidate, championed most recently by G. W. Ahlström (1980: 7–9) is Tell 'Etun near Beit 'Auwa; but cf. now the response to Ahlström by G. Davies (1982: 25–28). Both possibilities are indicated on fig. 41.
Azekah	Khirbet Tell ez-Zakariyeh	
Zorah	Sar'ah	
Aijalon	Yalo	
Hebron	Hebron	Also called el-Khalil. Jebel er-Rumeideh, which overlooks the modern city, is the site of ancient Hebron.

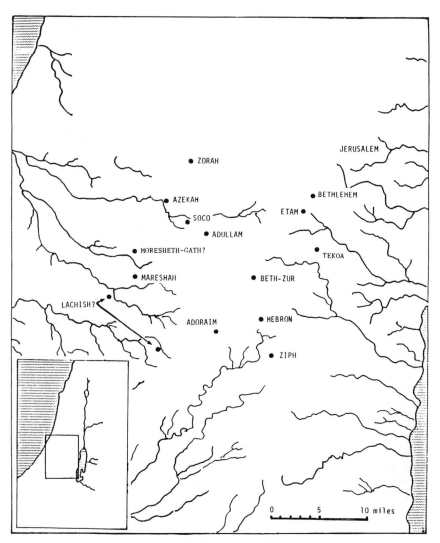

Fig. 41. Rehoboam's cities of defense.

B.C.E. invasion. Whereas Sennacherib had demonstrated that Judah was vulnerable to attack from the coastal plain, the defensive cities protected Judah against attacks from that direction. Yet Hezekiah, Manasseh, or Amon would hardly have been in a position to undertake a refortification program, which leaves Josiah as the likely candidate for the king who did.

(3) Building activities were recorded only for those kings whom the Chronicler regarded as good and righteous rulers, the idea being to complete and confirm this positive judgment. Such confirmation was not really necessary for Josiah, but it was particularly so for Rehoboam where something positive was needed to offset the negative implications of Shishak's invasion. In effect, then, the Chronicler simply transferred the list pertaining to Josiah's refortification program back to Rehoboam's reign. (Fritz depends heavily at this point on Welten 1973: 11–15.)

I wish to comment on these three points in reverse order, defend the generally accepted position that it was in fact Rehoboam, not Josiah, who fortified these cities, and propose a different explanation as to the purpose and strategy behind Rehoboam's fortification program.

Fritz' explanation as to why the Chronicler would have transferred the list from Josiah to Rehoboam does not correspond to my perception of how the ancient compilers of the biblical materials went about their work. Clear examples can be cited, to be sure, of where materials have been placed in improper historical context.[1] Also, as was stated at the beginning of this paper, the Chronicler was quite capable of a tendentious use of the available sources. However, to suggest that conscious transposition of a unit of material from one king to another occurred simply because the Chronicler wished to make one of them appear more successful seems to me rather farfetched. My impression is that, when the biblical compilers placed material in improper context, usually it was for less consciously manipulative reasons. In short, if one is to make a convincing case for assigning the list of defensive cities to Josiah, then a better explanation must be offered as to why the Chronicler transposed the list back to Rehoboam.

That the fortification program attributed by the Chronicler to Rehoboam covered the area devastated by Sennacherib in 701 B.C.E. is not to be disputed. More striking than the territorial overlap of Sennacherib's invasion with the list of defensive cities, however, is the fact that there is virtually no overlap (two cities out of fifteen) between this list and the list of Levitical cities recorded in Joshua 21:8–42 // 1 Chronicles 6:39–66 (RSV 6:54–81). The former fits almost hand in glove with the latter (noted first by Alt 1953: 313 and again by Aharoni 1967: 292). Fig. 42 shows the Levitical cities of Judah, Benjamin, and southern Ephraim. The site identifications in table 10 are presupposed here.

Earlier critical scholars tended to regard the Levitical city list as an ideal arrangement with little or no historical basis. Two characteristics suggested this. On the one hand, the list seems rather schematic in its present form—four cities listed for each of the twelve tribes. On the other hand, it presupposes extensive territory for Israel, more than the Israelite and Judean kings normally controlled. The more recent tendency has been to see the list as an authentic document, probably from David's or Solomon's reign, which may have been schematized by late editors (cf. esp. Mazar 1957; 1960 and bibliography provided there). Arguments for the latter position are as follows. (1) Israel probably did control the territory presupposed by the list during David's and Solomon's reigns. (2) While the presumption of twelve tribes with four cities to a tribe seems artificial, the cities which can be located tend to appear in clusters rather than being evenly spaced as one would expect if the list were entirely ideal. Moreover, the Levitical cities are situated primarily in frontier regions and areas which remained outside "Israelite" control until the emergence of the monarchy under Saul and David. (3) While the origin of the Levites remains obscure, some of the available evidence suggests that they were associated primarily with the Bethlehem-Hebron vicinity prior to David's rise to power and that he gave them a prominent role in the administration of his kingdom. E.g., 1 Chronicles 26:29–32 records that from the Levitical family of Izhar "Chenaniah and his sons were appointed to outside duties for Israel, as officers and judges." Of the Levitical family of Hashabiah from Hebron, we are told that an additional seventeen hundred men "had the oversight of Israel westward of the Jordan for all the word of the LORD and for the service of the king."

Returning now to Fritz' line of argument, his point of departure is that Rehoboam would have had no need to undertake such an extensive fortification program since he inherited a good fortification system from Solomon. A possibility which Fritz overlooks (and which commentators have overlooked all along to my knowledge) is that Rehoboam's cities of defense may have been designed less to protect Judah from external enemies than to secure Rehoboam's own control over the area. After all, most of the remainder of the kingdom which he inherited from Solomon, from the very outskirts of Jerusalem northward, had already accomplished a successful rebellion.

It is generally supposed, of course, that the Judeans would have been more inclined to loyalty toward the Davidic dynasty than the northern tribes, since David himself was Judean. However, there is no reason to believe that the Judeans would have been intensely loyal either. Moreover, Judah was not the only tribal group to be taken into account for this southern area. Actually, it is the Levites whom the Chronicler remembers as being particularly loyal to Rehoboam, and it is perhaps significant that the Chronicler mentions them in the same context as Rehoboam's fortification program. The other item which is

Table 10. Ancient Hebrew Place Names and Related Arabic Names.

Hebrew	Arabic	Comment
Hebron	Hebron	Included among Rehoboam's defensive cities. Location uncertain. Must have been somewhere in the Shephelah, on the frontier between Judah and Philistia (Josh. 15:42; 2 Kings 8:22). Eusebius places it in the district of Eleutheropolis (present-day Beit Jibrin). Tell Bornat is a likely candidate.
Jattir	Khirbet 'Attir	
Eshtemoa	es-Semu'	
Holon/Hilen		Location unknown. Joshua 15:51 seems to place it in the southernmost part of the hill country; i.e., in the vicinity of Estemoa and Debir.
Debir ·		Location uncertain. Must have been in the hill country south of Hebron (Josh. 15:15–19, 49; Judg. 1:11–15). Khirbet Rabud is a likely candidate.
Ain/Ashan		Location unknown. Read Ashan with 1 Chronicles 6:44 (RSV 6:59). Probably identical with Borashan in 1 Samuel 30:30, which would suggest the southern end of the hill country.
Juttah	Yatta	
Beth-shemesh	'Ain Shems	Tell er-Rumeileh nearby represents the ancient site.
Gibeon	el-Jib	
Geba	Jeba'	
Anathoth	Anata	Ras el-Kharrubeh nearby represents the ancient site.
Almon/Slemeth	Khirbet 'Almit	
Gezer	Tell Jezer	
Kibzaim/ Jokmeam		Location(s) unknown. Joshua 21:22 reads Kibzaim; 1 Chronicles 6:53 (RSV 6:68) reads Jokmeam. Possibly the "original" list included both.[2]
Beth-horon	Beit 'Ur el-Foqa Beit 'Ur et-Tahta	Some biblical passages distinguish between Upper and Lower Beth-horon which would correspond to Beit 'Ur el-Foqa and Beit 'Ur et-Tahta respectively.
Eltekeh		Location unknown. Somewhere in the vicinity of Ekron (which is probably to be identified with Khirbet el-Muqanna') and Timnah (possibly Tell el-Batashi).
Gibbethon		Location uncertain. Somewhere on the Philistine frontier. Often identified with Tell Melat.
Aijalon	Yalo	Included also among Rehoboam's defensive cities.
Gath-rimmon		Location unknown. Somewhere in the territory assigned to Dan in Joshua 19:40–48.

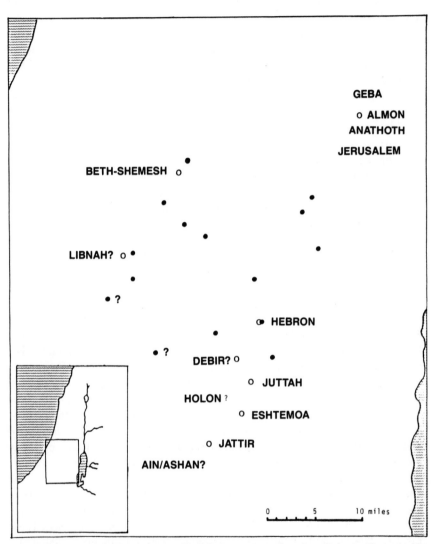

Fig. 42. Positions of the Levitical cities of Judah, Benjamin, and southern Ephraim (designated by "O") in relation to the positions of Rehoboam's cities of defense (designated by "●"); Aijalon and Hebron appear on both lists.

mentioned in the same context is that Rehoboam placed his own sons (of which he had many) in the fortified cities, gave them abundant provisions, and married them well.

In conclusion, I see no reason to doubt that it was actually Rehoboam who undertook the fortification program reported in 2 Chron. 11:5–12 or to doubt the essential accuracy of the information provided in the continuation of the pericope, verses 13–23. The following scenario seems reasonable.

(1) David was anointed king first by the elders of Judah (2 Sam. 2:1–4) and then, some years later, by the elders of Israel (2 Sam. 5:1–3). In neither case, it would seem, were the elders acting entirely voluntarily. The Judeans and other southern tribes clearly had regarded David as more of a nuisance than a potential leader while he was on the run from Saul (cf., e.g., 1 Sam. 23:6–14; 25:9–11; 26:1–2). After Saul's death, when David and his men moved into the Hebron area, this apparently was not by invitation and must have involved the confiscation of lands for his men and their families. Once there, the elders of Judah had little choice but to recognize his authority (2 Sam. 2:1–4a). The account of how David achieved recognition as king over Israel (i.e., the remnant of Saul's Ephraim-based kingdom) suggests that there, too, it was a matter of behind-the-scenes intrigue and power politics rather than popular appeal (2 Sam. 2:4b—5:3).

(2) It was the city of Jerusalem, however, rather than the tribal structures of either Judah or Israel, which became the real center of David's kingdom. There emerged a Jerusalem-based military elite and administrative structure. For all practical purposes the Jerusalem cult became the national cult. Also, David incorporated into his Jerusalem-centered kingdom other Palestinian cities and territories which had never been regarded as part of Judah or Israel. In short, while Judah and Israel remained important constituents of the kingdom, it became increasingly apparent that they were no more than that— constituents of an extended Jerusalem city-state. It is not surprising that David had to contend with attempted revolts on the part of Judah and Israel, probably not long after he had transferred from Hebron to Jerusalem (2 Sam. 15—20).

(3) The military system with which David maintained control of the kingdom and engaged in foreign wars was dominated at the top by relatives and foreign mercenaries. For civil administration, on the other hand, especially in the non-Judean/Israelite areas, he seems to have relied heavily on Levites. The list of Levitical cities probably derives from his or Solomon's reign. Presumably certain Levitical families were given lands associated with these cities and charged with local administrative and cultic responsibilities. Solomon continued, refined, and expanded David's administrative policies, especially in the area of corvée and taxation. Many, perhaps most, of Solomon's subjects must have found the circumstances distasteful. In fact, there was

opposition even among Solomon's administrative officials, an example being Jeroboam's self-imposed exile to Egypt. The situation which Rehoboam inherited at Solomon's death, therefore, was volatile to say the least.

(4) The very fact that Rehoboam went to Shechem suggests that the people of the north had already given signals of disloyalty to Jerusalem and the Davidic dynasty, one clear signal being their failure to send representatives to Jerusalem confirming Rehoboam in the first place. Whatever chances Rehoboam had of holding the kingdom together were dashed at Shechem. The whole northern part of his kingdom rebelled and established itself as an independent state under the same Jeroboam who had opposed Solomon. One of Jeroboam's first moves would have been to remove cultic and administrative officials, particularly the Levites, with known pro-Jerusalem/Davidic leanings (1 Kings 12:31). Many of these Levites fled to Jerusalem (2 Chron. 11:13–17).

(5) On the advice of the prophet Shemaiah, Rehoboam decided against any military attempt to challenge the rebel move. An important factor behind Shemaiah's advice, as well as Rehoboam's willingness to comply, may have been uncertainty regarding the loyalty of the remaining constituency of the kingdom. In any case, it was imperative that Rehoboam secure his position in Jerusalem, Judah, and the other southern territories. In Jerusalem he could count on the loyalty of numerous religious, military, and administrative officials who had achieved their positions and prospered under the Davidic dynasty, their ranks now inflated by Levitical refugees from the north. Loyalists would have been scattered more thinly outside of Jerusalem. Chief among the latter were the Levites who dominated certain key cities where David and Solomon had settled them; i.e., the Levitical cities. Rehoboam's cities of defense were designed primarily to secure the interior of the kingdom and, therefore, the heartland of Judah where the Levites had relatively little strength. He fortified these non-Levitical cities, supplied them with provisions, and placed them in the charge of relatives.

(6) Whether Rehoboam's fortification program is to be dated before or after Shishak's campaign probably is an irrelevant question. This program would have been an ongoing project, while Shishak's campaign was more on the order of a plundering raid than a systematic invasion. Rehoboam probably had little advance warning and the results were temporary. Shishak's roster of conquered cities, which is very difficult to interpret,[3] suggests a march up through Philistia followed by attacks primarily on cities in the rebel kingdom of Israel. Entries 23–26 (Gibeon, Beth-horon, Kiriathaim, Aijalon) indicate activity northwest of Jerusalem in what was then to become disputed territory between Israel and Judah. Presumably, Rehoboam chose to ransom Jerusalem with the temple treasury rather than to attempt to defend the city (1 Kings 14:6). Otherwise Shishak seems to have bypassed Judah.

(7) Hebron and Aijalon are exceptions in that they appear in both of the lists under discussion. They are also exceptions in other ways, which may explain why Rehoboam included specifically these two Levitical cities in his fortification program.

Aijalon, located northwest of Jerusalem in the area which received the full force of Shishak's attack, is among the cities which Shishak claims to have conquered. The question to be asked, therefore, is not why Rehoboam would have found it necessary to fortify or refortify this Levitical city, but why he did not also restore the other cities in that area which had fallen to Shishak; e.g., Gezer and Beth-horon. The answer is probably that he no longer had an entrée to the other cities: the area northwest of Jerusalem had become disputed frontier between Judah and Israel.

Hebron required special attention, on the other hand, because it, of all the cities in Rehoboam's then much-reduced kingdom, could be considered a legitimate and powerful rival to Jerusalem. Hebron had its own ancient traditions (Num. 13:22) and the Hebronites had good reasons to oppose the Davidic kings. First, David and his men had moved into and taken over their city. Then, within a few short years he had elevated Jerusalem above Hebron as the new capital and administrative center of the kingdom. Is it any surprise, therefore, that Absalom selected Hebron as the place to proclaim his rebellion (2 Sam. 15:7–10) or that Rehoboam would have undertaken special measures to secure the city? Probably these measures involved the building or strengthening of a fortified position in the city and placing the fortification in the charge of a son or some other relative whose loyalty to the crown could be trusted.

NOTES

1. A prime example is the Elisha complex in 2 Kings 2; 4:1—8:15. Cf. A. Jepsen 1942; C. F. Whitley 1952; and J. M. Miller 1966.

2. Where the Joshua version of the list reads Kibzaim the Chronicles version reads Jokmeam. It remains uncertain whether these are variant names for the same place (Mazar 1960: 198) or whether both Kibzaim and Jokmeam appeared in the "original" list. In the latter case, Jokmeam would have been dropped from the Joshua version at some later stage of the transmission of the text, and Kibzaim dropped from the Chronicles version (Aharoni 1967: 269–73).

3. The place names on Shishak's list do not appear in any coherent geographical order. Mazar (1957) has proposed a tempting but also very hypothetical rearrangement of the names which, if correct, would suggest a second thrust of Shishak's raid into the southern Negeb.

BIBLIOGRAPHY

Aharoni, Y.
1967   *The Land of the Bible*. Philadelphia: Westminster.

Ahlström, G. W.
1980   Is Tell Ed-Duweir Ancient Lachish? *Palestine Exploration Quarterly* 112: 7–9.

Albright, W. F.
1929   The American Excavations at Tell Beit Mirsim. *Zeitschrift für die alttest- amentliche Wissenschaft* 47: 1–18.

Alt, A.
1953   Festungen und Levitenorte im Lande Juda. Pp. 306–15 in vol. 2 of *Kleine Schriften*. München: C. H. Beck.

Beyer, G.
1931   Beiträge zur Territorialgeschichte von Südwestpalästina im Altertum I. Das Festungssystem Rehabeams. *Zeitschrift der Deutschen Palästina- Vereins* 54: 113–34.

Davies, G. I.
1982   Tell ed-Duweir = Ancient Lachish: A Response to G. W. Ahlström. *Palestine Exploration Quarterly* 114: 25–28.

Fritz, V.
1981   The "List of Rehoboam's Fortresses" in 2 Chr 11:5–12—A Document from the Time of Josiah. *Eretz-Israel* 15: 46–53.

Jepsen, A.
1942   Israel und Damaskus. *Archiv für Orientforschung* 14: 153–72.

Junge, E.
1937   *Der Wideraufbau des Heerwesens des Reiches Juda unter Josia*. Bei- träge zur Wissenschaft vom Alten und Neuen Testament 75. Stuttgart: W. Kohlhammer.

Mazar, B.
1957   The Campaign of Pharaoh Shishak to Palestine. Pp. 57–66 in vol. 4 of *Supplements to Vetus Testamentum*. Leiden: E. J. Brill.

Mazar, B.
1960   The Cities of the Priests and the Levites. Pp. 193–205 in vol. 7 of *Supple- ments to Vetus Testamentum*. Leiden: E. J. Brill.

Miller, J. M.
1966   The Elisha Cycle and the Accounts of the Omride Wars. *Journal of Biblical Literature* 85: 441–54.

Noth, M.
1957   *Überlieferungsgeschichtliche Studien. Die sammelnden und bearbei- tenden Geschichtswerke im Alten Testament*. Tübingen: Max Niemeyer.

Rainey, A. F.
1966   Gath of the Philistines. *Christian News from Israel* 17/2: 30–38; 17/4: 23–34.

Rudolph, W.
1955 *Chronikbücher*. Handbuch zum Alten Testament 21. Tübingen: J. C. B. Mohr (Paul Siebeck).

Welten, P.
1969 *Die Königs-Stempel. Ein Beitrag zur Militärpolitik Judas unter Hiskia und Josia*. Abhandlungen des Deutschen Palästina-Vereins 4. Wiesbaden: Harrassowitz.

Welten, P.
1973 *Geschichte und Geschichtsdarstellung in den Chronikbüchern*. Wissenschaftliche Monographien zum Alten und Neuen Testament 42. Neukirchen-Vluyn: Neukirchener.

Whitley, C. F.
1952 The Deuteronomic Presentation of the House of Omri. *Vetus Testamentum* 2: 137–52.

Chapter 18

THE LAST YEARS OF THE KINGDOM OF JUDAH

Abraham Malamat
Hebrew University

The Subjugation by Egypt and Babylonia

The defeat of King Josiah by Pharaoh Necho II (610–595 B.C.E.) at Megiddo in 609 B.C.E. was a pivotal moment in the latter years of the kingdom of Judah: national prosperity and high hopes for a renewed Judean Empire dissolved into incessant turmoil, with Judah caught in a political bipolar system between Egypt and Babylonia until it finally fell in 586 B.C.E.[1] The background of the Judean-Egyptian clash in 609 lay in the geopolitical changes resulting from the disintegration of the Assyrian Empire, which provoked rivalry between Judah and Egypt over the inheritance of the Assyrian provinces in Palestine.[2] Psammetichus I (664–610), Necho's father, apparently imposed his suzerainty on the Philistine cities and the Assyrian province of Magiddu (covering the Jezreel plain and Galilee), including the city of Megiddo itself which by then must have become an Egyptian base. Josiah (639–609), on the other hand, managed to extend his rule only over the province of Samerina and apparently to establish a corridor to the coast in the northern Shephelah.

With the weakening of the Assyrian Empire Egypt, traditional enemy of Assyria, now became its ally (probably between 622 and 617) as a result of the rise of Babylonia and Media, which had captured one Assyrian center after another (the city of Ashur in 614, Nineveh in 612, and Harran in 610). The Babylonian Chronicle of Nabopolassar, founder of the neo-Babylonian kingdom, shows that the Egyptians rushed military assistance to the Euphrates region in order to support the Assyrians in their struggle against the Babylonians in 616, 610, and 609.[3]

Josiah's attempt to stem the Egyptian thrust northward in 609 placed Judah in a common front with Babylonia, although it is uncertain whether this resulted from overall strategy preplanned by the two countries. The details of the encounter between Necho and Josiah are not adequately clarified (2 Kings 23:29–30; and a fuller version in 2 Chron. 35:20–24); it appears, however, that Josiah's move was based on carefully calculated political and strategic considerations. The Egyptian king, less than a year on the throne, lacked military experience; at the time of the sudden attack in the Megiddo plain, the Egyptian army was not only far from home but also still beyond reach of its stronghold at Megiddo. It is also possible that Egypt had somewhat earlier been humiliated by the Scythians who, according to Herodotus (I.105), burst out of the north to Philistia and whose threat to Egypt proper was removed only through payment of a bribe by Psammetichus.[4] Josiah's daring move might have been occasioned by the Egyptian blunder in the Euphrates region in 610, six months or so before the battle of Megiddo, when the army had had to abandon Harran and retreat to the west bank of the Euphrates.

The disastrous outcome of the battle of Megiddo in the summer of 609 led to radical political fluctuations in Judah and, along with them, alternate subjugation by and rebellion against each of the major powers, Egypt and Babylonia. The rapidly changing international scene demanded of the rulers of Judah both skillful maneuvering and exceptional adaptability and frequently confronted them with ominous political situations.

The first decisive step, the selection of Jehoahaz to succeed Josiah, ran counter to the principle of primogeniture. Jehoahaz was twenty-three years old at his accession; his brother Jehoiakim was twenty-five. That this was an exceptional occurrence seems borne out by the specific biblical reference to his anointment as king and perhaps by the name change from Shallum (Jer. 22:11; cf. 1 Chron. 3:15) to the significant throne name Jehoahaz (i.e., "Yahweh has taken hold of"), like other name changes such as Eliakim to Jehoiakim and Mattaniah to Zedekiah, which were also prompted by unusual circumstances of accession. The enthronement of Jehoahaz was thus a minor coup d'etat occasioned by the intervention of the ʿam hāʾāreṣ ("the people of the land"; 2 Kings 23:30; 2 Chron. 36:1), that body of landed gentry in Judah whose influence was tangible whenever the natural succession of the Davidic line was at stake. The political significance of the step is made clearer by the intense anti-Egyptian attitude of the ʿam hāʾāreṣ during this period, which undoubtedly affected Josiah's policy.[5]

It becomes apparent that Jehoahaz was chosen because his mother, Hamutal, daughter of Jeremiah of Libnah (2 Kings 23:31; the "lioness . . . among lions" of Ezek. 19:2), traced her lineage to the rural nobility of Judah and thus to the ʿam hāʾāreṣ. Similarly, eleven years later, Nebuchadnezzar enthroned Zedekiah, son of the same mother, who therefore also represented the anti-Egyptian faction of the Davidic house. On the other hand, the notables of Judah probably loathed the maternal lineage of Jehoiakim since his mother,

Zebudah (Zebidah), daughter of Pedaiah, originated from Ruman (2 Kings 23:36) apparently in the Beth Netophah Valley in Galilee. Jehoiakim's wife (mother-to-be of his heir), Nehushta, daughter of Elnathan (2 Kings 24:8), was chosen from among the Jerusalem nobility rather than from the ʿam hāʾāreṣ.[6]

Despite the defeat at Megiddo the leadership of Judah continued its anti-Egyptian policy, adopted prematurely at the cost of independence. Three months after his accession Jehoahaz was summoned to Necho's headquarters at Riblah in the land of Hamath in central Syria. His destiny from the beginning seemed so uncertain that Jeremiah proclaimed: "He shall return no more nor see his native country" (Jer. 22:10–12; cf. Ezek. 19:1–4). Jehoahaz was indeed deposed and exiled to Egypt, probably because of pressure from his brother Jehoiakim (also indicated in 1 Esdr. 1:5–38) who sought recognition of his rights as firstborn. Necho's appointment of Jehoiakim as king served their mutual interest: Jehoiakim's claims as legitimate heir to the throne were realized at the same time that he became Necho's vassal and loyal ally. Necho punished Judah, apparently in concurrence with Jehoiakim, by imposing a levy on the anti-Egyptian ʿam hāʾāreṣ (2 Kings 23:35) rather than upon the Temple or the palace treasury in Jerusalem; the latter was hardly affected and the king of Judah still had means to erect luxurious royal buildings (cf. below p. 293 and n. 21). Jehoiakim seems to have ascended the throne in Tishri 609,[7] reigning for eleven years until the winter of 598, although he himself and his circle of followers may have calculated his regnal years from the death of Josiah, entirely disregarding the regency of Jehoahaz.[8] The summer and autumn of 609, therefore, were days of great turmoil in Judah in view of the political vicissitudes and three kings rapidly succeeding each other under extraordinary circumstances.

Egypt now controlled the entire region west of the Euphrates or, in biblical phraseology, "from the Brook of Egypt unto the river Euphrates, all that pertained to the king of Egypt" (2 Kings 24:7, author's translation).[9] But its hegemony was short-lived. In 607, when the Babylonians attempted to seize the western bank of the Euphrates, they were repelled by the Carchemish-based Egyptians,[10] but in 605 Nebuchadnezzar, while still heir-apparent, defeated the Egyptians in the famous battle of Carchemish and routed the remnants of their forces in the land of Hamath. This battle, which resounds in the prophecies of Jeremiah (Jer. 46:2–12), in Josephus (Ant. X.6.1; X.11.1), and in Nebuchadnezzar's Babylonian Chronicle,[11] determined the future of Syria and Palestine. The leaders of Judah nonetheless failed to understand, either then or later, the shift in the balance of power on the international scene and adopted a high-risk policy, with fatal consequences. Persons of the stature of a Jeremiah, gifted with prescience and historical insight, had, in contrast, no semblance of doubt. Shortly after the battle of Carchemish the prophet was already expressing his stern belief that Nebuchadnezzar would rule over Judah and all of Hither Asia (Jer. 25:1–14). For him the salvation of the nation lay solely in voluntary submission to Babylonia, a belief to which he clung until the end (Jer. 21:8–9; 38:2ff.).

Babylonia soon subjugated Judah although the exact date is still disputed. Even Nebuchadnezzar's Chronicle, which records his annual military campaigns to the west from 605 to 601, remains vague as to the precise date, since it fails to specify the names of the tributary kingdoms (except Ashkelon; cf. below). Some scholars, relying on evidence in the opening of the book of Daniel and in Josephus (quoting Berossus), surmise that Judah was conquered immediately after the battle of Carchemish. It is difficult, however, to accept the chronological veracity of these traditions which are unsupported by the Babylonian Chronicle.[12] Others maintain that Judah surrendered either the following winter, when Nebuchadnezzar returned to the west to collect tribute, or the winter thereafter, when, already king of Babylon, he conquered Ashkelon in the month of Kislev, the first year of his reign (December 604). The latter date coincides with the ninth month of the fifth regnal year of Jehoiakim, when a general fast-day was proclaimed in Jerusalem (Jer. 36:9ff.) and an emergency session of ministers convened. To them was brought Jeremiah's forecast of national doom, the intrinsic drama of which can now be more fully appreciated by virtue of the Babylonian Chronicle. The stubborn Jehoiakim, however, dismissed Jeremiah's warning—"the king of Babylon will certainly come and destroy this land" (Jer. 36:29)—and burned the prophet's scroll, emphasizing Judah's tenacious determination to remain free of Babylonia.

Judah seems to have surrendered in the autumn or winter of 603 during Nebuchadnezzar's campaign in his second regnal year, which was undoubtedly conducted to the west.[13] The Babylonian king started out in the month of Iyyar with "a mighty army" supported by siege towers in anticipation of strong resistance. Although the continuation of the Babylonian tablet is damaged, we can nevertheless assume that Nebuchadnezzar intended to subdue all Philistia and gain control of Judah in preparation for his ultimate objective, the defeat of his rival, Egypt.[14] If this surmise is correct, the missing portion of the tablet would have recounted first the conquest of a specific Philistine city, such as Ashdod, Ekron, or Gaza (cf. Jer. 25:20; 47:5; Zeph. 2:4), then the surrender of Jehoiakim (cf. 2 Chron. 36:6–8 and Dan. 1:1–2, which seem to refer to this event).[15] Moreover, this proposed dating for the subjugation of Judah accords well chronologically with the circumstances leading to Jehoiakim's rebellion against Babylonia. According to 2 Kings 24:1, Jehoiakim was a vassal of Nebuchadnezzar in Babylonia for three years; in other words, he thrice paid annual tribute. If he made his first payment in the fall or winter of 603, the third installment fell due in the fall or winter of 601, during the expedition in Nebuchadnezzar's fourth regnal year. In Kislev of that year (December 601), the Babylonian king led an attack on Egypt proper, a significant international event now unexpectedly disclosed by the Babylonian Chronicle. The Chronicle does not conceal the shortcomings of the Babylonian army in its most ambitious campaign, reporting heavy losses on both sides and the return of the Babylonians empty-handed to their own country. The Babylonian blunder motivated Judah and several neighbors to throw off the Babylonian yoke.

Egypt was vitally interested in nurturing and supporting the uprising of the peoples in Palestine against Babylonian rule, and therefore the polarity between the pro-Babylonian and pro-Egyptian factions gradually intensified. Unlike the "true" prophets, who saw Egypt as a "broken reed," many of Judah's leaders placed their faith in the futile Egyptian promises of military assistance. That other states in Palestine also sought Egyptian aid against Babylonia is recorded in an Aramaic letter from Saqqara (Memphis in Egypt). In this letter, a ruler from Ekron, Gaza, or Ashdod approaches Pharaoh for urgent military assistance against the impending Babylonian onslaught.[16] If this supposition is correct, the document concerns one of the Babylonian expeditions against Philistia either in the summer of 603 or the winter of 601/600.

From Revolt to Revolt

The abortive campaign against Egypt prevented the Babylonians from taking action against Jehoiakim's insolence for the next two years. In his fifth regnal year (600/599) Nebuchadnezzar stayed at home to rehabilitate his chariot force and in the winter of 599/598 made raids only against the Arabian tribes.[17] These raids and the vast spoils captured by the Babylonians seem to be echoed in Jeremiah's oracle on "Kedar and the kingdoms of Hazor which Nebuchadrezzar king of Babylon smote" (Jer. 49:28–33). For the time being, therefore, Nebuchadnezzar was forced to resort solely to punitive measures against Jehoiakim, employing Chaldean garrisons stationed in the west as well as "bands of the Syrians [some read Edomites here], and bands of the Moabites, and bands of the Ammonites" (2 Kings 24:2).

These events seem to be reflected both in Jeremiah's reference to the Rechabites seeking sanctuary in Jerusalem "for fear of the army of the Chaldeans and the army of the Syrians" (Jer. 35:11) and in Zephaniah's wrathful charges against Moab and Ammon who "have taunted my people and made boasts against their territory" (Zeph. 2:8–10). If the LXX versions of 2 Chronicles 36:5 is historically reliable, then the incursion into Judah also included contingents from Samaria, implying that this region, previously annexed by Josiah, had, in Jehoiakim's time, once again been cut off from Judah by the Babylonians.[18] In any event, these were not sporadic, disorganized bands which attacked Judah but regular military units and auxiliary forces incited by Nebuchadnezzar to prepare Judah for the decisive strike a year later.

In the winter of 598/597, his seventh regnal year, Nebuchadnezzar struck at Judah in a show of strength that also served warning on Egypt and its allies. The biblical account of Jerusalem's surrender under Jehoiachin has been fully borne out by the Babylonian Chronicle:

> In the seventh year, the month of Kislev, the king of Akkad [Nebuchadnezzar] mustered his troops, marched to the Hatti Land [Syria-Palestine], and encamped against the city of Judah [Jerusalem], and on the second day of the month of Adar he seized the city and captured the king [Jehoiachin]. He appointed there a king of his own choice [Zedekiah], received its heavy tribute and sent (them) to Babylon (B.M. 21946, rev., ll. 11–13).

The precise date of the conquest of Jerusalem on 2 Adar (March 16, 597) and the almost simultaneous replacement of the Judean ruler serves now as a chronological reference point for this entire period as well as for the clarification of the reckoning of the regnal New Year in Judah.[19] Because of this date, moreover, the actual course of the siege of Jerusalem and the resulting exile can be more fully appraised.

In the month of Kislev Nebuchadnezzar marshaled his troops and set out from Babylon for Jerusalem, a 1600 km. (1000 mi.) march requiring some two months (assuming an average daily advance of 25 km. or 17 mi.), which brought him to Jerusalem during the month of Shebat, shortly before the city's surrender. By then, since Jerusalem was already under siege by Nebuchadnezzar's "servants" (to be inferred from 2 Kings 24:10–11), we must assume that Babylonian as well as other forces were stationed in the west. The entry in the Chronicle for the previous year suggests this, reporting merely that Nebuchadnezzar returned to Babylon and thus implying that most of his army was left behind to reinforce the garrison in the west. It therefore seems likely that when the king of Babylon suddenly appeared at the head of his choice troops before the gates of besieged Jerusalem, frustrated for want of Egyptian aid (cf. 2 Kings 24:7), the spirit of the defenders failed and Jehoiachin and his retinue were prompted to give themselves up.

Since Jehoiachin surrendered on the second of Adar after a reign of only three months (2 Kings 24:8; according to 2 Chron. 36:9, three months and ten days), his father must have died at the end of Marchesvan 598. By this time Jerusalem was probably already under siege, which may explain the various biblical versions concerning the strange circumstances of the death and interment of Jehoiakim. Although 2 Kings 24:6 describes his demise in unusually general terms, the LXX (Lucianic recension) here and in 2 Chronicles 36:8 records that he was buried in the garden of Uzza (as were his forebears Manasseh and Amon; 2 Kings 21:18, 26) outside the walls of Jerusalem. Interment here, certainly lackluster because of the heavy siege, may be what Jeremiah meant when he prophesied the king's ignoble end: "He shall be buried like the burial of an ass drawn and cast beyond the gates of Jerusalem" (Jer. 22:19, author's translation; cf. 36:30).[20] Even though the king's behavior deserves this prophetic vision of his final lot (in contradistinction to his condemnation of Jehoiakim; cf. Jeremiah's consoling words about Zedekiah, conditioned upon the latter's submission to divine command in Jer. 34:4–5), we should not exclude the possibility that the utterances about Jehoiakim's death and burial echo actual events (cf. the prophecies about the destiny of Jehoahaz and Jehoiachin, Jer. 22:10–12, 24–30). In any case, Jeremiah (22:13–17) and the author of 2 Kings 24:1–4 disparage Jehoiakim for both his foreign and his domestic policy, which led him to oppress the populace in order to erect splendid royal edifices[21] and to condemn and pursue mercilessly his opponents (he executed the prophet Uriah of Kiriath-jearim and sentenced Jeremiah to death, Jer. 26; cf. 36:26).

We can now reasonably reconcile the seeming biblical contradiction concerning the number of deportees and the dates of deportation during Jehoiachin's time by assuming two consecutive stages.[22] The first stage is probably represented by the list of deportees in Jer. 52:28 (which seems to be based on an official record), according to which 3,025 "Judeans" were carried off in Nebuchadnezzar's seventh year. This apparently limited deportation comprised the provincial elements of Judah, outside the capital, captured either during the siege of Jerusalem or immediately after its surrender (cf. the allusion in Jer. 13:18–19). The subsequent and major exile described in 2 Kings 24:12 included the higher echelons of Jerusalem, headed by King Jehoiachin and his retinue, along with thousands of the city's defenders. The city fell on 2 Adar and, since organizing such a mass deportation took several weeks, it must have occurred by the time Nebuchadnezzar's eighth regnal year began (2 Kings, loc cit) on 1 Nisan 597. Further, 2 Chronicles 36:10 ("when the year was expired," author's translation) also indicates that Jehoiachin's exile took place at the time of the civil New Year (Nisan). The assumption of a two-phase exile may also serve to resolve the discrepancies in the numbers of deportees listed in 2 Kings 24: 10,000 in one case (vs. 14) and 7,000 in the other (vs. 16), to each of which must be added 1,000 armorers and sappers,[23] the auxiliary technical personnel. The number 7,000 might refer to the later main deportation and the figure 10,000 to the total, including the 3,000 captives from the first stage.

The effects of Jehoiachin's exile were of greater qualitative than quantitative significance, however, for the elite of Judah were forced out—the royal family, high officials, the upper class as a whole, and the choice military personnel and artisans (2 Kings 24:12–16; cf. Jer. 24:1; 27:20; 29:2). Deportees also included the religio-spiritual leadership—priests and prophets (Jer. 29:21ff.), among them the prophet Ezekiel. Jeremiah's vision of the two baskets of figs thus justifiably equates Jehoiachin's exile with the "good figs" (Jer. 24, esp. vs. 5).

Indeed, the exilic community itself considered this deportation the decisive event in the progressive disintegration of the land of Judah, signaled by the inauguration of a new dating system (cf. 2 Kings 25:27 and the chronological calculation employed throughout the book of Ezekiel). Whereas the prime calamity at the end of Zedekiah's rule was the complete devastation of many Judean cities, above all Jerusalem (cf. Jer. 34:7; 44:2), the surrender of Jehoiachin had virtually saved the country from total physical destruction. Although the archaeological evidence for the partial destruction of certain sites in the time of Jehoiachin such as Tell Beit Mirsim and, in particular, Lachish is questionable,[24] some outlying districts can be presumed to have been taken away from the Judean kingdom, probably at its northern rather than at its southern perimeter as is generally assumed.[25] In fact, Nebuchadnezzar may have annexed Benjamin to the province of Samerina and thus saved the area from destruction a decade later, during the period of the final disaster (cf. below). Certain notables of Benjaminite origin were actually deported, however, such as the forebears of Mordecai, even though his family was exiled from the capital, Jerusalem (Esther 2:5–6).

The mass deportation of Judah's upper class and the heavy tribute exacted by Nebuchadnezzar, reported in the Babylonian Chronicle, undermined the very foundations of the kingdom during its final decade. Bereft of its experienced, authoritative political leadership, the country was becoming prey to unreliable and adventurous elements. After the land and property owners were exiled ("none remained, except the poorest people of the land"; 2 Kings 24:14), social and economic instability prevailed. In this respect Nebuchadnezzar's policy of deportation was surely shortsighted. Nevertheless, carrying off the bulk of the army and its ordnance and fortifications experts made Judah incapable of restoring its former strength and security.

These hindrances to Judah's recovery were increased by the coexistence of two kings of the Davidic line, the exiled Jehoiachin and his uncle Zedekiah, appointed in his stead, which raised the problem of the royal succession in Judah, created confusion within the kingdom, and undermined government authority. The biblical sources, now reinforced by the Babylonian Chronicle, tell us that Zedekiah was enthroned by Nebuchadnezzar himself in a coronation that included a ceremony and an oath of allegiance to the suzerain (Ezek. 17:12–14; cf. *Ant.* X.7.1), typical of the somewhat earlier Assyrian vassal treaties (Neo-Babylonian treaties have not been preserved) made with the subject states in the west. The vassal ruler was adjured not only by the suzerain's gods but also by his own—in our case, by Yahweh (cf. Ezek. 17:19–20; 2 Chron. 36:13). Furthermore, the frequent diatribes of Jeremiah and Ezekiel against Zedekiah for breach of fealty, as well as the Babylonian vengeance against the renegade Judean king (cf. passages below on p. 302), accord with the curses and punishments that the extant vassal treaties from the ancient Near East meted out to a rebel.[26]

Although Zedekiah was duly and properly installed as king by Nebuchadnezzar, his exiled nephew, Jehoiachin, was not divested of his royalty but enjoyed special status at the Babylonian court. The so-called Weidner Tablets, discovered at Nebuchadnezzar's palace, which list food rations for the various exiles, testify to this. Jehoiachin is mentioned in four documents as the "King of Judah" and in one of them, which is dated in the thirteenth year of Nebuchadnezzar (592/591), he is referred to when Zedekiah was, in fact, in power.[27] One should not, however, conclude from this that Jehoiachin actually remained king de jure of Judah, nor that Zedekiah was only regent or *locum tenens;* but rather he may have been regarded as titular head of the Jewish diaspora in Babylonia. Other exiled kings at the Babylonian court also retained their royal titles[28] and were perhaps to be used, inter alia, as a trump card against the new rulers appointed by Nebuchadnezzar. Equally unlikely is the claim that the seal impressions, "(Belonging) to Eliakim servant (*na'ar*) of Yaukin," found on jars from Tell Beit Mirsim, Beth-shemesh, and Ramat Rahel, prove that Jehoiachin maintained both his position as king and his royal estates in Judah even after his exile.[29] In fact, other seals bearing the epithet *na'ar* do not necessary indicate royal officials. It would seem, moreover, that the seal discussed should be dated paleographically considerably earlier than Jehoiachin's reign.

The duality of kingship during the last decade of the First Temple period undoubtedly caused dissension in Judah and created factions, of which one supported Zedekiah and the other Jehoiachin as the legitimate ruler, with the hope of his return to power. This question of legitimacy of royal succession seems to have been a cause for contention between the "true" and "false" prophets in the overall political and ideological controversy over relations with Babylonia, which raged within the prophetic circles.[30] In his ideological debate with Jeremiah at the Temple in Jerusalem, Hananiah son of Azzur, representative par excellence of the false prophets, boldly proclaimed that "two years hence" the exiles would be returned to Judah and Jehoiachin reinstated (Jer. 28:1–4).[31] Jeremiah unequivocally rejects, in contrast, the legitimacy of Jehoiachin's reign (Jer. 22:24ff.; cf. 36:30) and retains his allegiance to Zedekiah through the darkest hours of crisis and political divagations (cf. Jer. 38:14–26). Recognition of the legitimacy of Zedekiah's rule persists after the destruction of Jerusalem in the dirge for the king of Judah:

> The breath of our nostrils, the LORD's anointed,
>> was taken in their pits
> he of whom we said, "Under his shadow
>> we shall live among the nations" (Lam. 4:20).

Beyond the ideological controversy, however, the fact that Zedekiah ruled under foreign tutelage, contrary to the natural succession (unlike his step-brother Jehoiakim), and the threat of an alternative represented by Jehoiachin bespoke pressure on Judah's last king and restricted his maneuverability. In addition, the king's vacillating personality reduced him to hardly more than a puppet in the hands of his own ministers, as he himself confesses: "for the king can do nothing against you" (Jer. 38:5). This explains Zedekiah's paradoxical conduct in rebelling against the very power by whose grace he ruled Judah; by repudiating his own interests he nailed down his own coffin and that of his kingdom.

Zedekiah soon became entangled in the international scene. During his fourth regnal year, between Tishri 594 and Tishri 593, there convened in Jerusalem an anti-Babylonian conference attended by emissaries from the Transjordanian states, Edom, Moab, and Ammon, and the Phoenician coastal cities, Tyre and Sidon (Jer. 27:3; for the date, cf. 28:1). More precisely, this subversive gathering took place just prior to the confrontation between Jeremiah and Hananiah, which occurred in the fifth month of the same year (Ab 593). The anti-Babylonian plot loosed bitter charges between Jeremiah and those false prophets who advocated open revolt against Nebuchadnezzar not just in Judah (Jer. 27:9–16; 28) but even among the Judean exiles in Babylonia (Jer. 29:8–9; 21ff.). It is not unlikely that this intensified prophetic activity set the stage for the call of Ezekiel. The prophet's inaugural vision more or less coincided with the conspiratorial meeting held in Jerusalem, which boded ill no less for the exiles in Babylonia than it did for Judah.[32]

According to the Babylonian Chronicle, on the eve of the Jerusalem conspiracy the Babylonian Empire was beset by serious domestic and foreign problems, which gave the nations in the west the chance to rebel. In 596/595 the king of Elam attacked Babylonia but was roundly defeated (the inspiration, probably, for Jeremiah's invective against "Elam, in the beginning of the reign of Zedekiah" [Jer. 49:34]). In the winter of 595/594 an insurrection broke out even in Babylonia proper, but Nebuchadnezzar was able to quell it and depart immediately thereafter for a brief campaign to the west. Less than a year later (December 594), he set out once again for the west, an episode mentioned just before the Chronicle breaks off. If we assume correctly that the rebellion in Jerusalem started a few months later in the course of the following summer, then this last Babylonian campaign could not have been very impressive, or it might even have failed, thus aggravating the ferment in the west. During his fourth regnal year Zedekiah is said to have gone to Babylon (Jer. 51:59) or at least to have sent his "quartermaster" (cf. the LXX version). We do not know, however, whether this occurred before or in connection with Nebuchadnezzar's campaign to the west, or, conversely, whether this step was necessitated by the Babylonian response to the conspiracy against them.

The subversive schemes in Judah were no doubt once again fomented by Egyptian intrigue. The immediate cause of the anti-Babylonian alliance, however, was not, as is often assumed, Pharaoh Psammetichus II's ascent to the throne, since his reign now appears to have started in 595 not 594, more than two years before the Jerusalem plot.[33] During his third year (593) Psammetichus was engaged in a successful campaign in Nubia, probably with foreign mercenaries participating, including troops from Judah, to which the "Letter of Aristeas" alludes.[34] During this fourth year (592) he set out for Haru; i.e., Palestine and the Phoenician coast. The Egyptian sources make it clear that this expedition was essentially a pilgrimage, complete with priests, to holy sites in this area, perhaps including the Temple in Jerusalem.[35] Psammetichus' appearance in Asia certainly had strong diplomatic repercussions and undoubtedly stoked the latent anti-Babylonian sentiments smoldering within the Judean leadership.

These seeds of discontent, however, burgeoned into open rebellion against Nebuchadnezzar only after the accession early in 589 of Pharaoh Hophrah who continued relentlessly to undermine Babylonian hegemony over Palestine. No broad anti-Babylonian front in the west ever took shape, however, since apart from Judah only Tyre and the kingdom of Ammon seemed to have had the courage to rise up against the foreign oppressor. Tyre's attempt to rebel is proven by Nebuchadnezzar's siege, begun shortly after the conquest of Jerusalem and lasting for thirteen years (Ezek. 29:17–20; *Ant.* X.9.1; *Ag.Apion* I.21).[36] Ammon's rebellious designs are implied by Ezekiel's vision of Nebuchadnezzar's dilemma during his march, as to whether he should attack Rabbath-ammon or Jerusalem (Ezek. 21:18–31), and also by the scheme of King Baalis of Ammon to eliminate Gedaliah son of Ahikam, the governor of Judah appointed by the Babylonians after the destruction of Jerusalem at the hands of Ishmael son of Nethaniah (Jer. 40:14; 41:15).

The Destruction of Judah

When Nebuchadnezzar finally struck in the winter of 589/588, Judah had to stand up single-handedly to the awesome might of Babylonia. Diplomatic efforts to achieve an anti-Babylonian bloc had come to nothing, and Egyptian support was so minimal that Judah was virtually isolated in its hour of peril (cf. Lam. 1:2, 7). Judah was also less capable militarily of withstanding the Babylonian onslaught than it had been a decade earlier when it had select troops available for deployment, and the morale of the nation was undermined by the unresolved issue of total war with Babylonia or surrender. Among those who opted for surrender were Jeremiah and certain military figures who were convinced of the futility of armed confrontation. Given such prodigious obstacles, Jerusalem's ability to endure so long and so arduous a siege is all the more remarkable. The siege persisted for a year and a half, reckoning Zedekiah's regnal years from Nisan; if we adopt the autumnal Tishri calendar that has been used in this chapter, it lasted a full year longer.[37]

Whereas the books of Kings and, more significantly, Jeremiah and Ezekiel provide detailed accounts of the final struggle of Jerusalem, they do not specify what happened in the rest of Judah. Only an incidental remark is made about two Judean cities, Lachish and Azekah (Tell ez-Zakariyeh), which were in their turn to become battlegrounds, "for these were the only fortified cities of Judah that remained" (Jer. 34:7). These words, to be ascribed to the first year of the siege of Jerusalem prior to the dispatch of the Egyptian relief force, when Jeremiah still enjoyed freedom of movement and retained a flicker of hope for Zedekiah (Jer. 34:1-5, 21-22), testify to the speed with which the Babylonians had overrun Judah, except for those two cities which managed to maintain communication lines to the capital from the southwest. The lack of biblical data for the rest of the country is offset to some extent, however, by archaeological and Hebrew epigraphical evidence from several Judean sites which highlights the drama of the First Temple period.

Undoubtedly the most significant collection of Hebrew documents for our period are the ostraca from Lachish (Stratum II and Arad Stratum VI. The Lachish ostraca are mainly letters (or copies thereof)[38] dispatched to Joash, apparently the last commander of the city's garrison. Since they were found in the destruction layer of the city gate, they can be dated to the eve of the fall of Lachish. Although the letters do not explicitly mention the Babylonian invasion, they do attest the feverish activity in the southwestern part of the country—urgent orders, inspection of military guards, and installation of communication signal systems. Like the Bible, they also reflect the opposition and tension between activist leadership in the capital and the army in the outlying districts; moreover some prophets advocated appeasement, thus creating a situation destined "to weaken the hands of the soldiers . . . and the hands of the nation" (ostracon no. 6, l. 6; cf. Jer. 38:4). These documents record a relatively early stage of the war when the central government and high command in Jerusalem were still in full control of the situation, when the military services were functioning normally, and when communication between the capital and the southwestern front was still intact. Another letter, however, attests a genuine state of emergency and might have been written after the fall of Azekah (ostracon no. 4, ll. 10-13).

Unlike those of Lachish, the documents from the border fortress of Arad are essentially administrative, but found with these were several letters from the archive of Eliashib son of Oshiahu, probably the fortress commander. They generally deal with supplying provisions, mostly to the *kittiyim*, possibly mercenaries of Greek or Cypriot origin serving in the Judean army. A most instructive letter orders, in the king's name, the urgent dispatch of soldiers to the Edomite border to forestall an expected enemy invasion.[39] Although an Edomite attack on Judah could easily have coincided with the Transjordanian incursions just before the first Babylonian conquest of Jerusalem in 598/597 (cf. above), such an attack is more readily understandable in the context of the last Babylonian war. It also seems that the repeated wrath against Edom in biblical books was caused by the Edomite role in the final destruction of the Judean kingdom (cf. Jer. 49:7–22; Ezek. 25:12–14; Obad. 1:10–14; Joel 3:19; Ps. 137:7; Lam. 4:21–22).

The outcome of the final struggle with the Babylonians and the extent of the devastation of Judah are vividly illuminated by the archaeological excavations. While these excavations demonstrate that most of the fortress cities had begun to decline in an earlier era, there is unequivocal evidence that numerous sites in various parts of Judah were totally destroyed at the very end of the First Temple period: Lachish, Tell Beit Mirsim, Beth-shemesh, and Gezer on the border of the western slopes of the hill country and the Shephelah; Beth-zur, Khirbet Rabud (apparently the site of Debir), Ramat Rahel, and, above all, Jerusalem in the mountain region; apparently Arad,[40] Tel Malhata, and Tel Masos on the southern fringes; even remote 'En-gedi on the Dead Sea was not spared.[41] Thrust into the city walls of 'En-gedi were packs of arrows of the type used by the Babylonian army and a slingstone was found embedded in the wall of Lachish, undoubtedly thrown there by one of Nebuchadnezzar's slingers—"living" proof of the fierce battles these sites had witnessed.[42]

Totally different, however, was the situation north of Jerusalem where the Benjaminite settlements seemed to have fared much better. It has long been doubtful whether the archaeological evidence from Bethel and Mizpah (Tell en-Nasbeh) means that these places were destroyed by Nebuchadnezzar rather than at the end of the sixth or the beginning of the fifth century.[43] Recent excavations at Gibeah (Tell el-Ful) and Gibeon (el-Jib; mentioned even after the destruction of Jerusalem in Jer. 41:12, 16) also suggest that these sites were destroyed not at the hands of the Babylonians but considerably later. Neither at Anathoth (Ras el-Kharrubeh), Jeremiah's native town, nor at Mozah, is a break in settlement apparent during our period.[44] This may also apply to Ramah, headquarters of Nebuzaradan, the Babylonian commander during the final phase of the siege of Jerusalem, and a way station for Judeans going into exile after the fall of their capital (Jer. 40:1).

We can therefore assume that the settlement in Benjamin in fact survived unscathed by the Babylonian invasion. This may have been because Benjamin, a distinct entity (cf. Jer. 17:26; 32:44), was separated from Judah as early as 597 (cf. above) or because it surrendered to the Babylonians at the outset of their final invasion in 589/588. Whichever the case, after the destruction of the kingdom this area became the center of the remaining population, with

Mizpah the seat of Gedaliah, the Babylonian-appointed governor of Judah (cf. Neh. 3:7 on the continuation of Mizpah as the governor's seat right into the Persian period). An incident involving the prophet Jeremiah is instructive: during a temporary pause in the siege of Jerusalem, because an Egyptian relief force had arrived, the prophet, probably not unlike other inhabitants of the capital, tried to make his way to the land of Benjamin. Since Benjamin might by then have been under Babylonian control, such a move was bound to be called desertion to the enemy—exactly the accusation made against Jeremiah by the officer in charge of the Benjamin Gate: "You are deserting to the Chaldeans" (Jer. 37:13).

Further evidence that Benjamin escaped destruction is suggested by the list of exiles returning from Babylonia (Ezra 2:21–35; Neh. 7:25–38).[45] According to this list, the first returnees settled mainly in Benjaminite towns, which indicates that they were not in ruins. Special attention should be paid to the three Benjaminite cities listed in the Shephelah: Lod, Hadid, and Ono; situated as they were near the Via Maris, the vital route used by the Babylonian forces, they had no chance whatever to withstand the enemy and probably surrendered without a struggle. Besides Benjamin, the only localities mentioned in the list are the cities of Bethlehem and Netophah. As for the latter, it is of particular interest that the only army officers to join Gedaliah in Mizpah whose place of origin is stated explicitly—Seraiah son of Tanhumeth and the sons of Ephai and their men—are from Netophah (2 Kings 25:23; Jer. 40:8). From this we can conclude that the Judean army in this area had been neither completely disbanded nor completely exiled to Babylon. The same may perhaps be said for Bethlehem which apparently was not depopulated and, after the destruction of Jerusalem, continued to be an important transit station on the road to Egypt (Jer. 41:17). Thus, there remained throughout Judah proper population pockets neither destroyed nor destined for exile.

The siege of Jerusalem started on 10 Tebeth in Zedekiah's ninth regnal year (2 Kings 25:1; Jer. 52:4; Ezek. 24:1–2) and ended with the destruction of the Temple on 7 (or 10, according to another version) Ab, the eleventh year of the king of Judah and the nineteenth year of Nebuchadnezzar (2 Kings 25:8–9; Jer. 52:12). In absolute dates (adopting a Tishri calendar for the regnal year in Judah), the siege lasted from 15 January 588 until 14/17 August 586. The book of Kings focuses only on the final phase of the battle of Jerusalem and the destruction of the city (2 Kings 25:1–22; Jer. 52:4–27), but many details of the actual course of the siege can be gleaned from the prophecies of Jeremiah and Ezekiel. Faced with the enemy's threat, the king of Judah sent envoys to Egypt in order to enlist military aid, especially chariotry, as both Ezekiel (17:15) and possibly one of the Lachish Letters ("the commander of the army, Coniahu son of Elnathan had come down in order to go to Egypt" [ostracon no. 3, ll. 14ff.]) recount. Though Pharaoh was slow to respond, an Egyptian relief force did in fact compel the Babylonians to raise the siege of Jerusalem temporarily (Jer. 37:5, 11). This led to a false sense of security in the capital, which Jeremiah quickly warned against. The citizens went so far as to renege on the covenant made early in the siege for the manumission of slaves, an extreme measure probably intended to reinforce the city's potential defensive power (Jer. 34, esp. vss. 21–22).[46] The Egyptian task force, however, was too frail to be of any real consequence (Ezek. 17:17; 30:20–26; cf. Lam. 4:17). Ezekiel's prophecies of doom concerning Egypt, headed by chronological superscriptions, imply that the abortive operation took place in the spring of 587.[47] Hophrah's intervention occurred, therefore, only a year after the investment of Jerusalem; but even though it failed and the noose was newly tightened around the capital, the city's staunch defenders were able to hold out for more than a year.

That some of Jerusalem's inhabitants nevertheless yielded to the enemy during the final year of the siege is indicated by Zedekiah's reply to Jeremiah who, at the eleventh hour, urged Zedekiah's capitulation: "I am afraid of the Jews that are fallen to the Chaldeans, lest they deliver me into their hand and they mock me" (Jer. 38:19, author's translation). These deserters are probably among the 832 captives listed in Jeremiah 52:29 as exiled "from Jerusalem" in Nebuchadnezzar's eighteenth regnal year, while the city was still under siege. Analogous to the exile under Jehoiachin (cf. above p. 293), this small-scale deportation may reflect a preliminary wave followed after the fall of Jerusalem by a mass exile in Nebuchadnezzar's nineteenth year (2 Kings 25:8; Jer. 52:12).[48] Although the Bible does not mention the total number of deportees, it does suggest a multitude: "and the rest of the people who were left in the city . . . with the rest of the multitude, Nebuzaradan . . . carried into exile" (2 Kings 25:11; cf. Jer. 39:9; 52:15). Among the captives were the higher officialdom, the high priesthood, and the army command, whose punishment was far more severe than it had been in the days of Jehoiachin, for they were executed at Riblah, Nebuchadnezzar's headquarters in central Syria (2 Kings 25:18–21; Jer. 39:6; 52:10, 24–27).

Because the battle of Jerusalem was a formidable challenge for Nebuchadnezzar, he enlisted his choice commanders (Jer. 39:3, 13) who years later served in high positions in the Babylonian Empire (such as Nergal-sharezer, who was to become king of Babylon if only briefly). He also employed the most advanced techniques of siege-warfare of his day, throwing dikes around the city, raising ramps up to the walls, and using battering rams to breach the walls (2 Kings 25:1; Jer. 32:24; 33:4; Ezek. 4:1–2; 17:17; 21:22). Despite all this sophisticated siege technique, the Bible implies that the major cause for the fall of the city was the devastating famine which plagued the inhabitants (2 Kings 25:3; Jer. 52:6; cf. Jer. 37:21; Ezek. 5:10; Lam. 2:19–20; 4:4–10), whose number was probably swollen early in the Babylonian invasion by refugees from the countryside who sought safety within the capital.

Finally, on 9 Tammuz, in Zedekiah's eleventh regnal year (18 July 586), the wall of Jerusalem was breached (Jer. 39:2; 52:5–7; and, with the month omitted, 2 Kings 25:3–4), probably on its northern side, topographically the most vulnerable flank of the city. Penetration of the city from this direction is also implied by Zedekiah's position at the Benjamin Gate during a critical stage of the siege (Jer. 38:7) and by the gathering of the Babylonian officers upon the breach of the wall at the "Middle Gate," both in the north of the city. Under cover of darkness, however, Zedekiah and his retinue fled through the southern accesses of the city (by way of the king's garden near the Siloam pool), attempting to escape to Transjordania. The king was overtaken in the plain of Jericho, however, brought before Nebuchadnezzar at Riblah, subjected to cruel punishment, and led into Babylonian captivity (2 Kings 25:4–7; Jer. 39:4–8; 52:7–11; cf. Ezek. 12:12–14; 17:20; 19:9; Lam. 4:18–20) in accord with the breach of a vassal treaty. It was at this stage, apparently, that the Babylonian king decided to raze Jerusalem and its temple, and thus he sent his general, Nebuzaradan, to carry out this plan. From the time of the breaching of the walls, Zedekiah's flight, and his arrest and removal to Riblah until Nebuzaradan's arrival at Jerusalem, some four weeks must have passed.

Only then was the city thoroughly ransacked by the rampaging enemy; walls and houses were razed and the holy Temple and royal palace were burned (2 Kings 25:8–9; Jer. 52:12). The sacred vessels in the Temple and the palace treasures, which had been left behind following the Babylonian despoliation in the days of Jehoiachin, were pillaged and plundered (2 Kings 25:13–17; Jer. 27:6–22; 2 Chron. 36:18). Tangible evidence of the catastrophe which befell Jerusalem has been disclosed by the archaeological excavations both in the Upper City and on the eastern slopes of the southeastern hill of Jerusalem, where traces of once-demolished buildings have been uncovered.[49] The destruction in the latter region was so all-encompassing that Nehemiah, a century and a half later, was forced to abandon the ruins and leave the ravaged area outside his newly erected city wall (cf. Neh. 2:12–14). In the Upper City, at the northern defense line (south of the "Street of the Chain"), the burnt remains at the foot of a tower and finds of several arrowheads point to the violent battle with the Babylonians who attempted, as stated above, to break through from this direction.

With the conquest of Jerusalem and the cessation of the Davidic monarchy, Judah was divested of its polity, but the drama had not yet come to a close. Surviving remnants of the army and populace sought sanctuary across the Jordan river (Jer. 40:11) or possibly, if we may draw an analogy from the final events surrounding the destruction of the Second Temple, in hideouts and caves in the hills and the wilderness of Judah. For the latter, we can find support in the Bible and in epigraphical and archaeological discoveries. Indeed, the bitter reality enveloping the survivors is delineated in Ezekiel's grim vision at the news of Jerusalem's fall: "they that are in the wasteland shall fall by the sword, and him that is in the open field will I give to the beasts to be devoured, and they that be in *the forts* and in *the caves* shall die" (Ezek. 33:27, author's translation; cf. 7:15–16).[50] The cruel fate of those who escaped the sword is also tolled in the poet's lament:

> Our pursuers were swifter
> 	than the vultures in the heavens;
> they chased us on the mountains,
> 	they lay in wait for us in the wilderness (Lam. 4:19).

Such refugees, seeking shelter from the enemy, might well have left behind the Hebrew graffiti in a cave near Khirbet Beit-Lei, east of Lachish, where the names of Judah and Jerusalem appear with words of prayer.[51] The pottery and Hebrew papyrus[52] discovered in the caves at Wadi Muraba'at near the Dead Sea indicate that the fugitives found refuge there not only at the end of the Second Temple period but also during the seventh and, apparently, at the beginning of the sixth century B.C.E. In the Wadi ed-Daliyeh caves northeast of Ramallah, there were also discovered, alongside papyri from the end of the Persian period, several potsherds from Late Iron II, about the time of the destruction of the First Temple, perhaps hinting at the final tragedy.[53]

For want of testimony like that of Josephus' *Wars*, the Massada discoveries, and the Judean desert cave material, which illuminate the end of the Second Commonwealth and the Bar Kochba Revolt, we may never know the whole dramatic story of the tribulations of the rebels and refugees after the fall of Jerusalem.[54] Instead, Jer. 40ff. presents us with the epilogue to the catastrophe, allowing us to glance at the surviving population gathered around Gedaliah son of Ahikam, who tried to restore the last vestiges of the community. The assassination of Gedaliah and the annihilation of the Babylonian garrison at Mizpah (Jer. 41:3), however, shattered all hope for a resurgence of the Jewish community from within. Instead, the aspiration and yearning for national revival turned toward the Jewish diaspora in Babylonia and its yet unbudded potential.

NOTES

1. For this period cf. my previous studies (1968: 137–56; 1975: 123–45). These articles provide supplementary details and additional bibliographical references.
2. On the historical circumstances leading to the battle of Megiddo and on the battle itself, cf. Malamat (1973: 267–79).
3. Cf. C. J. Gadd (1923: 31ff.; B.M. 21901, ll. 10, 61, 66) and D. J. Wiseman (1956: 55ff.).
4. On the enigma of Scythian domination in Hither Asia and reflections of their

appearance in Palestine in the prophecies of Jeremiah and Zephaniah, cf. H. H. Rowley (1962: 206ff.), H. Cazelles (1967), and R. P. Vaggione (1973). For various opinions on the date of the Scythian invasion into Philistia, cf. Rowley (1962: 211 n. 3). Our suggestion to date it to the spring of 609 (1950/51: 154–59) is no longer tenable, since it has recently been established that Psammetichus died between the end of July and the end of September 610; cf. E. Hornung (1965). Possibly the Scythians advanced toward Egypt in 611, as proposed by T. T. Rice (1957: 45). For a suggested earlier date for this event, cf. recently A. R. Millard (1979: 119–22) and A. Spalinger (1978a: 49ff.).

5. On the irregularity of Jehoahaz' enthronement, cf. Malamat (1968: 140 and nn. 6–7) with literature on the 'am hā'āreṣ; on the anti-Egyptian stand of that body, cf. Malamat (1975: 126).

6. For similar notions concerning the relations between the 'am hā'āreṣ and the maternal lineage of the Judean kings, cf. also Ihromi (1974: esp. p. 427).

7. The assumption that Jehoiakim ascended the throne only after 1 Tishri 609, which is reasonable in itself, is essential to the chronological system used in the present essay. Regnal years in Judah, at least at this time, were reckoned from Tishri and not from Nisan, as was customary in Babylonia (even though the months of the year were counted from Nisan in keeping with the prevalent Judean civil calendar). This method, which obviously has certain implications for the reconstruction of the chain of events as presented below, is preferable to the alternate system, since it is reconcilable with a greater part of the variegated data of the period under discussion as we have sought to demonstrate elsewhere (1968: 146ff.; cf. n. 1 there for studies advocating a spring calendar, and n. 20 for an autumn one). For additional literature on both systems, cf. Malamat (1975: 124 n. 2). We cannot therefore readily accept the two most recent studies reiterating the claim for a Nisan calendar: E. Kutsch 1974; and E. Vogt 1975; the former arriving at the date of Jerusalem's destruction in 587 b.c.e., the latter in 586 b.c.e. An argument in favor of a Tishri reckoning not raised in the current controversy can, incidentally, be inferred from the chrono-logical superscription in Jeremiah 1:3, concerning the fall of Jerusalem: "until the end ['ad-tōm] of the eleventh year of Zedekiah . . . when Jerusalem was carried into exile in the fifth month" (author's translation). The juxtaposition of the fifth month (i.e., Ab) with the approximate termination here of the eleventh or, for that matter, any regnal year is feasible only on a Tishri basis (short of merely the sixth month before the actual year's end) and is discordant with a Nisan calendar (where the surplus would comprise almost half a year).

8. In this case the first official year of Jehoiakim's reign would have begun on 1 Tishri 609 (and not 1 Tishri 608, the lapse of time until then having been considered his accession year and, theoretically, Jehoahaz' first regnal year, countering Kutsch's main criticism of my contention [Kutsch 1974]). Such a reckoning indeed solves the chronological difficulty of the date of the battle of Carchemish in Jer. 46:2 (cf. below n. 11), but contradicts 2 Kings 23:36 according to which Jehoiakim reigned only eleven years and not the twelve now necessary. Even if we assume that Jehoiakim died before 1 Tishri 598 (and thus reigned only eleven years)—an assumption which in itself is not reasonable—a difficult chronological problem arises: the year which began in the autumn of 598 and ended in the autumn of 597 would then not be considered in the counting of the years (i.e., it was a "zero" year), a reckoning contrary to the chronological method of the Bible. It could not be accounted to Jehoiachin even theoretically, because he reigned only three months, and his reign

ended on 2 Adar 597 (cf. below). However, if the reckoning of the regnal years of Jehoiakim were begun only on 1 Tishri 608, as we assumed above, then the lapse in time from his assumption of the throne till this date would be considered an accession year (Akkadian *rēš šarrûti*). On the other hand, in purely chronological terms this period would be reckoned as the first year of Jehoahaz (in contrast to Kutsch 1974), for in this case Jehoahaz reigned till after the regnal New Year on 1 Tishri 609. A different chronological method has recently been put forth by H. Cazelles (1983). According to this method, regnal years were reckoned, under Egyptian influence, from the actual day of accession to the same date a year hence. Thus, Cazelles places the destruction of the temple in Ab 587 (rather than 586), for it occurred in Zedekiah's eleventh year, and he began his reign—based on the Babylonian Chronicle—around 2 Adar 597 (cf. below).

9. For Psammetichus I's and Necho's control of Syria and the Phoenician coast, cf. Malamat (1975: 128 n. 10).

10. Cf. Wiseman (1956: 64ff.; B.M. 22047, ll. 12ff.) and Vogt (1957: 72ff.).

11. For the Babylonian source, cf. Wiseman (1956: 66ff.; B.M. 21946). Jer. 46:2 places the battle of Carchemish in Jehoiakim's fourth, rather than in his third, regnal year and this is the only date of significance conflicting with a Tishri calendar (cf. Malamat 1968: 147 n. 21). For possible solutions, cf. Malamat (1975: 128 n. 11) and n. 8 above.

12. Cf. Malamat (1975: 129ff. and n. 15).

13. Cf. Malamat (1968: 141ff.; 1975: 131 and n. 19) for similar conjectures about the date of Judah's subjugation.

14. For the war between Babylonia and Egypt in the winter of 601/600 B.C.E. and on possible further evidence now available for this event, cf. E. Lipiński (1972) and Malamat (1973: 276–78 and nn. 31–33).

15. The relevant Babylonian passage is B.M. 21946, ll. 21ff. (Wiseman 1956: 70–71). The obliterated beginning of l. 22 seems to have mentioned one of the conquered Philistine cities (cf. Malamat 1975: 131 n. 18); names of other Philistine towns probably appeared in the following missing lines which almost certainly referred to Jehoiakim's surrender as well (Malamat 1968: 142 and n. 9).

16. Cf. the document in Donner-Röllig (1971: no. 266) and the additional literature in Malamat (1968: 143 n. 11; 1975: 131). Recently Demotic script was discovered written on the reverse of this papyrus, possibly giving the name of the place from which the letter was sent: "Ekron"; cf. Porten (1981).

17. Cf. Wiseman (1956: 31ff.). For the various Babylonian motives for campaigning against the Arab tribes, cf. I. Eph'al (1982: 171ff.) and W. J. Dumbrell (1972).

18. For this assumption, cf. A. Alt (1973b: 325 and n. 3). It is less likely that Necho had detached certain areas from the kingdom of Judah as early as 609. Equally unlikely is Y. Aharoni's suggestion that Necho's army then destroyed Arad, Stratum VII, which he sets forth on the basis of a hieratic inscription found in the destruction layer of this level (1981: 64, 150).

19. For the complex chronological problems and the means of determining the regnal New Year in Judah, raised now by the Babylonian Chronicle, cf. Malamat 1968: 44ff. and the extensive literature cited there and in Malamat 1975: 124 n. 2; cf. n. 7 above.

20. The garden of Uzza was actually situated "beyond the gates of Jerusalem," if we

accept B. Mazar's suggestion for locating this burial site on the slopes of the Mount of Olives near Silwan Village (cf. Mazar 1971: 23; 1958). On Jeremiah's prophecy, cf. inter alia, M. Cogan (1971: 29–34). The disgraceful burial of Jehoiakim is also intimated in Jer. 36:30: "and his dead body shall be cast out to the heat by day and the frost by night." This image recalls the curse formulae, in the neo-Assyrian treaties, to be leveled against a rebel; cf. D. H. Hillers (1964: 68ff.).

21. The description of the palace in Jeremiah 22:13–14 suggests imitation of Egyptian palaces; this style was admittedly not unknown in the northern Israelite kingdom; it, however, had long lain in ruins by the time of Jehoiakim. Y. Aharoni claims to have found remnants of Jehoiakim's palace at Ramat Rahel (1978). Difficulties in this identification, however, have been pointed out by Y. Yadin (1973: 59ff.). According to a suggestion of B. Mazar, Jehoiakim's palace was erected on the western hill of Jerusalem (near the present-day Tower of David), as he infers from Josephus' locating the Davidic palaces in the Upper City; cf. Nehemiah 3:25.

22. For the following solution cf. Malamat (1956; and, in greater detail, 1975: 133ff.).

23. For this term, Hebrew *masgēr*, cf. Malamat (1975: 133 n. 24). For the same term in Ugaritic, cf. M. Dietrich, O. Loretz, and J. Sanmartin (1975: 163).

24. There is marked disagreement among archaeologists as to whether in these sites the destruction level preceding the one from the very end of the First Temple period is to be attributed to Nebuchadnezzar's campaign of 598/597 or to Sennacherib's invasion of 701. For a recent discussion of this controversy, cf. D. H. Lance who postdates the relevant level to the period of Nebuchadnezzar, at least as far as Lachish III is concerned (1971). In the light of the recent excavations at Lachish D. Ussishkin rightly moves the destruction of Lachish III back to 701 B.C.E. (1977; 1978: 93).

25. On the basis of Jeremiah 13:19 some scholars conclude that the Negeb and the areas northward beyond Hebron were then cut off from Judah; cf. Alt (1973b: 327ff.) and P. Welten (1969: 166). This assumption, however, is without support. On the contrary, the excavations at Arad now prove that this site remained a Judean border fortress right down to the destruction of the First Temple (cf. below).

26. Cf. Malamat (1968: 145ff. and n. 8) for literature on the Assyrian vassal treaties and curse formulae. Add now E. Kutsch (1973: 10ff., 206). On the nature of Zedekiah's punishment, cf. F. E. Deist (1971).

27. Cf. E. F. Weidner (1939) and W. F. Albright (1942).

28. Cf. the list of deposed rulers in Babylonia, dating from about 570 (including the kings of Tyre, Gaza, Sidon, Arvad, and Ashdod), published by Unger (1925; 1926) and A. L. Oppenheim (1969: 308a–b). A possible parallel to the changeover of kings in Judah might be found at Tyre, whose king Ithobaal III was exiled in 573/572 and replaced by Baal, perhaps from the same local dynasty; cf. J. Klausner (1949: 38) and H. J. Katzenstein (1973: 326ff., 331).

29. On the Eliakim seals as indication of Jehoiachin's status in exile as official king of Judah, cf. Albright (1932) and H. G. May (1939). For reservations about this conclusion, cf. J. Liver (1958: col. 525), Malamat (1975: 138 n. 34), and N. Avigad (1976: 298–300).

30. On this matter, cf. Malamat (1951) followed by K. Baltzer (1961).

31. On the date of the redemption predicted by Hananiah and the possibility, not yet

considered, that this date is reflected in Ezekiel 20:1 and that Ezekiel, like Jeremiah, neglected the prophecy of redemption, cf. Malamat (1975: 137ff.).

32. On the anti-Babylonian parley in Jerusalem and its chronological correspondence to Ezekiel's appearance, cf. Malamat (1975: 137).

33. For the accession year of Psammetichus II and the revised Egyptian chronology of the Twenty-Sixth Dynasty in general, cf. the literature in Malamat (1975: 141 n. 40).

34. There is, however, a difference of opinion as to whether the "Letter of Aristeas" refers to Psammetichus I or II. Cf. S. Sauneron and J. Yoqette (1952) and K. S. Freedy and D. B. Redford (1970: 476ff.).

35. On Psammetichus II's campaign to Asia, cf. M. Greenberg (1957) who assumes that Pharaoh's appearance in Palestine aroused Zedekiah to open rebellion against Babylonia. For a recent study of this expedition, emphasizing its peaceful rather than its frequently assumed military nature, cf. Freedy and Redford (1970: 479ff.) and, more recently, A. Spalinger (1978b: 22–33). As for the possibility that Pharaoh or his priests visited Jerusalem during their journey, a pilgrimage somehow reflected in Ezekiel 8, depicting ritual abominations performed in the Jerusalem temple, cf. Malamat (1975: 142).

36. On the siege of Tyre, cf. W. Zimmerli (1969: 603ff., 718), M. Weippert (1971: 375 and n. 1260), Freedy and Redford (1970: 481ff.), and esp. Katzenstein (1973: 318–32). For the proximity of Nebuchadnezzar's attack against Judah on the one hand and against the Phoenicians on the other, there is enlightening testimony from Berossus, quoted only in Tatianus (cf. M. Stern 1974: 60ff.).

37. On the chronological dilemma as to the duration of the siege of Jerusalem and supplementary details on the course of its events, cf. Malamat (1968: 150ff.).

38. As suggested by Y. Yadin.

39. On this letter, cf. Y. Aharoni (1981: 46ff., no. 24).

40. Aharoni contends that Arad was destroyed by the Edomites in 595, Zedekiah's third regnal year. His conclusion is based on an inscription (no. 20) on a jar from the destruction layer of this site, starting with the word "bšlšt . . ."; "in the third [year of Zedekiah?]" (1981: 151). This assumption, however, is extremely dubious if only because of Edom's alliance with Judah in the anti-Babylonian plot one year later (cf. above).

41. On these sites, cf. the relevant entries in *Encyclopedia of Archaeological Excavations in the Holy Land*. Vol. I–IV, Jerusalem 1975–78; on Tel Malhata, cf. M. Kochavi (1970); on Khirbet Rabud, cf. Kochavi (1974); on Gezer, cf. W. G. Dever (1970b: 6, 33); on Beth-zur, cf. P. W. Lapp (1968a: 8, 28ff.), and on Tel Masos, cf. Aharoni, Fritz, and Kempinski (1981: 71).

42. Oral information from E. Stern. Concerning the so-called "Scythian" arrows, cf. Dothan, Dunayevski, and Mazar (1963: 55 and pl. XXIII, 26/7). For Lachish, cf. now Ussishkin (1978: 54).

43. On the basis of the excavation reports on Bethel and Tell en-Nasbeh, as well as of various data in Jeremiah, Ezra, and Nehemiah (mentioned below), I assumed a long time ago that the district of Benjamin surrendered to the Babylonians and was thereby spared destruction (Malamat 1950). Additional support for this assumption can now be found in the excavation report from Bethel (Kelso 1968: 37, 51), but cf. the reservations expressed by Dever (1970a: 469 and n. 16). Since then our con-

clusion has been reinforced by further excavations in the territory of Benjamin (cf. the following note; also Weinberg 1972: 47ff.).

44. On the excavations at Tell el-Ful, cf. P. W. Lapp (1965; 1970); on Gibeon, cf. Lapp (1968b), R. Amiran (1974/75), and the remarks of D. Barag (1967: 143) and E. Stern (1973: 34–37, and the bibliographical references on p. 256). On Anathoth, cf. A. Bergmann (1936); and on Mozah, cf. N. Avigad (1972: 9).

45. On the various lists of the returnees in the books of Ezra and Nehemiah and the possibility that they may mirror the historical situation prior to the exiles' return, cf. Z. Kallai (1960: 82ff.) and E. Stern (1973: 241ff.).

46. For the legal background of the manumission of the slaves in Jeremiah 34, add to the literature cited in Malamat (1968: 152ff., n. 30): M. Kessler (1971), N. Sarna (1973), and N. P. Lemche (1976).

47. Cf. Malamat (1968: 152). Freedy and Redford (1970: 470–72, 481) date the Egyptian expedition four or five months earlier on the erroneous assumption, in our opinion, that the dates in Ezekiel do not refer to the events per se but rather to the time when news of them reached Babylon.

48. Cf. Malamat (1968: 154 and n. 32).

49. On the excavation of the eastern slopes, cf. K. M. Kenyon (1974: 170ff.) and esp. the new excavations in this area, since 1978, under Y. Shiloh (1979; 1980: 13). For excavations in the Upper City and the traces there of the destruction, cf. now N. Avigad (1983: 53ff., and the map there on p. 58). According to Professor Avigad's most recent theory, the tower noted there served as the corner of a gate in the northern wall of the Upper City. This might have been the "Middle Gate" of Jeremiah 39:3, where Nebuchadnezzar's officers gathered after penetrating into the city (R. Grafman has orally suggested that the "Middle Gate" be located on the Temple Mount between the Temple and the palace; cf. Ezekiel 43:8 for a possible oblique reference to this connecting gate).

50. For the historical background of Ezekiel 33:23ff., cf. W. Zimmerli (1969: 818ff.) and W. H. Brownlee (1970).

51. The inscriptions were published by J. Naveh (1963). For a newly proposed reading and their attribution to refugees of the last Babylonian war, cf. F. M. Cross (1970).

52. Cf. P. Benoit, J. T. Milik, and R. de Vaux (1961: 26–28, 93–100). On the Hebrew papyrus, a palimpsest of a mid-seventh century letter, superimposed by a list of personal names with measures of capacity, cf. J. C. L. Gibson (1971: 31ff.).

53. For archaeological finds from Wadi ed-Daliyeh, cf. P. W. and Nancy Lapp (1974: 56 and n. 12).

54. Another rebellion in the west is to be inferred both from Jeremiah 52:30, which notes the exile of 745 Jews in Nebuchadnezzar's twenty-third regnal year (582), and from Josephus (*Ant.* X.9.7), who attributes a Babylonian campaign in the same year to Coele-Syria, Moab, and Ammon.

BIBLIOGRAPHY

Aharoni, Y.
1978   Ramat Raḥel. Pp. 1000–1009 in vol. 4 of *Encyclopedia of Archaeological Excavations in the Holy Land*, ed. M. Avi-Yonah and E. Stern. Jerusalem: Massada.
1981   Fritz, V. and Kempinski, A. Excavations at Tel Masos (Khirbet el-Meshâsh). *Tel Aviv* 1: 64–74.

Albright, W. F.
1932   The Seal of Eliakim and the Latest Pre-exilic History of Judah, with Some Observations on Ezekiel. *Journal of Biblical Literature* 51: 77–106.
1942   King Jehoiachin in Exile. *Biblical Archaeologist* 5: 49–55.

Alt, A.
1973a   Judas Gave unter Josia. Pp. 276–88 in vol. 2 of *Kleine Schriften zur Geschichte des Volkes Israel*. Munich: C. H. Beck.
1973b   Die Rolle Samarias bei der Entstehung des Judentums. Pp. 316–37 in vol. 2 of *Kleine Schriften zur Geschichte des Volkes Israel*. Munich: C. H. Beck.

Amiran, R.
1974/75   A Note on the "Gibeon Jar." *Palestine Exploration Quarterly* 107: 129–32.

Avigad, N.
1972   Two Hebrew Inscriptions on Wine-Jars. *Israel Exploration Journal* 22: 1–9.
1975   Jerusalem, The Jewish Quarter of the Old City, 1975. *Israel Exploration Journal* 25: 260–61.
1976   New Light on the *Naʿar* Seals. Pp. 294–300 in *Magnalia Dei. The Mighty Acts of God: Essays in the Bible and Archaeology in Memory of G. E. Wright*, ed. F. M. Cross, W. E. Lemke, and P. D. Miller. Garden City, NY: Doubleday.
1983   *Discovering Jerusalem*. Nashville: Nelson.

Baltzer, K.
1961   Das Ende des Staates Juda und die Messias-Frage. Pp. 33–43 in *Studien zur Theologie der alttestamentlichen Uberlieferungen*, ed. R. Rendtorff and K. Koch. Neukirchen-Vluyn: Neukirchener.

Barag, D.
1967   Review of J. Pritchard, *Winery, Defenses and Soundings at Gibeon*. *Journal of Near Eastern Studies* 26: 142–43.

Benoit, P., Milik, J. T., and de Vaux, R.
1961   *Discoveries in the Judean Desert*. Vol. 2. Oxford: Clarendon Press.

Bergmann, A.
1936   Soundings at the Supposed Site of Old Testament Anathoth. *Bulletin of the American Schools of Oriental Research* 62: 22–24.

Brownlee, W. H.
1970   The Aftermath of the Fall of Judah According to Ezekiel. *Journal of Biblical Literature* 89: 393–404.

Cazelles, H.
1967   Sophonie, Jérémie, et les Scythes en Palestine. *Revue Biblique* 74: 24–44.
1983   587 or 586? Pp. 427–35 in *The Word of the Lord Shall Go Forth: Essays in Honor of D. N. Freedman*, ed. C. L. Meyers and M. O'Connor. Winona Lake, IN: Eisenbrauns.

Cogan, M.
1971   A Note on Disinterment in Jeremiah. Pp. 29–34 in *Gratz College Anniversary Volume*, ed. I. D. Passow and S. T. Lachs. Philadelphia: Gratz College.

Cross, F. M.
1970   The Cave Inscriptions from Khirbet Beit Lei. Pp. 299–306 in *Near Eastern Archaeology in the Twentieth Century: Essays in Honor of Nelson Glueck*, ed. J. A. Sanders. Garden City, NY: Doubleday.

Deist, F. E.
1971   The Punishment of the Disobedient Zedekiah. *Journal of Northwest Semitic Literature* 1: 71–72.

Dever, W. G.
1970a   Archaeological Methods and Results. A Review of Two Recent Publications. *Orientalia* 40: 459–71.
1970b   *Gezer*. Vol. 1. Jerusalem: Hebrew Union College.

Dietrich, M., Loretz, O., and Sanmartin, J.
1975   Zur ugaritischen Lexikographie XIII. *Ugarit-Forschungen* 7: 157–69.

Donner, H. and Röllig, W.
1971   *Kanaanäische und aramäische Inschriften*. Third edition. Wiesbaden: Harrassowitz.

Dothan, T., Dunayevski, I., and Mazar, B.
1963   Ein-Gedi: Archaeological Excavations, 1961–62. Chapter 2: The Excavations at Tel Goren (Tel el-Jurn). *Yediot* 27: 20–82.

Dumbrell, W. J.
1972   Jeremiah 49:28–33; An Oracle Against a Proud Desert Power. *Australian Journal of Biblical Archaeology* 2: 99–108.

Eph'al, I.
1982   *The Ancient Arabs*. Jerusalem: Magnes Press.

Freedy, K. S. and Redford, D. B.
1970   The Dates in Ezekiel in Relation to Biblical, Babylonian and Egyptian Sources. *Journal of the American Oriental Society* 90: 462–85.

Gadd, C. J.
1923   *The Fall of Nineveh*. London: Oxford University.

Gibson, J. C. L.
1971   *Textbook of Syrian Semitic Inscriptions*. Vol. 1. Oxford: Clarendon Press.

Greenberg, M.
1957   Ezekiel 17 and the Policy of Psammetichus II. *Journal of Biblical Literature* 76: 304–9.

Hillers, D. H.
1964   *Treaty Curses and the Old Testament Prophets*. Biblica et Orientalia 16. Rome: Pontifical Biblical Institute.

Hornung, E.
1965 Die Sonnenfinsternis nach dem Tode Psammetichs I. *Zeitschrift für Agyptische Sprache und Altertumskunde* 92: 38–39.

Ihromi
1974 Die Königinmutter und der 'Amm Ha'arez im Reich Juda. *Vetus Testamentum* 24: 421–29.

Kallai, Z.
1960 *The Northern Boundaries of Judah.* Jerusalem: Magnes Press (Hebrew).

Katzenstein, H. J.
1973 *The History of Tyre.* Jerusalem: The Schocken Institute for Jewish Research.

Kelso, J. L.
1968 *The Excavation of Bethel.* Annual of The American Schools of Oriental Research 39. Cambridge, MA: American Schools of Oriental Research.

Kenyon, K. M.
1974 *Digging Up Jerusalem.* New York: Praeger.

Kessler, M.
1971 The Law of Manumission in Jer 34. *Biblische Zeitschrift* 15: 105–8.

Klausner, J.
1949 *History of the Second Temple.* Vol. 1. Tel Aviv: Massada (Hebrew).

Kochavi, M.
1970 The First Season of Excavations at Tell Malhata. *Qadmoniot* 3: 22–24 (Hebrew).
1974 Khirbet Rabûd = Debir. *Tel-Aviv* 1: 2–33.

Kutsch, E.
1973 *Verheissung und Gesetz.* Beihefte zur Zeitschrift für die alttestamentliche Wissenschaft 131. Berlin: Walter de Gruyter.
1974 Das Jahr der Katastrophe: 587 v. Chr. *Biblica* 55: 520–45.

Lance, D. H.
1971 The Royal Stamps and the Kingdom of Judah. *Harvard Theological Review* 64: 315–32.

Lapp, P. W.
1965 Tell el-Fûl. *Biblical Archaeologist* 28: 2–10.
1968a *The 1957 Excavation at Beth-Zur.* Annual of the American Schools of Oriental Research 38. Cambridge, MA: American Schools of Oriental Research.
1968b Review of J. Pritchard, *Winery, Defenses and Soundings at Gibeon. American Journal of Archaeology* 72: 391–93.
1970 The Pottery of Palestine in the Persian Period. Pp. 179–97 in *Archäologie und Altes Testament.* Festschrift für K. Galling, ed. A. Kuschke and E. Kutsch. Tübingen: J. C. B. Mohr.

Lapp, P. W. and Lapp, N.
1974 *Discoveries in the Wâdī Ed Dâliyeh.* Annual of the American Schools of Oriental Research 41. Cambridge, MA: American Schools of Oriental Research.

Lemche, N. P.
1976　　　The Manumission of Slaves—The Fallow Year—The Sabbatical Year—
　　　　　The Jubel Year. *Vetus Testamentum* 26: 38–59.

Lipiński, E.
1972　　　The Egypto-Babylonian War of Winter 601/600 B.C.E. *Annali dell'*
　　　　　Instituto Universitario Orientale di Napoli 32: 235–41.

Liver, J.
1958　　　Jehoiachin. Cols. 522–26 in vol. 3 of *Encyclopedia Miqra'it*. Jerusalem:
　　　　　Bialik Institute (Hebrew).

Malamat, A.
1950/51　The Historical Setting of Two Biblical Prophecies on the Nations. *Israel*
　　　　　Exploration Journal 1: 149–59.
1951　　　Jeremiah and the Last Two Kings of Judah. *Palestine Exploration*
　　　　　Quarterly 83: 31–37.
1956　　　A New Record of Nebuchadrezzar's Palestinian Campaigns. *Israel Explo-*
　　　　　ration Journal 6: 246–56.
1968　　　The Last Kings of Judah and the Fall of Jerusalem. *Israel Exploration*
　　　　　Journal 18: 137–56.
1973　　　Josiah's Bid for Armageddon. The Background of the Judean-Egyptian
　　　　　Encounter in 609 B.C.E. *Journal of Ancient Near Eastern Studies* 5: 268–
　　　　　78.
1975　　　The Twilight of Judah: In the Egyptian-Maelstrom. *Vetus Testamentum*
　　　　　Supplement 28: 123–45.

May, H. G.
1937　　　Three Hebrew Seals and the Status of Exiled Jehoiakim. *American Jour-*
　　　　　nal of Semitic Languages and Literatures 56: 146–48.

Mazar, B.
1958　　　Pereș 'Uzza. Col. 624 in vol. 6 of *Encyclopedia Miqra'it*. Jerusalem: Bialik
　　　　　(Hebrew).
1971　　　The Excavations in the Old City of Jerusalem Near the Temple Mount—
　　　　　Second Preliminary Report, 1969–70 Seasons. *Eretz Israel* 10: 1–34.

Millard, A. R.
1979　　　*Glimpses of Ancient Egypt*. Warminster: Aris & Phillips.

Naveh, J.
1963　　　Old Hebrew Inscriptions in a Burial Cave. *Israel Exploration Journal* 13:
　　　　　74–96.

Oppenheim, A. L.
1969　　　Babylonian and Assyrian Texts. Pp. 265–317 in *Ancient Near Eastern*
　　　　　Texts. Third edition, ed. J. B. Pritchard. Princeton: Princeton University
　　　　　Press.

Porten, B.
1981　　　The Identity of King Adon. *Biblical Archaeologist* 44: 36–52.

Rice, T. T.
1957　　　*The Scythians*. London: Thames and Hudson.

Rowley, H. H.
1962　　　The Early Prophecies of Jeremiah in Their Setting. *Bulletin of the John*
　　　　　Rylands Library 45: 198–234.

Sarna, N.
1973   Zedekiah's Emancipation of Slaves and the Sabbatical Year. Pp. 143–49 in *Orient and Occident: Essays Presented to Cyrus H. Gordon on the Occasion of his Sixty-fifth Birthday,* ed. H. A. Hoffner, Jr. Alter Orient und Altes Testament 22. Kevelaer: Butzon & Bercker.

Sauneron, S. and Yoqotte, J.
1952   Sur la politique palestinienne des rois saïtes. *Vetus Testamentum* 2: 131–36.

Shiloh, Y.
1979   Jerusalem, The City of David, 1979. *Israel Exploration Journal* 29: 244–46.
1980   Excavating Jerusalem: The City of David. Archaeology 33: 8–17.

Spalinger, A.
1978a   Psammetichus, King of Egypt, II. *Journal of the American Research Center in Egypt* 15: 49–57.
1978b   The Concept of the Monarchy during the Saite Period—An Essay of Synthesis. *Orientalia* 47: 18–36.

Stern, E.
1973   *The Material Culture of the Land of the Bible in the Persian Period.* Jerusalem: Israel Exploration Society.

Stern, M.
1974   *Greek and Latin Authors on Jews and Judaism.* Vol. 1. Jerusalem: Israel Academy of Sciences and Humanities.

Unger, E.
1925   Namen im Hofstaate Nebukadnezars II. *Theologische Literaturzeitung* 50: 482–86.
1926   Nebukadnezar II. und sein Sandabakku (Oberkommissar) in Tyrus. *Zeitschrift für die alttestamentliche Wissenschaft* 44: 314–17.

Ussishkin, D.
1977   The Destruction of Lachish by Sennacherib and the Dating of the Royal Judean Storage Jars. *Tel Aviv* 4: 28–60.
1978   Excavations at Tel Lachish—1973–1977. *Tel Aviv* 5: 1–97.

Vaggione, R. P.
1973   Over All Asia? The Extent of the Scythian Domination in Herodotus. *Journal of Biblical Literature* 92: 523–30.

Vogt, E.
1957   Die neubabylonische Chronik über die Schlacht bei Karkemisch und Einnahme von Jerusalem. *Vetus Testamentum Supplement* 4: 67–96.
1975   Bemerkungen über das Jahr der Eroberung Jerusalems. *Biblica* 56: 223–30.

Weidner, E. F.
1939   Jojachin, König von Juda, in Babylonischen Keilschrifttexten. Pp. 923–25 in *Mélanges syriens offerts à R. Dussaud.* Vol. 2. Paris: Paul Geuthner.

Weinberg, J. P.
1972   Demographische Notizen zur Geschichte der Nachexilischen Gemeinde in Juda. *Klio* 54: 45–59.

Weippert, M.
1971   *Edom*. Tübingen: Eberhard-Karls-Universität (Habilitationsschrift).

Welten, P.
1969   *Die Königs-Stempel*. Wiesbaden: Harrassowitz.

Wiseman, D. J.
1956   *Chronicles of Chaldean Kings (626–556 B.C.) in the British Museum*.
         London: Trustees of the British Museum.

Yadin, Y.
1973   The "House of Baal" in Samaria and in Judah. Pp. 52–66 in *Eretz
         Shomron*, ed. Y. Aviram. Jerusalem: Bialik and The Israel Exploration
         Society (Hebrew).

Zimmerli, W.
1969   *Ezechiel*. Biblischer Kommentar: Altes Testament 13. Neukirchen-Vluyn:
         Neukirchener.

Chapter 19

A BIBLIOGRAPHY OF EARLY BRONZE AGE SITES IN PALESTINE

James F. Ross
Virginia Theological Seminary

Glenn Rose was intensely interested in the Early Bronze Age, particularly as it is manifested at Tell el-Hesi. We had many interesting discussions of the remains there. This essay is in remembrance of those happy times and in tribute to his memory.

The following is a checklist with bibliographical notes of those EB sites in Palestine which have received publication in some form. The area covered is roughly that of the great British surveys, with some more attention to Transjordan and the Negev.

The sites are arranged in two groups: I. Excavated Sites and II. Surveyed Sites. Included in the former are those which have seen a major expedition, even though EB materials have been found only on the surface or in soundings. Occasionally soundings have also been made at surveyed sites (e.g., Tell Habil), so in some cases the distinction is rather arbitrary.

Names given are usually those provided by the original investigators; in a few cases alternatives are provided. In the case of well-known biblical sites, the biblical name is used, even though certain anomalies thus occur (e.g., Samaria). Where no modern or biblical name is known, the designation given is that of the principal author (e.g., Zori 1962: n). Following the usual custom, initial Tell, Khirbet, etc., as well as the Arabic definite article, are ignored in the alphabetization (cf., however, "Tell Aviv").

Following the name of each site is a parenthesis containing E-W/N-S map references and an indication of the subperiods of the Early Bronze Age represented. Where possible map coordinates have been checked on modern maps; on occasion, however, I have had to rely on sketch maps, thus introducing a certain element of uncertainty.

As for the subperiods, I accept the suggestions of the original investigators.

The system used is that made popular by G. Ernest Wright (1961; 1971); thus the "Proto-Urban" of Dame Kenyon and her followers becomes "EB I." On these matters cf. Ross 1980: 150–57. Sometimes I have drawn my own conclusions from the data; e.g., if "Khirbet Kerak" ware is reported, I posit "EB III."

Any work of this sort is bound to be incomplete, both because excavations and surveys continue and because some sites and/or bibliographical references were simply missed. The serious reader will also want to consult the excellent bibliographies prepared by Eleanor Vogel and her associates (*HUCA* 42 [1971] 1–96; 52 [1981] 1–96). However, Thompson's studies (1975; 1979) should be used with great care. There are a great many cases of confusions of sites with the same name, duplicate entries for sites with more than one name, and mistaken bibliographic information. Every reference must be checked. Unfortunately the excellent article by M. Broshi and R. Gophna on EB II–III, *BASOR* 253 (1984) 41–53, came to me too late to be used here.

EXCAVATED SITES

Bibliographical entries are in approximate order of appearance, with the exception of references to the *EAEHL* (*Encyclopedia of Archaeological Excavations in the Holy Land*). There are occasional references to the bibliography at the end of this article and to surveys.

Abu el-Alayiq, Tulul
(191/140–1)

EAEHL 571–73 (Foerster and Bacchi).

Pritchard, J. *The Excavations at Herodian Jericho* (AASOR 32/33; New Haven, 1958).

De Vaux, R. Revue de Pritchard, *The Excavations at Herodian Jericho*. *RB* 66 (1959) 155ff.

Acre (Tell el-Fukhkhar)
(158/259—1)

Jerusalem Post, August 25, 1983, reports EB 1.

Ader
(223/067—2;3;4)

EAEHL 31–32 (Kochavi).

Albright, W. F. The Archaeological Results of an Expedition to Moab and the Dead Sea. BASOR (1924) 2–12 (10 on Ader).

Albright, W. F. Soundings at Ader, a Bronze Age City of Moab. *BASOR* 53 (1934) 13–18.

Cleveland, R. The Excavation of the Conway High Place (Petra) and the Soundings at Khirbet Ader. *AASOR* 34–35 (1960) 79–97.

Mattingly 1981: 9060.

Affula
(177/223—1;2;3;4)

EAEHL 32–36 (Dothan).

Sukenik, E. Late Chalcolithic Pottery from 'Affuleh. *PEFQS* (1936) 150–54.

Sukenik, E. Archaeological Investigations at 'Affula. *JPOS* 21 (1948) 1–79.

Dothan, M. The Excavations at 'Afula. *Atiqot* 1 (1955) 19–74.

Zori 1977: 76.

Ai
(175/147—1;2;3)

EAEHL 36–52 (Callaway).

Yeivin, S. The Masonry of the Early Bronze People. *PEFQS* (1934) 189–91.

Marquet-Krause, J. La deuxième campagne de fouilles à 'Ay (1934): Rapport sommaire. *Syria* 16 (1935) 325–45.

Dussaud, R. Note additionnelle. *Syria* 16 (1935) 346–52.

Vincent, L. Les fouilles d'et-Tell = 'Ai. *RB* 46 (1937) 231–66.

Marquet-Krause, J. *Les fouilles de 'Ay (et-Tell), 1932–35;* 1 vol. text, 1 album (Bibliothèque archéologique et historique 45; Paris, 1949).

Prausnitz, M. 'Ay and the Chronology of Troy. *Eleventh Annual Report,* Institute of Archaeology, University of London (1955) 19–28.

Callaway, J. The 1964 'Ai (et-Tell) Excavations. *BASOR* 178 (1963) 13–40.

Callaway, J. *Pottery from the Tombs at 'Ai* (London, 1964).

Amiran, R. Khirbet Kerak Ware at Ai. *IEJ* 17 (1967) 185–86.

Callaway, J. The 1966 'Ai (et-Tell) Excavations. *BASOR* 196 (1969) 2–16.

Amiran, R. The Egyptian Alabaster Vessels from Ai. *IEJ* 20 (1970) 170–79.

Callaway, J. The 1968–69 'Ai (et-Tell) Excavations. *BASOR* 198 (1970) 7–31.

Wright, G. E. The Significance of Ai in the Third Millennium B.C.E. *Archaeologie und das Alte Testament* (Galling Festschrift; Tübingen, 1970) pp. 299–319.

Ben-Tor, A. An Ivory Bull's Head from 'Ay. *BASOR* 208 (1972) 24–29.

Callaway, J. *The Early Bronze Sanctuary at 'Ai* (London, 1972).

Callaway, J. and Schoonover, K. The Early Bronze Age Citadel at Ai (et-Tell). *BASOR* 207 (1972) 6–53.

Wagner, N. Early Bronze Houses at 'Ai (et-Tell). *PEQ* 104 (1972) 5–25.

Amiran, R. Reflections on the Identification of the Deity at the EB II and EB III Temples at 'Ai.I BASOR (1973) 9–13.

Ben-Tor, A. and Netzer, E. The Principal Architectural Remains of the Early Bronze Age at Ai. *EI* 11 (1973) 1–7 (Hebrew); English summary, 22°.

Callaway, J. A Second Ivory Bull's Head from Ai. *BASOR* 213 (1974) 57–61.

Callaway, J. and Wagner, N. A Re-examination of the Lower City at Ai. *PEQ* 106 (1974) 147–55.

Amiran, R. and Kempinsky, A. Review of Callaway, *The Early Bronze Sanctuary at Ai. IEJ* 27 (1977) 57ff.

Callaway, J. New Perspectives on Early Bronze III in Canaan. *Archaeology in the Levant,* ed. P. Moorey and P. Parr (Kenyon Festschrift; Warminster, 1978) pp. 46–58.

Callaway, J. *Ai II: The Early Bronze Citadel and Lower City at Ai (et-Tell)* (ASOR Excavation Reports; Cambridge, 1980).

Ain el-Qudeirat
(096.0/007.2—2)

Beit-Arieh, I. and Gophna, R. Earlay Bronze Age II Sites in Wadi el-Qudeirât (Kadesh-Barnea). *Tel Aviv* 3 (1976) 142–50.

Beit-Arieh, I. and Gophna, R. The Early Bronze Age Settlement at 'Ain el-Qudeirât. *Tel Aviv* 8 (1981) 128–35.

Aiyadiya, Khirbet
(164/257—1)

Ben-Tor, A. Excavations at Horvat 'Uṣa. *Atiqot* 3 (1966) 1–24 (Hebrew); English summary, 1°–3°.

Amman (citadel)
(239/151—1;2;3)

Dornemann, R. *The Archaeology of the Transjordan in the Bronze and Iron Ages* (Milwaukee, 1983) p. 12 and fig. 46.

Anafa, Tell
(210/286—3)

Herbert, S. Tel Anafa, 1978. *IEJ* 28 (1978) 271–74.

Arad
(162/076—1;2)

EAEHL 75–81 (Amiran).

Aharoni, Y. and Amiran, R. Excavations at Tel Arad: Preliminary Report on the First Season. *IEJ* 14 (1964) 131–47.

Amiran, R. A Preliminary Note on the Synchronism between the Early Bronze Strata of Arad and the First Dynasty. *BASOR* 179 (1965) 30–33.

Aharoni, Y. Excavations at Tel Arad: Preliminary Report on the Second Season, 1963). *IEJ* 17 (1967) 233–49.

Amiran, R. and Aharoni, Y. *Ancient Arad: Introductory Guide to the Exhibition Held at the Israel Museum, January—April 1967* (Jerusalem, 1967).

Amiran, R. and Aharoni, Y. Arad: An Early Bronze Age City and a Biblical Citadel. *Archaeological Discoveries in the Holy Land* (New York, 1967) pp. 89–99.

Amiran, R. Early Bronze I–II: The City of Arad. *AJA* 72 (1968) 316–18.

Amiran, R. and Baumgartel, E. A Second Note on the Synchronism between Early Arad and the First Dynasty. *BASOR* 195 (1969) 50–53.

Amiran 1970.

Amiran, R. A Cult-Stele from Arad. *IEJ* 22 (1972) 86–88.

Amiran, R., Beit-Arieh, Y., and Glass, J. The Interrelationship between Arad and Sites in Southern Sinai in the Early Bronze Age II. *IEJ* 23 (1973) 193–97.

Amiran, R. An Egyptian Jar Fragment with the Name of Narmer from Arad. *IEJ* 24 (1974) 4–12.

Amiran, R. The Narmer Jar Fragment from Arad: An Addendum. *IEJ* 26 (1976) 45–46.

Amiran, R., Alon, D., and Cohen, C. A Public Buildings Area in the Ancient Canaanite City of Arad (Report on the Ninth and Tenth Seasons of Excavations, 1974–75). *The Israel Museum News* 11 (1976) 35–40.

Amiran, R. Excavations in the Early Bronze Age City of Arad, 11th Season 1976. *The Israel Museum News* 12 (1977) 58–60.

Amiran, R. *Early Arad: The Chalcolithic Settlement and Early Bronze City.* Vol. I: *First-Fifth Seasons of Excavations, 1962–66* (Jerusalem, 1978).

Amiran, R. The Date of the End of the EB II City of Arad: A Complementary Note to Early Arad, I. *IEJ* 28 (1978) 182–84.

Amiran 1980.

Araq el-Emir
(222/147)

Lapp, P. The 1961 Excavations at Araq el-Emir. *ADAJ* 6–7 (1962) 80–89.

el-Areini, Tell
(129/113—1;2;3)

EAEHL 89–97 (Yeivin).

Yeivin, S. Tell Gath. *IEJ* 6 (1956) 258–59.

Yeivin, S. Tell Gath. *IEJ* 7 (1957) 264–65.

Yeivin, S. Tell Gath. *IEJ* 8 (1958) 274–76.

Yeivin, S. Tell Gath (Tell Sheikh el-'Areini). *IEJ* 9 (1959) 269–71.

Yeivin, S. Early Contacts between Canaan and Egypt. *IEJ* 10 (1960) 193–203.

Yeivin, S. Tell Gath. *RB* 67 (1960) 391–94.

Yeivin, S. Tell Gath. *IEJ* 11 (1961) 191.

Yeivin, S. and Ferembach, D. *First Preliminary Report on the Excavations at Tel "Gat" (Jerusalem, 1961).*

Ciasca, A. Tell Gat. *Oriens Antiquus* 1 (1962) 23–39.

Yeivin, S. Tell "Gath." *RB* 69 (1962) 395–97.

Yeivin, S. Further Evidence of Narmer at "Gat." *Oriens Antiquus* 2 (1963) 205–13.

Yeivin, S. A New Chalcolithic Culture at Tel 'Erany and its Implications for Early Egypto-Canaanite Relations. *Fourth World Congress of Jewish Studies. Papers*, Vol. I (Jerusalem, 1967) pp. 45–48.

Yeivin, S. Additional Notes on the Early Relations between Canaan and Egypt. *JNES* 27 (1968) 37–49.

Aroer
(228/098—4)

EAEHL 98–100 (Olávarri).

Olávarri, E. Fouilles à Arô'er sur l'Arnon. *RB* 72 (1965) 77–94.

Olávarri, E. Fouilles à Arô'er sur l'Arnon. *RB* 76 (1969) 230–59.

Arqub el-Dhahr
(219/228—1)

Parr, P. A Cave at Arqub el-Dhahr. *ADAJ* 3 (1956) 61–73.

Glueck 1939: 93.

el-Asawir, Tell
(152/209—1)

EAEHL 100–02 (Dothan).

Dothan, M. Notes and News. *IEJ* 3 (1953) 263.

Amiran 1969: Pl. 9, nos. 15, 21–23; photos 25, 38.

Dothan, M. *Assawir Manasseh* (Tel Aviv, 1970; Hebrew).

Hadashot 65–66 (1978), 14ff. (Hebrew).

Ashdod
(117/129—2)

EAEHL 103–19 (Dothan).

Dothan, M. Ashdod of the Philistines. *New Directions in Biblical Archaeology*, ed. D. Freedman and J. Greenfield (Garden City, 1971) p. 16.

Azor
(131/159—1)

EAEHL 144–48 (Ben-Tor).

Dothan, M. Preliminary Report on the Excavations at Azor. *BIES* 23 (1959) 68–69 (Hebrew).

Dothan, M. Excavations at Azor, 1960. *IEJ* 11 (1961) 171–75.

Dothan, M. The Excavation at Azor, 1960. *BIES* 25 (1961) 24–30.

Dothan, M. An Inscribed Jar from Azor. *Atiqot* 3 (1961) 181–84.

Ben-Tor, A. Excavation of Two Burial Caves at Azor. *Qadmoniot* 6 (1973) 48–50 (Hebrew).

Ben-Tor, A. Two Burial Caves of the Proto-Urban Period at Azor 1971. *Qedem* 1 (1975) 1–53.

Bab edh-Dhra
(203/072—1;2;3;4)

EAEHL 149–51 (Ben-tor).

Kyle, M. and Albright, W. F. Results of the Archaeological Survey of the Ghor in Search for the Cities of the Plain. *BS* 81 (1924) 278–85.

Albright, W. F. The Archaeological Results of an Expedition to Moab and the Dead Sea. *BASOR* 14 (1924) 5–9.

Albright 1926: 58–62.

Abel, F. Chronique. *RB* 38 (1929) 243–46.

Albright, W. F., Kelso, J., and Thorney, J. Early Bronze Pottery from Bâb edh-Dhrâ' in Moab. *BASOR* 95 (1944) 3–11.

Saller, S. Bab edh-Dhra'. *Liber Annuus* 15 (1964/65) 137–219.

Lapp, P. Bâb edh-Dhrâ'. *RB* 73 (1966) 556–61.

Lapp, P. The Cemetery at Bâb edh-Dhrâ', Jordan. *Archaeology* 19 (1966) 104–11.

Lapp, P. Bâb edh-Dhrâ' Tomb A76 and Early Bronze I in Palestine. *BASOR* 189 (1968) 12–41.

Lapp, P. Bâb edh-Dhrâ', Perizzites and Emim. *Jerusalem Through the Ages* (Jerusalem, 1968) pp. 1°–25°.

Lapp, P. Bâb edh-Dhrâ'. *RB* 75 (1968) 86–93.

Tadmor, M. Excavations at Bab edh-Dhra'. *Qadmoniot* 2 (1969) 56–59 (Hebrew).

Schaub, R. T. An Early Bronze IV Tomb from Bâb edh-Dhrâ'. *BASOR* 210 (1973) 2–19.

Adovasio, J. M., Andrews, R., and Carlisle, M. R. Textile Remains and Basketry Impressions from Bâb edh-Dhrâ', 1975. *AASOR* 43 (1978) 57–60.

Finnegan, M. Faunal Remains from Bâb edh-Dhrâ', 1975. *AASOR* 43 (1978) 51–54.

Johnston, R. and Schaub, R. T. Selected Pottery from Bâb edh-Dhrâ', 1975. *AASOR* 43 (1978) 33–49.

Rast, W. and Schaub, R. T. A Preliminary Report of Excavations at Bâb edh-Dhrâ', 1975. *AASOR* 43 (1978) 1–32.

Richardson, J. and McCreery, D. Preliminary Analysis of the Plant Remains from Bâb edh-Dhrâ', 1975. *AASOR* 43 (1978) 55–56.

Rast, W. and Schaub, R. T. Preliminary Report of the 1979 Expedition to the Dead Sea Plain, Jordan. *BASOR* 240 (1980) 21–61.

Rast, W. Patterns of Settlement at Bab edh-Dhra. *AASOR* 46 (1981) 1–5.

Schaub, R. T. Ceramic Sequences in the Tomb Groups at Bab edh-Dhra. *AASOR* 46 (1981) 69–118.

Schaub, R. T. Patterns of Burial at Bad edh-Dhra. *AASOR* 46 (1981) 45–68.

Cf. also specialists' reports in *AASOR* 46.

Rast, W. and Schaub, R. T. The Dead Sea Expedition to Bâb edh-Dhrâ' and Numeira. *ASOR Newsletters* (January 1982) 4–12.

Lee, J. R. Early Bronze Age Gaming Stones from Bab edh-Dhra, Jordan. *Levant* 14 (1982) 171–74.

Froehlich, B. and Ortner, D. Excavations of the Early Bronze Age Cemetery at Bab edh-Dhra Jordan, 1981. *ADAJ* 26 (1982) 249–65.

Batashi, Tuleilat
(142/132)

EAEHL 1204–5 (Kaplan).

Beit Sahur
(171/123—1;2)

Hennessy, J. B. An Early Bronze Age Tomb Group from Beit Sahur. *ADAJ* 11 (1966) 17–40.

Beit Mirsim, Tell
(141/096—4)

EAEHL 171–78 (Albright).

Albright, W. F. *The Archaeology of Palestine and the Bible* (New York, 1932) pp. 63–126.

Albright, W. F. *The Excavation of Tell Beit Mirsim. I. The Pottery of the First Three Seasons* (AASOR 12; New Haven, 1932).

Albright, W. F. The Excavation of Tell Beit Mirsim. IA. The Pottery of the Fourth Campaign. *AASOR* 13 (1933) 55–127.

Kyle, M. *Excavating Kiriath-Sepher's Ten Cities* (Grand Rapids, 1934).

Albright, W. F. *The Excavation of Tell Beit Mirsim, II: The Bronze Age* (AASOR 17; New Haven, 1938).

Dever, W. G. and Richard, S. A Re-evaluation of Tell Beit Mirsim Stratum J. *BASOR* 226 (1977) 1–14.

Bethel
(172/148—3)

EAEHL 190–93 (Kelso).

Albright, W. and Kelso, J. *The Excavation of Bethel (1934–60)* (AASOR 39; Cambridge, 1968) pp. 22, 54ff. on EB.

Beth Emeq
(164/263—1)

Frankel, R. and Kempinski, A. Beth Ha-ʻEmeq. *IEJ* 23 (1973) 242–43.

Beck, P. The Cylinder Seal Impressions from Beth-ha-ʻEmeq. *Tel Aviv* 3 (1976) 120–26.

Ben-Tor 1978: 115.

Beth-shan
(197/212—1;2;3)

EAEHL 207–12 (James).

Rowe, A. *The Topography and History of Beth Shan.* Vol. I (Philadelphia, 1930).

FitzGerald, G. Excavations at Beth-shan in 1931. *PEFQS* 1932 138–48.

FitzGerald, G. Excavations at Beth-shan in 1933. *PEFQS* 1934 123–34.

FitzGerald, G. The Earliest Pottery of Beth Shan. *Museum Journal* 24 (1935) 5–22.

Beth-shemesh
(147/128)

EAEHL 248–53 (Wright).

Grant, E. and Wright, G. E. *Ain Shems Excavations.* Vols. 4–5 (Haverford, 1938–39); Vol. 4, pp. 92–95, Pl. XXIII; Vol. 5, p. 27.

Beth Zur
(159/110)

EAEHL 263 (Funk).

Funk, R. The Bronze Age—Iron I Pottery. *The 1957 Excavation at Beth-Zur* (AASOR 38; Cambridge, 1968) p. 35.

Dalit, Tell
(147/153—1;2)

Cresson, B. and Gophna, R. Tel Dalit, 1978–1979. *IEJ* 29 (1979) 122–23; cf. also idem. *RB* 86 (1979) 459ff. (includes plan).

Gophna, R. An Early Bronze Town at Tel Dalit. *Qadmoniot* 14 (1981) 22–25 (Hebrew).

Dan
(211/294—3)

EAEHL 313–21 (Biran).

Biran, A. Tel Dan, 1977. *IEJ* 27 (1977) 245–46.

Biran, A. Tell Dan Five Years Later. *BA* 43 (1980) 168–73.

Biran, A. Tel Dan, 1979, 1980. *IEJ* 31 (1981) 103–5.

Biran, A. Tel Dan, 1981. *IEJ* 32 (1982) 138ff.

Dibon
(224/101)

EAEHL 330–33 (Tushingham).

Winnett, F. Excavations at Dibon in Moab, 1950–51. BASOR 125 (1952) 12, 16, 18.

Winnett, F. and Reed, W. The Excavations at Dibon (Dhibân) in Moab. Parts I and II (AASOR 36–37; New Haven, 1964) pp. 24, 66.

Dothan
(173/202—1;2;3)

EAEHL 337–39 (Ussishkin).

Free, F. The First Season of Excavation at Dothan. BASOR 131 (1953) 16–20.

Free, J. The Second Season of Excavation at Dothan. BASOR 135 (1954) 14–20.

Free, J. The Third Season o f Excavation at Dothan. BASOR 139 (1955) 3–9.

Free, J. The Excavation of Dothan. BA 19 (1956) 43–48.

Free, J. The Fourth Season of Excavation at Dothan. BASOR 143 (1956) 11–17.

Free, J. The Fifth Season of Excavation at Dothan. BASOR 152 (1958) 10–18.

Free, J. The Sixth Season of Excavation at Dothan. BASOR 156 (1959) 22–29.

Free, J. The Seventh Season of Excavation at Dothan. BASOR 160 (1960) 6–15.

Free, J. The Seventh Season of Excavation at Dothan. ADAJ 6–7 (1962) 117–20.

Helms, S. Early Bronze Fortifications at Dothan. Levant 9 (1977) 101–14.

Ein Samiya
(182/155)

EAEHL 357–58 (Yeivin).

Lapp, P. The Dhahr Mirzbaneh Tombs: Three Intermediate Bronze Age Cemeteries in Jordan (New Haven, 1966) p. 6.

Dever, W. Middle Bronze Age I Cemeteries at Mirezbaneh and Ain-Sâmiya. IEJ 22 (1972) 95, 109.

Zohar, M. Tell Marjamah ('Ein Samiyeh). IEJ 30 (1980) 219–20.

En Besor
(101/079—1;2)

Gophna, R. A First Dynasty Egyptian Site near 'En-haBesor. Qadmoniot 5 (1972) 14–15 (Hebrew).

Gophna, R. Excavations at 'En Besor. Atiqot 11 (1976) 1–9.

Schulman, A. Egyptian Seal Impressions from 'En Besor. Atiqot 11 (1976) 16–25.

Ben-Tor 1978: 15.

Gophna, R. Excavations at 'En Besor. Atiqot 14 (1980) 10–16.

Schulman, A. R. More Egyptian Seal Impressions from 'En Besor. Atiqot 14 (1980) 17–33.

En Gedi
(187/097)

Kempinski, A. The Sin Temple at Khafaje and the En-Gedi Temple. IEJ 22 (1972) 10–15.

Esdar, Tell
(147/064—1;2)

EAEHL 1169-71 (Kochavi).

Glueck, N. The Fifth Season of Exploration in the Negev. BASOR 145 (1957) 14.

Kochavi, M. Excavations at Tel Esdar. Atiqot 5 (1969) 14-48 (Hebrew).

Cohen, R. Tel Esdar, Stratum II. IEJ 28 (1978) 185-89.

el-Farah, Tell
(181/188—1;2)

EAEHL 395-404 (de Vaux).

De Vaux, R. and Stève, A. La première campagne de fouilles à Tell el-Far'ah, pres Naplouse: Rapport préliminaire. RB 54 (1947) 394-433, 573-89.

De Vaux, R. and Stève, A. La deuxième campagne de fouilles à Tell el-Far'ah, pres Naplouse: Rapport préliminaire. RB 55 (1948) 544-80; 56 (1949) 102-38.

De Vaux, R. La troisième campagne de fouilles à Tell el-Far'ah, pres Naplouse: Rapport préliminaire. RB 58 (1951) 566-90.

De Vaux, R. La quatrième campagne de fouilles à Tell el-Far'ah, pres Naplouse. RB 59 (1952) 551-83.

De Vaux, R. Les fouilles de Tell el-Far'ah, pres Naplouse. Cinquième campagne. RB 62 (1955) 541-89.

De Vaux, R. The Excavations at Tell el-Far'ah and the Site of Ancient Tirzah. PEQ 1956 125-40.

De Vaux, R. Les fouilles de Tell el-Far'ah, pres Naplouse. Sixième campagne—Rapport préliminaire. RB 64 (1957) 552-80.

De Vaux, R. Les fouilles de Tell el-Far'ah. Rapport préliminaire sur les 7e, 8e, 9e campagnes, 1958-60. RB 68 (1961) 557-92; 69 (1962) 212-53.

Huot, J.-L. Typologie et chronologie relative de la céramique du Bronze Ancien à Tell el-Fâr'ah. RB 74 (1967) 517-64.

De Vaux, R. Tirzah. Archaeology and Old Testament Study, ed. D. W. Thomas (Oxford, 1967) pp. 371-83.

Gezer
(142/140—1;2;3)

EAEHL 428-43 (Dever).

Macalister, R. The Excavation of Gezer (London, 1911-12) 3 vols.

Rowe, A. Excavations at Gezer. PEFQS (1935) 19-33.

Wright, G. E. The Trogdolytes of Gezer. PEQ (1937) 67-79.

Amiran, R. The "Cream Ware" of Gezer and the Beersheba Late Chalcolithic. IEJ 5 (1955) 24-45.

Callaway, J. The Gezer Crematorium Re-examined. PEQ 94 (1962) 104-17.

Dever, W. Gezer—A City Coming to Life. Qadmoniot 3 (1970) 57-62 (Hebrew).

Furshpan, A. The Gezer "High Place" (Cambridge, 1970; Harvard dissertation) pp. 51-68, 151.

Dever, W. G., Lance, H. D., and Wright, G. E. Gezer I. Preliminary Report of the 1964-66 Seasons (Jerusalem, 1970).

Dever, W., et al. Further Excavations at Gezer. BA 34 (1971) 94-132.

Dever, W. The Gezer Fortifications and the "High Place." PEQ 105 (1973) 69.

Dever, W., et al. *Gezer II. Preliminary Report of the 1967–70 Seasons, Fields I and II* (Jerusalem, 1974).

Kempinski, A. Review of *Gezer II. IEJ* 26 (1976) 210–13.

Rast, W. Review of *Gezer I* and *Gezer II. AJA* 80 (1976) 307ff.

Ben-Tor 1978: index of geographical names.

Gibeon
(168/139—2)

EAEHL 446–50 (Pritchard).

Pritchard, J. *Gibeon: Where the Sun Stood Still* (Princeton, 1962) pp. 149–51.

Pritchard, J. *The Bronze Age Cemetery at Gibeon* (Museum Monographs; Philadelphia, 1964) p. 10.

Givatayim
(132/164—1)

EAEHL 451–52 (Kaplan).

Sussman, V. and Ben-Arieh, S. Ancient Burials in Giv'atayim. *Atiqot* 3 (1966) 27–39 (36–39 on EB) (Hebrew; English summary, 4°).

Halif, Tell
(137/088—2;3)

Seger, J. and Borowski, O. The First Two Seasons at Tell Ḥalif. *BA* 40 (1977) 156–66.

Seger, J. Tel Halif (Lahav), 1976. *IEJ* 27 (1977) 45–47.

Cole, D. Tell Halif (Lahav), 1977. *IEJ* 28 (1978) 119–21.

Seger, J. Tel Halif, 1980. *IEJ* 30 (1980) 223–26.

Seger, J. Lahav Research Project: Excavations at Tell Halif, 1980. *BA* 44 (1981) 183–86.

el-Hammeh, Tell
(212/232—1;2;3)

EAEHL 469–73 (Avi-Yonah).

Glueck, N. The Archaeological Exploration of el-Hammeh on the Yarmûk. *BASOR* 49 (1933) 22ff. = *QDAP* 3 (1934) 174.

Glueck, N. Tell el-Hameh. *AJA* 39 (1935) 321–30.

el-Harbaj, Tell
(158/240—3)

EAEHL 23–24 (Prausnitz).

Garstang, J. Tell el Harbaj. *BBSAJ* 2 (1922) 12–14.

Garstang, J. El Harbaj. *BBSAJ* 4 (1924) 45–46.

Hazor
(203/269—2;3)

EAEHL 474–95 (Yadin).

Yadin, Y., et al. *Hazor*. Vols. III–IV (Jerusalem 1961); Pls. IV, 1–3; V, 1; XXVIII, 2; CLIV–CLVI; CXCII; CXCVII; CXCVI, 1–4; CCC.

Yadin, Y. Excavations at Hazor, 1968–1969. *IEJ* 19 (1969) 5.

Yadin, Y. *Hazor* (Schweich Lectures; London, 1972) pp. 119–20.

Hazorea
(160/227—1;2)

Anati, E., et al. *Hazorea I* (Archivi 5; Capo di Ponte, 1973) pp. 72–74, 99, 103–4.

Mayerhof, A. Hazorea. *Hadashot* 78–79 (1982) 23 (Hebrew).

Cf. also sub Tell Qiri.

Hebron
(160/105—2)

Hammond, P. Hebron. *RB* 73 (1966) 567–68.

Hammond, P. Hebron. *RB* 75 (1968) 253–58.

Hepher, Tell
(141.0/198.0—1;2;3)

EAEHL 1071–74 (Gophna).

Gophna and Kochavi 1966.

Paley, S., Porath, Y., and Stieglitz, R. The 'Emeq Hefer Regional Project. *IEJ* 32 (1982) 66ff., 259ff.

Hadashot 78–79 (1982) 36ff. (Hebrew).

el-Hesi, Tell
(124/106—3)

EAEHL 514–20 (Amiran and Worrell).

Petrie, W. M. F. *Tell el-Hesy (Lachish)* (London, 1891).

Bliss, F. *A Mound of Many Cities: or, Tell el Hesy Excavated* (London, 1898).

Kenyon, K. A Crescentic Axehead from Jericho and a Group of Weapons from Tell el Hesi. *Eleventh Annual Report*. Institute of Archaeology, University of London (1955) 10–18.

Matthers, J. *A Reassessment of the Early Bronze Age Material Excavated at Tell Hesy 1890–1892*. Unpublished M.A. dissertation, University of London, 1974.

Toombs, L. Tell el-Ḥesi, 1970–1971. *PEQ* 106 (1974) 19–31.

Rose, D. G. and Toombs, L. Tell el-Hesi, 1973 and 1975. *PEQ* 108 (1976) 41–54.

Fargo, V. and O'Connell, K. Five Seasons of Excavation at Tell el-Ḥesi (1970–77). *BA* 41 (1978) 165–82.

O'Connell, K., Rose, D. G., and Toombs, L. Tell el-Hesi, 1977. *PEQ* 110 (1978) 75–90.

Rose, D. G., Toombs, L., and O'Connell, K. Four Seasons of Excavation at Tell el-Hesi: A Preliminary Report. *AASOR* 43 (1978) 109–49.

Ross, J. F. Early Bronze Age Structures at Tell el-Ḥesi. *BASOR* 236 (1980) 11–21.

Fargo, V. Early Bronze Age Pottery at Tell el-Ḥesi. *BASOR* 236 (1980) 23–40.

O'Connell, K. and Rose, D. G. Tell el-Ḥesi, 1979. *PEQ* 112 (1980) 73–91.

Betlyon, J. Tel el-Ḥesi, 1981. *IEJ* 32 (1982) 67ff.

Toombs, L. Tell el-Ḥesi, 1981. *PEQ* 115 (1983) 25–46.

el-Husn
(232/210—1)

EAEHL 526–27 (Kochavi).

Harding, G. and Isserlin, B. Four Tomb Groups from Jordan. *PEF Annual* 6 (1953) 1–13.

Iktanu
(213/210—1)
Prag, K. The Intermediate Early Bronze—Middle Bronze Age: An Interpretation of the Evidence from Transjordan, Syria and Lebanon. *Levant* 6 (1974) 69–116 (77–78, 97–98 on Iktanu).

Ira, Tell
(148/071—2;3)
Biran, A. and Cohen, R. Tel Ira. *IEJ* 29 (1979) 124–25.

Beit-Arieh, I. Tell 'Ira. *IEJ* 31 (1981) 243–45.

Iskander, Khirbet
EAEHL 531–32 (Kochavi).

Glueck 1939: 127–28.

Parr, P. Excavations at Khirbet Iskander. *ADAJ* 4–5 (1960).

Richard, S. Report on the 1981 Season of Survey and Soundings at Khirbet Iskander. *ADAJ* 26 (1982) 289–97.

Jamid, Tell
(233/236—1)
Mellaart 1962: 1.

De Contenson 1964: 30ff.

Ben-Tor 1978: 7.

Kerestes 1980: 14.

Leonard 1981: Pls. XXXIV–XXXV.

Jenin
(178.5/207.5—1;2)
Glock, A. Tell Jenin. *RB* 86 (1979) 110–12.

Jericho
(192/142—1;2;3)
EAEHL 550–75 (Foerster and Bacchi).

Sellin, E. and Watzinger, C. *Jericho: Die Ergebnisse der Ausgrabungen* (Leipzig, 1913).

Garstang, J. Jericho: City and Necropolis. *AAA* 19 (1932) 8ff., 19ff., 38ff.

Garstang, J. Jericho: City and Necropolis (Fifth Report). VII. General Report for 1935; The Early Bronze Age. *AAA* 22 (1935) 143–68.

Garstang, J. Jericho: City and Necropolis. Report for Sixth and Concluding Season, 1936. I. General Survey and Special Features. *AAA* 23 (1936) 67–76.

FitzGerald, G. Jericho: City and Necropolis. III. Pottery of the Early Bronze Age. *AAA* 23 (1936) 91–100.

Garstang, J. and Garstang, J. B. E. *The Story of Jericho*, rev. ed. (London, 1948).

Kenyon, K. *Excavations at Jericho. Volume One: The Tombs Excavated in 1952–54* (London, 1960).

Kenyon, K. *Excavations at Jericho.* Volume Two: *The Tombs Excavated in 1955–58* (London, 1965).

Hennessy, J. B. *The Foreign Relations of Palestine during the Early Bronze Age* (London, 1967).

Kenyon, K. *Excavations at Jericho.* Volume Three: *The Architecture and Stratigraphy of the Tell.* Text and Plates, ed. T. A. Holland (London, 1981).

Jerishe, Tell
(132/166)

EAEHL 575 (Avigad).

Sukenik, E. Tell Jerishe. *QDAP* 4 (1935) 208; 10 (1944) 198.

Geva, S. Tell Jerishe. *IEJ* 27 (1957) 47.

Geva, S. *Tell Jerishe: The Sukenik Excavations of the Middle Bronze Age Fortifications* (Qedem 15; Jerusalem, 1982) p. 3.

Judeideh, Tell
(141/115—3)

EAEHL 694–96 (Broshi).

Bliss, F. and Macalister, R. *Excavations in Palestine during the Years 1898–1900* (London, 1902) pp. 7, 8, 44ff., 89–90, 107, 195, 199.

Kefar Monash
(142/195—3)

EAEHL 1071–72 (Gophna).

Hestrin, R. and Tadmor, M. A Hoard of Tools and Weapons from Kfar Monash. *IEJ* 13 (1963) 265–88.

Yeivin, S. Additional Notes on the Early Relations between Canaan and Egypt. *JNES* 27 (1968) 40–48.

Gophna, R. A Crescentic Axehead from Kfar Monash. *IEJ* 18 (1968) 47–49.

Ben-Tor, A. The Date of the Kfar Monash Hoard. *IEJ* 21 (1971) 201–6.

Watkins, T. The Date of the Kfar Monash Hoard Again. *PEQ* 107 (1975) 53–63.

Keisan, Tell

Rowe, A. Tell Keisan. *QDAP* 5 (1936) 207–9.

Reports on 1935–1936 seasons printed in J. Briend, J.-B. Humbert, et al. *Tell Keisan (1971–76)* (Fribourg, 1980) pp. 381–92.

Kerak, Khirbet
(203/236—1;2;3)

EAEHL 253–62 (Hestrin).

Guy, P. L. O. Bet Yeraḥ. *Alon* 3 (1951) 32–33 (Hebrew).

Maisler, B., Stekelis, M., and Avi-Yonah, M. The Excavations at Beth Yeraḥ (Khirbet Kerak) 1944–46. *IEJ* 2 (1952) 183–87.

Bar-Adon, P. Beth Yeraḥ. *IEJ* 3 (1953) 132.

Bar-Adon, P. Beth Yeraḥ. *IEJ* 4 (1954) 128–29.

Bar-Adon, P. Beth Yeraḥ. *IEJ* 5 (1955) 273.

Bar-Adon, P. Beth Yeraḥ. *Alon* 5–6 (1957) 29–30 (Hebrew).

Bar-Adon, P. Another Ivory Bull's Head from Palestine. *BASOR* 1965 (1962) 46ff.

Ben-Tor 1978: index of geographical names.

Sussman, V. A Relief of a Bull from the Early Bronze Age. *BASOR* 238 (1980) 75–77.

Tel Beth Yeraḥ. *Hadashot* 76 (1981) 11–13 (Hebrew).

Kinneret (tomb)
(203/235—2)

EAEHL 717–18 (Mazar).

Maisler, B. An Earlya Bronze Tomb at Kinneret. *BJPES* 10 (1942) 1–9 (Hebrew).

Albright, W. F. Review of Maisler, "Early Bronze Tomb." *BASOR* 93 (1944) 26.

Amiran, R. Connections between Anatolia and Palestine in the Early Bronze Age. *IEJ* 2 (1952) 100–101.

Mazar, B., Amiran, R., and Haas, N. An Early Bronze Age II Tomb at Beth-Heraḥ. (Kinneret). *EI* 11 (1973) 176–93; England summary, 28°.

Kinrot, Tell
(200/252—1;2)

Fritz, V. Kinneret und Ginnosar: Voruntersuchung für eine Ausgrabung auf dem *Tell el-ʿOrēme* am See Genezareth. *ZDPV* 94 (1978) 32–45.

Yakar, J. Tel Kinrot, 1982. *IEJ* 32 (1982) 255ff.

Fritz, V. Notes and News. *IEJ* forthcoming.

Kittan, Tell
(204/221—1;2;3)

Hadashot 57–58 (1976) 14–16 (Hebrew).

Hadashot 61–62 (1977) 15 (Hebrew).

Lachish
(135/108—1;2;3)

EAEHL 735–52 (Tufnell, Aharoni, and Ussishkin).

Tufnell, O., et al. *Lachish III: The Bronze Age* (London 1958).

Lod
(140/151—1)

EAEHL 753–54 (Kaplan).

Maahaz, Tell
(131/102—1;3)

Cohen, R., Amiran, R., et al. Tel Maahaz. *IEJ* 25 (1975) 162.

Amiran, R. Excavations at Tel Ma'ahaz 1975, 1976. *Israel Museum News* 12 (1977) 63–64.

Schulman, A. and Gophna, R. An Archaic Egyptian *Serekh* from Tel Ma'ahaz. *IEJ* 31 (1981) 165–67.

el-Mahruq, Khirbet
(198/170—1)

EAEHL 766–68 (Yeivin).

Yeivin, Z. Khirbet el-Mahruq. *IEJ* 24 (1974) 259–60.

Malhata, Tell
(152/069—1)

EAEHL 771–74 (Kochavi).

Kochavi, M. Tel Malḥata. *IEJ* 17 (1967) 272–73.

Kochavi, M. The First Season of Excavations at Tell Malhata. *Qadmoniot* 3 (1970) 22–24 (Hebrew).

Megadim, Tell
(145/236—1;2)

EAEHL 823-26 (Broshi).

Broshi, M. Tel Megaddim. *IEJ* 17 (1967) 277-78.

Broshi, M. Tel Megadim. *IEJ* 18 (1968) 256-57.

Broshi, M. Tel Megaddim. *IEJ* 19 (1969) 248.

Broshi, M. Tel Megadim—A Phoenician City and Roman-Byzantine Road-Station. *Qadmoniot* 2 (1970) 124-26 (Hebrew).

Megiddo
(167/221—1;2;3)

EAEHL 830-56 (Aharoni and Yadin).

Schumacher, G. *Tell el-Mutesellim.* Vol. 1 (Leipzig, 1908).

Watzinger, C. *Tell el-Mutesellim.* Vol. 2 (WVDOG 22; Leipzig, 1913).

Fisher, C. *The Excavation of Armageddon* (Chicago, 1929).

Engberg and Shipton 1934.

Guy, P. L. O., Engberg, R., et al. *Megiddo Tombs* (OIP 33; Chicago, 1938).

Shipton, G. *Notes on the Megiddo Pottery of Strata VI-XX* (SAOC 17; Chicago, 1939).

Loud, G. *Megiddo II: Seasons of 1935–1939* (OIP 62; Chicago, 1948) 2 vols.

Dothan, M. Some Problems of the Stratigraphy in Megiddo XX. *EI* 5 (1958) 38-40 (Hebrew; English summary, 85°).

Kenyon, K. Some Notes on the Early and Middle Bronze Strata of Megiddo. *EI* 5 (1958) 51°-60°.

Dunayevsky, I. and Kempinski, A. The Megiddo Temples. *ZDPV* 89 (1973) 161-87.

Epstein, C. The Sacred Area at Megiddo in Stratum XIX. *EI* 11 (1973) 54-57 (Hebrew; English summary, 23°-23°).

Brandfon, F. The Earliest City Wall at Megiddo. *Tel Aviv* 4 (1977) 79-86.

Meser
(154/205—1)

EAEHL 864-65 (Dothan).

Dothan, M. Excavations at Meṣer, 1956, Preliminary Report on the First Season. *IEJ* 7 (1957) 217-28.

Dothan, M. Excavations at Meṣer, 1957, Preliminary Report on the Second Season. *IEJ* 9 (1959) 13-29.

Miqne, Tel
(136.0/131.7—2)

Dothan, T. and Gitin, S. Tel Miqne (Ekron), 1981. *IEJ* 32 (1982) 150-53.

el-Mukhaiyet, Khirbet
(220.5/129.0—3)

EAEHL 923-24 (Bagatti).

Saller, S., in S. Saller and B. Bagatti, *The Town of Nebo (Khirbet el-Mekhayyat)* (Jerusalem, 1949) pp. 20-24.

Munhata
(201/233—1)

EAEHL 871–74 (Perrot and Zori).

Zori 1958: 47.

Zori 1962: 9.

Nagila, Tell
(126/101—2;3)

EAEHL 894–98 (Amiran and Eitan).

Aharoni, Y. and Amiran, R. Tel en-Najilah. *BIES* 17 (1953) 53–54 (Hebrew).

Amiran, R. and Eitan, A. Tel Nagila. *IEJ* 13 (1963) 144, 333–34.

Amiran, R. and Eitan, A. Two Seasons of Excavations at Tell Nagila (1962–63). *Yediot* 28 (1964) 193–203 (Hebrew).

Amiran, R. and Eitan, A. Tel Nagila. *IEJ* 14 (1964) 291–31.

Amiran, R. and Eitan, A. A Canaanite-Hyksos City at Tell Nagila. *Archaeology* 18 (1965) 113–23.

en-Nasbeh, Tell
(171/143—1;2)

EAEHL 912–19 (Broshi).

McCown, C., Wampler, J., et al. *Tell en-Nasbeh* (Berkeley/New Haven, 1947) 2 vols.

Albright, W. F. Review of C. McCown, J. Wampler, et al., *Tell en-Nasbeh,* vols. I and II. *JNES* 7 (1948) 202–5.

Numeira
(200.2/060.0—3)

Rast and Schaub 1974: 8ff.

Rast, W. and Schaub, R. T. Preliminary Report, 1979, (cf. sub Bab edh-Dhra) 40–47.

Rast, W. Settlement at Numeira. *AASOR* 46 (1981) 35–44.

Ophel
(172/130—1)

Vincent, L. H. *Jérusalem sous terre. Les récentes fouilles d'Ophel* (London, 1911).

Vincent, L. H. *Underground Jerusalem: Discoveries on the Hill of Ophel, 1909–1911* (London, 1911).

Vincent, L. H. Les récentes fouilles d'Ophel. *RB* N.S. 8 (1911) 566–91; 9 (1912) 86–111, 424–53.

Pella
(207.8/206.3—1;2;3)

EAEHL 939–43 (Levine).

Smith, R. H., Hennessey, J. B., et al. Preliminary Report on the 1979 Season of the Sydney-Wooster Joint Expedition to Pella. *ADAJ* 24 (1980) 14.

McNicoll, A., Smith, R. H., et al. *Pella in Jordan 1* (Canberra, 1982) vol. 1, p. 35.

Poran, Tell
(113/124—2)

Gophna, R. Fortified Settlements from the Early Bronze and Middle Bronze II at Tel Poran. *EI* 13 (1977) 87–90 (Hebrew; English summary, 293*).

el-Qassis, Tell
(160/232—1;2;3)

Garstang, J. (?) Tell el Kussîs. *BBSAJ* 2 (1922) 16–17.

Albright 1926: 6, 28 n. 55.

Ben-Tor, A., Portugali, Y., and Avissar, M. The First Two Seasons of Excavation at Tel Qashish 1978–1979: Preliminary Report. *IEJ* 31 (1981) 137–64.

ASI/N 11.

Qedesh, Tell
(200/279—1;2;3)

EAEHL 406–8 (Aharoni).

Albright 1925: 12.

Qiri, Tell
(161.1/227.4—1)

Ben-Tor, A. Tell Qiri (Hazorea). *IEJ* 25 (1975) 168ff.

Ben-Tor, A. Tel Qiri (Hazorea), 1976. *IEJ* 26 (1976) 200ff.

Ben-Tor, A. Tell Qiri (Ha-Zorea). *RB* 83 (1976) 272.

Ben-Tor, A. Excavations at Tell Qiri in Kibbuts Hazorea, 1975–76. *Qadmoniot* 10 (1977) 24–27 (Hebrew).

Ben-Tor, A. Tell Qiri—A Look at Village Life. *BA* 42 (1979) 105–13.

Qishyon, Tell
(187/229—1;2;3)

Zori 1977: 110–13.

Amiran, R. and Arnon, C. Tell Qishyon. *IEJ* 27 (1977) 164–65.

Hadashot 69–71 (1979) 38ff. (Hebrew).

Arnon, C. and Amiran, R. Excavations at Tel Qishon: Preliminary Report on the 1977–1978 Season. *EI* 15 (1981) 205–12 (Hebrew; English summary, 82*).

Arnon, C. Tell Qishyon – 1981. *Hadashot* 78–79 (1982) 18 (Hebrew).

el-Qom, Khirbet
(146/104—1;2;3)

EAEHL 976–77 (Dever).

Holladay, J. Khirbet el-Qom. *IEJ* 21 (1971) 176.

ASI/J 135.

Quneitira
(199/245—1;2;3)

Albright 1926: 6, 26.

Amiran, R. Connections between Anatolia and Palestine in the Early Bronze Age. *IEJ* 2 (1952) 93.

Yeivin, S. Archaeology in Israel (November 1951—January 1953). *AJA* 59 (1955) 164.

Cf. Prausnitz sub Ai for bone handle.

Prausnitz, M. *Alon* 5–6 (1957) 35ff. (Hebrew).

Rabud, Khirbet
(151/093—1)

EAEHL 995 (Kochavi).

Kochavi, M. Khirbet Rabud—Ancient Debir. *Excavations and Studies,* ed. Y. Aharoni (Yeivin Festschrift; Tel Aviv, 1973) pp. 49–75 (Hebrew; English summary, x–xii).

Kochavi, M. Khirbet Rabud. *Tel Aviv* 1 (1974) 1–32.

Raddana, Khirbet
(169/146)

Callaway, J. and Cooley, R. A Salvage Excavation at Raddana, in Bireh. *BASOR* 201 (1971) 9–19.

Ras el-Ain
(143/168—1;2;3)

EAEHL 70–73 (Eitan).

Ory, J. and Iliffe, J. Pottery from Ras el- 'Ain. *QDAP* 5 (1936) 111–26.

Ory, J. Excavations at Ras el-'Ain. *QDAP* 6 (1937) 99–120.

Eitan, A. Tel Aphek (Rosh ha-'Ayin). *IEJ* 12 (1962) 151–52.

Eitan, A. Rosh Ha'ayin. *RB* 69 (1962) 407–8.

Eitan, A. Excavations at the Foot of Tel Rosh Ha'ayin. *Atiqot* 5 (1969) 49–68 (Hebrew; English summary, 6°–7°).

Kochavi, M. Tel Aphek (Ras el-'Ain). *IEJ* 22 (1972) 238–39.

Kochavi, M. Tel Aphek. *IEJ* 23 (1973) 245.

Kochavi, M. Tel Aphek. *IEJ* 24 (1974) 261.

Kochavi, M. *Excavations of Aphek-Antipatris* (Tel Aviv, 1978).

Kochavi, M. The History and Archaeology of Aphek-Antipatris. *BA* 44 (1981) 75–86.

Rosh ha-Niqra
(160/277—1;2;3)

EAEHL 1023–24 (Tadmor).

Tadmor, M. and Prausnitz, M. Excavations at Rosh Hanniqra. *Atiqot* 2 (1959) 72–88.

Helms, S. The Early Bronze Gate at Rās en-Naqūra (Rōš ha-Niqrā). *ZDPV* 92 (1976) 1–9.

Ben-Tor 1978: index of geographical names.

er-Ruweisa, Khirbet Tell
(181/271—1)

Amiran, R. Khirbet Tell er-Ruweisa in Upper Galilee. *EI* 2 (1953) 117–26 (Hebrew).

es-Safi, Tell
(135/123—4)

EAEHL 1024–27 (Stern).

Bliss, F. and Macalister, R. *Excavations in Palestine during the Years 1889–1900* (London, 1902) pp. 28–43.

Aharoni, Y. and Amiran, R. Archaeological Survey of the Shephelah. *BIES* 19 (1955) 222 (Hebrew).

Sahab
(245.5/142.5—1)

Ibrahim, M. Archaeological Excavations at Sahab, 1972. *ADAJ* 17 (1972) 23–36.

Ibrahim, M. Second Season of Excavation at Sahab, 1973 (Preliminary Report). *ADAJ* 19 (1974) 55–61.

Ibrahim, M. Third Season of Excavations at Sahab, 1975 (Preliminary Report). *ADAJ* 20 (1975) 64–82.

es-Saidiyeh el-Gharbi, Tell
(204/186—1)

EAEHL 1028 (Pritchard).

De Contenson 1960: 49–56.

De Contenson 1964: 38.

Pritchard, J. B. *The Cemetery at Tell es-Sa'idiyeh, Jordan* (Museum Monographs; Philadelphia, 1980).

Samaria
(169/187—2)

EAEHL 1032–50 (Stern).

Kenyon, K., in J. W. Crowfoot, et al., *The Buildings at Samaria* (Samaria-Sebaste 1; London, 1942) pp. 91–93.

Kenyon, K. Early Bronze Pottery in J. W. Crowfoot, et al., *The Objects from Samaria* (Samaria-Sebaste 3; London, 1957) pp. 91–94.

esh-Sharia, Tell
(119/088)

EAEHL 1060 (Oren).

esh-Shunah, Tell
(207/224—1;2;3)

EAEHL 656–58 (de Contenson).

De Contenson 1960: 12–31.

Mellaart 1962: 132.

Mittman 1970: 88.

Ibrahim 1976: 4.

Leonard 1981: Pls. I–XII.

Taanach
(171/214—3)

EAEHL 1138–47 (Glock).

Sellin, E. *Tell Ta'anek* (Denkschriften der Kaiserliche Ak. d. Wissenschaften, Phil.-hist. Kl., Band L, 4. Abh., Vienna, 1904).

Lapp, P. The 1963 Excavation at Ta'annek. *BASOR* 173 (1964) 4–44.

Lapp, P. Taanach by the Waters of Megiddo, *BA* 30 (1967) 2–27.

Lapp, P. The 1966 Excavations at Tell Taanek. *BASOR* 185 (1967) 2–39.

Lapp, P. The 1968 Excavations at Tell Taanek. *BASOR* 195 (1969) 2–49.

Lapp, P. *The Tale of the Tell* (Pittsburgh, 1975) pp. 91–103.

Tel Aviv

EAEHL 1159–1168 (Kaplan) cf. esp. 1161, 1163ff.

ha-Bashan St. (130.2/166.6—1): Kaplan, J. The Archaeology and History of Tel Aviv-Jaffa. *BA* 35 (1972) 72.

Abbatoir Hill (129.5/166.7—1): Kaplan, J. loc cit.

Nordau Boulevard (129.5/166.6—1): Kaplan, J. An EB Tomb at Tel Aviv. *BIES* 16 (1952) 20–25 (Hebrew; English summary, vi).

el-Hasas, Tell (130.9/166.9): Kaplan, J. Arachaeological Survey of the South Bank of the Yarkon. *EI* 2 (1953) 160 (Hebrew).

Qirya (130.2/164.3—1): Kaplan, H. Tel Aviv, A Burial Cave in the Qirya. *IEJ* 29 (1979) 241.

Exhibition Grounds (132.0/168.3): *Hadashot* 41–42 (1972) 27 (Hebrew).

Bodenheimer (130.4/166.8—1): Kaplan, H. Tel Aviv, No. 8 Bodenheimer Street. *IEJ* 29 (1979) 238ff.

Ramat Aviv "C" (130.8/168.8—1): Kaplan, H. ibid., 240.

Tirat Zvi
(199/203)

Zori 1962: 189.

Yarmuth, Tell
(147/124—1;2;3)

EAEHL 544–45 (Ben-Tor).

Ben-Tor, A. The First Season of Excavations at Tell Yarmuth (1970). *Qedem* 1 (1975) 55–87.

De Miroschedji, P. Tel Yarmut, 1980. *IEJ* 31 (1981) 121–24.

De Miroschedji, P. Tel Yarmut, 1981. *IEJ* 32 (1982) 159–61.

De Miroschedji, P. Un objet en céramique du Bronze ancien à représentation humaine. *IEJ* 32 (1982) 190–94.

Yinam, Tell
(198/235—1)

Liebowitz, H. and Folk, R. L. Archaeological Geology of Tel Yin'am, Galilee, Israel. *Journal of Field Archaeology* 7 (1980) 23–42.

Liebowitz, H. Excavations at Yin'am: The 1976 and 1977 Seasons: Preliminary Report. *BASOR* 243 (1981) 79–94.

Hadashot 67–68 (1978) 15; 72 (1979) 20 (Hebrew).

Yoqneam
(160.5/230.0—1;2)

Ben-Tor, A. and Rosenthal, R. The First Season of Excavations at Tel Yoqne'am, 1977: Preliminary Report. *IEJ* 28 (1978) 57–82.

Ben-Tor, A., Portugali, Y., and Avissar, M. The Second Season of Excavations at Tel Yoqne'am, 1978: Preliminary Report. *IEJ* 29 (1979) 65–83.

ASI/N 16.

Zakariya, Tell
(144/123—2;4)

EAEHL 141–43 (Stern).

Bliss, F. and Macalister, R. *Excavations in Palestine during the Years 1889–1900* (London, 1902) pp. 12–27.

Dagan 1982: 51.

SURVEYED SITES

Abalis, Tell (206.9/274.1): Yalqut.

Abda, Khirbet (165/272): Yalqut.

Abil, Tell (204.2/296.0): Yalqut; Guy, P. L. O. *BBSAJ* 6 (1924) 75; Albright 1926: 16.

Abu Alubah, Tell (206.0/203.1): Ibrahim 1976: 10; few EB.

Abu edh-Dhahab, Tell (207.2/186.6): Ibrahim 1976: 91; one EB.

Abu el-Fukhar, Tell (211.5/215.2): Glueck 1951: 125.

Abu el-Kharaz, Tell (206.0/200.2): Ibrahim 1976: 7; Glueck 1951: 159a.

Abu en-Naml (207/231): Yalqut.

Abu Faraj, Tell (199.4/203.5): Zori 1962: 68.

Abu Hamed, Khirbet (233.7/166.0): Glueck 1939: 275.

Abu Hayet, Tell (207/204): Mellaart 1962: 24.

Abu Hureira, Tell (112/087): Amiran, R. and Aharoni, Y. *BIES* 17 (1953) 56–60 (Hebrew); Aharoni, Y. *IEJ* 6 (1956) 31.

Abu Musarrah, Khirbet (177.3/137.3): ASI/BE 147; few EB.

Abu Nijras, Tell (202.9/200.0): Ibrahim 1976: 62; possible EB.

Abu Qarf, Tell (213.7/138.9—1): Glueck 1934: 18; Glueck 1951: 211.

Abu Sharif, Tell (129.5/071.0): Kuschke, A. *ZDPV* 70 (1954) 119.

Abu Shawmar (228/177): Kerestes 1978: 128.

Abu Shuqeir, Khirbet (155.4/220.1): ASI/D 163.

Abu Sifri, Tell = Tell el-Hilu (197.8/192.5—1;2): Mittmann 1970: 336; ASI/EM 86.

Abu Sultan, Tell (125.9/147.5): Dothan, M. *IEJ* 2 (1952) 108.

Abu Sundeih (143.0/118.5): Yalqut.

Abu Sus, Tel (203.0/197.8—1/2): Zori 1977: 56; de Contenson 1964: 41ff.; Zobel, H.-J. *ZDPV* 82 (1966) 97–100.

Abu Zara, Tell (171.9/167.9): ASI/BE 36.

Abu Zebna, Khirbet (229.5/177.2): Glueck 1939: 307.

Abu Zureiq, Tell (162/226—1): Engberg and Shipton 1934: 61 n. 15.

Adamit (170.3/276.0—1): Amiran 1970: fig. 5.

el-Adanin, Khirbet (205.9/037.2): MacDonald 1982: 173.

el-Adasa, Khirbet (172.7/137.2): Wibbing, S. *ZDPV* 78 (1962) 164ff.

Adashim, Tel (179.5/228.7—1/2): Zori 1977: 81.

Adasiyyah (Lower) (207.5/229.0): Ibrahim 1976: 2; few possible EB.

Adasiyyah (Upper) (208.0/231.0): Ibrahim 1976: 1.

Adeimeh (209.0/132.5): Stekelis, M. *Les monuments mégalithiques de Palestine* (Paris, 1935), ch. III; Stekelis, M. *EAEHL* 828ff.

Agra, Tel (137.9/101.1—2/3): Dagan 1982: 51ff.

Ahdir, Horvat (138.6/036.5—2): *Hadashot* 53 (1975) 32 (Hebrew); Cohen, R. *IEJ* 28 (1978) 185 n. 4; ASI/SB 52.

el-Ain, Tell (250.1/187.0): Glueck 1951: 305.

el-Aineh (223.7/043.0): Glueck 1935: 221, cf. Pl. 25B; Glueck 1939: 72.

Ain el-Alaq (155.8/219.7): Yalqut.

Ain el-Jirani (199.5/221.8): Yalqut.

Ain Faz (201.5/225.9): Yalqut.

Ain Mehna (220.8/197.3): Glueck 1951: 40.

Ain Naura (187.3/224.8): Alt, A. *PJB* 23 (1927) 40.

Ain Riyashi, Khirbet (238.1/184.6): Glueck 1951: 270.

Ain Saubala, Khirbet (211.2/040.3—1): MacDonald 1980: 172.

Ain Umm el-Amud = Ein ha-Naziv (197.4/208.6): Zori 1962: 92; cf. Amiran 1970: fig. 5; *IEJ* 4 (1954) 129 for burials.

Ain Zagha, Khirbet (211.5/288.2): Yalqut.

Ajje (168.5/196.5): ASI/EM 56; only one EB.

Ajlun (220.7/193.7): Glueck 1951: 129; cf. Wright 1937: 61.

Akhin, Khirbet (199.1/225.7—1/2): Zori 1977: 185.

Ala-Safat (c. 210/150): Stekelis, M. *EAEHL* 829ff.; Stekelis, M. La necropolis megalitica de Ala-Safat, Transjordania *Ampurias* 22–24 (1961) 49–128.

Allaq, Khirbet (155.5/135.5): Kuschke, A. *ZDPV* 70 (1954) 124.

Al Manaqid (204.2/039.2—1;2): MacDonald 1980: 173.

Al Mazar (184.1/214.7—1/2;3): Zori 1977: 3.

el-Alya, Tell (199.9/200.9): Zori 1962: 67.

Ameidat (209.3/212.8): Glueck 1951: 126.

Amriyeh, Khirbet (217.2/188.6—1;3): Mittmann 1970: 206.

Aqrabah (225/239—1;2): de Contenson 1964: 32ff.

Aqrabah, Khirbet (226.0/098.3): Glueck 1939: 151.

el-Arab, Horvat (143.0/123.4—2/3): Dagan 1982: 54.

Araq er-Rashdan, Khirbet (207.2/214.0): Glueck 1951: 146; Ibrahim 1976: 44.

el-Arbain, Tell (205.6/213.9): Ibrahim 1976: 34; Glueck 1951: 144.

el-Arida, Tell (198.5/205.7): Zori 1962: 74.

Arjum (217.2/073.7—1;2/3;4): Mattingly 1981: 9047.

Arqub Umm Tell (217.5/179.0): Glueck 1939: 347; cf. Albright 1929: 12.

Arq el-Amar (170.5/116.5): Neuville, R. *QDAP* 1 (1932) 157ff.; 2 (1933) 185ff.

Arsa, Khirbet (114.2/116.2): *Alon* 2 (1950) 11 (Hebrew).

Ashan, Khirbet (125/076—2): Cohen, R. *IEJ* 27 (1977) 163ff.

el-Ashari, Tell (243/236): Albright 1925: 15–16.

Ashkelon (Afridar) (108.7/121.2): Gophna, R. *IEJ* 18 (1968) 256.

Ashtarah, Tell (243/244): Albright 1925: 15; Alt, A. *PJB* 29 (1933) 21.

ASI/D 115 (150.9/222.6).

ASI/D 131 (155.9/220.0).

ASI/D 150 (154.3/221.3).

ASI/EM 41 (166.8/199.2).

ASI/EM 94 (166.9/190.5).

ASI/EM 175 (162.8/177.7).

ASI/EM 223 (155.3/153.2).

ASI/G 93 (211.3/263.2—2).

ASI/G 144 (215.5/250.3—2).

ASI/G 192 (220.2/240.3).

ASI/G 206 (210.8/234.3).

ASI/JD 4 (198/171—2).

ASI/JD 153 (187/110—2).

ASI/N 77 (169.8/233.9—1).

ASI/N 82 (169.9/235.6—1).

Atar Har Harif (107.5/988.7—2): Cohen, R. *IEJ* 29 (1979) 253ff.

Avot, Khirbet (193.3/276.3—2): Braun, E. *IEJ* 31 (1981) 107–8.

Awarwareh (219.0/091.4): Mattingly 1981: 8013.

Ayateh, Tell (224.5/211.5): Glueck 1951: 12.

Bab en-Naqb = Tell Hadad (190.1/182.0): ASI/EM 159; Knierim, R. *ZDPV* 85 (1969)
   53–59, quoting P. Lapp.

Balame, Khirbet (177.7/205.8): ASI/EM 18.

Baluah (N) (224.5/086.0—4): Mattingly 1981: 8004.

Baluah (S) (224.5/085.5): Mattingly 1981: 8014.

Baluah (SE) (225.7/084.3—1;2/3;4): Mattingly 1981: 9272.

Bani Fadil, Khirbet (186.0/165.3): Herrmann, S. *ADAJ* 6–7 (1962) 91.

Baqurah (206.5/228.0): Ibrahim 1976: 13, north and middle sites; possible EB.

el-Bardawil (219.8/247.5—2): ASI/G 171.

Barta, Tell = Tell Huga (200.5/213.5): Zori 1962: 19; Zori 1958: 46.

el-Bassa, Khirbet (196.1/237.7): Saarisalo 1927: 35ff.

el-Battiha, Tell (206/292): Yalqut.

Bat Yam (126.6/156.7): *Hadashot* 33 (1970) 22; 34–35 (1970) 24 (Hebrew).

el-Bayada, Khirbet (236.1/219.2—1): Mittmann 1970: 19.

el-Bedha, Khirbet (220.5/201.4—1;2;3): Mittmann 1970: 168.

Beer Naweh (144.6/110.0—2/3): Dagan 1982: 53.

Beerot Adullam (150.2/118.2—1): Dagan 1982: 50.

Beer Resisim (106/020—2): Cohen, R. and Dever W. *IEJ* 29 (1979) 254–55.

Beer Resisim, Site 126 (106/019—2;3): Cohen, R. and Dever, W. *IEJ* 30 (1980) 230.

el-Beheirah (235.0/195.0): Glueck 1951: 286.

el-Beida, Tel (197.8/198.6—1;2;3): Zori 1977: 54; Mittmann 1970: 338.

el-Beida, Tell (168.8 /231.6—1;2): ASI/N 67.

Beider Radwan (212.5/044.3—1;2;3): MacDonald 1980: 173.

Beit Sallum, Khirbet (166.7/182.5): Bach, R. *ZDPV* 74 (1958) 48ff.

Benat, Khirbet (236.2/177.5): Glueck 1939: 331.

Bes, Horvat (162.7/082.1—2): Amiran 1980: 11ff.

Beqerah, Khirbet (125.8/028.9—1;4): Glueck/Vogel 66.

Beseileh (207.0/213.5): Ibrahim 1976: 43.

Besor Bridge "Site H" (101.7/079.4): Gophna, R. *IEJ* 26 (1976) 199.

Beth Elem, Horvat (144.9/109.7—2): Dagan 1982: 53.

Beth Qad (183.7/208.4—1/2): Zori 1977: 59.

Beth Yosef (200/221): Zori 1962: 13.

Bint Jubeil (190.4/280.5): Amiran 1970: fig. 5.

Biqat Uvda, Site 124 (146.3/928.3—2): Amiran, R., Arnon, C. and Avner, U. *IEJ* 29 (1979) 256.

Biqat Yavnael (195.7/237.8): *Hadashot* 14 (1965) 4 (Hebrew).

Bir Deir el-Asal (144.4/097.7—2): ASI/J 181.

el-Bireh, Khirbet (246.2/173.7): Glueck 1939: 320.

el-Bir el-Gharbi, Tell (166/256—4): Prausnitz, M. *EAEHL* 25; Prausnitz, M. *IEJ* 30 (1980) 3ff., 206ff.

Bir Hasan (172.0/205.9): ASI/EM 17; few EB.

el-Birketen (234.1/189.8—1;3): Mittmann 1970: 251.

Bir Safadi (130.5/069.8—1): Glueck/Vogel 379.

Bir Shenek, Khirbet (105.3/069.9—2): Glueck/Vogel 508.

el-Biyad, Khirbet (226.6/230.9): Glueck 1951: 71.

Bleda (198.6/282.2): Amiran 1970: fig. 5.

Bornat, Tel (138.0/115.3—2): Dagan 1982: 51.

el-Breitawi, Khirbet (251.2/165.7): Glueck 1939: 312.

Burga, Tel (147/215): *Hadashot* 21 (1967) 10–11; 41–42 (1972) 15–16 (Hebrew); Kochavi, M., Beck, P., and Gophna, R. *ZDPV* 95 (1979) 142–51.

Buweib, Khirbet (205.8/182.6): Ibrahim 1976: 105.

el-Buweida, Khirbet (156.7/225.4): ASI/D 71.

Dabayib en-Nawar (196.2/205.6): Zori 1962: 99.

Dabburiya (186.8/233.6—1/2): Zori 1977: 157.

Dagan 1982: 48 1 (131.5/102.2—1).

Dagan 1982: 51 4 (133.0/132.5—2/3).

Dagan 1982: 53 10 (139.3/106.0—2/3).

Dagan 1982: 53 5 (135.9/131.8—2/3).

Dagan 1982: 53 6 (142.8/115.0—2/3).

Dagan 1982: 53 7 (144.7/114.6—2/3).

Dagan 1982: 55 3 (138.3/109.2—2/3).

Dagan 1982: 57 11 (136.6/102.5—2).

Dagan 1982: 57 5 (136.3/108.2—2/3).

Dagan 1982: 57 6 (136.4/108.0—2).

Dagan 1982: 57 7 (138.2/106.8—2).

Dagan 1982: 57 8 (139.7/106.1—2).

ed-Daliyah, Khirbet (206/207): Ibrahim 1976: 50; few EB.

Dalton (196/269): Amiran 1970: fig. 5.

ed-Damiya, Khirbet (194.0/239.4): Saarisalo 1927: 31ff.

ed-Debab (205.4/218.5): Ibrahim 1976: 73.

ed-Deia, Khirbet (210.5/293.3): Yalqut.

Deir Abu Said (211.5/208.7—1): Mittmann 1970: 101.

Deir Burak (229.7/204.0—1;3): Mittmann 1970: 141.

Deir ed-Domeh (148.7; 093.2): ASI/J 213.

Deir Kharuf, Tel (137.5/102.1—2/3): Dagan 1982: 54.

Deir Qequb (211.5/208.7—1): Mittmann 1970: 103.

Deir Saaneh, Tell (220.8/217.0): Glueck 1946: 5ff. (equated with Mekhlediyeh); Glueck 1951: 112.

Deragot, Horvat (157.4/079.0—2): Amiran 1980: 11ff.

Derah (253.2/224.2): Albright 1925: 16.

edh-Dhaheriyeh, Tell (147/092): Albright 1938: 2 n. 1, 5 n. 7; *QDAP* 2 (1933) 193ff.

Dhahrat el-Iraq (157.5/228.8): ASI/D 27.

Dhahr el-Khirbe (225.7/193.3—2;3): Mittmann 1970: 194.

Dhahr et-Tell (163.3/268.2): Saarisalo 1929: 38.

edh-Dhiyabeh, Tell = Tell Abu Hashi (204.0/211.7): Glueck 1951: 150; cf. Zori 1962: 50; Glueck 1946: 3ff.

edh-Dhuq (198.7/209.8): Zori 1962: 89.

Dishon, Khirbet (198.6/276.6): Amiran 1970: fig. 5.

ed-Dura (212.4/266.4): ASI/G 83.

Ebal (176.5/180.1—1) Clamer, C. *IEJ* 27 (1977) 48.

Edan (219.7/225.7): Glueck 1951: 95.

Eder, Tell = Ein Hur, Khirbet (167/276): Ben-Tor 1978: 8; Aharoni, Y. *EI* 4 (1956) 57 (Hebrew).

Ein el-Hawwara (167.6/236.5—1): ASI/N 57.

Ein el-Jarbah (162.1/226.8—1): Mayerhof, A. *Hadashot* 78–79 (1982) 23ff. (Hebrew).

Ein er-Ruzz (182.5/225.9—1/2): Zori 1977: 99.

Ein Fara, Khirbet (179.6/138.0): ASI/BE 137; Saller 1961/62: 156.

Ein Kuniyeh (218.4/293.6): Ben-Tor 1978: 5.

Ein Shahal "A" (197/225—1;2): Zori 1977: 178; Ben-Tor 1978: 6.

Ein Shahal "B" (197.4/225.8—1/2): Zori 1977: 179.

Ein Shahal "C" (197.8/226.2—1/2): Zori 1977: 180.

Ein Umm el-Adam (212.0/239.7—2): ASI/G 194.

Ein Yizreel (181.9/218.2—1/2;3): Zori 1977: 33.

En Shadud (172/229—1): Braun, E. *IEJ* 29 (1979) 234ff.; *Hadashot* 77 (1981) 9ff. (Hebrew); Braun, E. and Gibson, S. *BASOR* 253 (1984) 29–40.

el-Fakhat (213.3/228.4—3): Glueck 1951: 98, Pl. 120:12; de Contenson 1964: 3.

Faqahiyeh, Tell (238.0/176.7): Glueck 1939: 329.

Faqqas, Tell (235.0/180.0): Glueck 1939: 332.

Faria el-Jiftlik (197/172): ASI/JD 2.

Feifa (194.5/038.7—1): Rast and Schaub 1974: 11ff.

Feinan (197.0/004.7): Glueck 1935: 14.

Felah, Khirbet (204.7/183.7): Ibrahim 1976: 101; possible EB.

Fendi, Tell (205.0/212.0): Glueck 1951: 145; doubtful.

Feqeiqes (211.0/054.1): Glueck 1939: 109.

Freiji, Tell (230/178—2): Kerestes 1978: 127.

el-Fuhar, Tell (239.8/221.9—2;3): Mittmann 1970: 14.

Gesher = Tell esh-Shemdin (202.0/225.2): Zori 1962: 30; Zori 1958: 48.

el-Ghaba et-Tahta (163.8/223.7): Yalqut; *Alon* 5–6 (1957) 10 (Hebrew).

Ghadir en-Nahas (219.5/267.4): ASI/G 79.

Ghalta, Tell (166.6/232.1—1): ASI/N 49.

Givat Gad (139.2/104.9—2): Dagan 1982: 57.

Givat Hammoqeshim (202.5/224.4—3): Zori 1962: 8; Zori 1958: 47.

Givat Yehonatan (184.7/216.4—1/2;3): Zori 1977: 5.

Glueck Negev 79 (125.4/028.9): Glueck, N. *BASOR* 137 (1955) 16.

Glueck Negev 80 (126.4/028.9—1): Glueck, N. *BASOR* 137 (1955) 16.

Glueck Negev 234b (125.8/990.4—4): Glueck, N. *BASOR* 142 (1956) 19ff.

Glueck/Vogel 37 (130.6/013.7—4).

Glueck/Vogel 123 (139.8/044.2—1;4).

Glueck/Vogel 124 (138.9/045.6—2).

Glueck/Vogel 147 (124.6/001.7—4).

Glueck/Vogel 149C (125.2/003.2—4).

Glueck/Vogel 152 (123.2/001.8).

Glueck/Vogel 369 (101.9/026.4—4).

Glueck/Vogel 374 (160.2/038.5—4).

Glueck/Vogel 416 (124.6/078.0—1).

Glueck/Vogel 437 (139.1/026.7—2).

Glueck/Vogel 441 (136.5/027.5—4).

Glueck/Vogel 445A (146.9/042.4—1).

Glueck/Vogel 507 (105.9/069.7—1).

Glueck/Vogel 511 (097.5/066.8—2).

Glueck/Vogel 512 (096.5/065.6–2).

Gophna and Kochavi I (145/196): Gophna, R. *EAEHL* 1071–74.

Gophna and Kochavi II (141.5/196.5): Gophna, R. *EAEHL* 1071–74.

Gush-Halav (191/270): Amiran 1970: fig. 5; Aharoni, R. *EAEHL* 408.

Habil, Tell (204.5/197.2): de Contenson 1960: 31–49; Leonard 1981: Pls. XXVIII–XXX; cf. Ibrahim 1976: 65; Glueck 1951: 161a and b.

Habra, Wadi (180/094): Aharoni, Y. *IEJ* 4 (1954) 126ff.; 5 (1955) 222ff.

el-Habsa, Tell (198.6/198.8—1): Mittmann 1970: 340.

el-Hadab (155.3/098.3): ASI/J 176.

el-Hadid (202.7/224.3—3): Zori 1962: 7; Zori 1958: 47.

el-Hajj Mahmud, Khirbet (202.7/207.3): Zori 1962: 57.

Hallat el-Misri (152.7/213.3): *Hadashot* 3 (1962) 16 (Hebrew).

Ham, Tell (225.3/214.1): Glueck 1951: 9.

Hamid, Khirbet (222.8/190.3—2;3): Mittmann 1970: 196 and n. 63.

el-Hammam (N) (198.5/212.5): Zori 1962: 25.

el-Hammam, Tell (213.9/139.1): Glueck 1951: 212; Glueck 1943: 17ff.; Wright 1937: 61; de Contenson 1964: 39.

el-Hamme, Tell (197.4/197.7): ASI/EM 55.

el-Handaquq, Tell (206.1/189.7): Ibrahim 1976: 83; Glueck 1951: 168; cf. Engberg and Shipton 1934: 62; EB dominant; de Contenson 1964: 36.

Hannoar, Khirbet (159/238): Yalqut.

Har ha-Mearah (107.3/981.7—2): Haiman, M. *IEJ* 32 (1982) 266.

Har Haruvim = el-Khureiba (152/240): Ben-Tor 1978: 8.

Har Shaul (185.3/215.8—1/2): Zori 1977: 4.

Harzia, Khirbet (218.0/079.2—2/3): :Mattingly 1981: 9027.

el-Hashshash, Tell (130.5/166.0): Yalqut.

Hassan, Khirbet (220.8/214.9): Glueck 1951: 113; doubtful.

Hawaja, Khirbet (241.0/172.7): Glueck.1939: 311.

Hejaj, Tell (214.5/173.7): Glueck 1939: 303; de Vaux 1938: 411.

Hejeijeh, Khirbet (207.5/194.0): Ibrahim 1976: 76; may = Glueck 1951: 163.

el-Hemer, Khirbet (226.3/188.4—1): Mittmann 1970: 262.

Heneideh, Tell (207.2/193.4): Ibrahim 1976: 78; two sites, both EB dominant.

Heraqla (228.2/199.3): Glueck 1951: 322.

Heshbon (226.3/134.3): Ibach 1976: 126; cf. Waterhouse and Ibach 1975: 232.

Hilyah, Tell (227.9/236.9—1;2): Mittmann 1970: 33.

Hisas (208/292): Yalqut.

Hisham, Horvat (145.7/126.2—2/3): Dagan 1982: 54.

el-Hosh (217.6/189.1—1;3): Mittmann 1970: 208.

el-Hudeira, Khirbet (152.4/217.8): Aharoni, Y. *IEJ* 9 (1959) 117ff.

Hujfa (224.4/071.0—2/3): Mattingly 1981: 9043.

Humeimat (N) (222.6/080.3—2/3;4): Mattingly 1981: 9004.

Humeimat (S) (222.7/079.8): Mattingly 1981: 9005.

Humeimat (NE) (223.5/079.9): Mattingly 1981: 9008.

Hunizar (199.9/214.3): Zori 1962: 174.

el-Hunud, Tell (200.1/251.8): Turville-Petrie, F. *BBSAJ* 3 (1923) 33.

el-Husn, Tell (232.5/211.2—2): Glueck 1951: 1.

Huweishan, Tell (239.0/190.2): Glueck 1951: 282.

Ibach 1978a: 139 (233.5/140.3): one EB.

Ibach 1978a: 140 (233.6/137.2—4).

Idmah, Tell (200.9/226.2—1): Zori 1962: 27; Zori 1958: 47–48.

Imra (215.3/084.5—2/3;4): Mattingly 1981: 8017.

Irbid (230.1/219.3): Glueck 1951: 153ff.; Albright 1929: 10.

el-Ishshe, Wadi (203.2/217.5): Yalqut.

Ismail "B", Tell (203.2/217.5): Zori 1962: 16; Zori 1958: 49.

Iztabba, Tell (198.3/212.4—3): Zori 1962: 43, Pl. zayin, b.

Jalul (231.0/125.0): Ibach 1978b: 221.

Jamain, Tell (202.5/201.7): Zori 1962: 63; Zori 1958: 49.

Jatt (154/201—1;2;3): Gophna and Kochavi 1966; *Hadashot* 17 (1966) 10–13 (Hebrew); Gophna, R. *EAEHL* 1071–74.

Jazirat Daoud (152.9/221.7): ASI/D 147.

Jebel Abu Thawab (230/174—1): Grant, E. and C. *Levant* 15 (1983) 187–91.

Jebel el-Ain (175.2/237.2): Yalqut; Ben-Tor 1978: 10.

Jebel el-Qafze (178.8/231.1): Neuville, R. *QDAP* 4 (1935) 202.

Jebel es-Saqa, Tell (210.6/200.7—1;2): Mittmann 1970: 116.

Jenabe, Tell (238.4/177.5—1;2;3): Mittmann 1970: 290; Glueck 1939: 330.

Jerash (234.6/188.1): Glueck 1951: 275.

Jisr el-Majami (202.7/226.0): Yeivin, S. and Maisler, B. *BJPES* 11 (1944) 18 (Hebrew); Ibrahim 1976: 29; possible EB.

Jisr esh-Shid (203.2/234.1): Yeivin, S. and Maisler, B. *BJPES* 11 (1944) 19 (Hebrew).

Jisr Quleid (221/238): Mellaart 1962: 7.

el-Jukhadar, Tell (230.2/295.5): ASI/G 106.

Juret el-Khazneh, Khirbet (226.7/168.2): Glueck 1939: 291.

Kabri (164/268—1;2): Amiran 1970: fig. 5; *Hadashot* 2 (1962) 25.

Kafr el-Ma (227.2/246.4): ASI/G 178.

el-Karantina, Tell = Karpas (202.8/207.9): Zori 1962: 52.

el-Karm (202.9/207.5): Zori 1962: 54; Ben-Tor 1978: 12.

Kefar Ata (161.8/246.0—1): Amiran 1969: 58–59, photos 51, 54–56; *Hadashot* 16 (1965) 22 (Hebrew).

Kefr Kuz, Khirbet (178.2/182.3): Campbell 1968: 6; few EB.

Kerestes 1978: 124 29 (230/237).

el-Khabiah, Khirbet (223.7/168.0): Glueck 1939: 293.

Khaif (215.3/077.1—4): Mattingly 1981: 9280.

Khanazir (192/032—1;2;3): Rast and Schaub 1974: 12–13.

Khandaq, Khirbet (220.5/155.7): Glueck 1939: 220; cf. de Vaux 1938: 406.

el-Khirbeh, Tell (191/277): Aharoni, Y. *EAEHL* 408.

Khrea (226.4/081.5—2/3;4): Mattingly 1981: 9041.

Kilkit, Khirbet (131.2/102.8): Yalqut.

Kom Yajuz (237.7/160.0): Glueck 1939: 250.

el-Kom (235.4/228.5): Glueck 1951: 51.

Kufin, Khirbet (160.9/114.3—1): Smith, R. H. *Excavations in the Cemetery at Khirbet Kūfin, Palestine* (London, 1962) pp. 6–8.

Kufr Rakib (215.0/207.0—1;2;3): Mittmann 1970: 106.

el-Kuhl (190.3/229.5—1/2): Zori 1977: 169.

Kuma (170.7/183.2): Campbell 1968: 39; possible EB.

el-Kurum (167.9/136.5): ASI/BE 151; few EB.

Lawieh (214.9/251.4): Ben-Tor 1978: 10–11; ASI/G 141, 142.

el-Lehun (230.5/097.0): Glueck 1934: 48; Naster, P. and Homs-Frédericq, D. *ADAJ* 23 (1979) 51–56.

Lejjun (232.5/072.2—2/3;4): Glueck 1934: 44–47; Mattingly 1981: 9066.

Maabarot (145/196): Yalqut; Sussman, V. and Ben-Arieh, S. *Atiqot* 3 (1966) 39 n. (Hebrew).

Maadh, Khirbet (207.5/223.6): Ibrahim 1976: 27; few possible EB.

MacDonald 1980: 62 (211.2/040.9—1).

MacDonald 1980: 64 (211.2/041.6—1).

el-Madraseh, Tell (206.6/221.2): Ibrahim 1976: 21.

el-Maghajja, Khirbet (193.2/229.1—1/2): Zori 1977: 209.

el-Maghar (129.8/138.9—1): Kaplan, J. *BIES* 17 (1952) 140ff.

Maghuz, Tell (196.6/201.1): Zori 1962: 95; may = Kabr Ehsen in Zori 1958: 49.

Mahrama, Khirbet (224.2/202.9—1;3): Mittmann 1970: 138.

Main, Khirbet (162.7/090.9): ASI/J 231; few EB.

Majdal (149.6/201.7—1): Gophna and Kochavi 1966.

el-Maliha, Tell (199.4/211.3): Zori 1962: 85.

el-Malat, Tell (137.4/140.5): Mazar, B *BIES* 16 (1951) 49ff.

el-Manshiya, Tell (198.9/210.5): Zori 1962: 88.

el-Mansura (229.0/192.0—1): Mittmann 1970: 241.

el-Mansura, Khirbet (202.1/233.8): Saarisalo 1927: 50ff.

Maqbarat es-Sleikah (206.6/192.9): Ibrahim 1976: 79.

el-Maqlub, Tell (214.6/201.5—1;2): Glueck 1951: 234.

el-Marajim (216.0/224.5—1;2;3): Mittmann 1970: 83.

el-Marqaah, Khirbet (207.1/212.5): Ibrahim 1976: 45; possible EB.

Masada, Khirbet (137/103): Amiran 1969: photos 46–47.

el-Masalle, Tell (168.7/205.7): ASI/EM 14.

el-Mashakhkha, Khirbet (196.5/219.6—1/2): Zori 1977: 136.

Mashmil, Khirbet (213.5/033.5): Glueck 1935: 232.

Masna (222.3/076.7—2/3;4): Mattingly 1981: 8024.

Mattingly 1981: 8010 (225.5/087.9—4).

Mattingly 1981: 9007 (216.7/079.4—3).

Mattingly 1981: 9009 (218.4/078.8).

Mattingly 1981: 9160 (231.5/080.3—1).

el-Mazar (201.2/224.1): Zori 1962: 171.

el-Mazar, Tell (196.0/171.9): ASI/JD 3.

el-Meghaniyeh, Tell (244.5/180.9): Glueck 1951: 261; doubtful.

el-Meidan (231.2/223.0): Glueck 1951: 43.

el-Meidan, Tell (208.2/175.5): Glueck 1951: 191.

Mellaart 1962: 6 (227/237).

Mendah (212.8/218.7): Glueck 1951: 120a.

Meqbereh, Tell (203/201): Mellaart 1962: 25; = Ibrahim 1976: 6 and Glueck 1951: 159.

Meron (191/265): Amiran 1970: fig. 5.

Merqab Azn, Khirbet (233.7/194.5): Glueck 1951: 279.

el-Meshobesh, Khirbet (230.0/172.7): Glueck 1939: 310.

el-Metwi, Khirbet (242.4/192.4): Glueck 1951: 300.

el-Mintar, Tell (207.6/224.5): Ibrahim 1976: 14.

Misar, Khirbet (221.3/086.5): Glueck 1934: 58; Mattingly 1981: 8011.

Miske, Tell (187.3/182.5—3): ASI/BE 3; Glueck 1951: 254a.

el-Misna (223.0/077.0): Glueck 1934: 137.

Momghareh, Khirbet (241.3/177.5): Glueck 1939: 325.

Mudawwar, Tell (207.7/219.1): Ibrahim 1976: 32; few EB; Glueck 1951: 140.

Mudowwerah (212.5/051.2—1;2;3): Glueck 1939: 95.

Mughaiyir, Khirbet (188.4/232.8—1/2): Zori 1977: 158.

Mugharat esh-Shababik (197.3/254.8): Binford, S. *IEJ* 16 (1966) 21.

Mugheyir, Tell (237.9/223.9—1;2;3): Mittmann 1970: 10.

el-Muhafar, Tell (170.6/205.7): ASI/EM 16; major EB.

Muharakat (N) (221.6/073.3—2/3;4): Mattingly 1981: 9115.

Muharakat (S) (221.7/072.9—4): Mattingly 1981: 9114.

Mukhnah el-Fokah, Khirbet (175.4/175.9): ASI/BE 26.

Mumani (229.5/167.0): Glueck 1939: 277; doubtful.

Muntar Zibdeh (233.8/207.0): Glueck 1951: 289; doubtful.

Murhan (188.5/217.6—1/2): Zori 1977: 112.

el-Musheirifa, Khirbet (169.7/239.0—1;2): ASI/N 69; Saarisalo 1929: 38.

el-Musherfeh, Khirbet (215.4/190.7—2;3): Mittmann 1970: 211.

Musrara, Khirbet (163.8/232.5—1;2): ASI/N 33.

el-Muzeble, Khirbet (223.1/194.9—1;2;3): Mittmann 1970: 193.

Nahalal (168.7/233.4—1): ASI/N 65.

Nahal Mitnan (102.0/009.0—1): Haiman, M. *IEJ* 21 (1982) 265ff.

Nahal Tavor (c. 200/225): Amiran 1969: 47, photo 36; 49 n. 9; Ben-Tor 1978: 13; Sussman, V. and Ben-Arieh, S. *Atiqot* 3 (1966) 39 n. (Hebrew).

Nahf (179/260): Amiran 1970: fig. 5; Yalqut.

en-Nahl, Tell (156.90/244.95): Saarisalo 1929: 38.

en-Naima, Tell Khirbet (205/286): Yalqut; Albright 1926: 18–23; 1925: 12.

en-Najjar, Khirbet (178.2/205.6): ASI/EM 19.

Naur (228.5/143.0): Waterhouse and Ibach 1975: 229.

Nebi Yusha, Khirbet (216.2/163.0): Glueck 1939: 284.

Nein (182.5/226.3—1/2): Zori 1977: 98.

en-Nimrah (248.0/172.7): Glueck 1939: 319.

Nimrud, Tell (202.3/210.1): Zori 1962: 79.

Oreimeh, Khirbet (226.0/175.2): Glueck 1939: 289.

el-Oreimeh, Tell (225.0/167.7): Glueck 1939: 292.

Parur, Tell = Khirbet Fureir (159/226): Ben-Tor 1978: 4; ASI/D 58.

Peqiin (181/264): Amiran 1970: fig. 5.

Qabr el-Faras = Galed (157.8/217.8): Ben-Tor 1978: 5, 11.

el-Qadish, Khirbet (202.4/237.9): Kochavi, M. *BIES* 27 (1963) 169 (Hebrew).

Qadum (165.0/179.3—1): Magen, I. *Qedem Museum* (Qedumim, 1982); *Hadashot* 80–81 (1982) 19 (Hebrew).

el-Qahwa, Tell (163/237—4): Prausnitz, M. and Kempinski, A. *IEJ* 27 (1977) 165ff.

Qamm (218.4/221.3—1;2): Mittmann 1970: 79.

Qaq, Tell (213.0/223.8): Glueck 1951: 105.

el-Qarn (222.3/132.4): Ibach 1976: 19; cf. Waterhouse and Ibach 1975: 232 n. 54.

Qarqaf, Khirbet (164.3/185.9): ASI/EM 133; few EB.

Qasr Mahrun (174.3/202.1): ASI/EM 33.

Qasr Sabihi (226.2/187.0—2;3): Mittmann 1970: 265.

Qasr Umm el-Harmil (177.7/086.2): Aharoni, Y. *IEJ* 11 (1961) 13.

el-Qelaya, Tell (206.2/186.8): Glueck 1951: 171; de Contenson 1964: 36ff.

el-Qeseibeh, Tell (208.3/218.3): Ibrahim 1976: 33.

el-Qeseir (225.0/163.7): Glueck 1939: 282.

el-Qitaf, Tell (202.6/207.6): Zori 1962: 55.

el-Qos, Tell (208.5/183.3): Glueck 1951: 175; de Contenson 1964: 37ff.; Ibrahim 1976: 102.

Qumiya, Khirbet (187/219): Yalqut.

el-Quneye, Khirbet (N) (244.5/182.5—2;3): Mittmann 1970: 298.

el-Qureiya, Khirbet (216.1/124.1): Kuschke, A. *ZDPV* 77 (1961) 27ff.

Qurn el-Kibsh, Khirbet (223.5/128.0): Glueck 1935: 240, Pl. 25A.

Qurn Hattin (194.8/244.8): Albright 1928: 5; Jirku, A. *ZDPV* 53 (1930) 148.

Qurs, Tell (230.6/236.8): Glueck 1951: 89; Mellaart 1962: 3; de Contenson 1964: 31ff.; Ben-Tor 1978: 4; Kerestes 1978: 124.

el-Qutt, Khirbet (173.0/163.4): ASI/BE 37; few EB.

el-Quweijiya, Khirbet (220.7/126.4—3): Stoebe, H. *ZDPV* 82 (1966) 29.

el-Quweilbi (231.8/232.2): Maayah, F. *ADAJ* 4–5 (1960) 16.

er-Radgha, Tell (199.8/200.6): Zori 1962: 66.

er-Rafid, Khirbet (176.7/161.8): ASI/BE 42.

er-Rahub, Khirbet (237.5/224.1—1;2): Mittmann 1970: 11.

Ramat Matred (c. 120/020—2): Cohen, R. *IEJ* 30 (1980) 231–34.

Ras Abu Lofeh (212.0/219.0): Glueck 1951: 120.

Ras Abu Murra, Khirbet (147.3/135.5): Yalqut.

Ras Ali, Khirbet (164.5/241.5): Yalqut.

Ras ed-Diyar (185.5/177.8): Campbell 1968: 15; few EB.

Ras el-Kuwem (230.6/183.9—1): Mittmann 1970: 282.

Rashuni (221/171): de Vaux 1938: 415.

er-Rasiyyah (206.2/204.1): ASI/EM 226.

er-Ras, Khirbet (168.7/154.1): ASI/BE 68.

Rasm Gibbor, Horvat (139.4/109.8—2): Dagan 1982: 55.

Ras Umm ez-Zureq (230.2/198.1—1;2;3): Mittmann 1970: 186.

er-Rayan, Tell (199.1/204.9): Zori 1962: 73.

er-Rayy, Tell (N) (207.9/224.1): Ibrahim 1976: 30.

er-Rayy, Tell (S) (207.7/223.8): Ibrahim 1976: 28; few EB.

er-Reheil (249.5/170.5): Glueck 1939: 314; Kerestes 1978: 128.

er-Reheil, Tell (226.2/177.2): Glueck 1939: 343.

Rekhesh, Tel (194.0/228.8—1;2): Zori 1977: 175; Gal, Z. *EI* 15 (1981) 213–15 (Hebrew; English summary, 83°).

Rekhmeh, Khirbet (140.7/045.5—4): Glueck/Vogel 120.

er-Reseifeh (248.0/158.7): Glueck 1939: 260.

er-Reseifeh, Khirbet (248.7/158.7): Glueck 1939: 261.

Rikabi, Tell (207.7/176.4): Glueck 1951: 192.

er-Rish, Tell (165.0/233.9—1;2): ASI/N 42.

er-Rufeif, Tell (208.1/212.1): Ibrahim 1976: 47; few EB.

Rujm el-Edam (226.9/233.0): Glueck 1951: 59.

Rujm el-Kom (235.0/193.7): Glueck 1951: 278.

Rujm el-Qadi (226.3/230.6): Glueck 1951: 70.

Rujm Saab = Debsa (219.8/221.6—1;2): Mittmann 1970: 77.

Rujm Umm el-Qleib (223.3/092.0—1;2/3;4): Glueck 1934: 57ff.; Mattingly 1981: 8008.

er-Rujum, Khirbet (153.8/198.3): ASI/EM 47; few EB.

er-Rumeimim, Khirbet = Ein Salim (210/102—3;4): Stoebe, H. *ZDPV* 82 (1966) 31ff.

er-Rumman, Khirbet (228.5/174.2): Glueck 1939: 304.

er-Rumman, Tell (204.8/278.0): Yalqut.

es-Sabaniyyeh (226.6/258.4): ASI/G 110.

Safi (193.0/049.3—1): Glueck 1939: p. 147; Rast and Schaub 1974: 9–11; Amiran 1969: photos 44, 55.

Safririm (144.75/118.65): Rahmani, L. *RB* 67 (1960) 403.

es-Safsafa, Khirbet (186.9/227.6—1/2;3): Zori 1977: 165; Zori, N. *PEQ* (1952) 114–17.

Sahne (220.0/184.4—1;2): Mittmann 1970: 228.

Sakhara, Khirbet (240.0/176.2): Glueck 1939: 326.

es-Sakhineh, Khirbet (207.9/227.2): Ibrahim 1976: 25; few EB.

el-Sakhineh, Tell (207.8/227.0): Ibrahim 1976: 26; EB dominant.

Sal (235.8/219.7—1): Mittmann 1970: 18.

Salim (181.4/179.5): Campbell 1968: 11.

Samar (224.0/231.5—1;2): Mittmann 1970: 43.

es-Sammam, Khirbet (212.2/286.8): Yalqut.

Sammar, Horvat (163.2/071.5—2): Amiran 1980: 11ff.

es-Sarim, Tell (197.0/207.0): Zori 1962: 102.

es-Sassiyah, Khirbet (205.8/222.6): Ibrahim 1976: 17; one possible EB.

es-Sauda, Khirbet (189/235—1/2): Zori 1977: 191.

Semunieh (169.9/234.0—1;2): ASI/N 83.

Seluqiyeh, Tell (219.0/265.3): ASI/G 87.

Seqaah, Tell (205.4/185.5): Ibrahim 1976: 99.

es-Serareh, Khirbet (213.0/048.0): Glueck 1939: 88.

Shaar ha-Golan (206/232—4): *IEJ* 2 (1952) 252ff.

Shabaneh (166.4/239.9—1;2): ASI/N 43.

Shahuah, Khirbet (196.4/219.7—1/2): Zori 1977: 137; = esh-Sheikha?

esh-Shamdin, Tell (193.7/211.4): Zori 1962: 135.

esh-Shammam, Tell (164.9/230.6—1;2): ASI/N 38.

Shamsin, Khirbet (199.5/232.6): Saarisalo 1927: 48ff.

esh-Shauk, Tell (193.3/211.5): Zori 1962: 134.

esh-Sheikha (196/219): Yalqut; = Khirbet Shahuah?

esh-Sheikh Ali, Khirbet (202.0/233.5): Yalqut.

esh-Sheikh Basum, Khirbet (195.5/237.8): Saarisalo 1927: 33ff.

esh-Sheikh Daud, Tell (203.0/207.6): Zori 1962: 53.

esh-Sheikh Dhiab, Tell (190.8/161.5—1;2): ASI/JD 13; Glueck 1951: 25.

esh-Sheikh es-Simad, Tell (199/209): Yalqut.

esh-Sheikh Mohammed, Khirbet (205.1/211.4): Ibrahim 1976: 40; possible EB; Glueck 1951: 149.

esh-Sheikh Muhammad (212/284): Yalqut.

Sheikh Muzeighit (199.8/230.8—1/2): Zori 1977: 202.

Sheikh Saad (247/249): Albright 1925: 15.

Shejeret el-Asherah (222.6/213.3): Glueck 1951: 122.

Shejeret el-Faqireh (237.6/232.5): Glueck 1951: 56.

esh-Shemdin, Tell (203.2/224.3): Zori 1958: 47; Zori 1962: 4.

Shem Tov, Horvat (143.9/107.5—1): Dagan 1982: 48.

esh-Shihab, Tell (240.5/233.0): Albright 1925: 16–17.

esh-Shiir, Tell (225.5/218.7): Glueck 1951: 80.

Shlomi (163.9/275.0—1): Amiran 1970: fig. 5; Yalqut.

Shuqba (154/154): Bar-Yosef, O. *EAEHL* 1109.

Sibya (215.0/215.5): Glueck 1951: 121.

Sihan (221/171): Noth, M. *ZDPV* 73 (1957) 34.

Siir (163.2/110.4—1): ASI/J 99; cf. Saller 1961/62: 156.

es-Simadi, Tell (196.3/170.9): ASI/EM 190.

Sitt Leila, Khirbet (150.5/215.5): Aharoni, Y. *IEJ* 9 (1959) 110ff.

Siyar el-Kherfan (211.1/264.2—2): ASI/G 90.

Som (225.0/221.7): Mittmann 1970: 70.

Subeia, Khirbet (145.0/118.0): Rahmani, L. *RB* 67 (1960) 403.

Sufan, Tell (173.2/181.7—2): ASI/BE 8; Nandrasky, K. *ADAJ* 8–9 (1964) 89ff.; Campbell 1968: 36ff. says no EB.

esh-Sumeiriya, Tell (159.1/264.2): Saarisalo 1929: 38.

Summaqa (218.2/284.8): ASI/G 39.

Sur el-Musheirifa (169.9/239.1): ASI/N 70.

Sur, Khirbet (172.3/178.7): Campbell 1968: 37.

es-Suwari, Khirbet (229.0/178.2): Glueck 1939: 340.

es-Suwwan, Khirbet (205.4/222.7): Ibrahim 1976: 22; one probable EB.

es-Suwwan, Tell (204.5/222.2): Ibrahim 1976: 22; few EB.

Tabaqat el-Abid (161.1/226.8): Yalqut.

Tabun, Tell (163.7/235.4—1;2): ASI/N 31.

et-Tahuneh, Ras (170.2/146.2): ASI/BE 94.

Tamrah (188.1/226.7—1/2): Zori 1977: 126.

Tannuriyye (224.6/262.6): ASI/G 95; few EB.

et-Taqa, Khirbet (198.5/225.2—1/2): Zori 1977: 186.

et-Tayyiba (151.4/186.1): ASI/EM 123.

Tekoa (170/115): Saller 1961/62: 153–56.

et-Tayyib, Khirbet = Horvat Tov (163.9/081.7—1;2): Aharoni, Y. *IEJ* 14 (1964) 146; Amiran 1980: 11ff.

et-Teleil (228.7/169.5): Glueck 1939: 294.

et-Tell (209.4/257.4—2): Albright 1928: 7; ASI/G 111.

et-Tell, Khirbet (174.9/158.7): ASI/BE 51.

Telma, Horvat (129.9/035.4—2): Cohen, R. *IEJ* 28 (1978) 185 n. 4; *Hadashot* 53 (1975) 34–35 (Hebrew).

Tevet, Khirbet (181.5/227.0—1/2): Zori 1977: 84.

Tiberias (200/243): Yeivin, S. *AJA* 56 (1952) 141.

et-Tira (144.8/158.2):*Hadashot* 8 (1963) 19 (Hebrew).

Tulkarm (152/190—2): Yeivin, S. *Eretz Shomron* (Jerusalem, 1973) p. 152 (Hebrew; English summary, p. xix), Pl. kaph–aleph, 2.

Turbiya (196.8/219.1—1/2): Zori 1977: 138.

et-Turmus, Tell (128.0/125.5): Yalqut.

el-Ubeidiya, Tell (202.9/232.8): Yeivin, S. and Maisler, B. *BJPES* 11 (1944) 19 (Hebrew).

el-Umeiri, Tell (234.2/142.0—3;4): Ibach 1978a: 149.

Umm Beteimeh (240.2/190.0): Glueck 1951: 302; doubtful.

Umm el-Amdan (200.4/198.1—1): Mittmann 1970: 343.

Umm el-Amdan, Tell (199.9/198.6—1;2): Mittmann 1970: 342.

Umm el-Bair (206.6/193.5): Ibrahim 1976: 74; probable EB.

Umm el-Ghuzlan, Khirbet (216.8/222.5—1;2;3): Mittmann 1970: 81.

Umm el-Habaj (223.0/081.0—4): Mattingly 1981: 9012.

Umm el-Hasinat (235/236): Kerestes 1978: 21.

Umm el-Kharwa (205.8/223.1): Ibrahim 1976: 16; few EB.

Umm el-Qetein, Tell (214.0/137.7): Glueck 1951: 221.

Umm es-Sedeirah, Khirbet (215.0/047.0): Glueck 1939: 87.

Umm es-Suddur (203.5/233.2): Yalqut.

Umm ez-Zuweitine, Khirbet (171/109): ASI/JD 154.

Umm Hamad Gharbi, Tell (205.2/172.2): Glueck 1951: 199b; Mellaart 1962: 136.

Umm Hamad Sherqi, Tell (205.1/172.2—1;2;4): Glueck 1951: 199a; Mellaart 1962: 135ff.; de Contenson 1964: 38; Leonard 1981: Pls. XIII–XXIII; Helms, S. *Levant* 16 (1984; forthcoming).

Umm Qala, Khirbet (161.8/124.3): Morawe, G. *ADAJ* 8–9 (1964) 89.

Umm Qreiqarah (215.2/038.6—1): MacDonald 1980: 171.

Umm Rujm, Khirbet (237.5/159.0): Glueck 1939: 246.

Umm Sabuna, Khirbet (201.1/221.4): Zori 1962: 38.

Umm Yanbuteh, Khirbet (214.2/161.5): Glueck 1939: 223a; de Vaux 1938: 408.

Umweis, Teleilat (207.2/132.4): Mellaart 1962: 65; Glueck 1951: 223.

Wadah, Khirbet (249.2/173.5): Glueck 1939: 318.

Waterhouse/Ibach 1975: 82 (225.8/136.5—3;4).

Yaaf, Tell = Tell el-Qasab (202.6/264.1): Yalqut.

Yaamun, Tell (236.5/201.2): Glueck 1951: 297; Albright 1929: 10.

Yabrud (173/154—1): Amiran 1969: 49, photos 39, 40; Ferembach, D., quoting K. O. Henckel, *IEJ* 9 (1959) 222.

Yalqut 46 (197.5/225.8).

Yalqut 47 (203.5/220.0).

Yalqut 64 (203.4/210.3).

Yamma, Khirbet (198.0/233.6—1;2;3): Yalqut.

Yanin, Khirbet (171.1/255.5): Saarisalo 1929: 38.

Yanuh (173.6/265.5): Saarisalo, A. *JPOS* 10 (1930) 7, 10.

Yaquq (195.3/254.6—2): Ravani, B. *Atiqot* 3 (1961) 121.

Yavneh Yam (Palmahim) (121/147—1): Gophna, R. *Atiqot* 5 (1969) 80 (Hebrew); Gophna, R. *EAEHL* 1114; Gophna, R. *IEJ* 18 (1968) 132f.

Yawbak, Khirbet (151.5/180.3): ASI/EM 164.

Yehudi, Horvat (135.9/109.7—2/3): Dagan 1982: 55.

Yizreel, Tel (181.2/218.1—1/2): Zori 1977: 34.

Yoqrat, Tell (176/275): Aharoni, Y. *EAEHL* 408.

Yosef, Tel (188.2/215.2—1/2;3): Zori 1977: 42.

Yotvata (153.7/921.7—1): Meshel, Z. and Saas, B. *RB* 84 (1977) 268ff.

Yov, Khirbet (196.5/219.6—1/2): Zori 1977: 136.

Yubla (194.3/220.3—1/2): Zori 1977: 132.

Zaba, Khirbet (200.4/217.4): Zori 1962: 39.

ez-Zajan, Tell (210.6/177.3–1;3): Stoebe, H., quoting S. Mittmann, *ZDPV* 82 (1966) 26.

Zaqqum, Tell (S) (206.2/205.3): Ibrahim 1976: 58.

ez-Zehara, Tulul (192.9/213.1): Zori 1962: 129.

Zerah, Tell (212.0/225.7): Glueck 1951: 100; Kerestes 1978: 129.

ez-Zeraqon, Khirbet (239.2/221.7—1;2;3): Mittmann 1970: 16.

Ziqim (104.3/112.6): Yalqut.

Ziwwan, Khirbet (200/222): Zori 1962: 36.

Zori 1962: 11 (203.2/222.0): Zori 1958: 47.
Zori 1962: 51 (203.2/211.1).
Zori 1962: 59 (203.4/206.9).
Zori 1977: 74 (169/217—1/2).
Zori 1977: 105 (186.2/217.1—1;2).
Zori 1977: 106 (184.8/217.4—1/2).

BIBLIOGRAPHY

Albright, W. F.
1925   Bronze Age Mounds of Northern Palestine and the Hauran: The Spring Trip of the School in Jerusalem. *BASOR* 19: 5–19.
1926   The Jordan Valley in the Bronze Age. *AASOR* 6: 13–74.
1928   Among the Canaanite Mounds of Eastern Galilee. *BASOR* 29: 1–8.
1929   New Israelite and Pre-Israelite Sites: The Spring Trip of 1929. *BASOR* 35: 1–14.
1938   *The Excavation of Tell Beit Mirsim, II: The Bronze Age.* AASOR 17. New Haven.

Amiran, R.
1969   *Ancient Pottery of the Holy Land from its Beginning in the Neolithic Period to the End of the Iron Age.* Jerusalem.
1970   The Beginnings of Urbanization in Canaan. Pp. 83–100 in *Near Eastern Archaeology in the Twentieth Century,* ed. J. Sanders. Glueck Festschrift. Garden City.

Amiran, R. et al.
1980   The Early Canaanite City of Arad: The Results of Fourteen Seasons of Excavations. *Qadmoniot* 13: 2–19 (Hebrew).

ASI/
        BE = Benjamin and Mt. Ephraim
        EM = Ephraim and Manasseh
        G = Golan
        J = Judah
        JD = Judaean Desert and the Plain of Jericho
        All of the above in Bar-Adon, P., Epstein, C., et al., ed. M. Kochavi, *Judaea, Samaria and the Golan: Archaeological Survey 1967–68.* Jerusalem, 1972.
        D = Daliya (Olami, Y., Jerusalem, 1981)
        N = Nahalal (Raban, A., Jerusalem, 1982)
        SB = Sede Boqer (Cohen, R., Jerusalem, 1981)
        All Hebrew with English summaries.

Ben-Tor, A.
1978   *Cylinder Seals of Third-Millennium Palestine* BASOR Supplement Series 22. Cambridge.

Campbell, E. F.
1968   The Shechem Area Survey. *BASOR* 190: 19–41.

De Contenson, H.
1960   Three Soundings in the Jordan Valley. *ADAJ* 4–5: 12–88.
1964   The 1953 Survey in the Yarmuk and Jordan Valleys. *ADAJ* 8–9: 30–46.

Dagan, Y.
1982   *The Shephelah of Judah: A Collection of Articles.* Tel Aviv. (Hebrew).

Engberg, R. and Shipton, G.
1934   *Notes on the Chalcolithic and Early Bronze Age Pottery of Megiddo.* SAOC 10. Chicago.

Glueck, N.
1934   *Explorations in Eastern Palestine I.* AASOR 14. New Haven.
1935   *Explorations in Eastern Palestine II.* AASOR 15. New Haven.
1939   *Explorations in Eastern Palestine III.* AASOR 18–19. New Haven.
1943   Some Ancient Towns in the Plains of Moab. *BASOR* 91: 7–26.
1946   Band-Slip Ware in the Jordan Valley and Northern Gilead. *BASOR* 101: 3–20.
1951   *Explorations in Eastern Palestine IV.* AASOR 25–28. New Haven.

Glueck/Vogel
1975   E. K. Vogel, "Negev Survey of Nelson Glueck." *EI* 12: 1–17.

Gophna, R. and Kochavi, M.
1966   An Archaeological Survey of the Plain of Sharon. *IEJ* 16: 143ff.

Ibach, R.
1976   Heshbon 1974: The Archaeological Survey of the Hesban Region. *AUSS* 14: 119–26.
1978   Expanded Archaeological Survey of the Hesban Region. *AUSS* 16: 201–13.
1978   An Intensive Surface Survey at Jalul. *AUSS* 16: 215–22.

Ibrahim, M. et al.
1976   The East Jordan Valley Survey, 1975. *BASOR* 222: 41–66.

Kerestes, T. M. et al.
1978   An Archaeological Survey of Three Reservoir Areas in Northern Jordan, 1978. *ADAJ* 22: 108–35.

Leonard, A.
1981   *Preliminary Plates from The 1953 Soundings in the Jordan Valley Conducted by James Mellaart.* Unpublished manuscript in ACOR library, Amman.

MacDonald, B.
1980   The Wadi el Hasa Survey 1979: A Preliminary Report. *ADAJ* 24: 169–83.
1982   The Wâdī el-Ḥasā Survey of 1979 and Previous Archaeological Work in Southern Jordan. *BASOR* 245: 35–52.

Mattingly, G.
1981   *A Reconstruction of Early Bronze Age Cultural Patterns in Central Moab.* Ann Arbor dissertation 81-01038.

Mellaart, J.
1962   Preliminary Report of the Archaeological Survey in the Yarmuk and Jordan Valley. *ADAJ* 6–7: 126–57.

Mittmann, S.
1970   *Beiträge zur Siedlungs- und Territorialgeschichte des nördlichen Ost-jordanlandes.* Abhandlungen des Deutschen Palästina-Vereins. Wiesbaden.

Rast, W. and Schaub, T.
1974   Survey of the Southeastern Plain of the Dead Sea, 1973. *ADAJ* 19: 5–53.

Ross, J. F.
1980   The Early Bronze Age in Palestine. Pp. 147–70 in *Essays in Honor of Kenneth R. Rossman*, ed. K. Newmyer. Crete, Nebr.

Saarisalo, A.
1927   *The Boundary between Issachar and Naphtali: An Archaeological and Literary Study of Israel's Settlement of Canaan.* Helsinki.
1929   Topographical Researches in Galilee. *JPOS* 9: 27–40.

Saller, S.
1961/62   Jerusalem and its Surroundings in the Bronze Age. *Liber Annuus* 12: 153–56.

Thompson, T. L.
1975   *The Settlement of Sinai and the Negev in the Bronze Age.* TAVO Beiheft. Wiesbaden.
1979   *The Settlement of Palestine in the Bronze Age.* TAVO Beiheft. Wiesbaden.

Vaux, R. de
1938   Exploration de la region de Salt. *RB* 47: 398–425.

Waterhouse, S. and Ibach, R.
1975   Heshbon 1974: The Topographical Survey. *AUSS* 13: 217–33.

Wright, G. E.
1937   *The Pottery of Palestine from the Earliest Times to the End of the Early Bronze Age.* New Haven.
1961   The Archaeology of Palestine. *The Bible and the Ancient Near East.* Albright Festschrift. Garden City.
1971   The Archaeology of Palestine from the Neolithic through the Middle Bronze Age. *JAOS* 91: 276–93.

Yalqut
     Reshumot Yalqut ha-Pirsumim (Official Gazette of Registered Archaeological Sites; Department of Antiquities, State of Israel), 1091 (1964) and supplements. For named sites, cf. index; for others (Yalqut n), cf. the appropriate paragraph, corresponding to a particular sector.

Zori, N.
1958   Neolithic and Chalcolithic Sites in the Valley of Beth-Shan. *PEQ:* 44–51.
1962   An Archaeological Survey of the Beth-Shan Valley. Pp. 135–98 in *Biq'at Beth-Shan*, ed. J. Aviram. Jerusalem. (Hebrew).
1977   *The Land of Issachar: Archaeological Survey.* Jerusalem.

I am particulary sorry not have access to various studies by Gerald L. Mattingly: Nelson Glueck and Early Bronze Moab *ADAJ* 27 (1984; forthcoming); The Early Bronze Sites of Central and Southern Moab *Near East Archaeological Society Bulletin* (Fall, 1983).

LIST OF CONTRIBUTORS

AVRAHAM BIRAN is Director of the Nelson Glueck School of Biblical Archaeology of Hebrew Union College-Jewish Institute of Religion, former Director of the Department of Antiquities, Israel, and Director of the Excavations at Tell Dan.

ROBERT G. BOLING is Professor of Old Testament, McCormick Theological Seminary.

JOSEPH A. CALLAWAY is Professor Emeritus of Biblical Archaeology at Southern Baptist Seminary, and former Director of the Joint Archaeological Expedition to Ai.

EDWARD F. CAMPBELL, JR. is Francis A. McGaw Professor of Old Testament, McCormick Theological Seminary and former Editor of *Biblical Archaeologist*.

RALPH W. DOERMANN is Professor of Old Testament, Trinity Lutheran Seminary and Project Archaeologist, Joint Expedition to Tell el-Hesi.

VALERIE M. FARGO is Professor at the Oriental Institute of the University of Chicago and Project Director of the Joint Archaeological Expedition to Tell el-Hesi.

FRANK S. FRICK is Professor of Old Testament, Albion College and Co-chair of the ASOR/SBL Sociology of the Monarchy Seminar.

PAUL F. JACOBS is Associate Professor of Old Testament, St. Thomas University and Associate Director of the Lahav Research Project (Tel Halif).

GARY L. JOHNSON is Associate Pastor, First United Methodist Church, Edmond, OK, and a current staff member of the Joint Expedition to Tell el-Hesi.

PHILIP J. KING is Professor of Old Testament, Boston College and former president of the American Schools of Oriental Research.

NANCY L. LAPP is Curator of Bible Lands Museum and Lecturer in Archaeology at the Pittsburgh Theological Seminary.

ABRAHAM MALAMAT is Professor of Jewish History, Hebrew University. An earlier draft of his article was published in *The Age of the Monarchies: Political History*, volume 4-I of *The World History of the Jewish People* and is reprinted with permission.

GEORGE MENDENHALL is Professor in the Department of Near Eastern Studies at the University of Michigan.

J. Maxwell Miller is Professor of Old Testament at Candler School of Theology, Emory University and Director of the Archaeology Survey of Central Moab.

Leo G. Perdue is Professor of Old Testament and Academic Dean, Phillips Graduate Seminary. He is a former Assistant Volunteer Director of the Joint Expedition to Tell el-Hesi.

Walter E. Rast is Professor of Old Testament, Valparaiso University, President of the American Center of Oriental Research in Amman, and Director of the Excavations at Bab edh-Dhra.

D. Glenn Rose is the late Darbeth Distinguished Professor of Old Testament and Archaeology, Graduate Seminary, Phillips University and former director of the Joint Expedition to Tell el-Hesi. His article was delivered at the Southwestern Regional ASOR meeting on March 14, 1981, in Denton, Texas.

James F. Ross is Professor of Old Testament, Virginia Theological Seminary and Field Archaeologist, Joint Expedition to Tell el-Hesi.

Joe D. Seger is former Director of the Nelson Glueck School of Biblical Archaeology of Hebrew Union College-Jewish Institute of Religion, former Director of the Excavations at Tell Gezer, and Director of the Lahav Research Project (Tell Halif). It was at Gezer in the 1960s that Glenn Rose was initiated into the disciplines of Palestinian archaeology. Moreover, it was largely from the Gezer experience that the Tell el-Hesi project, for which he served as Director at the time of his death, received its impetus for developing and adjusting its archaeological methods and purposes. It is thus most appropriate that a volume in his memory include a report of the Gezer results.

Yigal Shiloh is Professor of Biblical Archaeology in the Institute of Archaeology, Hebrew University, and Director of the City of David Project.

Ephraim Stern is Professor of Biblical Archaeology, Hebrew University, Editor of Qadmoniot, and former Director of Excavations at Tell Qadish, Gil'am and Tell Mevorakh.

Lawrence E. Toombs is Professor of Religion and Culture, Wilfrid Laurier University and former Project Archaeologist, Joint Expedition to Tell el-Hesi and Joint Expedition to Caesarea.

INDEX TO MODERN AUTHORS*

---

*This index does not include authors listed in the bibliography of Early Bronze sites prepared by James F. Ross, pp. 315–353.

INDEX TO BIBLICAL REFERENCES